MODERN PHILOSOPHIES OF EDUCATION

MODERN PHILOSOPHIES OF EDUCATION

John S. Brubacher

Professor of Education, The University of Michigan

FOURTH EDITION

McGRAW-HILL BOOK COMPANY

NEW YORK   ST. LOUIS   SAN FRANCISCO

TORONTO   LONDON   SYDNEY

MODERN PHILOSOPHIES OF EDUCATION

Library of Congress Catalog Card Number 68-30554
08539

1234567890   MAMM   7543210698

PREFACE

As might be expected, this revision of *Modern Philosophies of Education* includes new materials which have appeared since the previous edition and also restatements of old and familiar materials. Bibliographies, of course, have also been updated. But the most significant aspect of the revision is its quite different organization. I have literally pulled the whole previous structure apart and then put it together again in a new and, I think, an improved order.

The central theme of the new organization has been prompted by a growing conviction that there has been a misplaced emphasis in the exposition of educational philosophy. Hitherto that exposition has given priority to philosophical categories at the expense of educational ones. Thus, some authors have organized the field of educational philosophy around schools of philosophy—realism, idealism, pragmatism, existentialism, and the like. Others, myself included, have organized the field around subdivisions in the field of philosophy—metaphysics, epistemology, and axiology, for example. In both cases educational categories such as aim, curriculum, and method have been subordinated to the philosophical categories. Education merely fleshes out the philosophical skeleton. It illustrates philosophic principles.

No doubt these philosophical categories shed light on educational problems. But our main interest is *education;* philosophy is ancillary. From this angle philosophy enters education when disagreements occur on policy, ambiguities arise in the terms used, or practice proceeds on unexamined assumptions. The selection of and emphasis on philosophical materials, therefore, stems from the practice of education and not the systematic requirements of general philosophy. It is this viewpoint that I have taken as the basis of this revision. The reader will comprehend the change in viewpoint by no more than a cursory comparison of the table of contents of this and previous editions. He will recognize at a glance many of the old materials but note they are quite differently arranged. Many other old materials, however, will be less recognizable. Particularly is this true of the materials in the former chapters on knowledge and value theory. These have been combined with those of the chapters on the educative process and redistributed into new chapters headed by the educational categories of aims, curriculum, and method.

This reorganization may make it appear that educational philosophy is a kind of *ad hoc* affair and may seem to neglect the traditional aspect of philosophy as systematic and synoptic. But not so. If inquiry into the problems of education leads to wider and more far reaching strategies, then that is the point at which to consider such broad theories rather than to thrust them forward before their relevance to the tactics of educational practice has become evident. This conclusion will also put the reader on guard that although I grant a main function of educational philosophy is to clarify terms— and more reference will be made in this edition to the results of linguistic analysis—I do not side with the notion that a revolution has occurred in philosophy which makes clarification the exclusive function of the discipline. I do think ideological considerations are important for the teacher and administrator.

John S. Brubacher

CONTENTS

PART TWO AIMS

PART THREE   CURRICULUM

PART ONE
School and Society

CHAPTER ONE

The School and Social Change

Teachers and parents may well feel confused these days over the great variety of opinion which obtains on the subject of education. Indeed there is such a contrariety of even expert advice that it seems as if the learned talk in a Babel of voices when they give directions on rearing the young. Distressing as this situation may be, it is not unusual. Quite the opposite: the situation seems to be one of long standing. Twenty-five hundred years ago no less a sage than Aristotle wrote:

> As things are . . . mankind are by no means agreed about the things to be taught, whether we look to virtue or the best life. Neither is it clear whether education is more concerned with intellectual or moral virtue. The existing practice is perplexing: no one knowing on what principle we should proceed—should the useful in life, or should virtue, or should the higher knowledge be the aim of our training; all three opinions have been entertained. Again about the means there is no agreement: for different persons, starting with different ideas about the nature of virtue, naturally disagree about the practice of it.[1]

Aristotle and his contemporaries found it difficult to agree on a fitting sort of education for the young because contemporary social conditions were in a state of accelerated change. Political institutions had shifted from aristocratic to democratic forms. A commercial economy had rapidly lifted Greece to a position of leadership in the eastern Mediterranean. National preeminence brought in its wake international conflict and ultimately international war. Foreign trade and war, to say nothing of domestic political strife, gave rise to a whole new crop of ideas among the Greeks. In the field of education the fundamental question arose whether the traditional educational stereotype would longer fit the new world into which the Greeks were moving or whether new times demanded a revision of their educational ideal.

The situation in the twentieth century—not to mention intervening centuries—has been marked by similar and even more drastic changes. The political structure has been very fluid. Monarchistic institutions have

---

[1] Aristotle, *Politics*, Book VIII, Chap. 2.

given way to democratic, and democratic institutions in turn have been beset by fascistic and communistic ones. Industrial economies have rapidly outstripped agrarian and commercial ones. International war not once but twice has tested men's political and economic ideologies. Reinforced by the remarkable development of science, the intellectual turnover of ideas has never been so great. Consequently people today, as twenty-five hundred years ago, are raising the age-old questions about how to educate their children for the dynamic social conditions in which they live. If their answers are confused and faltering, there should be no occasion for surprise; uncertain times give rise to uncertain answers.

THE SOCIAL AS BASIC CATEGORY

Granted that "existing practice is perplexing" today no less than twenty-five hundred years ago; yet where does one begin to search for a "principle," to use Aristotle's phrase, that will enable us to thread our way through the changes and uncertainties that confront us? Most leading philosophers have treated education as a dimension of politics, as for instance, Plato in his *Republic*, Aristotle in his *Politics*, and Dewey in his *Democracy and Education*. From their example, perhaps, we are justified in concluding that the most perennial dimension of education is the social one. If this is so, it may well be an entrée to the principle (or principles) for which we are looking.

Even consideration of a view opposite to the social one seems to come to the same conclusion. Thus we often speak of a person as being self-educated. While no doubt it is possible for a person to learn through his own unaided efforts and while it is a credit to his resourcefulness when he does, yet the total amount that anyone can learn exclusively on his own is extremely limited. Except for association with its mother, the newborn child would not only learn little but more than likely would physically perish. Even the so-called self-taught adult would make snail's progress indeed if he did not have at hand the tools and books representing the funded capital of learning of others both of his own generation and of those of ages past. In view of this situation, it is probably not extravagant to claim that education is primarily a social process and that the social process constitutes one of the main dimensions of any philosophy of education.

Before examining the process of social change and the role of the school in this process, however, let us look into the nature of society itself. According to one view, individuals antedated society. In the presocial state they were free and independent. It was naturally a free and voluntary act, therefore, when subsequently they formed society. In forming society, of course, they necessarily encumbered themselves with limitations to their former freedom and independence. Yet since society resulted from a voluntary compact, individuals surrendered no more freedom than nominated in the bond of social union. Moreover, since society is contractual, its terms can be amended or even abrogated at the will of its members. From this guarded, almost mistrustful, attitude toward society, it is difficult to escape the conclusion that somehow there is a latent opposition between individual and social interests.

Another view of the nature of society purports to see grave difficulties in the way of independent individuals' coming together to form society. They ask, how can there be genuine meeting of minds in simple communication, let alone in formal contract? If individuality is unique, how can the pupil possibly enter into the experience of the teacher or the race? Or how can the teacher understand the difficulties which the child is experiencing? Because one's own experience is peculiar to himself, he seems precluded from ever knowing what his fellow's experience uniquely means to him. People's highly prized individuality would seem to keep them locked up in separate worlds and prevent the very existence of society, the school, or the class.

The idealist thinks he has a way of overcoming this impasse. In any given class there are at work not only the minds of the teacher and the individual pupils but, as he says, there is also a social mind.[2] The social mind is the corporate mind of the pupils and teacher organized around some principle of knowledge on which all minds are thinking as one. For an individual to learn the meaning of his lesson is equivalent to being a member of a class. There is a close relation here between class as a social grouping in school and class as a logical category or classification. So, defining what the individual has learned involves subsuming the species under the genus, the individual under the universal. The social tie which thus binds teacher and pupil together into a class is an ideal or spiritual factor. While the pupil and teacher are distinct from each other, yet neither achieves his full meaning except in contrast to the other. Thus a child can be a pupil only in relation to a teacher and an adult a teacher only in relation to a pupil.[3] This thesis and antithesis of the pupil-teacher relation is finally mediated—and so the Hegelian triad is completed—in a synthesis of a higher third, the spiritual, which in its highest manifestation is the source of mankind and binds mankind together.

Yet another view of society regards it in the nature of an organism.

---

[2] Cf. Alexander Meiklejohn, *Education between Two Worlds* (Harper & Row, Publishers, Incorporated, New York, 1942), Chap. 14.
[3] For a questioning of this view, see *infra*, p. 235.

Just as a biological organism is a whole consisting of many parts, each performing its unique function in integration with the rest, so society too is a whole consisting of many individual persons or social strata, each making his unique contribution toward an integrated totality. In general, this has been the theory of totalitarian states. According to this view, society is a corporate entity in addition to the individual entities which compose it. As any whole is greater than its parts, so the social organism takes precedence over the individual organisms which compose it. While this does not deny the freedom or independence of the individual, it insists that the individual realizes freedom only through merging his identity with the organic whole.[4] In totalitarian practice any nonconforming individual who by his nonconformity contradicts the theory must be either regimented or liquidated.

Since there can be but one social whole, the state is that whole. It is not surprising, therefore, that in the totalitarian state the education of the individual is subordinated to that of the state. He is educated as a citizen rather than as a man. This is as it should be, for the state has ends of its own—cultural, religious, linguistic, economic, territorial—which, if in conflict with those of the individual, must be deemed superior because more farseeing and less selfish. The state itself thus becomes an end in the educational process. The individual becomes a means to its realization. His personality is made to emerge out of its narrow isolation into this larger social consciousness, which in the totalitarian ideology thus inspires and gives meaning to his life. The group culture which thus forms the core of the curriculum is in turn the expression of the will of the totalitarian state. Progress is a social rather than an individual phenomenon.

A final theory of the nature of society rejects its formation either through mere human efforts at communication and contract or through such figments as a social mind and a social organism. According to this last view individual and society are coeval, for society originates in human nature itself. The individual is regarded as endowed with a social nature; he is social by instinct. Conceived in a social situation necessitated on account of bisexual reproduction, the individual is born with such undeveloped potentialities that he would die if it were not further instinctive for the parents to prolong their temporary association into the more enduring society of the family. While the society of the family is necessary to offset the deficiencies of the child's early immaturity, it meets this requirement with only varying degrees of success because of the unavoidable limitations of the parents. If the child is to actualize the full potentialities with

---

4 Cf. Denton L. Geyer, "Three Types of Education for Freedom," *School and Society*, 36:406–407, November, 1947. See also *infra*, pp. 205–206.

which he is born, he needs a larger society than the family to help him do so. To achieve this end, it is necessary, it is instinctive, that man form the larger society of the state.

To reason that society is rooted in nature carries a twofold advantage. On the one side, this reasoning reveals society as definitely subordinated to the individual. It is the means to his self-realization. It supports and benefits from his creativity. The educational converse—that society is the end and the individual a means to the realization of that end—is never true. On the other side, if we add that God is the author of nature, this reasoning leads to the conclusion that society is not only a generic trait of nature in general and of human nature in particular, but it is also divinely ordained. The advantage that some see in this conclusion is that the kind of education to which an individual is entitled by right stems from God and cannot be abrogated by society as it could be if society were formed in any of the other foregoing ways.

THE SOCIAL BASIS OF HUMAN NATURE

Some students of human nature have been inclined to look askance at the notion that man is instinctively social. To ascribe man's social behavior to a social instinct, they say, is like ascribing the effects of morphine to a dormitive power in the drug. In the end this approach toward understanding human nature merely begs the question under inquiry. It leads nowhere except to learned ignorance.

Instead of seeking to understand the social basis of human nature through endowing it with social instincts, perhaps the educator will do better to commence with the empirical fact that man seems everywhere and always to be caught up in an intricate web of social relations. Without them, as already noted, the newborn babe would almost surely perish. But even after the child grows to relative physical independence, he enters, in complex civilizations, a long period of social infancy in which he is dependent on others for tutelage in the folkways or culture of his social group. The greater the division and specialization of labor in this group, the more adults are interdependent on each other. Mutual dependence, then, is a characteristic of human culture, so deep-rooted that the memory of man runneth not to the contrary. Indeed, it is so ingrained over the centuries that it is easy to see how social habits become, as we say, second nature.

It is of the utmost educational importance whether we regard the social basis of human nature as instinctive or habitual. We often hear men despair, for example, of correcting some of society's worst social ills. War as a means of settling international disputes, they say, cannot be eliminated so long as human nature is what it is. If man is pugnacious by instinct, why of course then he must fight as a child in the schoolyard and later as an adult on the battlefield. There is little or nothing that education can do. But if, on the other hand, fighting is just a bad habit, presumably we can rearrange social circumstances so that war will be superseded by the institution of international courts. In that event education could do much by way of creating a new outlook on an ancient abuse and by way of attaching to the administration of international justice the individual's present habits of self-restraint in submitting to the administration of domestic justice.

The social view one takes of human nature also turns on one's view of the nature of the relations of individuals to each other. Here we must raise the question whether to conceive of relations as internal or external.[5] According to the view that relations are external, reality can be analyzed into basic particles or atoms. These units can be moved about into a variety of relations, but each is so fundamentally discrete and indigenous that its character does not depend on its relationship to other units. Extended to society, this view treats individuals as the atoms of social relations. Society is a compact in which individuals freely contract to form society. Individuals, therefore, will be able to take on or throw off a variety of social yokes without impairment of their own unique identity or personality.

This approach to the social basis of human nature has led to various kinds of educational practice. It is probably fundamental to the whole *laissez faire* position on education.[6] Since the nature of the individual is external to his relations, his only social obligations should be those of his own free choice. Therefore the government should allow him to arrange for the education of his offspring privately and should not force him to pay taxes for public schools.[7] Similarly, when the student goes to school his curriculum should be elective, freely chosen, and not prescribed. With such a theory, furthermore, it will be no surprise if ultraprogressive or ultrademocratic schools show such reverence for pupil individuality that they give it almost unbridled freedom to express itself.[8]

If one takes the view that relations are internal, then one commences, not with independent atoms, but with an initial state in which everything is so related to other things that a disturbance of relations would affect an alteration in the nature of the things related. Experimental studies in biology reveal that the kind of organ a cell grows into depends only in

[5] *Infra*, pp. 136–138.   [6] *Infra*, pp. 78–79.   [7] *Ibid*.   [8] *Infra*, pp. 204–205.

part on what kind of cell it is, for fully as important is the location of that cell. That is, a given cell may grow into the head or foot of an organism, depending on its being transplanted near the head or near the foot.

It is the same with individuals as with atoms or cells; relations are all important.[9] At the very outset, what the human embryo becomes may be radically conditioned by prenatal influences on it. Furthermore, when individuals grow up they do not voluntarily form society; rather are they found almost unavoidably in society. Their normal environment is in association with each other. It is by shared purposes that they constitute society. In fact society may be said to exist *in* and *by* communication between individuals. The social process and the educational process are essentially one and the same. By the same token individuals are in large part what they are by virtue of what they share in communication with others. Each is so much a part of the other that we may regard society as a category which actually transforms physical and animal nature into what it is.[10]

If this analysis of the social quality of human nature is sound, we as educators are justified in reversing the age-old notion that human nature is unchanging. It may change very, very slowly as in the category of physical structure, but if Darwin is right, change it does. In social category it may change no faster than the social relations or conventions in which it is enmeshed. But we could greatly accelerate change in this category by being open-minded to change ourselves. The individual nature of human nature, then, depends on the kind of human nature which is emerging in others. The concepts of *ego* and *alter*, self and other, emerge simultaneously in the educative process. That is, learning to know oneself is not just an affair of private introspection. It is also an affair of seeing how others behave and of recognizing and identifying feelings of theirs with feelings of one's own. Each is indispensable to the other.

PROGRESS AND "STATUS QUO"

The fact that fundamental change is continually afoot does not mean that everyone embraces it enthusiastically. As a matter of fact the social order at any time comprises a vast variety of interacting forces. In the action and reaction of these forces, stresses and strains occur, which in the long run tend to offset each other and thus result in a sort of balanced state of

[9] Cf. Raymond H. Wheeler, "The Crisis in Educational Objectives," *Educational Administration and Supervision*, 20:19–25, January, 1934.
[10] John Dewey, "The Social as a Category," *Monist*, 38:176, April, 1928.

affairs. This condition is often referred to as the *status quo*. Such an equilibrium, however, is usually uneasy and seldom static. The pressures of old forces wax and wane, or new ones intervene so that both the locus and direction of social tension are always shifting to a greater or less extent. If this dynamic quality were not present, social progress would be impossible.

On the whole, most people have their lives pretty well adjusted to the *status quo*. Of course, they expect progressive improvement, but usually piecemeal inside the *status quo* as a frame of reference. More than likely they will resist any major disturbance requiring a redistribution of social energies of so general a nature as to require a radically new over-all frame of reference. Such extensive adaptation is quite too inconvenient or even precarious for them. What they fear, of course, is that the advantages which they presently derive from the *status quo* will be jeopardized. Superficially they do obeisance to the idea of progress, but inwardly they view it with suspicion and trepidation.

The individualities of some people, however, are so marked that they cannot be made congruent with things as they are. They cannot abide the *status quo*. Such people are likely to become aggressively restless. Sometimes they are disgruntled with the *status quo* because the existing balance of forces is weighted against their own interests. Sometimes they produce novel ideas or inventions which require thoroughgoing readjustment of the tension of social forces. But, although they press their views in the name of progress, they are more than likely to antagonize their neighbors, who either are satisfied with the *status quo* or disagree as to what direction progress should take.

Sometimes schools or individual teachers in a school are the incubators of social unrest. Till the recent past this has only infrequently been the case because the traditional school has been preoccupied with the cultural spoils of antiquity. As a result the school indirectly, if inadvertently, was a supporting pillar of the *status quo*. Since the First World War, however, the curriculum has increasingly and intentionally drawn its inspiration from the grinding forces of contemporary social life. The school no sooner added this new source for curriculum materials than it was instantly recognized as a powerful potential force for changing as well as preserving the *status quo*. Both progressives and conservatives perceived this, and both immediately tried to capture the school as an agent of their point of view. The struggle to make the school an ally of contemporary social forces has led to much discussion of the proper role of the school in the social order and of the proper method of teaching controversial issues in the schoolroom.

Some have thought that the school should hold aloof from the cauldron of social controversy or at least be neutral toward it. Others have thought that the school should plunge right into the area of contention. But those who have taken the latter view have divided on whether the school should be an agent for consolidating the *status quo* or whether it should be an instrument for social change. Those who take the first view think the teacher should adopt methods which will indoctrinate loyalty to the *status quo*. Those who hold to the second view think the teacher should be free to adopt a more critical attitude in his teaching. If the teacher is to be free to deviate from the *status quo*, he is almost sure to make enemies. Some think that the teacher should enjoy the protection of academic freedom in saying unpopular things, others that he should have no more protection than the average citizen when he exercises his civil liberty in advocating an unpopular cause.

CONSERVATIVE FUNCTION OF THE SCHOOL

By far the oldest theory of the mutual relations of the school and the social order, and the one most widely honored in practice, is that the school should conserve the existing social culture. This culture was won only at a great cost of time and suffering. Confronted with the enigmas of life, mankind has only laboriously and at great sacrifice accumulated a stock of solutions. It would, obviously, be a great pity if any of these were to be lost through chance failure to teach them to the oncoming generation. Moreover, except as culture patterns are conserved through the school, there is no way to shorten the period of trial and error which is incident and precedent to social progress. Especially is it important for the school to perform this conservative function if other social institutions neglect to do so. Formerly, each institution like the family, church, and state tended to perpetuate its own mores. Latterly, however, these mores have become too complex for informal transmission, and these institutions have become too busy to attend to their educational duties adequately. Hence the evolution of the school as a residual institution to catch up and preserve social patterns otherwise in danger of loss or neglect.

Such a description of the conservative function of the school should lead one to be very wary of inferring that, therefore, the role of the school is reactionary. It may have been so in times past. But "conservative" and "reactionary" are not synonymous terms, though they sometimes are treated as such. To treat them as synonymous is to confuse the difference in degree they represent. Proceeding on the conservative theory, it is entirely possible for the school to preserve social systems of the left as well as those of the right, radical as well as reactionary patterns of culture.

Indeed, with this qualification, it is perhaps not too much to assert that nearly all educational philosophers agree that, to some extent at least, the school must be conservative in function.

Even after conceding that conservation is indispensable, it must at once become evident that in an advanced civilization the school cannot conserve the whole social heritage through instruction. The total social culture is far too extensive to be crammed into the short span of years that even advanced students spend in school, to say nothing of the short period of compulsory attendance. And even if this were possible, it would probably be undesirable for the curriculum to mirror impartially both the good and the bad in racial experience. The school must exercise a normative function coincident with its conservative one.

This may take several directions. In the first place, the culture of an advanced civilization is not only overwhelming in quantity, but it is also baffling in complexity. One of the things that a school will have to do, therefore, is to simplify what is to be presented to the immature. Furthermore, not only will it have to simplify, it may also have to balance it. The conjunction of time and place at which a child is born inescapably causes accidental limitations. Fortunately, he need not be wholly at the mercy of his epoch or locality, for the school can compensate for this disadvantage through balancing the diet of the curriculum. Especially can the school transcend both time and place through such studies as history and geography. The more diverse the elements to which the school introduces the child, the more will there be need for yet another service from the school, that of coordinating the various pulls which different environments make upon him. Coordination, however, implies some system of values. This leads to the last and perhaps most controversial aspect of the normative function of the school, that of purifying the cultural heritage. It requires but a moment's reflection to realize the tremendous improvement which could be brought about through sifting out those culture patterns which are unworthy to be perpetuated. The potentialities are great even if the actualization has been somewhat short of expectation.

There are several difficulties with this normative aspect of the conservative function of the school. At the outset, one must beware of simplifying the school environment so that it becomes a pallid attenuation of the real society it represents or of purifying it so that it becomes an impractical idealization of the *status quo*. But next, if there is to be a norm, the question arises, what shall be the norm, what kind of mesh shall the school use to screen the social culture? It is one thing to say that school and college have a telic function, but it is quite another to gain general agreement on any particular direction. Perhaps most general acceptance would go to a screen that is representative of the values of the *status quo*. Then, whether the *status quo* is democratic or fascistic, capitalistic or communistic, there will be relatively little ambiguity on the norm of conservation.

PROGRESSIVE FUNCTION OF THE SCHOOL

Conservatives offer little or no objection to the normative function of the school so long as it seeks to approximate a more purified form or ideal of the *status quo.* The major difficulty arises when the school adopts a norm radically different from the *status quo.* Nevertheless, there are liberals and progressives who think that the school is not just a residual institution to catch up and maintain things as they are but a vehicle by which to forge ahead as well. To them it is as absurd to think that education can preserve civilization from decaying as it is to think that the science of medicine can keep one from dying. Rather must education be the source of new ideas, of a social program that is constantly undergoing reconstruction. In other words, they think that the normative function of the school may also involve originating major changes, changes possibly in the norm or frame of reference itself.

In this phase, the normative function of the school is creative rather than conservative. It introduces, therefore, the second outstanding theory on the relation of the school to the social order, namely, that it is the duty of the school to take some initiative and responsibility for social progress. Among the supporters of this theory there are two very distinct subdivisions of opinion. One is content to have the school an independent critic of the *status quo,* with any social progress an indirect or incidental outcome of critical instruction. The other would be much more direct, purposeful, and aggressive. It would have the school form a definite conception of the better social order and then work with might and main to bring it into being.

First to regard the school as a pioneer of social progress were the organizers of the "progressive education" movement. Usually taking a dynamic, changing universe as their frame of reference,[11] they attempted to gear education to it. Since nothing can be accepted as final in a world ruled by flux, they taught children not so much what to think as how to solve problems which this flux presented. Children learned to regard conclusions from their problem solving as tentative and subject to amendment in the light of future events. In the struggle to meet a contingent

[11] *Infra*, pp. 139–141. See also William H. Kilpatrick, *Education for a Changing Civilization* (The Macmillan Company, New York, 1926).

future, "progressive educators" laid great store by individual differences among pupils in the hope that out of this rich variety of talent successful adaptation to the precarious quality of a dynamic universe would more likely occur.

By introducing such ideas into the schools, progressive education could hardly avoid creating a ferment in the social order. Yet, although progressive educators kept sharp watch for signs indicating the probable future direction of social change, they did not identify themselves with any particular political and economic program or party. On the contrary, they tried to actualize the long-standing utopian theory that in a mature society education and politics should be one and the same thing, that is, the study of how to manage public affairs intelligently.[12] Instead of aligning the school with any single reform group, they took the view that the school should be a place where all sorts of social programs would be studied no matter how varied or contradictory they might be. They tried to institutionalize the continuous reconstruction of social theory and practice.[13]

To have a governmental agency such as the school or university stand off and criticize the actions of the state will require a great amount of self-imposed restraint on the part of the sovereign. Under a monistic theory of the state[14] it would probably be too much to expect. With a pluralistic state,[15] however, it is quite possible, even desirable. Indeed, one can make a strong case that education should not suffer its objectives to be externally imposed, but that it should be autonomous, free to erect its own ends.[16] Every profession enjoys considerable autonomy in determining its own character. Therefore the public school, although maintained by the state, should not be its supine servant. On the contrary, it should have some freedom in determining its own function in, and its own relation to, the social order.

There are some who would go so far as to set up the school as an

12 John Dewey, "Education as Politics," New Republic, 32:140–141, October, 1922.
13 Isaac L. Kandel, "Education for Social Change," Journal of Social Philosophy, 1:23–35, October, 1935; Edward H. Reisner, "Can the Schools Change the Social Order?" Teachers College Record, 36:388–396, February, 1935; James T. Adams, "Can Teachers Bring About the New Social Order?" Progressive Education, 10:310–314, October, 1933; John Dewey, "Educational and Social Change," Social Frontier, 3:235–238, May, 1937; William H. Kilpatrick, "Public Education as a Source for Public Improvement," School and Society, 41:521–527, April, 1935; George A. Coe, "Education as Social Engineering," Social
14 Infra, p. 75.
15 Infra, pp. 75–76.
   Frontier, 1:25–27, January, 1935.
16 John Dewey, Sources of a Science of Education (Liveright Publishing Corporation, New York, 1929), pp. 73–75; Raymond J. McCall, "The Autonomy of Education," Educational Theory, 1:248–250, December, 1951.

independent branch of government.[17] Ordinarily we think of government as divided into legislative, judicial, and executive branches, with education as a department in the executive branch. But perhaps education should be a fourth branch of government. The various reasons which might be adduced for such a policy can be summed up in the statement that political interests are ephemeral, while the cultural interests of the school far outrun annual or even quadrennial elections. The cycle for maturing a new school generation with its set of ideas is much longer. Moreover, the transition from one political regime to the other would be much less of a shock to the schools if the administration of the latter had a long-term, independent status.

On first examination, it may seem as if the independence which this critical theory of the responsibility of the school for social progress demands may result in a remoteness of the school from the social order. But not so. The formulation of educational ends should grow out of whatever is incomplete in the everyday lives of those who are learning. Indeed they undoubtedly will, if, as usual, participation in the vital activities of a social group leaves a sense of the unfinished. Under such circumstances, any vital education will inescapably have a share in building the social order of the moment. Proceeding on such premises, we may conclude that education as well as politics is a process of discovering what values are of most worth. The school is one of the community's resources for social experimentation and, as such, should not be neglected. What the supporters of this critical theory seek is not an alienation of the school from life, but protection in a freedom to study life independently. If freedom were the settled policy of the schools no matter what faction commanded a political majority, the educational policy of the schools would not suffer convulsions when political power periodically changes hands.

If the state cannot be objective about criticism directed at itself from the public school, there is the possibility that it may be willing to take criticism from the private school. The public school, committed in the great majority of cases to the theory of conservation, acts as the flywheel of the social order. The private school, however, addicted to deviations from any official stereotype, might act as the source of experimental ideas. This possibility would be attractive were it not for the fact that the chief progress which has resulted from private schools has been in educational techniques rather than radical schemes of social progress. Naturally private schools, generally drawing the sinews of their strength from the vested

[17] National Education Association, Department of Superintendence, Twelfth Yearbook, *Critical Problems of School Administration*, Washington, 1934, pp. 65–66.

economic interests of privileged social classes, are not likely to bite or even seriously threaten to bite the hand that feeds them.

In the course of experience, however, many educational frontiersmen and subsequently reconstructionists became disappointed in the outlook for social progress under progressive education. To assure progress, they claimed, society and the school must have a definite plan.[18] It is just this that progressive education lacks. Through stressing individualism, progressive education waits for progress to occur by chance variation. But these educational frontiersmen had no patience to wait for progress to occur in such casual, haphazard fashion. Furthermore, progressive education seems overawed by the precariousness of the future. On the one hand, this leads to its being cautious. It seems unwilling to make any but ad hoc disposition of each problem as it comes into view from behind the heavy veil of the future. On the other hand, the contingencies of circumstance have led progressive education to the cultivation of the agile, adaptable mind to a point where it appears incapable of attachment to any abiding plan or purpose. In place of such a policy of intellectual drift and laissez faire, they would recognize or substitute a deep loyalty to some fundamental social plan. If insistence on such a plan seems to smack of imposition and an infringement of freedom, they would not cringe from the indictment but frankly affirm that imposition is inescapable and the only assured road to vital achievement.

If the school undertakes to sponsor a social program, the only remaining question concerns the authorship of the plan. In the past the school has at different times taken its direction from clergy, soldiers, statesmen, and businessmen. Not a few educational frontiersmen think it is high time that the teachers themselves should exercise leadership. Through the curriculum and methods of instruction, the power lies in their hands to achieve major social reconstruction. The only way for teachers to influence the course of human events is boldly and unblushingly to take advantage of the strategic position in which they find themselves. If their competence to do this is challenged, it needs but be pointed out that no other class is in such complete possession of the wisdom of the ages, or under such heavy duty to use it in the interests of all the people. But this is just a matter of degree. To act on such an audacious theory of the relation of the school to the social order undoubtedly courts danger. It is to the credit of those subscribing to it that they appreciate its risks. If they would be in the vanguard of social progress, they realize teachers must accept re-

---

[18] George S. Counts, *Dare the School Build a New Social Order?* (The John Day Company, Inc., New York, 1932.)

sponsibility for their actions, surrender their security in large measure, and suffer any consequent jeopardy to reputation and fortune.

Courageous and challenging though such a point of view may be, many objections have been entered against it. Some have pointed out that it is preposterous to think that so enormously vast a task as the building of a new social order could be undertaken wholly or even mainly by any single social institution such as the school. As a matter of fact, the world is far too complex for such an undertaking. Moreover, there are other institutions as powerful as the school which are equally interested in the amelioration of human ills. Certainly it would be fantastic to think that the school could inaugurate a new social order in opposition to, or without the assistance of, business, the family, or the church.

A closely allied objection raises the question whether the rank and file of teachers are well enough trained to assume the responsibilities of leadership, which the creative theory of the school's relation to the social order would demand. Many sincere friends of education have grave doubts.[19] The conduct of public affairs is an art as well as an academic discipline. One can become skillful in this art only by actual participation in those affairs. Many teachers are well trained academically, but distressingly few of them have had experience in practical affairs as a background for better teaching, let alone for making them competent in the formation and execution of public policy. Indeed, in the Catholic parochial school, where teachers are largely drawn from teaching orders, it has been regarded an advantage that the teacher is withdrawn from the turmoil of life.[20] But, even conceding this questioned proficiency, the further objection may still be advanced that teachers probably could not agree among themselves as to the line along which social reconstruction is to occur. As a matter of fact, there seems no more reason to expect unanimity among them than among any other group of lay or professional people.

Realistic as the educational frontiersmen attempt to be in giving concrete space-time location to the social plan which is to command the loyalty of the school, it is surprising to some how close they hover to an unrealistic program. Thus, to adopt a frame of reference markedly different from the *status quo* is to make the school discontinuous with its social milieu.[21] So, too, a curriculum pitched in advance of the society contemporaneous

---

[19] John C. Chapman and George S. Counts, *Principles of Education* (Houghton Mifflin Company, Boston, 1924), p. 624. The difference in Counts's position here and in his *Dare the School Build a New Social Order?* pp. 27–31, is noteworthy.

[20] Thomas E. Shields, *Philosophy of Education* (Catholic Education Press, Washington, D.C., 1921), pp. 424–425.

[21] Albert P. Pinkevitch, *The New Education in the Soviet Republic* (The John Day Company, Inc., New York, 1929), pp. 153–154.

to it, may be as unrealistic as one that lags too far behind it. Furthermore, if the public refuses to accept the reform program in the school, serious maladjustment may result for pupils who are prepared for a new social order but who are required to live in an old one. Moreover, there is danger that the educators who would reform the social order too rapidly or too radically will defeat their own ends and that, at the conclusion of their struggle with the community, they will be worse off than at the beginning. When one bears in mind the slow and halting progress that has been made in achieving the limited freedom which the school has come to enjoy in democratic countries, one should be very cautious in provoking a public resentment which would wipe out the gains already made.

But foremost among objections is the oft-repeated argument that in a democratic society it is the adult community first and last which must decide what kind of social order the schools shall nourish. Where the sense of the community is ultimate, it is certainly too much to expect that the community will long support a school which undermines the very foundation of that support. In fact, to teach contrary to its dictates, almost behind its back, so to speak, is positively unethical.[22] The state has an instinct of self-perpetuation, as the individual has one of self-preservation. Moreover, it can be pointed out that, as a matter of the constitutional framework of government, it is the legislature and not the school that is entrusted with deciding broad matters of social policy like changing the social frame of reference. The school is a department or subdivision in the executive not the legislative branch of government. So, if the reform of the social order is a school matter at all, it seems that the only recourse is to adult education in its widest meaning.

A good argument can be made that the real source of social change is not to be found in the schools at all, but in much more powerful and elemental forces. The really basic factors which compel the alteration of social mores are such things as mechanical invention, military conquest, the strife of economic classes, racial segregation, political revolution, and crusading religion. Certainly the school can hardly hope to harness the tides of such basic energies to its leadership. Rather is the school more likely to be carried in and out with them.

From these objections to the school's attempt to give direction to social progress, it would be unfair to infer that the objectors think the school has no role to play in social progress. On the contrary, they assign a very important part to the school. This part is to complete and consolidate changes in social policy once they have been decided upon—whether

---

22 Thomas H. Briggs, "Should Education Indoctrinate?" *Educational Administration and Supervision*, 22:571–572, November, 1936.

by bullets or by ballots.[23] In this view the school is the servant of social change, not its master. Or, perhaps more accurately yet, one should set aside as futile any discussion of which is cause and which effect, education or social change. The two are mutually interactive, circular, never ending. Each cross-fertilizes the other.

But many adherents of this more moderate position will admit that it would be unfortunate indeed if educational policies and programs were to shift with every variation in the social weather. Certainly the school must be more than a weather vane. Yet it would be their further opinion that, if the school could even slightly modify the great elemental forces of society, it should exercise its influence to reduce the extremes of social oscillation. In times of rapid change, they feel that the function of the school is to stabilize the period of transition, rather than to accelerate the flux of disturbing forces.[24] It is a time to emphasize the fundamental values which have maintained their position of eminence in the cultural heritage over long stretches of time. This does not mean that they favor a rigid static social order, but rather that they would prefer stability to instability, security to insecurity. They would make haste slowly, realizing that one of the most puzzling of all social problems is how to build new institutions out of old ones and yet keep the old institutions open for business during alterations.

NEUTRAL FUNCTION OF THE SCHOOL

Seeing that it is no easy task for society to be at one and the same time stable and progressive, free and secure, and seeing that the community may vent its wrath on the school if it dislocates or even threatens to dislocate the *status quo* by its teaching, many educators think it advisable that the school take the high stand of neutrality on controversial social issues. To some of these educators neutrality means a strict aloofness not only from politics but also from the market place. They claim that the school should not be interested in useful knowledge or the practical clash of philosophic systems. They rather think it the austere role of the school, standing high above these temporal concerns, to pursue eternal values and to master universal truths. Governed by such laws and principles, education, they think, is the private possession of the individual, the esoteric art of an initiated intelligentsia.

---

[23] David Snedden, "Education and Social Change," *School and Society*, 40:311–314, September, 1934.

[24] William C. Bagley, *Education and Emergent Man* (Thomas Nelson & Sons, New York, 1934), p. 155.

Other neutralists concede that the school must be concerned with the affairs of men and exclude such problems from the curriculum only when they are so controversial that their discussion would divide the community and endanger its wholehearted support of the school. This is the only consistent position to take, they claim, in a pluralistic culture, where the public school belongs to all the people. Still other educators would even admit controversial issues of economy and politics into the curriculum but ensure that the school maintain its neutrality by having the teacher impartially present all sides of these issues, taking strict care not to commit himself or the school to one side or another.

To judge by the criticism it has received, the position of neutrality is not nearly the secure haven of retreat that it would appear on first impression. Many scout as idle pretension the idea that any school teacher or administrator can be completely nonpartisan or altogether objective about the fundamental issues which agitate society.[25] Human beings are individuals. Individuality points to differences and limitations in human nature. Differences and limitations inevitably result in unique attitudes and preferences. Thus an individual by his very nature stands for this or that and not "neither" as the etymological derivation of the word neutral would indicate. Since this is the case, neutrality is at best a remote possibility even when consciously sought. To avoid hypocrisy and self-deception, it would seem in the best interests of all concerned for the teacher and the school to be forthright in declaring their philosophic predilections. Needless to add, these are the scruples of a democratic state. In a totalitarian state of either the fascist or communist model, neutrality is neither possible nor a desideratum.

Yet, even if we concede the possibility of achieving neutrality by the teacher or the school, there are still difficult criticisms to surmount. On the one hand, there is the misfortune that, if controversial issues are left out, some of the best places in the curriculum will have to be left blank.[26] On the other hand, if the teacher seeks to weigh the pros and cons of some controversial issue impartially, the student may come to suffer a kind of academic paralysis. He may come to think either that the pros and cons are so evenly balanced that it is impossible to come to a decision or that one argument is about as good as another so that he is disinclined to commit himself to act.

Again, there is the grave moral criticism against the neutral school

---

25 Max Weber, *Methodology of the Social Sciences* (The Free Press of Glencoe, New York, 1949).
26 William E. Hocking, *Human Nature and Its Remaking* (Yale University Press, New Haven, Conn., 1923), p. 260.

that it paradoxically becomes the unwitting partisan of the *status quo.* For anyone to stand on the side lines and refuse to take sides is a negative or implied approval of things as they are. Thus a failure or refusal to think or act on social alternatives has moral consequences just as definitely as a willing commitment to thought and action.[27] We must be aware that thinking, even behind the four walls of the school, does not occur in a vacuum. If it did occur in a vacuum, totalitarian governments would not be so afraid of academic freedom.

Imagine it be granted now that neutrality on the part of the school, if not impossible, is at least undesirable. If decision and preference are unavoidable, the main concern of the public should be in seeing that action be based on preferences and decisions *fairly* arrived at. This is the case with the courts. No one expects the courts to be neutral, that is, to refuse to decide for the plaintiff or defendant. But he does expect the courts to arrive at their decisions openly and without fear or favor. It is fairness rather than neutrality, therefore, which the public should expect of the schools in dealing with controversial issues in the curriculum.

Some critics of the neutral school would reject even this concept of judicial fairness. To them, the judge whose bias does not creep into the "weight of the evidence" is a fiction.[28] Or, they ask, how can all sides be fairly represented, when one side is entrenched in the prejudices of the *status quo?* Certainly there should be no illusions about the difficulty of gaining fairness of instruction on controversial issues. It is, perhaps, only less difficult than being neutral. But if confidence could be established in a human amount of it, the school might bear some modest responsibility for social progress.[29]

THE SCHOOL AND REVOLUTIONARY CHANGE

So far we have proceeded on the assumption that social change and progress would take place in orderly fashion. We have assumed that children and adults could learn to discuss alternative social policies and come to some rational conclusion as to a plan of action. To effect social progress,

---

[27] John Dewey, "Education and Social Change," *Social Frontier,* 3:236–237, May, 1937; William O. Stanley, B. Othanel Smith, and Kenneth D. Benne, "Progressive Essentialism in Education," *Frontiers of Democracy,* 9:212, April, 1943. For a further analysis of the position of these authors, see Robert H. Ennis, "Is It Impossible for the Schools to Be Neutral?" *Harvard Educational Review,* 29:128–136, Spring, 1959.

[28] Horace M. Kallen, "Controversial Social Issues," *Progressive Education,* 10:188, April, 1933.

[29] Cf. John L. Childs, "Should the School Seek Actively to Reconstruct Society?" *Annals of the American Academy of Political and Social Science,* 182:1–9, November, 1935.

however, is not always so simple a matter. There are many times when, after the most elaborate study of an issue, the parties thereto cannot agree on what action to take. To break such an impasse it is generally the policy of democracies to take a vote and then let the majority organize the whole group for action. Letting the majority have its way does not mean that the minority agrees with them on principle; it merely means that the minority submits to this way of breaking a deadlock where it is imperative that some action be taken one way or another. Because the minority voluntarily consents to majority rule, social changes can be brought about in orderly peaceable fashion with a minimum show of force.[30] This orderly process of change is one of the chief things children must master in learning the ways of democracy.

By making only such changes as the minority consents to, change not only occurs in orderly fashion, but it usually comes about very gradually. As it is often remarked, social progress takes place through evolution rather than revolution. Fortunately or unfortunately, there are times when it seems to some people that the gradual evolutionary pace of social progress is not fast enough. Supremely confident of the justice of the reform they seek, they feel justified in forcing the pace. They are willing to use the slower processes of education to effect the changes they have in mind, but they will not hesitate to abandon them for more forcible measures if the results are not quick and striking.

Such an occasion may arise where there is some obstruction to the usual orderly process of social change. As an instance, we may take the strike. Teachers want both better salaries and better working conditions. Boards of education may be reluctant to agree or are opposed to alleviating these complaints. Resentment builds up at what seems callous exercise of public power, and teachers feel driven to abandon or at least augment rational procedures with more forceful ones such as the strike. Indeed, it is perhaps not too much to say that only where power is approximately equally distributed can we be assured that people will willingly or necessarily resort to reason and persuasion as the means of easing social tensions.

The demand for accelerated social change may also arise on more theoretical grounds. Suppose the change demanded is not just a readjustment of the balance of forces within the accepted *status quo* but a fundamental shift from an old to a new frame of reference. A number of laymen and educators think that such a shift or transition cannot be made gradually. They reject gradualism because it is atomistic; it brings social recon-

---

30 Horace M. Kallen, *op. cit.*, p. 188; John S. Brubacher, "Education and World Order," *Educational Forum*, 8:195–196, January, 1944.

struction piecemeal, in installments. They very much doubt, furthermore, that qualitative changes like jumping from one frame of reference to another can be brought about quantitatively. Gradualism would mean, for instance, that over a period of time society could move from capitalism to communism. This would imply that, however far apart these two extremes, the difference between them is only one of degree, not of kind. But the opponents of gradualism regard the difference between the frames of reference of capitalism and communism as a difference in kind rather than degree. The change from one to the other can occur only through a drastic reorganization of outlook. It is like jumping a broad stream; we must do it in a single jump and all at once and not in a series of leaps spread over a period of time. Instead of a slowly rising learning curve there must be nothing short of vertical ascent. Socially there must be a revolution.

Some educators take the Marxian view that this social revolution is to be brought about through the "class struggle." They favor an education which capitalizes on social discontent for revolutionary purposes. They would even sharpen the lines of the class struggle by the formation, inside school and out, of militant organizations of teachers, pupils, and parents. While they would put an initial trust in the modifiability of human nature through logical persuasion, they would have little confidence that old habits of class interest would be readily reached by such means. Consequently, the solution of the struggle will not always proceed along pleasant lines. Power will have to be met with power. Coercion, unfortunately, will be necessary at times.[31] It will be postponed as long as possible, but when it comes, blame for it will fall, not on the teachers and working class, but on the shoulders of the upper class who could not gracefully surrender undeserved privileges. If the use of force in disobedience of law seems inconsistent with the office of being a teacher, it can only be said that successful insurrection against the capitalist class is altogether moral from the proletarian frame of reference.[32]

Other educators are greatly disappointed at this conclusion, for it means that ultimately education has no important role to play in social tensions. It merely conserves whatever social order happens to obtain. In Plato's *Republic*, education was to conserve social justice when by some happy accident a philosopher-king came to rule. But both the philosophies of waiting for chance occurrence to produce the ideal society and

[31] Reinhold Niebuhr, *Moral Man and Immoral Society* (Charles Scribner's Sons, New York, 1932), p. 15; C. M. Fischer, "The Place of Religious Education in the Social Revolution," *Religious Education*, 31:46–52, January, 1936; Theodore B. Brameld, "Karl Marx and the American Teacher," *Social Frontier*, 2:53–56, November, 1935.
[32] Boris P. Esipov and N. K. Goncharov, *I Want to Be like Stalin* (The John Day Company, Inc., New York, 1947), pp. 141–144.

of forcing its advent with violence break down, because they fail to effect social reconstruction through the more gradual processes of education. No revolution can have real enduring success unaccompanied by the whole-hearted transformation of the mental and moral habits of people as well as the outward transfer of power from the old to the new order. Otherwise, the new order is sadly compromised at the very outset. By using force to bring in the new order of today, it has already prepared the way for counterrevolution by force tomorrow. If the rebuilding of society is to be spared the setbacks of periodic revolutions which shake it to the very foundation, it must employ education before and during change and not just ex post facto to entrench changes brought about by force.[33]

Yet other educators, whose philosophies of education clearly recognize the claims of the proletariat in the collision of class interests, fail to see why these terms of the social problem also constitute the method of its solution. They do not think that an ongoing clash of classes must necessarily be solved by open advocacy of class struggle. For those who have little or no faith in education as a means of social reconstruction, the class struggle may be a consistent procedure. But how can those who have adopted education as a career possibly subscribe to such doctrine? To do so is to repudiate and belittle their profession. On the contrary, educators should maintain faith in discussion and persuasion. Instead of intensifying class antagonisms or widening the breach between classes, they should endeavor to keep open the channels of communication between them. To pin their reliance on rational procedures does not necessarily lead to apathy or complacency. Although teachers neither need to be nor can be neutral in the conflict of social interests, they can and should energetically undertake the reduction of tension in comprehensive social rather than in narrow class interest.

Of course the conciliation of social cleavages is extraordinarily difficult and will take a considerable time to learn. But learning rarely occurs suddenly. All one may learn, even under the pressure of a revolution, is to hate enforced accelerated change. Indeed, how could it be otherwise? If the lamp of reason is not lit or if the light is blown out, it but remains to struggle to a decision in darkness. When rational processes are put aside, it is only too likely that clubs and machine guns will become the social arbiters. Bullets will replace ballots. What a confession of intellectual and moral bankruptcy! And at what a cost! Yet, confidence that rational and educational processes can supplant physical force in the long run is a consummate adventure in faith.

[33] John Dewey, "Education and Social Change," Social Frontier, 3:237, May, 1937.

SELECTED BIBLIOGRAPHY

American Historical Association: *Report of the Commission on Social Studies: Conclusions and Recommendations* (Charles Scribner's Sons, New York, 1934), Chap. 8.

Brameld, Theodore: *Cultural Foundations of Education* (Harper & Row, Publishers, Incorporated, New York, 1957).

Counts, George S.: *Dare the School Build a New Social Order?* (The John Day Company, Inc., New York, 1932).

Nash, Paul: *Authority and Freedom in Education* (John Wiley & Sons, Inc., New York, 1966), Chap. 4.

Newmann, Fred M. and Donald W. Oliver: "Education and Community" in Theodore R. Sizer (ed.), *Religion and Public Education* (Houghton Mifflin Company, Boston, 1967), Chap. 11.

Slesinger, Zalmon: *Education and the Class Struggle* (Covici, Friede, Inc., New York, 1937).

CHAPTER TWO

The Economic Order
and Education

Of the social assumptions which underlie a philosophy of education perhaps those which escape with the least notice and criticism are the economic. Not infrequently teachers and laymen are altogether unaware of the way economic bias conditions school practice. If they have a philosophical frame of reference, they will likely have constructed it with such dimensions as politics and religion in mind but not economics. They will subscribe, for instance, to the idea of equalizing educational opportunity for children but remain quite obtuse to equalizing the economic conditions of men to the extent necessary to achieve their educational ideal. Some who see this connection fail to see that the remedy is more than a matter of financial engineering, that it is also a moral problem of what kind of coordinated educational system and economic order we want. It well behooves us, therefore, to bring to the spotlight of attention just what economic presuppositions are operating underneath various educational practices.

To illustrate our problem, we might note the effect of a changing environment. It is surprising how different democracy in education can be when scaled to an agrarian society and when designed for an industrial one. A nation of small scattered landholders will have an independence and resourcefulness which is bound to be reflected in their schools. But in a nation whose population is predominantly congested in cities and employed in factories, the people have a mutual interdependence which eventually is certain to find a different educational expression. Furthermore, an agrarian society with free land to challenge initiative, perseverance, and resourcefulness may well develop a rugged individualism in its pupils. But a highly compact industrial society offers little or no such chance. There organization and cooperation, rather than individualism, become school objectives. Finally, to mix these ideologies in the same educational prescription, as for instance to infuse education with the optimism of free economic opportunity after the frontier which gave it birth has disappeared, will surely brew educational confusion and social injustice.

Whether one works behind a plow, beside a machine, or at a desk, it is necessary to notice differences in educational practice which arise out of the way in which work is motivated. Ask the parents of children of almost any generation in the nineteenth or twentieth centuries the purpose of going to school, and it is better than an even chance that they will answer "to get ahead." Homework and the work of making a living are stoked by the same urge, personal profit. Just as one competes in business for profits, so too in many schools there is competition for marks. But older and newer schools differ widely on the employment of competition as the motivation for improving the range and quality of learning. The prominent place awarded to examinations and marks in the older type of school finds its counterpart in a highly competitive capitalistic economic system. The newer schools, which insist that no one shall fail, that a curriculum must be found in which the humblest can succeed, are only truly realistic in an economic system based on collectivistic effort.

Perhaps nothing has increased the economic perplexities honeycombing education so much as the twentieth-century struggle between capitalism and communism. The conflict between the two economic systems leaves important educational issues very unsettled. Perhaps at the core of this struggle is the class structure of society and the ownership of land, together with the instruments of production. Is ownership to be public or private? Is it to repose in the middle and upper classes or in the proletariat? The educational consequences of taking sides here are far-reaching. In the capitalist system, the middle and upper classes are likely to look on their superior educational opportunities as merited by their abilities and the services they render society. To the communist, the *bourgeoisie,* entrenched behind the private ownership of capital, appear not only to exploit the laboring proletariat but to establish their own class values as the educational norm for the lower classes as well. How is this conflict to be resolved? Let us consider its relation to educational philosophy under three headings—the production, the distribution, and the ownership of wealth.

SUBSISTENCE AND PROSPERITY ECONOMIES

At the very outset, it is interesting to note the direct relation which exists and always has existed between education and the production of wealth. It is nowhere better illustrated than in the etymological derivation of the word "school." The Old English spelling was "schole," which was borrowed with the change of but one letter from the Latin *schola.* The Romans in turn were indebted to the Greek σχολή. The primary meaning of this Greek word is "leisure"; only secondarily has it been associated with formal education. It came to this derived meaning because leisure time was an indispensable prerequisite to schooling. In early days most people operated on a bare subsistence economy; that is, they consumed practically everything which they produced. Not only that, but with unremitting toil they barely produced enough to ensure a wavering balance between income and outgo. Fortunately, not everyone was so precariously situated. There were a few who had the advantage of a surplus of production over consumption. From time to time these people could relax their bent position over the economic grindstone without endangering the equilibrium of subsistence because they had this reserve to fall back upon. In other words, they could afford to interrupt their work with moments of leisure. It is to the undying credit of the Greeks that, instead of idling away their hard-purchased leisure time, they spent it in self-improvement, in education. So customary did this practice become, that in the course of time the very word for leisure came to be adopted as the word for school. And schooling ever since has flourished chiefly in economies of abundance where the standard of living is high.

Perhaps tracing the ancestry of the word "school" incidentally reveals the reason why school has so often been thought of as academic, as an institution set apart from the workaday concerns of men. But, even in culture patterns where the school incorporates the dominant modes of economic production into its curriculum, there is still need for recognizing a prolonged period of social infancy, during which the child will have economic leisure. The immediate consequences of earning a living can be learned on the job. To learn the more remote ones, however, the child must have more time and freedom than steady employment yields. So it has come to be accepted in a complex civilization that education requires a period of social as well as biological infancy, when the young will live off the labor of others and be released from self-support.

The relation of the school to the standard of living must now be reversed to see how the standard of living is reciprocally conditioned by the school. Suppose one starts with the rather simple Malthusian formula that the standard of living is a function of the ratio between the total amount of wealth of various kinds and the total number of people who are to be supported by that wealth. Most obviously, the school improves the standard of living either by increasing the total stock of wealth or by decreasing the birth rate. Of course it can hardly increase the amount of land or raw materials. But it can go a long way in developing the technical skills which will increase their yield and productivity. It is also admirably suited to promoting such personal qualities as thrift, industry, and efficiency, so important in the exploiting of natural resources. Yet this assistance will be at least partially nullified unless education at the same time encourages wise and discriminating consumption. In spite of full production and wise consumption, the standard of living may still fall and the quality of schooling with it, if the growth of population outdistances the discovery and de-velopment of natural resources. To thwart this, much might be done by the school in disseminating information about birth control, if that were not taboo in important sectors of public opinion. Prevented from influencing the birth rate directly, nevertheless the school perhaps affects it indirectly. It not only widens the range of human economic values, but it also re-arranges their order of urgency. As education teaches people to want better housing, wider travel, finer art, but above all ampler education of higher quality, the size of families shrinks in order to stretch the family income to cover these items.

Here, then, appears a happy formula—the higher the standard of liv-ing, the better the education, the higher still the standard of living, etc., indefinitely. It seems like a panacea. But looks are often deceiving. Perhaps periods of economic prosperity and educational advance have frequently, even generally, been coincident. But none of them has lasted indefinitely. Why is this? There are at least three answers. First, there seems to be a human limit at which "wealth accumulates and men decay." Perhaps this is because, when education is highly developed, it fosters mental activity far above what is required for bare subsistence. Such activity requires great effort, an effort which humans, being what they are, find burden-some to sustain.[1] Consequently, the fact that they lapse and employ their excess wealth in physical ease instead of in increased educational endeavor is regrettable but not altogether surprising.

In the second place, the production of wealth is apparently not limit-less. For one thing, it seems to check itself. Especially in industrial so-cieties does it appear subject to the infirmity of economic cycles. Surplus wealth is reinvested in further machinery for production, but shortly the market's capacity to consume is exhausted, and a period of readjustment follows. Production is slowed down till consumption can catch up again. Producers are thrown out of work, and the standard of living falls. The subsequent public and private financial retrenchment results in a lowered standard of living and curtailment of the educational program.

To break out of this cycle some educators urge a new social ethic. Since science and machines seem to guarantee society against the age-old fear of insufficient production—and that with fewer workers, as automation expands—new educational aims seem in order. The previous emphasis on production should now be subordinated to one of consumption; expendi-ture should rival saving in importance. The vocational aim in education to produce workers should be tempered to the new economic age. Since

---

[1] A. Lawrence Lowell, *At War with Academic Traditions in America* (Harvard University Press, Cambridge, Mass., 1934), p. 51.

there will be need for fewer workers and since they will work fewer hours, much more schooltime should be devoted to turning out consumers, especially consumers in the arts of leisure. The free pursuit of the good, the beautiful, and the true should be encouraged as never before. If these ends are sound, children should be kept out of early employment and in school longer.

The same point can be made more positively against a background of relative prosperity rather than of economic depression. Instead of investing its economic surplus in further production, thus risking overproduction, society should invest more and more in personal services, especially education.[2] To spend money on education is to make an investment in human capital. There are two reasons for such investment. On the one hand, we may regard man as an instrument of production and on the other, as an end in himself. As men eat both to improve their productivity and to enjoy their appetites, so too they have a double interest in education—to increase their technical proficiency and to become well-rounded individuals.

Unfortunately, such an investment in people has yet to establish itself as a social value in comparison with investment in physical capital. The reason people are not regarded as more important than things is because society has long been accustomed to placing a higher value on the accumulation of capital than on its expenditure, on restraining the desire to consume rather than on indulging it. Expenditures for education, especially for consummatory satisfaction, seem to deplete rather than to increase the store of capital goods. If hardheaded, shortsighted, practical men look askance at private investment in human rather than physical capital, it may fall within the public sector of government to readjust this balance of investment.

A third limit to education's riding on the wings of a constantly expanding economy is even more serious. It is to be found in the relatively fixed amount of natural resources. By the careful application of science, raw materials may be forced to make a more efficient yield, but the possibility of their increase in absolute amount seems out of the question. People differ on how to interpret these facts for education.[3] Traditionally, the American system of education has expanded as if there were no bottom to the nation's purse. Three centuries of an open frontier have left an almost indelibly optimistic mark upon the mind of the American educator. Even the disappearance of free land has not discouraged him. He has confidence

[2] John K. Galbraith, "The Social Balance," in Association for Higher Education, *Current Issues in Higher Education*, 1959, pp. 45–47.
[3] George T. Renner, "Education and the Conservation of Resources," *Social Frontier*, 5:203–206, April, 1939.

that the school will so develop the arts and sciences through the inventive genius of its pupils that resultant increased production will more than compensate for the end of the Western frontier. But there is also a more sober educational estimate of the economic facts.[4] There is foreboding that not only geographic but perhaps also industrial frontiers will disappear. Should this prove true, education like industry may have to curtail its expectations.

TYPES OF ECONOMY

The values propounded by an educational philosophy vary not only with the amount of surplus wealth and leisure which an economy can scrape together but also with the type of economy by which that surplus is produced. That is, it makes a further difference to educational values whether the basic way in which people make a living is agricultural or industrial. On the whole, educational values are lower and less widespread in an agrarian than in an industrial society. This is not difficult to understand. Agriculture involves hard physical labor and long hours of work. As a result there is relatively little time to take off to attend school. Furthermore, agrarian surpluses are always uncertain in amount on account of the weather, and even at their peak do not provide for the maintenance of large segments of the population in leisure so that they can attend school for extended periods of time. For long, too, agriculture was an art carried on by empirical rule of thumb and consequently had little need of book learning. More recently, of course, agriculture has become a science as well as an art, which, together with its mechanization, has called for considerably more schooling than formerly. But even at best, predominantly agricultural societies are not renowned for the intensity with which they cultivate the arts and sciences in general.

An economy which in addition to a base in agriculture also has a base in commerce generally places a higher value on education and also makes greater demands on it. The principal form of wealth in a commercial economy is stock in trade. Because this stock is convertible into currency, it is easier for the merchant than the farmer to buy such services as formal teaching represents. Not only that, but the merchant has greater need for formal schooling, for his business has an overhead in the form of records, accounting, and commercial law, which requires book knowledge. Add to this the fact that in the market place he comes to exchange ideas as well

4 J. Anton De Haas, "Economic Nationalism and Education," *Harvard Teachers Record*, 4:69, April, 1934; Ross Finney, *Sociological Philosophy of Education* (The Macmillan Company, New York, 1928), p. 380.

as goods with those from foreign parts, and you have a final reason why a commercial economy makes a greater and more varied demand on education.

It is industrial rather than agricultural society which most enhances the regard for education. In the first place, modern industry is extremely technical. Its intricate machinery and its complicated processes are the result of the tremendous expansion of science. Consequently, if one is just to understand, let alone have the skill to manage modern industry, he must be well trained in science. To gain command of science at its present level of industrial development, one must go long years to school. There is just no other way. In the second place, industrial economy has advanced the cause of education by enormously increasing society's economic surplus. Machines today both in the factory and on the farm are capable of turning out economic surpluses which, according to the standards of yesterday, are nothing short of fantastic. Indeed these machines, these mechanical slaves, are able now to provide enough economic leisure to afford universal education for many who in an earlier period would have been bound to the unremitting toil of human slavery or serfdom.

Even within a given economy, but particularly within an industrial economy, there are further distinctions in making a living which profoundly affect educational values. The principal distinction is earning one's living either chiefly with his hands or chiefly with his head. Of course the head directs the hand, but clearly in some jobs the directive function of the head is more important than the executive function of the hand, and vice versa in other jobs. Not always but on the whole, the more one's job emphasizes mental functions, the more one's education will be a tutelage in the use of symbols and abstractions, and the more one's job emphasizes manual handling of concrete materials, the more his education will be an apprenticeship in the development of manual or motor skills. Such specialization in economic function is not only inevitable but on the whole very desirable if the high standard of living of modern industrial society is to be maintained. But with specialization comes differentiation in social rewards. We live in a society which historically has inherited a system of values that attaches greater worth and prestige to occupations involving the directive work of the mind than it does to those involving executive work with the hands, to cultural rather than to vocational education.[5] Yet we also live in a day when the rising importance of the laboring classes is sharply challenging this hierarchy of value both in economics and in education.

[5] John Dewey, "Culture and Professionalism in Education," *School and Society*, 18:421–424, October, 1923.

The sharpness of this issue was not so great while industrial culture was still in the manu-facture stage. Then both on the farm and in the crafts, all forms of work and learning to work were closely articulated with family life. Consequently it was an easy and natural thing for children to learn by observing and participating in economic production. Personal knowledge and ingenuity could be developed because tools were under the general command of the worker. And not least was the fact that the enterprise was usually of such a size that the setting of one's labor in the total undertaking of production, distribution, and consumption could easily be held in mind as the worker labored.

But when industrial culture passed into the machino-facture stage, the economic enterprise became so large that the directive and planning functions became separated from the productive ones. The former became the badge of a class known as management and the latter the badge of a class known as labor. Specialization in economic function led to specialization in education. As the machines of industry became more complex, labor came to specialize in the parts of the machine they tended. Indeed workers often became mere appendages of machines which others owned. From an education under manu-facture which included an overview of the whole economic process, labor became reduced under machino-facture to an education limited to the specialized skill of tending one small part of the machine. This shrinking of the scope of education seems a pity since the over-all intellectual possibilities of machine civilization, based as they are on science, so far exceed the educational opportunities based on crafts and prescientific agriculture.

THE ROLE OF WORK IN EDUCATION

After seeing the educational values actually generated by existing economies of production, we may well pause to examine normatively what these values ought to be. The oldest and perhaps most persistent position regards work or labor principally as the means whereby leisure is purchased to devote to education. Stated succinctly, the good life depends on labor but consists in leisure. It is a thinly veiled inference of this view that leisure occupies a position morally superior to that of labor. Its superiority lies in the fact that man is compelled to work to live but is uncoerced in the exercise of his leisure; he works for a wage, but he engages in leisure activity because it is worth while on its own account. Of course man may praise voluntarism and still choose to use his leisure for relaxation and play. While this use may be justified on occasion, man must be on his guard against dissipating his leisure in this fashion. If he has a serious sense of responsibility to himself and society he will more often choose to devote his leisure to self-improvement.

Some have regarded this higher form of activity as, indeed, a form of work—moral work, to be exact. Others claim it is a contradiction in terms to regard education as work in any form. As already stated, work implies coercion and the motivation of an extrinsic reward. But enhancement of the humane in man is worth while on its own account. If the student, therefore, regards his education as work, if he must be driven to his studies by teacher threats and scholastic marks, his recalcitrance is a measure of his immaturity and the confusion of his values.[6]

The educational theory that work is the servant of leisure suits itself perfectly to an aristocratic form of society, where one class of men works and another class is maintained in leisure. The opposite of this theory is one which gives work the role, not of servant, but of master in the educational household. This is notably the view of Marx and his followers and also, to an extent, of Gandhi. Since workers dominate communist society, it is not surprising that the role of work dominates communist educational policy. Thus the cultural problems of production, distribution, and consumption become the central ideological axis of the school. Around this axis are concentrated and integrated the scientific, artistic, and social aspects of labor.

In prescribing work, Marx had in mind real work, that is, the production of economic goods. Yet, at the same time that work had the dual objective of industrial efficiency and the humanization of man, it also sought to avoid the twin educational evils of exclusive vocationalism as well as of exclusive verbalism. In both these respects Gandhi was of a similar mind. Indeed, he went even a point further in ascribing to work the added role of partially defraying the cost of the schools. Nor was this insistence merely a virtue born of necessity in a poverty-stricken economy. Gandhi not only strongly opposed a purely literary education because it unfitted youth for the manual work in which most of them would be engaged the rest of their lives, but he believed education through economic work to be a great moral resource as well.[7]

In between the aristocratic and communistic theories of the role of work in education is a theory which takes its cue not so much from the economic as from the epistemological and ethical aspects of work. If work is a necessary evil, it holds the fault is not inherent in work but in

[6] Mortimer J. Adler, "Labor, Leisure, and Liberal Education," *Journal of General Education,* 6:35–45, October, 1951.
[7] T. A. Priest, "The Concept of Sarvodaya in Ghandian Education," *Educational Theory,* 10:148–160, April, 1960.

the conditions surrounding it.[8] Instead of looking on man's expulsion from the Garden of Eden and his condemnation to work as a calamity, this third theory views it as a heaven-sent opportunity, because it was only as man learned to use tools and read signs that he began his long upward evolution. From this angle, work finds its educational significance in its humanization of man. Its educational function is not primarily economic— the tool of a business economy—but epistemological and ethical. On the one hand, work as response to the problematic introduces the student to the need for logical method, and on the other, it involves him in social collaboration through which moral character takes form.

A school which builds its educational program upon this theory is concerned with the child's active occupation. Occupations, however, are not formal as with Froebel but quite pragmatic as with Dewey. With Dewey there are three notable species of the genus "occupation"—work, play, and art. Of the three, work is most important since nearly everyone at some time or other has to earn his bread by the sweat of his brow. It is then that he learns to govern his occupation by its outcome, by the product of his work. And it is only when this connection between work and product is severed that man becomes a robot, preoccupied with his compensation, wages, or leisure. Since play and art present the same opportunity as work to govern occupation by its outcome, no sharp difference is to be made in the educational significance of the three. With its shorter-term goals, play generally does not concentrate on its product with quite the business-like intensity of work. Indeed, it takes more joy in the activity itself. Thus men who first hunted for a livelihood later hunted for sport. Art, not to forget it, is work permeated with the play attitude. Consequently, if work inside or outside school seems toilsome or futile, it but needs to be infused with the spirit of play and art. Therefore work ought to be a congenial and humanizing part of education.

One does not need to be cynical or especially hardheaded to realize the probable impossibility of this ideal under the factual conditions already described.[9] Yet, if the wheels of modern industry driven by modern power plants whir too swiftly to be a satisfactory school, one can recollect nostalgically the kind of school the more leisurely family constituted when it housed handicrafts. Work was humanizing in that era because the school of apprenticeship could easily make plain the relation of work to the end product. Hence if modern industry persists in dehumanizing the educa-

---

[8] John Dewey, "Learning to Earn," *School and Society*, 5:331–335, March, 1917.
[9] Nevertheless, Hugh Hartshorne has insisted that if work is an important part of education, then industry should be planned so that the younger generation can find happy expression in it, even at the expense of slowing it down and rendering it less technically efficient. See his *Character and Human Relations* (Charles Scribner's Sons, New York, 1932), p. 288.

tional role of work by training for specific trades, emphasizing routine duties, turning guidance into job placement, it may afford justification for returning to school those archaic forms of work which do humanize its role.

Many are apprehensive over the consequences of introducing a note of play into what should otherwise be serious work. If children learn to play at their studies, they will later on be inclined to play at their work, and it goes almost without saying that the adult world will not tolerate that frivolity. Play is all right on the playground at recess and after school, but it should not be imported into the regular curriculum. This does not mean that the academic curriculum should not be lightened with spontaneity, but it does warn the teacher not to forget that getting an education is serious business.

Implicit in this complaint is a dualistic theory of work and play. They are viewed as separate activities, as separate attitudes. The common view is that work is serious while play is fun, that work is wearisome while play relaxes. Indeed, play is a relief from work; it is a diversion from the tedium and strain which work engenders. In play, fortunately, there is an absence of the discipline so inherent in work. Of course, both work and play consume energy, but while work depletes the individual's energy, play seems to provide recreation and recuperation of his energy. With work and play so opposite to each other it is not surprising that some educators think that they should be kept separate in school.

Other educators think that a close examination of work and play reveals them as overlapping rather than as disparate categories. Thus they point out that it is quite possible to take one's play very seriously. Some take it so seriously, in fact, that they become professionals and earn their living by it. Even amateurs "work" hard, as we say, at perfecting their form. They discipline themselves by rigid training. Furthermore, cases are not unknown where play ceases to be fun, where men drill so steadily at a sport that it becomes drudgery. Work, conversely, is not without an aspect of play. Some people seek relief and diversion at the end of the day by working in their gardens, on their radios, or at their antiques. But others come home to "play around," as they say, with these same occupations. They find fun and recreation in doing what under other circumstances might well be boring and tiring.

The more one multiplies cases the more difficult it appears to be to classify activities as either work or play or even to tell when any given activity is work or when it is play. For educational purposes perhaps the best way to distinguish between work and play is in terms of the temporal length of one's purposes. The longer these purposes—the more remote the ends in view—the more likely an activity is to be considered work. Conversely, the shorter these purposes—the more immediate the ends—

the more likely the activity is to be of the nature of play. If a boy engages in baseball after school and if when the game is over that is that, we clearly have an instance of play. But if this same boy engages in baseball with a long look beyond the end of the afternoon, possibly to steady employment in the sport, then the game begins to take on an aspect of work even though still doubtless retaining an aspect of play.

The case is no different with academic studies. Suppose teacher and pupil improvise a store as part of an activity program. If the arithmetic learned incidental to this activity is learned just to enjoy the project, then the educational aims are very short-run and the activity becomes little more than a game. If, on the other hand, the children see beyond playing store to the long-range usefulness of the arithmetic learned, then their endeavors take on the more serious character of work. With very young children, whose interest span is very short, it may be necessary to start serious instruction with a game and then withdraw this prop when they grow older. The teacher should feel free to form the daily program as either play or work, whichever circumstances seem to dictate. The chief pedagogical sins to avoid are activities with aims so short-lived as to be trivial and activities so shorn of purpose from the pupil point of view that their performance becomes drudgery.

Finally it needs pointing out that both work and play have a larger pedagogical significance than their mere relation to motivation. The educational significance of economic work has already received considerable attention. But play and work also have epistemological significance. They are the two principal channels for the operation of an activity theory of learning. Thus play and work offer unexcelled opportunities for manipulating and constructing materials, activities of the utmost importance if one holds to a pragmatic view of truth. As long as play was justified in the curriculum as an opportunity for working off surplus energy and thus of keeping out of worse mischief, play had but a tenuous hold on the curriculum. But given pragmatic significance, play has come to have a much more secure place in pedagogical theory.

SOCIOECONOMIC CLASS STRUCTURE

It is one thing to note the differences in educational philosophy which grow out of the production of wealth. The more serious clash of philosophies, however, runs on from this point. The surplus wealth necessary for leisure and schooling is very unevenly distributed throughout the mass of the population. While no strict lines can be drawn to divide the populace, it is common to recognize three different strata—the wealthy, the poor, and the middle classes. The differences in the standards of living at these levels eventuate in corresponding divergencies of cultural outlook. Not infrequently these differences run at cross purposes in the demands they make on education.

How the various class interests set up mutually incompatible tensions in the educational program can be illustrated at several points. Doubtless it may be taken for granted as ethically appropriate that every child should achieve the optimum development of his individuality. Perhaps this ideal could be reasonably reached if there were an unlimited economic surplus that could be spent on education. Since the limitation actually is severe, there has been more or less of a mad scramble for each to get as much of the goods of education as he could. In a capitalist society, the economically powerful have generally been most successful in attaining self-realization for their children. In a proletarian society, the converse has obtained. In both cases, the oppressed class has had to content itself with a half or an even less portion. In neither instance has the dominant class been noted for the tenderness with which it has regarded the educational interests of other classes, especially where any concession might impair or threaten its own aspirations.[10]

The chief educational goods, control and possession of which is the object of class strife, are the length of time one's children shall stay in school and the kind of curriculum they shall study there. Some argue for a larger portion of these goods on the ground that the distribution of intelligence among children generally coincides with the social privilege of their parents. Others stoutly rebut this justification for entrenching the dominant economic class of the moment. While children usually inherit the social privileges or handicaps of their parents, they really seem too young and innocent to have done anything to deserve such social baggage. For just this reason society provides schooling which is free to all. Yet, much as this works for equality of opportunity, it really goes only half far enough. The offspring of the economically favored can make a prolonged stay in school, while all too frequently the children of the underprivileged must be withdrawn at the earliest possible moment in order to go to work.

Indeed, a student will be fortunate if his prospects for staying in school, rather than his native endowment, are not made the main basis for selecting his educational program. Those who can expect a long social and economic infancy usually elect a liberal or cultural education which has traditionally fitted men for the governing and directive offices of life. The rest, since they must leave early, are often shunted off into trade education

---

[10] Percy E. Davidson, "The Socialists on the Equality of Educational Opportunity," *School and Society*, 13:405, April, 1921.

and a position of social subordination. Hard as these circumstances seem to be, they do not lack at least a qualified defense in underlying theory.[11] This theory holds schools should cultivate a privileged leisure class because of the scholarship which its leisure makes possible, the protection its propriety affords ethics and morals, and the wealth with which it can patronize the fine arts. This does not imply that those who labor continuously learn nothing at all. But it does mean that they learn what is immediately useful. The special distinction of the leisure class is that it can afford to study that which is more remotely significant. A great civilization does not live from hand to mouth, from moment to moment, but often centuries beyond its economic working period. Obviously, in such a defense of a leisured class, leisure is not to be confused with idleness. Leisure is to be put to use, notably as the Greeks did, by devotion to education.

But the recurrent danger of such an educational theory is that, in perusing a curriculum dealing with the more remotely significant bearings of daily occupations, a leisure class may lose all contact with their immediate meanings. It may become so aloof in its ivory tower that it is not aware of pressure for fundamental changes in basic conditions. And so, undisturbed, it continues to pursue meanings which, though they once had their origin in a socially significant situation, are no longer so firmly based. From this point on, the culture of this class runs the grave risk of becoming merely ornamental. This may even be socially very wasteful, as where once useful studies are continued as a badge of social class. To dissipate one's time on useless studies marks a person for extravagance. At the same time, however, it permits the subtle inference that he must belong to an upper social class, for only such a class could afford such conspicuous waste. This is why some subjects in the curriculum derive their prestige from the social class that studies them rather than from the uses to which they are put.

Even at its best, the culture of a leisure class involves a vulnerable dualism. Its antithesis is the culture of the working class. Whether the latter be slave or free, peasant or factory-hand, its training has almost from time immemorial been held at a discount in comparison with that of the upper class. Although the necessity of work is universally recognized, nevertheless it is generally thought of as a disagreeable experience; witness "toil" and "drudgery" as synonyms for work. Even religion, condemning man to work in the sweat of his brow, has lent its sanction to some of the disesteem in which work is regarded. Yet, however much the education

---

[11] William E. Chancellor, *Motives, Ideals, and Values in Education* (Houghton Mifflin Company, Boston, 1907), pp. 11–13; John S. MacKenzie, *Outlines of Social Philosophy* (The Macmillan Company, New York, 1921), pp. 105–107.

of a leisure class may have been the admiration and envy of agrarian and commercial societies, its position of preferment is energetically challenged by the proletarian culture of industrial society. Of course, this challenge has been pressed most vigorously under communism. But even under capitalism the culture of the common man has risen to a new prominence. The moral sentiment of democratic capitalism has come to demand that men and women assume responsibility for making a social return for their support. As a result there has developed an increased esteem for labor.[12] No work now is thought shameful except that which is slipshod.

Yet, in spite of the fact that the slowly growing political and economic emancipation of the masses has destroyed the notion that leisure and erudition are the monopoly of a small class, a strong tendency still persists to discount the vital connection between head and hand, between processes and materials. Curriculums built upon the workaday culture of the common man incline to be narrowly confined to the routine and practical. Perhaps this is inescapable, in view of the fact that the results which industrial workers achieve are done for a wage and are the results of working for their employers' ends and not their own. If this degradation of the workers' culture is accepted as the unavoidable consequence of mechanical invention, then educational salvation must be found in shorter hours of work and a compensating leisure life.

No separate attention has been paid so far to the cultural objectives which the middle class is struggling to realize. On the whole, this group feels itself superior to the poorer classes. It further prides itself on its liberality and humaneness.[13] But though it usually is genuinely distressed at the sight of misery and suffering, it is disinclined to make any great sacrifice of its own material comforts to ameliorate the acerbities of the economic order. In severe crises it is most likely to be found on the side of the "haves," rather than the "have nots." Generally the number of children in its families is low, its standard of living correspondingly high. Far from being a class maintained in leisure, this group has a standard of living high enough to appreciate the advantage of superior educational opportunities for its children, yet low enough to need help to realize its educational ambitions. The wealthy have been able to gain their educational ends through private schools. The purse of all but a few of the middle class has been unequal to such a strain. Hence they call upon the state to provide through public schools what they themselves could not

[12] J. Frank Day, "Education and Labor's Reward," *Journal of Educational Sociology*, 4:434–442, March, 1931, and 4:625–633, June, 1931.
[13] George S. Counts, *Dare the School Build a New Social Order?* (The John Day Company, Inc., New York, 1932), pp. 7–9.

through private means. Thus they have long continued the great bulwark of the public school system.

Maybe just because the public school was largely exploited in middle-class interest, it has not enjoyed the full confidence of the proletarian group. Thus, one would prefer to think of the administration behind the public school as being impartial and without the bias of economic class, but the contrary seems more nearly to represent the truth of the matter. Not only is it true that the state is generally controlled by dominant economic interests of the moment, but careful study has revealed that boards of education, instead of being drawn from all three economic strata, have their membership heavily weighted in favor of the middle and upper classes.[14] These two classes themselves do not regard their class as a barrier to disinterested public service but rather count the superior education they have enjoyed as enabling them to rise above class and formulate educational policies in terms of the common weal. Whether there are any board members who could be so disinterested is certainly a moot point.

TEACHERS AND ECONOMIC CLASS ORIENTATION

The question is now in order as to the class point of view from which the teacher should make up his educational philosophy. Granted that social-class structure is bound to condition educational values, should the teacher's educational philosophy have a class orientation? On the whole, the tendency of teachers has been to identify themselves with the two upper classes. This affiliation is probably very natural, since the teaching personnel is most usually recruited from the middle class. Equally influential is the fact that they prefer to think of themselves as one of the learned professions, and the learned professions are notoriously identified with the middle and upper classes.

Persistent influences have been at work, however, to convince teachers that their true interests really lie with the laboring proletariat.[15] Teaching, it is argued, fails of status among the professions because teachers have no control over their remuneration, hours, and conditions of work, as do other professions. Furthermore, because they do not own their own tools and equipment, it is contended they are wage earners pure and simple

---

[14] George S. Counts, *The Social Composition of Boards of Education* (The University of Chicago Press, Chicago, 1927); and Hubert P. Beck, *Men Who Control Our Universities* (King's Crown Press, New York, 1947).

[15] John Dewey, "The Teacher and the Public," *The American Teacher*, 19:3–4, March–April, 1935; and Theodore Brameld, "The Teacher and Organized Labor," *Educational Forum*, 4:253–261, March, 1940.

and should be organized as a skilled trade.[16] Instead of organizing academically, they should organize along economic lines. Just as it is a false dualism in epistemology to separate knowing and doing, so it is also a false dualism to organize teachers as intellectual workers apart from those who work with their hands.[17] Only by joining with the workers, furthermore, can teachers maneuver themselves into a position where they will be effective in future social reconstruction, especially if that reconstruction takes a radical turn. Teachers have so long been wont to think of themselves as professional people that a labor orientation on their part would doubtless require quite an intellectual and emotional readjustment.

That class division and dualism in epistemology have anything in common seems to some philosophers a far cry. But in addition, they argue, since the schools, at least the public schools of a democracy, belong to all the people, the teachers should not play favorites with any economic class. Teachers may unconsciously or uncritically betray a bourgeois orientation, but when they consciously take thought as to their class sympathy they should strive beyond the ordinary to escape any and all class preference. How else can the school maintain its public character? As for thinking themselves an intellectual proletariat oppressed by supervisors and administrators, who, to continue the analogy, constitute a sort of pedagogical capitalistic class, teachers could do nothing which would more quickly disrupt the close cooperation necessary between these two groups for successful learning experiences by the younger generation.[18] Certainly such an interruption of free communication between the two groups would be educationally disastrous.

To soft-pedal class barriers is, in large measure, to press for the cause of democracy in education. Democracy has frequently been said to stand for the abolition of class distinctions. The Marxian class struggle aims at a classless society in which everyone receives education according to his abilities. On the surface, it would appear as if the two educational philosophies of communism and democracy were not so far apart after all. The apparent common ground between them is, however, quicksand. The Marxian society would be classless because only one class, the proletarian, would survive the class struggle.[19] The dictatorship of a single class, however, indicates a certain rigidity of principle. It implies that the evidence on social conflict is all in and that it all points one way. The educational

---

[16] R. Bruce Raup, *Education and Organized Interests in America* (G. P. Putnam's Sons, New York, 1936), pp. 222–223.

[17] John Dewey, "United We Stand," *Social Frontier*, 1:11–12, April, 1935.

[18] William L. Ettinger, "Democratized School Administration," *School and Society*, 12:265–272, October, 1920.

[19] Cf. Ross Finney, *op. cit.*, p. 375, where the middle class is to be the only class.

corollary of such a position is to teach by inculcation. Ultimately, such a method could have little in common with democracy where it is recognized that no dominant class, whether it be a priesthood, a military clique, a political party, the *bourgeoisie*, or the proletariat, is without its own peculiar limitations when it comes to shaping educational policy. Hence the educational corollary of democracy is to socialize intelligence so that no group could, on account of superior knowledge, exploit another.[20]

PRIVATE PROPERTY AND THE PROFIT MOTIVE

Basic to the class structure of education is a problem which remains to be analyzed, that of the ownership of property and the motivation of production. An epitomized description of the capitalist system of private ownership and the quest for profit might run as follows. Ownership is a reward for one's labor. Unless a man can be secure in the possession of the fruits of his toil, he will question whether work is worth the endeavor. Furthermore, man wants to be free, in competition with his fellows, to accumulate as much wealth as he can or wants. If one man works for another, the latter as employer is entitled to pay the former as employee a wage and to keep the balance for himself as profit. Indeed, without the prospect of profit, it is said, business cannot go on. Lastly, having acquired wealth, the owner reserves the right to dispose of it as he wills. Even in death his testamentary will reaches on into the future to control the uses to which his accumulated wealth will be put.

The educational counterpart of the free competition to gain profits is to be found in the appeal to pupil interest, pupil initiative, pupil self-reliance, and freedom for pupil self-expression. More concretely, the preeminent purpose for going to school seems to be that of making money, improving one's economic class status, "getting on." Not only is education to get on, but it is to get ahead as well. Competition in commerce is matched in school with competition for marks, honors, prizes.[21] The young learn to glory not in their strength but in the fact that they are stronger. The less capable often develop a debilitating sense of inferiority. Indeed, it is a school crime for a student to be detected in the act of helping a faltering fellow. When people insist that education be practical, it is the narrow sense of making a material living that is connoted. The wider meaning of practical, the way in which education may enlarge the horizon

[20] John Dewey and James S. Tufts, *Ethics*, rev. ed. (Holt, Rinehart and Winston, Inc., New York, 1932), p. 408.
[21] John Dewey, *School and Society* (The University of Chicago Press, Chicago, 1900), pp. 29–30.

of action, is obscured from view. The individual success motive reigns so supreme that education for personal advancement is thought to coincide with ensuring the common weal.

Not only that, but the system has been thought to be in the interest of children.[22] Some have cited Darwin's theory of evolution in support of competitive practices in business and in school. But it is more likely that Darwin is indebted to the competitive economic doctrine of his day for his theory of the struggle for survival. Again, the worth of self-interest in trade can best be appreciated as a relief from the excessive regimentation of economic life under feudalism and later mercantilism. Correspondingly, in education it proved a boon to develop the individual's powers of self-reliance and self-expression.[23] Finally, in a frontier society, the appeal to individualistic energy rendered a genuine social service in furnishing the enterprise to subjugate the empire of natural resources to be found there. The contrast it provided between the ambitious and the lazy, the thrifty and the ne'er-do-well, even afforded a commendable moral significance. It is no great wonder, therefore, that in a capitalistic society personal traits like industry and thrift have become cardinal objectives of religious as well as secular education.

One of the peculiar features of the private-profit system, whose incidence on education must not be overlooked, is the fact that capitalist production is for profit primarily and for use only secondarily. Goods are produced for use, but only if a profit can be anticipated. Generally, too, only those goods are produced which will yield the greatest profit. One of the points at which this characteristic of business is most pregnant with meaning for education is that of extraschool educational agencies, such as the cinema, radio, and television.[24] Although the main purpose of these great instruments of public opinion is to provide commercial services, their incidental educational consequences are admittedly profound. The critical point, for present purposes, is to note that those who control the educational consequences are governed too often, not by educational ends, but by the necessity of producing profit. Whether this assures the development of the best type of human personality in both the younger and the older generations is frequently open to question.

Sometimes this confusion of commercial and educational interest infiltrates into the school itself. The pursuit of academic freedom, for in-

[22] Merle Curti, "The Social Ideas of American Educators," *Progressive Education*, 11:28–29, January–February, 1934.
[23] Arthur T. Hadley, "Educational Methods and Principles of the Nineteenth Century," *Educational Review*, 28:332–334, November, 1904.
[24] William H. Kilpatrick, "Educational Ideals and the Profit Motive," *Social Frontier*, 1:9–13, November, 1934.

stance, may bring out points which, when taken seriously as a basis for student and popular action, threaten the flow of some entrepreneur's stream of profits. If he thinks of entering a protest, the entrepreneur must decide which is more valuable in the long run, his personal gain or the next generation's education. His usual confusion in distinguishing between selfish and social interests leads many to fear that the profit system is one of the greatest enemies of the free employment of intelligence. Another effect of the profit system is the quality of work it encourages students to do. Since the profit system looks first to the sale and only secondarily to the quality, so too, it is alleged, students are thereby encouraged to do only a grade of work which will "get by."[25] Perhaps this is as much the fault of pragmatism's influence in education as it is the profit system's. Although it was probably only figuratively that pragmatism was early described as raising the question of the "cash value" of an action, nevertheless the pragmatic quality of profits has not escaped popular attention. In either event, the stimulating ideal of fine workmanship as an end in itself is in real danger of being lost.

When profits occur in a private market economy, it is much easier to effect their reinvestment in material capital than in human beings—in the production of further capital goods than in the education of people. The reason is that our economy places a higher value on production than on consumption for it is by saving, refraining from consumption, that capital accumulates. The expenditure of profits on education, unfortunately, seems like consumption rather than the promise of increased future production. Consequently it is downgraded as an investment. While private profits almost automatically find their way back into capital investment, there is no similar automatic process by which they find their way into education. Except for private charity it takes an act of levying taxes by the state to transfer these private profits to education. Perhaps there would be no difference between private and public investment if the return on education could be calculated as objectively as is the return on material capital. But the return on human investment in education is so subjective that there is always present the danger of underestimating, even depreciating, its possibilities.[26]

When the state does decide to channel part of the gross national product into education, it does so in the form of taxation. Private schools, endowed universities, foundations for the promotion of research are a consistent offshoot of a society built on an economy of private property. What

---

25 William C. Bagley, *Education and Emergent Man* (Thomas Nelson & Sons, New York, 1934), pp. 171–172.
26 John K. Galbraith, *op. cit.*, pp. 47–48.

claim, however, has the public school on property vested with private rights? Very often the owning class supports taxes for the public schools because they themselves are assured of a return on their investment. This return consists in the more productive workers that educated employees make. Furthermore, it is estimated that people educated to a humble stake in the economic order will be less likely to commit crimes of violence against property so that, in the end, the support of public education decreases the population that has to be supported in prisons and poorhouses. Private property thus is assumed to be the stabilizing keel of a civilized system of education.[27] Conversely, it can be argued that much of the value of private property is due to the stability which culture gives to the social order. If that be the case, then not all of property's value is due to managerial capacity, but a large portion is a sort of unearned social increment. Of this the owner is not owner, but trustee. When the public taxes, then, it but appropriates that which is its own. It may very well levy a school tax, therefore, on the principle that individuals should give according to their ability and receive according to their need.

As long as there was free land on the frontier, no one took occasion to question the competitive system critically. Indeed, its infirmities were obscured by a sort of natural equality of opportunity it presented. Misgivings began to arise, however, when such a view continued to condition the aims of education in the more compact society engendered by industrial capitalism. In a more settled, congested society, men may fail to achieve an economic subsistence through no faut of their own and in spite of being educated to be industrious and thrifty. Under such conditions, to continue to motivate the school from the competitive point of view may result in the excessive stimulation of the strong and the corresponding oppression of the weak. If so, it is high time to put this philosophy of education in its proper perspective.[28] That the past century and a half has been a period when school could perhaps be revered as an instrument to make wealth in order to gain private profit must not obscure the eras when broader social motives were dominant—when economic success was even irrelevant to the main purpose of life and education.

In fact, some see signs anticipating a return to circumstances which will incline the school toward social service rather than individual success. Since industrial capitalism leads in the direction of concentration and com-

[27] Francis G. Blair, "Education in Relation to Material Values," *School and Society*, 31:422–423, March, 1930.
[28] Rex Tugwell and Leon H. Keyserling, *Redirecting Education* (Columbia University Press, New York, 1934–1935), Vol. I, pp. 100–101; George S. Counts, *The American Road to Culture* (The John Day Company, Inc., New York, 1930), pp. 68–69; Harold F. Clark, "Economic Forces and Education," *Teachers College Record*, 32:326–327, January, 1931.

bination, a planned or collectivistic economy becomes increasingly necessary.[29] Under such a dispensation child interest will be secondary to social
necessity as a gauge for the school program. Children's duties will be emphasized, as well as their rights. It will be of first importance to teach them
how to organize and cooperate in the struggle against poverty and political
knavery, rather than to sharpen their powers and prospects for individual
success. The young will learn to find as much zest in pulling their weight
in one big boat as in paddling their individual canoes. Indeed, they must
learn that in a modern highly specialized and interdependent society more
freedom is to be gained by planning for it through collective action than
by *laissez faire* individual action, where each looks after his own interests
independently, even in disregard of others.

It is communism which has gone farthest down the road of collec-
tivism and has most thoroughly worked out its implications for education.
Central in communist thought is the economic factor in human history.
And central in this economic factor is the dialectical conflict, active all
through history, between the limited number possessed of private property
—notably the *bourgeoisie* and upper classes—and the vast dispossessed
and disinherited masses. As long as the labor of the latter is exploited by
the former there can be no prospect of labor playing its proper role in the
educative process. In fact, how can it when the social-class system nurtures
a sham dualism between manual and intellectual work? Sweep these class
distinctions away, and it will be possible to assign the worker his rightful
place in the educational scheme. And there is no reason why these distinctions should not be swept away, seeing that a class-ridden society
started as an accident in history and continues today as an anachronism.
When the mass of men become owners of what they produce as well as of
the instruments of production, they will be able to learn joyfully, inspired
by the intrinsic value of their labor.

But, even under these advanced circumstances, there are some among
both capitalists and communists who are unwilling to see competition
completely disappear from the educative process. They prefer the motivation of cooperation as more economical and more moral but, nevertheless,
they do not shut their eyes to the dangers of regimentation. In a reconstructed view of things, their design would be to socialize the competitive
incentive. Thus they would have competition among groups, as among two
or more schools or classes in a school, to see which could first complete
its portion of a large, planned, cooperative enterprise. In such a rivalry no
individual would be outstripped and thrown into the social discard because

---

[29] J. Anton De Haas, *op. cit.*, pp. 63–72.

his group would feel obliged to come to his assistance. Care would have to be taken here only that the aid rendered him would be truly educational and would not impoverish his scholastic abilities further.

SELECTED BIBLIOGRAPHY

American Historical Association: *Report of the Commission on Social Studies: Conclusions and Recommendations* (Charles Scribner's Sons, New York, 1934), Chaps. 2–3.

Bukharin, Nikolai, and Evgeni Preobrazhensky: *The ABC of Communism* (Workers' Party of America, Lyceum Literature Department, New York, 1921), Chap. 10.

Counts, George S.: *The Challenge of Soviet Education* (McGraw-Hill Book Company, New York, 1957).

Davis, Jerome: *Capitalism and Its Culture* (Holt, Rinehart and Winston, Inc., New York, 1935), Chap. 18.

Donohue, John W.: *Work and Education* (Loyola University Press, Chicago, 1959).

Hook, Sidney: *Education for Modern Man* (The Dial Press, Inc., New York, 1963), Chaps. 5, 9.

John Dewey Society: Fifth Yearbook, *Workers' Education in the United States* (Harper & Row, Publishers Incorporated, New York, 1941), Chap. 12.

Kallen, Horace M.: *The Education of Free Men* (Farrar, Straus & Cudahy, Inc., New York, 1949), Chaps. 16–18.

Kilpatrick, William H. (ed.): *The Educational Frontier* (Appleton-Century-Crofts, Inc., New York, 1933), Chap. 2.

Nash, Paul: *Authority and Freedom in Education* (John Wiley & Sons, Inc., New York, 1966), Chap. 1.

Patel, M. S.: *The Educational Philosophy of Mahatma Gandhi* (Navajivan Publishing House, Ahmedabad, India, 1953), Chap. 6.

Pinkevitch, Albert P.: *The New Education in the Soviet Republic* (The John Day Company, Inc., New York, 1929), Chaps. 7–8.

Pring, Beryl: *Education, Capitalist and Socialist* (Methuen & Co., Ltd., London, 1937).

Russell, Bertrand: *Education and the Modern World* (W. W. Norton & Company, Inc., New York, 1932), Chaps. 10, 11, 13.

Shore, Maurice J.: *Soviet Education: Its Psychology and Philosophy* (Philosophical Library, Inc., New York, 1947).

Slesinger, Zalmon: *Education and the Class Struggle* (Crown Publishers, Inc., New York, 1937).

Veblen, Thorstein: *The Theory of the Leisure Class* (The Viking Press, Inc., New York, 1922), Chap. 14.

CHAPTER THREE

Politics and Education

The schoolmen in this country are wont to deplore the entrance of politics into school affairs. They fear that educational policies will then be determined by considerations oblique or even irrelevant to the meritorious development of education itself. In some quarters this studied attempt to keep the schools unsullied by politics is viewed as grave misfortune. In the communistic ideology—and probably in the fascistic ideology as well—it is unthinkable that the schools should lie outside the political sphere. Since the school trains the future citizen, education is far too strategic an instrument to fall into the hands of any save the state. Politics so conceived is not a term of opprobrium; it is rather synonymous with statesmanship. It is that phase of ethics which treats of the duties of states. In this sense probably even bourgeoise societies will agree that education can hardly be divorced from politics. In any event, it is the theory of politics conceived in its highest terms with which the philosophy of education has now to deal.[1]

Politics in this sense concerns the aim or design according to which social arrangements are made. Some think that the origin of such an aim or design is the result of premeditation antedating the practice of politics itself. Indeed, it is this priority in time and independence of events which recommends it as a guiding principle. If founded in natural law as well, it carries that much greater weight. Others take the view that political theory is rather the outcome of political activity. A political ideology must be seen not as a premeditated beginning of civic activity but as a theoretical statement of historical traditions. To be sure, the American Declaration of Independence did foreshadow educational policy by assuming that all men are created equal, but the idea did not spring full-born from the brow of Thomas Jefferson. As a matter of fact the idea represented much cogitation by many minds on the day-to-day experience of generations of Europeans as well as Americans. It was thus an abbreviated abstract of a long historical process.

If one allows himself to reflect on educational practice of the present century, he will note a number of problems whose solution at bottom in-

[1] William P. Warren, "Philosophy, Politics, and Education," *International Journal of Ethics,* 47:342–344, April, 1937; Theodore Brameld, "The Philosophy of Education as the Philosophy of Politics," *School and Society,* 68:329–334, November, 1948.

volves political ideologies. At the top or close to the top of the list is the one just mentioned as foreshadowed by the Declaration of Independence— how shall educational opportunities be distributed? Primarily, shall there be equality of opportunity? If so, what does that golden phrase mean for races of different colors? What does it mean in regard to the eradication of individual poverty or where there are vast differences in the economic ability of states to support optimum educational programs? Again, what does it mean in terms of honors and advance-placement programs for superior students?

Another educational problem at or near the top of importance concerns the distribution of political power. The twentieth century seems marked by a worldwide drift toward popular forms of government. What are the educational implications of rule by the people? To what extent should educational decisions be shared by, and with the consent of, the governed? For instance, does this notion include students where their interests are involved? And how are "people" conceived? Will governments and schools respect them as persons and treat them ethically as ends? Will they recognize them as having singular and unique individualities? And if so, will they accord individuality the freedom and the right to dissent? Coincidentally, will they maintain the autonomy of the university with its tradition of criticizing tradition? These are the major issues to which we now turn.

AUTOCRACY

We begin with the effect which the distribution of political power has on educational philosophy. For convenience we shall note the educational consequences of vesting political power in the one, the few, or the many. This threefold division of political power represents a classification of political theories which is as old as Aristotle and as modern as today.

As for rule by the one, there have been various types. Whether the ruler has been a king, tyrant, despot, or dictator, however, will make little difference, for the educational consequences of all will be much the same. Where one rules, the final decision on public policy rests with him. Obviously, such a ruler must have the best education that his times afford in order to make wise choices. While it would be a happy coincidence for all the ruler's subjects to have an equally fine education, it is clearly not a necessity, as in the case of the ruler himself. Since a first-rate education for all is not indispensable, it is an easy step to point out that neither is it desirable. Where there is differentiation of social function, it may well be claimed that there should be specialization in educational preparation. Thus, the ruler should have one kind of training, but the ruled another. The former should learn to choose and to lead, while the latter should learn not to question, but to follow.[2] The teachers under an absolute ruler will propagandize and indoctrinate the decisions made higher up. As in the army, the schools of an autocracy will more than likely emphasize drill and obedience at the expense of initiative and criticism.

The merits and demerits of such an educational philosophy are the same as those of the political theory after which it is patterned. There is undoubtedly an efficiency and expedition that is deserving of praise. The respect paid to the expert is indeed admirable. On the other hand, educational outcomes for the people as a whole are heavily staked on the superior education of just one person. This might fail at several points. If the ruler inherits his office, of course his education for leadership can commence very early. But there is no guarantee then that he has the native hereditary qualities which will improve or deserve the opportunities of his environment. If the ruler rises to power relatively late in life, as a dictator often does, it is too late to educate him formally for his task. And this is to say nothing of the waste of the undeveloped talent of the mass of the population.

ARISTOCRACY, OLIGARCHY, AND PLUTOCRACY

It is rare that rule by the one is found in pure and simple form. Generally, the sovereign power is shared with a selected group of others. This minority group may rule with or without elevating one of their number above the rest. In either event this distribution of power results in oligarchy, rule by the few. These few may be variously recruited. Among the Greeks they were the οἱ ἄριστοι, the best people—hence our word "aristocrats." For long the nobility of the aristocrats was thought to be hereditary. Under modern capitalism, the few have sometimes formed a plutocracy, rule by the wealthy. Communism and fascism also result in rule by the few because the ruling party is a minority group. Obviously, whatever way the few are constituted will have definite educational implications.

When the few have been a nobility, education has notoriously been an upper-class affair. The nobility and the wealthy *bourgeoisie* have virtually had a monopoly of education beyond the rudiments. European education, even as late as the twentieth century, still exhibits this influence in its two-class system of schools, one set for the masses and another for the classes. The reasons are clear. Governmental policy is determined by a

[2] Fred Clarke, *Essays in the Politics of Education* (Oxford University Press, Fair Lawn, N.J., 1923), p. 34.

ruling class. Naturally they must have an education consonant with their responsibilities. The education of the rest of the people beyond what is absolutely necessary can be relatively neglected.

The fascistic philosophy of education has some points in common with this view. Here, education is chiefly for a dominant elite. The leadership principle of feudal times is central. Sovereignty rests with a group of leaders who do not derive their power from the populace or its elected representatives, but from their ability to rule by rising above their own immediate private interests. It is no chance affair that those of exceptional endowment become the elite of power and influence in the affairs of life. This is but the inexorable logic of events. Furthermore, like produces like. Consequently, it is no mere accident that the great majority of gifted children are born in the families of the privileged classes. Education, therefore, does not make or unmake the dominant elite. It merely accentuates their excellence and in so doing increases their social distance from the masses. It equips them to wield the power which is their lot. In this there should be nothing depressing. On the contrary, there is a sort of Platonic justice about it. Each person will be educated to the full extent of his potentialities, but none for a role beyond what his native endowment warrants. If some are discontented, it will be a simple exercise of educational technique to condition them to be content with what they have and to perform their role in the social whole.

Members of this select minority validate their choice of values by their power to enforce them. It is bluntly admitted that this is the only way to terminate the protracted arguments to which the more democratic methods of discussion and persuasion lead. Those in the adult generation who cannot see it this way must be repressed. In the younger generation, education can take the place of repression. But even with them, what is taught is fixed in advance by the leaders. There is no free discussion of the educational ideal. Universities are no longer autonomous seats of learning where an argument can be pursued in Socratic fashion whithersoever it may lead. A science so pure and objective as not to reflect national bias has no place in the curriculum. Educational freedom in such a state does not mean self-realization or emancipation of the individual, but rather the sublimation of the individual in the interests of the state. Liberty is not a right but a concession of the state, contingent on what it deems its own interests. Consequently, the virtues in which the individual is schooled are those of discipline, duty, and self-sacrifice.

The communistic philosophy of education appears to court many of the same objectives that fascism does. Yet there are some notable differences. One may perhaps take a very serious exception, at the start, to communism as an instance of the rule by the few. Since most communists agitate for the dictatorship of the proletariat, and since the proletariat far outnumbers any other class in society, this classification of communism may seem somewhat incongruous. On the other hand, whatever the manifold paper theories of communism call for, the fact is that in Russia, communism's most conspicuous exponent, sovereign power has been narrowly held by a minority political party, whose head is a personal dictator. The educational corollaries of this paradoxical situation require some further elucidation.

On the point of educational method, the dictatorship of the proletariat seems to have most in common with the fascistic type of dictatorship. Communism just as frankly warps the school to its peculiar ideology as does fascism. The rising generation is instilled with the proletarian point of view through just as authoritarian indoctrination. Academic freedom or self-determination for other minorities can be tolerated only within the confines of communist doctrine.

Not everywhere, of course, is the proletariat powerful enough to dictate educational policy so unquestionably. In countries where communism is a hope rather than a fact, methodology must be modified during the inevitable period of transition. For the evangelical teacher, persuasion is the first line of attack.[3] He will openly persuade his pupils toward his viewpoint if the community does not interfere but will not hesitate to exercise his influence subtly if necessary. But, even so, the Marxist will have much less confidence than liberal educators as to what can be achieved through a democratic educational process. When balked by opposition to communism, he will readily abandon education altogether as a means of social reform and rely on force and violence just as the fascist does. If disobedience to law seems highly inconsistent for the teacher in the capitalist system, it may be looked upon as highly moral when viewed from the Marxist frame of reference.[4]

In the matter of the creation of educational opportunities, the two types of dictatorship commence to diverge considerably. Rule by a minority political party is said to be only a temporary phase of communism. The benevolent despotism of fascism apparently was to last indefinitely. When communism has been made entirely secure, sovereignty is expected to be put on the widest possible base. Consequently, while opportunities for the best education may be narrowly limited at first, later it is hoped they will be extended to all. Far from cutting the educational pattern to meet the needs of a dominant elite, communism aims ultimately at a classless so-

---

[3] Theodore B. Brameld, "Karl Marx and the American Teacher," *The Social Frontier*, 2:54, November, 1935.
[4] *Ibid.*

ciety where the limits of schooling will be set by ability alone. This recognition of the proletariat as the center of gravity in the communistic philosophy of education is also emphasized in the curriculum, where the cultural problems of peasants and industrial workers are the absorbing interest. This is true even of the transition stage of rule by personal dictator and party leaders.

At this point, the philosophy of education consequent to rule by the few almost merges with that attendant upon rule by the many. Before taking up this next point, however, it will be well to glance at some objections to the philosophy of the education of the few. Several severe criticisms have been aimed at supposedly vulnerable points in this theory. One of the chief snares said to lurk in this point of view is the assumption that only the few are capable of intellectual training. Certainly one must beware the insidious ease with which the holding of such a hypothesis can color one's estimate of the data it seeks to interpret.

No less misleading, so it is claimed, is the plausible way in which the ruling class justifies its superior education. The stock argument has it that superior educational opportunities for the few are to be justified in the superior service which the few are thereby enabled to render to the masses and to society as a whole. If they have educational privileges not shared by the majority, these privileges are a compensation or reward for the meritorious social function this minority performs. But one must be on guard against hypocrisy here.[5] While educational privileges may originate in this fashion, more than likely after the lapse of time they will be accepted as rights, due to hereditary superiority. Superior educational advantages so readily increase one's social distance from his fellows that he all too quickly rationalizes his outstanding opportunity as something due to innate endowment. For the argument to be really plausible, proof should be required that the underprivileged classes could not do as well if given equal educational opportunities. The privileged classes have usually asserted the futility of any social maneuver to find this out because they claim the masses on the whole have given practically no evidence of abilities worth cultivating. As a matter of fact, there is a serious lack of evidence for this claim. First the privileged classes oppress the masses by denying them an enriched opportunity and then turn about and accuse them of lacking the very abilities they have been refused a chance to display.

But, even granting that the maximal education of the few is but commensurate with their peculiar function as rulers, there is still objection to such a philosophy of education. The further difficulty with this argument

[5] Reinhold Niebuhr, *Moral Man and Immoral Society* (Charles Scribner's Sons, New York, 1932), pp. 117–118.

is that it is so dangerously easy, even with the best of intent, to mistake the selfish interests of one's class for the welfare of the whole. In practice, it must be admitted that only too frequently individuals use the educational gifts conferred on them by society for their own self-aggrandizement and correspondingly often fail to recognize the social obligation which such privilege creates. Indeed, in some instances, the privilege is even looked upon as a means of avoiding some of the more onerous social burdens. As a matter of fact, it ought to be axiomatic that it is a good thing for any man that his fellows obtain a superior education.

DEMOCRACY AS RESPECT FOR DIGNITY OF THE PERSON

An instance has already been noted where the educational pattern is cut after the interests of the many, although the many do not, at least as yet, participate broadly in the exercise of sovereign power. It is now in order to inspect a philosophy where not only are the many the center of educational gravity, but where the government, too, is of the many, by the many, and for the many. This variance in political base does make a significant difference in educational theory. While the schools of benevolent despotism may be primarily devoted to the cultural concerns of the workers, they may still fall short of the development of personality found in a democracy, simply because they do not reach the moral autonomy which is possible with a universal franchise.

Democracy makes the many of such paramount political and educational importance because it believes in the essential dignity of all persons.[6] It enjoins that every person be treated always as an end.[7] This injunction holds no matter to which sex a person belongs, no matter what his color or race, no matter whether he is highborn or low, and no matter what the economic condition of his parents is. Whatever these accidental circumstances, a man is to be educated as man because of his humane nature, because "a man's a man for a' that." Since every individual counts, it would be a cosmic miscarriage for his capacities to go undeveloped. Failure to realize his peculiar potentialities not only would pauperize him but would in so far pauperize the society of which he is a member.

The personal virtues which democracy's schools inculcate can easily be imagined. Since the measure of a man is what he is and what he can do, the individual is under the duty of making the most he possibly can out of

---

[6] William H. Kilpatrick, "Democracy and Respect for Personality," *Progressive Education*, 16:83–90, February, 1939; Edward H. Reisner, "The Quality of School Experience Appropriate to a Democracy," *Teachers College Record*, 40:698–700, May, 1939.
[7] *Infra*, p. 298.

himself. Teachers will encourage qualities of initiative, enterprise, self-reliance, and perseverance in their pupils. On the economic side, there will be emphasis on hard work, the dignity of labor, and scorn of idleness and a leisure class.[8] On the political side, provisions for education will be conditioned by a deep devotion to our common patrimony of civil rights and by a no less deep regard for civic responsibilities. To fulfill these specifications nothing less than universal education will suffice, the education of each and all to the limit of their capacities or at least to a point of diminishing returns of instructional effort expended on them.

What is the warrant for the democratic faith in the dignity of the person?[9] Some support their faith with largely secular arguments.[10] Democratic regard for human dignity, they claim, pays off in a richer quality of living for all concerned. This is not simply the conclusion of unsupported theory; it is attested by the hard facts of human experience. Furthermore, these facts are not of just recent origin; they have been accumulating through long centuries of history. From pre-Christian times right down to the present there has been an age-long struggle to guarantee the respect for personality—long accorded to the one and the few—to the many as well. The struggle has waxed and waned in different periods of history, but over the centuries democracy has slowly been emerging the victor over autocracy and aristocracy. People aware of their stake in the struggle and the price at which it has been bought evidence a staunch and abiding confidence in their democratic faith.

Others feel anxious about the security of their democratic faith in the dignity of the person unless it is anchored in something more than the precedents of history and the habits of men. To them the proud claim that the dignity of man is guaranteed by "inalienable" rights to life, liberty, and happiness is hollow indeed unless it is rooted in religious rather than purely secular principles. Operating on Judeo-Christian convictions, they find the dignity of the individual assured through the universal fatherhood of God. To acknowledge the fatherhood of God implies that all men are brothers. If all men are brothers, then they must all be objects of infinite worth in the sight of their divine Parent. Having a capacity for infinite love, God is not likely to play favorites with his children. In any event, whatever

---

[8] Isaac L. Kandel, "The Philosophy Underlying the System of Education in the United States," International Institute, *Educational Yearbook*, 1929 (Teachers College, Columbia University, New York, 1930), p. 518.

[9] John S. Brubacher, "Democracy, Education, and the Judeo-Christian Tradition," *Religious Education*, 38:353, November–December, 1943.

[10] William H. Kilpatrick, *op. cit.*, pp. 83–84; Frederick S. Breed, National Society for the Study of Education, Forty-first Yearbook, Part I, *Philosophies of Education* (Public School Publishing Company, Bloomington, Ill., 1942), p. 136.

their worth, it is intrinsic in their nature. Democracy and Christianity are not just congenial; they are congenital.

Obviously, these two approaches to authenticating the dignity of man lead to different consequences. In the one case, "consent of the governed" is the ultimate authority in determining educational policy. This implies that authority is immanent in man and requires us to place tremendous confidence in our fellows that they will neither impair nor rescind man's fundamental rights, especially his right to an education which will enable him to realize the fullness of his nature. In a world that could produce the Nazi philosophy of education, this seems an optimistic if not unwarranted expectation. In the other case, it is not society that is sovereign but God. And it is He who gives ultimate validity to educational policy. If the right to command man came from God instead of man, society might disregard man's fundamental rights, but it could never alienate them from him. On the contrary, as is often stated, these most precious rights are "inalienable" because God-given.

DEMOCRACY AS FREEDOM

Not the least aspect of the dignity of the person is his individuality, that is, the manner in which he is different from others. Every one possesses individuality because, being sexually produced, he is unique, the first and last of his kind.[11] Because it is of the very nature of man's individuality to be different from his fellows, he wants to be free. He wants to assert his individuality, his unique nature, with a minimum of let and hindrance from his fellows.[12] If men were born with equal talents, they would not feel this yearning for freedom, for the wants of all would be much if not altogether alike. But the scientific fact is that they are born different, and it is this fact which lends significance to the oft heard claim that they are born free.

When we use the word "freedom," it is usually followed by the preposition "from." On the whole, this is the sort of freedom with which we have identified democratic education so far. We have emphasized the importance of establishing the independence of the individual from environmental circumstances which would restrict or interfere with his individuality. But "freedom" is also often followed by the preposition "to" or "for."[13]

[11] Edwin G. Conklin, "Contributions of Biological Research to Education," *School and Society*, 31:752, June, 1930.

[12] Cf. Isaac L. Kandel, "Liberalism and Education," *Educational Forum*, 1:261–270, March, 1937; William H. Kilpatrick, *op. cit.*, pp. 85–90.

[13] James L. McConaughy, "Education in a Democracy," *School and Society*, 46:391, September, 1937.

Mere severance from encroachments of the social environment would give democratic education a rather narrow and principally negative quality. There are many who like to think of democratic freedom in more affirmative terms. They want freedom "from" constraint, to be sure, but they also want to be free "to" take action in the belief that freedom to take action is a factor in the outcome of events. The more thoroughly educated people are in a field the more free they are to take positive action. Hence no one should think of democratic freedom in a whimsical or capricious sense. On the contrary, only the well-disciplined should be entitled to enjoy democratic freedom.[14]

There are a number of points in educational practice at which democracy emerges in the form of an emphasis on freedom. Perhaps first to leap to mind would be academic freedom.[15] Academic freedom is an excellent illustration of a freedom which involves both the prepositions "from" and "to." The teacher must be free "from" influences which prevent his stating the truth as he sees it, but he must also be thoroughly competent in his field "to" investigate the truth. The basis for such competence generally rests in part on a sound liberal education. In liberal education we have another emergence of freedom.[16] Liberal education, as the etymological derivation of liberal from the Latin *liber* implies, is the education of the free man, the man who enjoys political freedom.[17] Obviously, in a democracy in which all men are politically free, all should have a liberal education. But this liberal education should further be conceived in the spirit of liberalism—or individualism, as de Tocqueville put it. As a last instance, since all men in a democracy are free, education must be free, that is, there must be no economic barriers to its acquisition.[18] It is this freedom which is incorporated in the idea of a "public" school, a school open and free to all.

In modern democracies numbers are so enormous that entrusting political powers to the many would all but defeat itself if it were not for the selection of leaders or experts to guide and execute the common will. Since modern democracies are representative rather than simple or direct

14 Cf. William Stanley, B. Othanel Smith, and Kenneth D. Benne, "Progressive Essentialism in Education," *Frontiers of Democracy*, 9:209–210, April, 1943; Isaac L. Kandel, "The New School," *Teachers College Record*, 33:505–514, March, 1932.

15 James L. McConaughy, *op. cit.*, pp. 287–389.

16 Harold Taylor, "Individualism and the Liberal Tradition," in Willis D. Weatherford (ed.), *Goals of Higher Education* (Harvard University Press, Cambridge, Mass., 1960), Chap. 1. See also Ralph Barton Perry, *Realms of Value* (Harvard University Press, Cambridge, Mass., 1954), pp. 425–436.

17 Cf. Mortimer J. Adler, "Liberalism and Liberal Education," *Educational Record*, 20:422–436, July, 1939.

18 For further illustrations of what democracy means in practice, see Charles F. S. Virtue, "Are Our Schools Really Democratic?" *School and Society*, 51:425–428, April, 1940.

democracies, some think it the proper function of the schools on the one hand to select and educate the capable for leadership and on the other to train the balance of the population for intelligent followership. While this is undoubtedly a gain in freedom for the individualities of the few educated to lead, it is not, as some fear, an infringement on the freedom of the individualites of those educated to follow. It is really a gain in freedom for all. The obvious advantage in the education of a democratic elite is the greater freedom they make possible for the masses through making available for them insights they have not the wit to see. Indeed, such an educational practice falls neatly within Plato's ethic of justice, in that each group in society is being educated in line with its talents and in such a fashion as to benefit the whole group.

The contribution of an educated leadership to the advantage of the social whole is generally well recognized. Less well understood, however, is the need for well-educated followership. The two are complementary aspects of a democratic education for freedom. The mere fact that leaders are provided is far from a guarantee that the rest of the people will follow. They must know enough to see that their advantage lies that way. On the other hand, leaders cannot expect the populace to follow their initiative blindly. The danger here would be that the leaders might soon lull themselves into the easy self-assurance of infallibility. After all, leaders and led are one society. In a democracy where there is rule by the many, the many must have the final word on what direction social activity shall take. The leaders must, therefore, convince them what is best to do. Their only hope for this lies in well-educated followers, people who can discriminate between the charlatan and the genuine leader. It has even been said that the best-educated people are the most led.

Education for the dual role of leadership and followership appears to run a perilously close parallel to the sort of education found fitting where political power is held by the few. In fact no small number are afraid that a democratic elite will abuse their freedom, that they will selfishly exploit it to develop their own individualities through education but not in such a way as to benefit the whole. If democratic schools foster an aristocracy of talent, there seem to be several safeguards to prevent this paradoxical situation from endangering an ultimate democratic outcome. The chief thing which seems to save democratic freedom is the democratic recruitment of future leaders. Thus democracy's aristocracy will not be artificially chosen on the basis of socially inherited privileges, but will rather be selected according to the excellence of native endowment. Moreover, it is hoped that a further safeguard on the side of democracy will be found in the debt of gratitude which the natural elite will feel toward the masses from whose flesh and blood they sprang and by whom their superior education was made possible. But perhaps the chief safeguard rests in avoiding the all too common mistake of drawing the lines between leaders and led too strictly and too rigidly. Those who have a competence to lead in politics may well be those to follow in scientific research, and those who should be captains of industry may well follow in aesthetic concerns. The democratic administration of the grading or grouping of pupils, therefore, indicates that groupings should be kept flexible, that they should be reviewed whenever the educational purpose of the group shifts.[19] Only so can the freedom of the individual be kept alive and flexible.

While this appears to be a sound theory of democratic freedom, we must not forget that historically the distinction between the education of leaders and the education of followers, the education of the upper and lower classes, was not predicated on democratic principles of justice and equity. Rather it was predicated on birth and economic privilege. Only after a prolonged struggle for power were the many, the lower classes, able to wrest a fair measure of educational freedom for their own individual interests. In this struggle, too, only rarely did the upper classes voluntarily make concessions to the distribution of politico-economic power and consequently to educational opportunity on ethical principles of justice. Interestingly enough, the upper classes have been quicker to yield to lower class pressure for greater educational freedom than for political and especially economic freedom. This is because education merely denotes privilege, while suffrage denotes both privilege and power. They have further preserved their tactical superiority in social affairs by magnanimously providing the masses with an education calculated to inculcate submissiveness. But the advantage promises to be only temporary. Education, if not power, is at least potential power. It equips the disinherited with the means of an ever more efficient protection of their own interests.[20]

So far we have taken an optimistic view of the uses of freedom in a philosophy of education. Sometimes it has unexpected and untoward results. Instead of encouraging a sturdy self-reliance and confidence in one's powers, the pursuit of freedom, especially in the wake of the two World Wars, has overwhelmed some people with such an oppressive sense of loneliness and insecurity, even of insignificance, that life becomes in the end meaningless for them. In this predicament, seeking an escape from the burdens of freedom, they generally beat a retreat along either one of

---

[19] *Infra*, pp. 266–267.
[20] Harold Laski, *A Grammar of Politics* (George Allen & Unwin, Ltd., London, 1925), pp. 114, 147.

two educational roads, one leading to conformity and the other to authoritarianism.

Other untoward results of an education based on free or liberal principles are the possible excesses to which it may lead. Some claim that when democracy's schools have liberated individuality they have succeeded in breeding a race of vigorous, self-confident men, but unhappily a race unworthy of the trust of wealth and power because they have been found wanting in self-criticism and unselfish politico-economic action.[21] In a limited economy, where the means are insufficient for all to achieve the full stature of their potentialities, individuals engage in a competitive struggle for economic and educational opportunities. With no greater loyalty than self, they frequently exploit the development of those less able to help themselves. Some even assail democratic rule by the majority as the attempt of pressure groups to gain control of the government for the time being to ensure their own cultural and educational interests. Furthermore, since government is subject to the whims of passing majorities, they attack it for being unsure of its own educational ends, for offering no steady object of allegiance.[22]

These are serious indictments of democratic freedom. They show a one-sided emphasis on justice, an emphasis that is only partly just. Apparently modern educators have not yet fully learned and applied Plato's concept of justice, educating the individual according to his talents, yes, but in such a way as to benefit the whole. However, learning to have regard for others as for oneself is an old problem of the human race. No doubt it will long continue to remain a standing challenge to democratic education.

Even when democracy is functioning at its virtuous best, it seems to suffer from inherent infirmities. These infirmities are most likely to disclose themselves when democracy clashes with autocracies or oligarchies. Then the very freedom for the individual, respected by democracy's school, may become a liability rather than an asset. Thus, taught to listen to a variety of opinion, democracy must take time out to educate itself on the merits of the clash and what to do about it. Meanwhile an autocracy or oligarchy, unhampered by parliamentary or educational safeguards, may strike at once and thereby gain an overwhelming initial advantage, not unlikely the advantage of driving a wedge into the ranks of democracy while it is divided into parties to discuss the pros and cons of the clash. Another danger arises from the agent of autocracy or oligarchy who bores from within democracy under the guise of a critic. Behind this pose he may tear

[21] William E. Hocking, "The Future of Liberalism," *Journal of Philosophy*, 32:234, April, 1935.
[22] Cf. Joseph A. Leighton, *The Field of Philosophy* (Appleton-Century-Crofts, Inc., New York, 1930), pp. 399–400.

down democracy's structure and, if challenged for his destructive work, take refuge in the academic freedom or civil liberty which democracy accords its citizens, to be sure that its shortcomings come to public attention.[23]

DEMOCRACY AS EQUALITARIANISM

The American Declaration of Independence states that "all men are created equal." At first glance it would appear that this new dimension of a democratic philosophy of education presents us with a paradox. After establishing the dignity of the person and the freedom to assert his unique individuality, is it not a contradiction in terms or at least a serious ambiguity to turn about and claim the equality of all men?[24] The answer to this question is very complex. An initial handle to it may be to ask how this clause of the Founding Fathers is to be interpreted. Were they making an empirical descriptive statement of fact, or were they rather laying down an ethical prescription of how men ought to be treated?

Some have accepted the former interpretation. Although the author of the Declaration of Independence himself seems not to have subscribed to this interpretation, some pre-revolutionary French writers such as Helvetius seem to have espoused it. Moreover it is easy to infer that Rousseau also subscribed to it, because in accounting for the all too evident inequalities in eighteenth-century education he ascribed them, not to the inequalities of native endowment, but to differences in education due to the accidental socioeconomic circumstances of children's parents. Communists who are products of the Russian revolution in the twentieth century are not much different. They reject entirely the psychological doctrine of individual differences, ascribing any failure to meet the educational norm to faulty motivation or to physiological impediments.

There are many who regard a literal equalitarianism as too naïve an interpretation of the democratic philosophy of education. For them it no longer fits the facts. It is sentimental rather than scientific. Educational psychology has so clearly proved the definite existence of marked individual differences that it has left literal equalitarianism without a leg to stand on. Individuals not only differ among themselves as to capacities and aptitudes but the capacities and aptitudes of each are unequal. The educator

23 John S. Brubacher, "Democratic Education: The Vices of Its Virtues," *Educational Trends,* 9:10–16, May–June, 1941. See also *infra,* Chap. 13.
24 Cf. A. Lawrence Lowell, "Democracy, Equality, and Education," *Harvard Educational Review,* 1:94–98, November, 1931.

is now no more justified in assuming that children have equal mental gifts than that they are all the same height and weight at birth. Furthermore, no amount of education will eliminate these differences. The conclusion follows that equality can no longer mean identity of education for all.

Even if the Declaration of Independence can no longer be thought to be descriptively accurate in its statement about equality, we must still consider whether to accept the statement prescriptively. Not a few, even though they recognize that education cannot endow a school generation with abilities it does not have, nevertheless persist in calling for equality of education. They reason that a child's ability cannot be justly represented by what it is at any given time but only by what it might become under favorable circumstances. To ensure favorable opportunities, the chance for an education must be passed around. Fairness in passing it around demands that the chance must be "quantitatively" equal. Otherwise, as has been already seen in another connection, to accuse a child of not having abilities which he never had a favorable chance to disclose is manifestly unjust.[25]

Easily yielding the naïve position of a literal equality of talent, other friends of democracy concentrate on endeavoring to equalize the external or material circumstances of obtaining an education. They fully recognize the differences among human individuals but think it ill-advised to increase the disparity between the extremes of talent in society. Something more must be done, for instance, than to give scholarships to promising children in the economically underprivileged masses. Such a procedure may provide an open-class society, wherein one may rise from the humblest to the highest ranks of life, but in the end it deprives the proletariat of its natural leaders and leaves the sterilized masses as subject to exploitation as before. Such practice results in plutocracy rather than democracy.

If such disparity becomes too great, there is danger that the extremes will not understand each other and will consequently fall out of communication with each other. A failure of communication, of course, would threaten the very existence of society. Hence, many think, a democratic society or state must be built on an education which emphasizes the likenesses of men rather than their differences. Accordingly, they would lay down the same minimum educational requirements for all. At the same time, however, they generally recognize that economic resources for commanding minimum educational opportunities are no more evenly distributed than are psychological talents. Not only are talented children accidentally born into families with low economic competence, but whole families by chance live in areas of the country where scanty or little-developed natural

[25] Thomas V. Smith, *The American Philosophy of Equality* (The University of Chicago Press, Chicago, 1927), pp. 308–309. See also Harold Laski, *op. cit.*, p. 114.

resources result in a low standard of living. Hence for them a democratic society must try to provide educational opportunity more equitably by taxing everyone according to his ability to pay but disbursing public funds according to educational need.

There is little or no objection to the way in which equalitarian theories and procedures tend to level up the school population. Exception is rather taken to the fact that they also have a tendency to level it down. Public effort seems to exhaust itself once it puts a floor under educational opportunities. If it does not exhaust itself, at least it all too often contents itself with meeting minimum requirements. This attitude neglects the ceiling toward which those of superior ability might stretch. While they generally exceed the average in spite of the failure of society to enrich their opportunities proportionately, there is no telling what they might do if democracy were not so tied to the idea of equalitarianism.

This last presents no problem to some equalitarians. They see equalitarianism as possessed of two meanings. One is that of sameness, the meaning emphasized so far. The other is "fittingness." According to this second meaning educational opportunities are equally distributed if "fitted" or suited to one's needs even though each one's needs are paradoxically quite different. Asking equalitarianism to take on this paradox compounds rather than clarifies ambiguity.[26] Better by far to express this second meaning by a different but related word. Happily the word equity does just that. Let equality stand for sameness, but let equity deal with difference.[27] Under this rubric none need be guilty in the name of equality of depriving an unusually capable young person of the greater opportunities he needs than his neighbor to accomplish what nature has endowed him to do.

If we forsake the egalitarian doctrine of treating all children alike and replace it with a doctrine of treating them all equitably, that is, taking account of the differences which make them unequal, it is appropriate to lay down some rules. First and most important, let it be said, distinctions must be relevant and proportionate to some accepted end. Indeed, distinctions are most invidious when they are irrelevant. Egalitarianism has endured as a great battle cry through history because it has been directed against privileges and distinctions which were irrelevant because inherited or otherwise unearned through any merit of the holder. And so, in the

26 Paul B. Komisar and Jerold R. Coombs, "The Concept of Equality in Education," *Studies in Philosophy and Education*, 3:223–244, Fall, 1964. See also Aharon F. Kleinberger, "Reflections on Equality in Education," *Studies in Philosophy and Education*, 5:293–340, Summer, 1967.

27 For the educational significance of the difference between equity and equality, see Benjamin F. Pittenger, "Some Relations of Education and Democracy," *Educational Administration and Supervision*, 8:424–428, October, 1922.

second place, let it be said, distinctions must be publicly arrived at and consistently applied among equals.[28]

A sample of instances will illustrate the rules. First take cases where unequals are treated equally because the differences making them unequal are irrelevant. Race, of course, is the leading instance. Color of skin seems quite irrelevant to educability. So too of sex. Men and women are different, to be sure, but again the difference is irrelevant to educability. Next take examples where unequals are treated unequally because the differences are relevant. Honors programs are a case in point. To distinguish between students of varying abilities is quite relevant to doing advanced work. Similarly of programs such as Head-start. Here giving advantages to the disadvantaged but not to others can be supported ethically because it is relevant to the set purpose of trying to overcome accidents of birth.

DEMOCRACY AS SHARING

A less individualistic conception of democracy and one with a greater social emphasis is that which takes its origin in the nature of society as communication, as mutually shared purposes. Advocates of this conception of democracy not only fasten on sharing as the nature of society but erect sharing into a norm of the good society. To them the good society, the one to which they attach the name democracy, has two dimensions. It is the one which on the one hand shares the largest number and variety of purposes among its own members and which on the other shares similarly with other groups.[29] And, as someone has added, it continually endeavors to widen the area of shared concerns, to grow in sharing.[30] Just as the measure of growth is more growth,[31] so the measure of democracy is more democracy, more sharing. Put in still another way, the only cure for the ills of democracy is more democracy.

The devotion of democracy to education is of long standing. When democracy made its political appearance, its success was expected to rest on education because a government built on the suffrage of the people demanded that the people be informed. But there is a more profound reason. Democracy is more than just a political form; it is a way of life. It is a mode of association which applies as well to other social groups such as the family, the church, and business. What characterizes this mode of

---

[28] Paul Nash, "Two Cheers for Equality," *Teachers College Record*, 67:217–223, December, 1965.

[29] John Dewey, *Democracy and Education* (The Macmillan Company, New York, 1916), p. 96.

[30] Boyd H. Bode, *Progressive Education at the Crossroads* (Newson and Company, New York, 1938), pp. 104–113.

[31] *Infra*, pp. 106–107.

living is that it gives a responsible share to each member in proportion to his capacity in shaping the policies of the group to which he belongs.[32]

There is an obvious advantage to a way of life which keeps open the channels of communication in this manner. Crises occurring anywhere in the social system can quickly become the concern of all. If all have been educated to self-reliance and inventiveness, formidable resources can be mobilized to solve common problems. The experience or insight of each is thus made freely available to give added meaning to the experience and insight of every other so that the cumulative effect is bound to be very formidable.

The danger to a democracy predicated on sharing arises when the channels for communication become shut off. Thus it can be seen that linguistic barriers are an impediment and that secrecy is an obstruction to understanding, as in the case of fraternities and sororities or classified information in research. People of different religious beliefs may also find it difficult to talk to each other, for example, on religious instruction in the public school. School segregation based on sex, race, skin color, or socio-economic circumstance is a constant threat to the kind of associated living that lies at the heart of democracy. The same holds for rank in the administrative hierarchy of the educational system. The more the administrative staff consults teachers and the more teachers can consult students, especially in college, the more democratic the system.[33]

Keeping channels of communication open and free, however, will not alone guarantee the solution of problems confronting democracy. There may be the freest exchange of opinion wherein the parties to the exchange still disagree. In such cases the democratic way to break the deadlock is to let the majority have its way—not that the majority is necessarily right, but rather that majority rule is the only way to get action. Of course there are some issues of such fundamental principle—chiefly religious—that it is better to have no action than to submit them to majority rule.[34] The danger of a vote on such issues is that the minority may not abide by it. Rather than offend its conscience by submitting to the majority, it may abandon educational procedures easing the tension and resist with physical force.[35] By the same token there are other issues, like desegregation of the

---

[32] John Dewey, op. cit., pp. 96–102. See also John Dewey, Reconstruction in Philosophy (Holt, Rinehart and Winston, Inc., New York, 1920), pp. 208–210.

[33] John Dewey, "Democracy in Education," Elementary School Teacher, 4:139–204, December, 1903.

[34] It is a question just how far to carry religious forbearance. In 1951 New York omitted questions on the germ theory of disease from its Regents examinations in deference to Christian Scientists. Might the same argument be used to exclude the germ theory of disease from the medical school?

[35] Theodore B. Brameld, "The Philosophy of Education as the Philosophy of Politics," p. 333.

races in public schools, which may be of such paramount ethical importance nationally and internationally that they must be resolved by majority rule even if it means regretfully abandoning orderly means of persuasion for enforcement through the power of the state.

To learn to free communication and to submit to majority rule wherever possible is, perhaps, one of the greatest arguments for the universal public school. By getting the youth of various races, national backgrounds, religious faiths, political convictions, and economic circumstances together in the same school, where they can rub cultural elbows, we have one of the best assurances for keeping open the highways of social intercommunication. But let a group establish a private or independent school on whatever grounds—to teach a particular point of view, political, economic, or religious; to exclude clientele whose social backgrounds are unacceptable; or what have you—and a difficult barrier is erected to the interpenetration of diverse ideas. No doubt within the private school there is a wide sharing of interests, particularly of those which brought the school into existence. But the real threat to democracy is the impediment which the independent school constitutes to sharing with other groups. The very fact that it withdraws its clientele from the public school shows it has something to share which is not shared in the public school or that there is something the public school shares they do not want to share. In either event the very existence of independent schools invites misunderstanding if not even misgiving.

Yet in defense of the private school, we may pertinently inquire whether it is not part of the birthright of freedom for minority groups, dissatisfied with the shortcomings of the public school, to set up independent schools of their own to form the kind of curriculum from the social heritage which they peculiarly want for their children. The answer theoretically and historically is definitely in the affirmative. At this point we are likely to find ourselves in something of a paradox. In the same name of democracy we are doubting and upholding the advisability of private schools. Hence we see that democracy as sharing and democracy as freedom are somewhat incompatible with each other.

The philosophic difference between these two kinds of schools in a democracy is not likely to produce a crisis in practice so long as the advocates of the public school do not insist that the public school is the sole institution for sharing culture with the young, or so long as the advocates of the private or independent school do not share doctrines so widely at variance with those taught in the public school as to imperil democracy itself or whatever the majority at any given time thinks democracy is. In other words democracy can put up with mildly contradictory educational practices, but there are definite limits to which such tolerance can go.

This conflict in the meaning of democracy raises the question whether democracy is a definite philosophy of education, whether it has any fixed, absolute principles, or whether it is only a more or less definite philosophy of education whose fundamental principles are constantly undergoing amendment in the light of experience.[36] Of course those who regard the essence of democracy as respect for the dignity of man, and found that respect on man's common fatherhood in God, are strongly inclined to think of the democratic philosophy of education in absolutistic terms.[37] There are some, too, who regard freedom and equality as inalienable rights of man embedded in the natural law. So strongly do absolutists cling to their views that they would not think of submitting them to vote by the majority. Those, however, who make the concept of sharing the norm of the democratic process in education are inclined to think of democracy in more relativistic terms. Thus democracy is constantly becoming whatever its members make it in the light of mutual criticism and reconstruction of their shared experiences.[38] Because of this emphasis on experience, it will not be surprising if some go so far as to claim that experimentalism is the educational philosophy which is peculiarly appropriate to democracy.[39] Yet, strangely enough—perhaps paradoxically—some of these people think the experimental method is so basic to the whole conception of democratic sharing that to give it up or even to restrict it would meet the utmost resistance from them. Indeed this resistance is so stubborn that one might well say even their conception of the democratic philosophy of education has absolutistic implications.[40]

SELECTED BIBLIOGRAPHY

Benne, Kenneth D.: A Conception of Authority (Teachers College, Columbia University, New York, 1943).
Berkson, Isaac B.: Ethics, Politics, and Education (University of Oregon Press, Eugene, 1968).
————: The Ideal and the Community (Harper & Row, Publishers, Incorporated, New York, 1958), Chap. 5.

[36] Sidney Hook, "Synthesis or Eclecticism," Philosophy and Phenomenological Research, 7:217–218, December, 1946.
[37] Cf. William E. Hocking, Human Nature and Its Remaking (Yale University Press, New Haven, Conn., 1923), pp. 11–13.
[38] John S. Brubacher, "Democratic Education: The Vices of Its Virtues," Educational Trends, 9:15, May–June, 1941.
[39] John L. Childs, Education and the Philosophy of Experimentalism (Appleton-Century-Crofts, Inc., New York, 1931), pp. 30, 93.
[40] John S. Brubacher, "The Absolutism of Progressive and Democratic Education," School and Society, 53:1–9, January, 1941; William J. Sanders, "Educators and the Democratic Principle," Educational Administration and Supervision, 27:692–697, December, 1941.

Bode, Boyd H.: *Democracy as a Way of Life* (The Macmillan Company, New York, 1921).

————— et al.: *Modern Education and Human Values* (The University of Pittsburgh Press, Pittsburgh, Pa., 1947), Chap. 1.

Brameld, Theodore B.: *Cultural Foundations of Education* (Harper & Row, Publishers, Incorporated, New York, 1957).

Dennis, Lawrence: *The Coming American Fascism* (Harper & Row, Publishers, Incorporated, New York, 1936), Chap. 17.

Gentile, Giovanni: *The Reform of Education* (Harcourt, Brace & World, Inc., New York, 1922), Chaps. 2–3.

Hutchins, Robert M.: *Education for Freedom* (Louisiana State University, Baton Rouge, La., 1943), Chap. 5.

Kallen, Horace M.: *The Education of Free Men* (Farrar, Straus & Cudahy, Inc., New York, 1949), Chap. 11.

Kandel, Isaac L.: *Comparative Education* (Houghton Mifflin Company, Boston, 1933), Chap. 3.

—————: *Conflicting Theories of Education* (The Macmillan Company, New York, 1938), Chaps. 1, 4, 11.

Kneller, George F.: *The Educational Philosophy of National Socialism* (Yale University Press, New Haven, Conn., 1941).

Nock, Albert J.: *The Theory of Education in the United States* (Harcourt, Brace & World, Inc., New York, 1932).

Peters, Richard S.: *Ethics and Education* (Scott, Foresman and Company, Chicago, 1967), Chaps. 3, 6, 7, 10.

Pinkevitch, Albert P.: *The New Education in the Soviet Republic* (The John Day Company, Inc., New York, 1929), Chap. 7.

Scheffler, Israel (ed.): *Philosophy and Education* (Allyn and Bacon, Inc., Boston, 1966), Chap. 16.

Smith, B. Othanel, and Robert H. Ennis (eds.): *Language and Concepts in Education* (Rand McNally & Company, Chicago, 1961), Chap. 9.

Smith, Huston: *The Purposes of Higher Education* (Harper & Row, Publishers, Incorporated, New York, 1955), Chap. 4.

Walsh, John E.: *Education and Political Power* (Center for Applied Research in Education, Inc., New York, 1964).

CHAPTER FOUR

The State and Education

The way in which various political forms of society condition the philosophy of education has been described at some length, with hardly any intimation whether the schools were to be supported and controlled by the government or by private effort. While this area is undoubtedly directly related to those we have discussed previously, in a sense it is independent of them. Whether education is a suitable enterprise for governmental support and regulation may be a moot point, regardless of a society's political pattern. While democracies, for instance, have usually been enthusiastic patrons of public education, there is nothing in the democratic principle which makes it mandatory for the public to maintain a system of schools. Historically, some democracies have been conspicuous for their governmental neglect of education. And equally, while societies governed by an aristocracy or plutocracy might be expected, through private schools, to monopolize education for their own children as the future rulers, many such societies have provided extended educational opportunities for the masses at public expense. From these instances, then, it should be clear that the relation of the government to education presents a discrete problem for the philosophy of education.

The foregoing illustrations not only delimit the present topic from preceding subjects of discussion, but they also serve to introduce us to the sort of conflicting educational practices we find in this region. Only a few of these need to be indicated here, to further define the problem of this area. The fundamental difference of opinion and practice here concerns what parts of education shall be allocated to the sphere of government and what parts to the liberty of the private citizen. At one time all education was under private supervision; latterly, more and more of it has come under the government. In some places, the government merely provides the school building and teacher. In others, it goes further and offers free textbooks and supplies. In still others, it furnishes such services as medical care, transportation to and from school, and noonday lunches. Probably no one today would like to see the government abandon any of these services. Nevertheless, there are many parents who still prefer to keep close control over the quality and amount of these services by sending their offspring to private schools of their own selection rather than to public schools.

PLURALISM AND TOTALITARIANISM

The practical consequences of maintaining both public and private schools seldom present serious conflicts till a case arises where both public and private agencies reach out for the same thing. Thus when the state has included religion in the public school curriculum, the church has regarded it as an invasion of a subject-matter field peculiarly falling within the precincts of the church and its Sunday or parochial schools. Similarly, when the church has sought a portion of public funds raised by taxation for the support of its schools, the state has generally objected. Most critical, of course, have been cases where the state has tried to establish a monopoly over education by abolishing private schools altogether. This clash of secular and religious interests in the sphere of education has been all the more severe where the secular state has been also strongly nationalistic. But to the forces of nationalism in education there is secular opposition as well. Here the competition is not only whether the church or state shall control educational policies but whether central or local secular authorities shall dominate.

The reason why the clash on the locus of educational control is of such import is that if one favors the state as the proper educational agency one puts tremendous potential power in the hands of those who control the state. Men form many societies such as the family, church, and school, but in forming the state they do something unique—they organize the physical force of the community. In fact, the state is the only society which can lawfully employ physical coercion to achieve its ends. It can, for instance, compel children to attend school, while private agencies have no such power. Even more important, it can levy a school tax and, if it is not paid, proceed against the property of the delinquent taxpayer. Obviously, to put the state back of the schools is to support their educational program with unmatchable power and resources. A fortiori, to put the national state back of the schools is to weight central authority heavily as over against local authority. It is small wonder, therefore, if we must be at considerable pains to examine the philosophic principles on which the control of such power should rest.

A matter of first importance here is to decide more precisely just what are the limits of the state. As already stated, men associate themselves together for a great many different purposes, such as business, recreation, politics, and worship. But the critical question arises whether political society, the state, is but one among many societies with limited objectives to which the individual belongs or whether the state is an overarching society which includes and dominates all the rest. Those who hold that the state is but one among many competing forms of society hold to a pluralistic theory of society and the state. On the other hand, those who regard the state as the all-inclusive social category hold to a monistic or totalitarian theory. The pluralistic theory of society and the state has found its chief advocates among democracies, while the monistic or totalitarian theory has been chiefly espoused by autocracies or oligarchies like communism and fascism.

The totalitarian theory proves attractive to its adherents because basically they hold to an organismic theory of society.[1] Just as the biologic organism must be studied as an integrated whole, so they think the social body must be approached as a whole or a totality. Of all the societies which men form, the state is the most inclusive in its membership. Some churches aim to be catholic, that is, all-inclusive, in their membership, but they fail of their objective because membership in them is ultimately on a voluntary basis, and some people do not choose to join. In the case of the state, on the contrary, the child is born into it. He cannot escape being a citizen. He may be an individual in addition to being a citizen, but it is only as he overcomes the necessary limitations of individuality through participation in the social whole, the state, that he really reaches the full stature of a man. The state represents the universal, and it is only as the individual draws inspiration from the universal that he amounts to anything worth while. Hence the totalitarian is inclined to regard society and the state as coterminous and citizenship as exhausting or absorbing the status of the individual.

With the state lifted to this pinnacle of importance, it will come as no surprise that all schools must be under governmental control. Private schools can have no autonomous standing. In such a system Rousseau's idea of educating the man rather than the citizen would be quite repugnant. On the contrary, the totalitarian would probably follow Hegel in believing that the child has no chance of becoming a full-fledged man except through education for citizenship. Similarly, the only way the child can make his will effective is to learn to will what the state wants him to will. Hence the child is educated not only exclusively by the state but ultimately exclusively for the state as well. Thus the state comes to assume ethical as well as political sovereignty in the education of its wards.

The pluralistic theory of society and the state appeals to its proponents because of the large measure of freedom it preserves for them. History has taught them to be very cautious about the aggrandizement of governmental power. The inherent danger of a state coterminous with society or even approaching such congruity is that it will bestride the life of

[1] *Supra,* pp. 5–6.

individuals like a colossus. To protect themselves from the shadow of such governmental tyranny they have persistently tried to reduce the pretensions of the state. One of the best ways of doing this, they have learned by experience, is by specifically delimiting the powers of government through a written constitution. By basing government on limited rather than absolute powers, the pluralist leaves many social enterprises to be undertaken by other forms of human association besides the state, such as the church and family. This not only provides relief from the uniformity of state regimentation, but it also affords welcome competition among a variety of different ways of doing things.

With the dimensions of the state scaled down materially where the conception of pluralism obtains, the social climate proves congenial to both public and private schools. The state may provide schools, but so also may the family, church, industry, and other voluntary agencies. Therefore the state must guard itself against claiming a monopoly in the education of children. If it exercises this restraint, public and private schools existing side by side become a mutual example and stimulus to each other's improvement. In this way, too, the student will be assured of being educated as an individual and not exclusively as a citizen. He will be educated as an end and not just as a mouthpiece or instrument of the state. This is not to imply that there is any necessary antithesis between the education of the good individual and the education of the good citizen, but it is a reminder that there are two different kinds of value here to which a democracy, at least, must be constantly sensitive. Furthermore, separating ethical sovereignty from the state and lodging it in the individual or the church will assure the state of a more honest estimate of its own vices and virtues when studied in the schools.

ANARCHISM

If the principle of pluralism be granted, it becomes a matter of expediency to decide which parts of the educational program should be assumed by government and which parts should be allocated to private effort. The two expedients found most frequently in practice are *laissez faire* and socialism. In the former case, the government holds aloof from education, leaving it to be provided by private agencies like the family and the church. In the latter instance, the state steps in to organize and maintain schools of its own. But there is also a third expedient, anarchism which, though less significant, must not be overlooked. Under anarchism education would be carried on, neither by the state nor merely at its sufferance, but with no state at all.

Only a theoretic statement can be made about education under anarchy, for practical instances of anarchism are all but nonexistent. In an anarchistic society, as already stated, there would be no political or civil state. Such social organizations as might obtain would be quite voluntary. In view of the shortcomings of human nature, many confidently believe that the absence of civil government with power to enforce law and order would lead to wild confusion, even chaos. Indeed, in the popular mind anarchy passes as a synonym for chaos and disorder. Whether or not anarchy would actually lead to such a social condition need not be a matter of moment here. The fact is that anarchists believe it possible theoretically to organize a society where each individual is able to hold his unruly animal nature in leash without constraint from the state. The least that can be said for such a theory is that it is a brave and lofty aspiration. If it is at all capable of realization it would certainly involve long and intensive schooling in the art of self-control. Since social control would be dependent on education rather than the coercion of government, it is probably true that in the utopia of anarchy there would be more need and regard for education than there would be in either the expedients of *laissez faire* or socialism.

It but remains to inquire how schooling would be provided in a society where people held to anarchistic principles. With no frame of public government on which to depend, providing educational opportunities would be a purely voluntary matter.[2] The right of a child to education and the duty of his parents to provide it would exist only in contract, that is, in voluntary agreement.[3] Of course the infant would be too young to make such arrangements and would therefore be at the mercy of his parents for an education until he grew older. Nevertheless, the anarchist is reluctant to coerce the parent in his educational duties toward his offspring, for he fully counts on parental instinct to fulfill its function at this point. Moreover the anarchist is no more ready to compel the child to go to school[4] than he is to compel the parent to provide him schooling. Even if the parent fails to fulfill his natural duty, the anarchist is more likely to blame this result on the inequitable distribution of wealth under capitalism than he is on parental defection of duty. Granted a suitable standard of living which would afford enough leisure for education, the anarchist is confident that those who are fond of teaching could not be kept from volunteering to

[2] For a recent statement of such a position, see William O. Reichert, "The Relevance of Anarchism: An Introduction to the Social Thought of Herbert Read," *Educational Theory*, 17:147–153, Spring, 1967.

[3] Benjamin R. Tucker, "Some Socialist and Anarchist Views of Education," *Educational Review*, 15:6–10, January, 1898.

[4] G. B. Kelly, "Some Socialist and Anarchist Views of Education," *Educational Review*, 15:13–16, January, 1898.

teach their fellows and that, consequently, voluntary associations for educational purposes would spring up everywhere.[5]

THE *LAISSEZ FAIRE* STATE

Only a negligible number of people think there is any possibility of dispensing with the state in the foreseeable future. Yet, while nearly every one recognizes that the state is indispensable, there are many who would severely restrict the state to a few basic functions, such as providing police and courts of law to protect the life and property of its citizens. With regard to other social enterprises they would have the state adopt a hands-off or *laissez faire* policy. Under such a regime the schools and colleges would in effect fare about as they would under anarchism. If there is a government but the government does not concern itself with education, there might almost as well be no government at all so far as the institutions of learning are concerned. Hence the younger generation would have to depend for their education on the family, church, and other voluntary philanthropic agencies as under anarchism.

As a matter of fact, few states are completely and undeviatingly *laissez faire* about education. While *laissez faire* is a general or basic policy, they are constantly making exceptions. Paupers and the children of paupers are a case in point. If parents or other private agencies do not voluntarily feel a responsibility here, then the state must almost perforce step in. But the question arises, what is the argument for having it step in just as little as it possibly can? Fundamentally the argument grows out of a general demand for freedom. Originally *laissez faire* was a protest against excessive government interference in private business and commerce. The feeling was that if the government would keep its hands off, not only would individuals be more prosperous, but the state itself would be better off. The best way to provide for the general welfare was for each individual to be free to look after his own. Self-interest is the law of nature. Government should tamper with it only where individual or group interests conflict and there only to be a referee and maintain a just balance among private interests.[6]

The rule applicable to business was supposed to be no less applicable to education. No one stated this view better than Herbert Spencer.[7] The child must be free to pursue his own self-interest in getting an education.

[5] Cyril E. M. Joad, *Introduction to Modern Political Theory* (Oxford University Press, Fair Lawn, N.J., 1924), p. 106.
[6] See also *infra*, pp. 204–206.
[7] Herbert Spencer, *Social Statics* (D. Appleton & Company, Inc., New York, 1878), pp. 360–362. [First edition, 1850.]

Only in the case of the infringement of this interest through conflict with others was the state justified in interposing on behalf of the child. Such a possible infringement, however, could arise only where some previously existing power of the child to get an education had been cut off or impaired. Now such a situation does not exist even where the parent fails to educate his offspring. In such a case the parent merely fails to enhance his development; he does not positively diminish or retard it. The child is no less free to exercise his native liberty after his parents neglect than he was before it. If the result of this rugged reasoning seems to risk leaving the immature to their own ineffective devices to obtain an adequate education, we must comfort ourselves, as does the anarchist, with the thought that no doubt some adult will find it to his self-interest to exercise his freedom in offering to care for the education of the young.

Just how assured this comfort is seems rather doubtful to critics of the *laissez faire* state. As a matter of history, private initiative and private philanthropy have been laggard in their provision of schools both in quantity and quality. Even with public subsidy, private philanthropy has been unable to expand educational facilities rapidly and extensively enough. Worse yet, the educational result is that some individuals have become more absorbed in their liberties than in their duties, in private economic gain than in civic responsibility. Under the banner of rugged individualism the strong have enjoyed the individualism and the weak have suffered the ruggedness. Not a few of those who have benefited from such a social policy have become so enamored of their success as to hold a vested interest in the doctrine of *laissez faire*. In fact they are so fanatically *laissez faire*, that they carry the doctrine to a *reductio ad absurdum*, that is, they are no longer *laissez faire* about *laissez faire* itself. Strangely enough, *laissez faire*, originating as a doctrine of freedom, becomes a bulwark of the *status quo*. Thus, according to their creed they should let the teacher alone and not interfere with his freedom to deal with controversial issues in the curriculum, but as a matter of fact they are often among the first to beseech the state to make the teacher take a loyalty oath to prevent his rocking the ship of state.

THE POSITIVE OR WELFARE STATE

Those who are impressed with the shortcomings of the doctrine of *laissez faire* generally think that the state should take a more positive attitude toward education. Much as they may admire a state that is a just and neutral umpire between the clashing interests of its citizens, nevertheless they think that the state must take positive as well as negative action to maintain a proper balance of social welfare for its citizens. As they see it, freedom is to be obtained not merely through independence from the restraints of state regulation but also through active social planning. This is no paradox to the socialist, the advocate of positive state action, for he would hold that social regulations which do not free more human energies than they restrain are ethically unsound. The state, hence, must have ends of its own.[8] Instead of being uncertain about its own ends, as an excessive emphasis on its neutrality would indicate, the state has a stake in the welfare of its citizen just as much as the individual citizens do themselves.

It is one thing to favor the positive or welfare state, but it is quite another to describe the precise nature of the state's interest in education. Perhaps the best way to look upon the state's interest in education is as a long-term investment.[9] This interest obviously runs far beyond the span of any single generation. The state must take affirmative steps to conserve its human resources just as it does its natural ones. Only so can it hope to perpetuate the vital virtues and skills which make it what it is. Such a crucial enterprise the state can hardly let hang on the liberty of the private citizen or on the uncertain benevolence of private philanthropies. The state must step forward from the outset and ensure not only an adequate amount of education but also education of an adequately high standard. Certainly we can trust no agency less universal than the state to accomplish such prophetic and unselfish ends.[10]

Now just how far may the state exert its power to achieve these ends? Certainly it must have the right to erect and maintain public schools. Moreover, these schools must be of all grades, from the nursery school to the university, with curriculums ranging from the simplest elements of liberal education to the most profound and recondite elements of professional specialization. If the state has an interest in establishing schools, it has a corresponding right to compel attendance at school and to regulate child labor so that attendance will be possible. To ensure that children get to school, it may provide transportation at public expense, and to ensure the tools of instruction when they get there, the state may provide children with free textbooks and supplies. Furthermore, to guarantee vigorous bodies as well as vigorous minds the state must have the right to give medical and dental examinations together with free meals if it wishes.[11]

[8] Cf. Bertrand Russell, "Socialism and Education," *Harper's Magazine*, 151:416, September, 1925.

[9] Thomas H. Briggs, *The Great Investment* (Harvard University Press, Cambridge, Mass., 1930), p. 8.

[10] Woodrow Wilson, *The State* (D. C. Heath and Company, Boston, 1889), p. 638.

[11] John S. Brubacher, "The Public School: An Example of the New Social Order," *School and Society*, 44:761–768, December, 1936.

There are those who think that the state should further reach forth and preside over childbirth, regulate the housing of children, advise them in courtship, and instruct them in parentage.[12]

All this, it almost goes without saying, the state is entitled to provide at public expense. This means that the state can tax the childless to educate the children of those blest with families, the Jew to educate the gentile, the Protestant to educate the Catholic, and the rich to educate the poor. But this does not mean that the state control of schools extends only to state-supported schools. The positive state may regulate private schools as well as public ones; for instance, it may require all children to be instructed in American history.

This scope and sweep of the positive or welfare state's interest in education frightens a few. They speak of it as socialistic, even communistic. And they do not think that they are just indulging in name calling when they so describe the public system. They honestly believe that the public school is paternalistic, that it so encroaches on the proper sphere of the family as to destroy the parents' sense of responsibility for their progeny. Furthermore, it works a real injustice on responsible and industrious parents to tax them for the education of the children of the shiftless and indolent as well as for the education of their own. Indeed, some critics claim the public school has a bad influence on the children as well as their parents. Making no personal financial sacrifice for their education, children fail to appreciate the benefits conferred upon them.[13]

THE FAMILY

In a pluralistic society, where the state, whether *laissez faire* or positive, is only one among several educational agencies, it will be well to examine the claims of these other agencies to sponsor the education of children and to see how these claims relate to those of the state. Of course all three principal educational agencies—the family, state, and church—are anxious to have the child grow into the very best possible kind of person. On some traits of what is the best possible kind of manhood and womanhood these three institutions are quite agreed. They reinforce each other in their educational endeavors to make the young courteous, industrious, generous, and the like. In some traits each institution specializes so that it supplements the others. The family develops affection; the state gives military

---

[12] William E. Chancellor, *Motives, Ideals, and Values in Education* (Houghton Mifflin Company, Boston, 1907), p. 254.
[13] James P. Munroe, "Certain Dangerous Tendencies in Modern Education," *Educational Review*, 3:145–155, February, 1892.

training; and the church teaches religion. But in still other areas all three institutions try to do the same thing but in such different ways as to lead to some confusion. All concern themselves with making the student a good citizen and with trying to make him a moral individual.[14] As we might expect, there will be difference of opinion, particularly between the church and the state, on how to achieve these ends.

Naturally each institution, confident of the worth of its own point of view, will wish to incline youth in its direction. The family, however, has the initial chance to win the child's loyalty. For one thing, the family begets the child and from time immemorial has been charged with his earliest training. That this is a sound vested interest has been recognized by both church and state. Whether it is necessary or even desirable to go so far as to say that the parent "owns" the child is perhaps a matter of some doubt.[15] Among other reasons which account for the priority of the family as an educational institution is the fact that it is unrivaled as society's basic affectional institution. Educational authorities at best are motivated by public spirit, a poor substitute for parental affection. It is doubtful whether even the teachers of the schools of the church, actuated by the deepest brotherly love, could do better. The security afforded by this family sentiment is simply invaluable.

But even when the strongest case has been built for reposing certain educational responsibilities in the discretion of the parent, it is generally recognized that the family has its limitations, that it does not contain within itself all the means for its own development. Worthy as the diversity of families is as a bulwark against the uniformity which state education too frequently imposes on children, nevertheless the diversity often amounts to abysmal deficiencies on the part of parents as educators. Capacity for parenthood is not by any means highly correlated with capacity for educating. Furthermore, fundamental sociological conditions are profoundly affecting the efficiency of the home as an educational agency. The passing of home industry, the frequent employment of both parents, the invention of the automobile, and the development of commercial amusement—to mention but a few of the changes—have greatly undermined the reverence and implicit obedience of the family discipline of not so long ago. In spite of these drawbacks, most families persist in educating the child through his tenderest years.

---

[14] John H. Ryan, "Limitations of Public Education," *Religious Education*, 22:582–585, June, 1927.

[15] William H. Kilpatrick, "Thinking in Childhood and Youth," *Religious Education*, 23:132, February, 1928; Bertrand Russell, *Education and the Modern World* (W. W. Norton & Company, Inc., New York, 1932), pp. 69–70; Nikolai Bukharin and Evgeni Preobrazhensky, *The ABC of Communism* (Workers' Party of America, Lyceum Literature Department, New York, 1921), pp. 233–234.

It is the rare family indeed, however, which would think itself competent to undertake the more formal instruction of later years. This the family generally delegates to some other agency, usually a public or private school. By their patronage families have encouraged roughly three types of private school. Some parents, concerned over the heterogeneity of the public school population, wish to have their children attend a school where the pupils will come from a more homogeneous background of manners, morals, health, and language habits. These often turn out to be socially select schools. They generally offer superior opportunities for an education of the conventional type. Other parents are discontented with the public school curriculum and prefer a school where a different content is offered. Most notable here are various parochial school systems, which expanded rapidly after the exclusion of religion from the public school offerings. Finally are to be noted private schools of a frankly experimental character. Not infrequently a few parents are dissatisfied with conventional educational stereotypes and are willing to undertake educational risks which the public or other more conservative private schools are unwilling to assume.

The obvious advantage of these private schools is the diversity of viewpoint they permit, to say nothing of the safeguard they are against tyrannies of the state. If society had always to depend on the level of popular enlightenment for its educational advances, the rate of progress would be distressingly slow. Historically, many of the most notable improvements in education have resulted from the establishment of schools with purposes different from those of the state. This virtue of private schools is at the very same time the origin of their vice. The danger is that they will stratify society along the very lines of their differences. Where this occurs, there is bound to be envy and misunderstanding. Some envisage a public school in which there will be both variety and socialization. Doubtless it is a noble ideal. Pending its achievement, however, the passing of education from the field of private enterprise should not be forced by legislation but should be the natural outcome of the improvement of the public school.

So far in our consideration of the family we have been looking at education from the perspective of the parents. After recognizing their right to direct the education of their offspring, the question arises: What about the child himself, has he any rights? Suppose, for instance, that his parents are very haphazard in exercising the right to direct their child's education. Does the child have any right to remedy or redress?[16] Yes, he does, but it is a rather weak one if he chances to live in a *laissez faire* state. At common law, for example, he has the right to demand only that his parents give him an education which will enable him to live in comfort in the con-

---

[16] Frank R. Paulsem, "Jurisprudence and Education," *Educational Administration and Supervision*, 43:65–82, February, 1957.

dition of his parents. If his parents are ignorant and poor, his prospects for educating himself beyond their miserable condition are not very promising. But suppose now that his parents grossly neglect his education or suppose that they are utterly corrupt morally, what is to happen then? Obviously it is very difficult to remain strictly *laissez faire* in the face of such impending disaster, and even *laissez faire* states have been known to take positive action here.

The embarrassment suffered by the *laissez faire* state when confronted by such an extreme case is not shared by the positive state. In such extenuating circumstances the positive state will not hesitate to step between parent and child by suspending the parent's supervision of his child's education and by making the child a ward of the state.[17] On the whole, the nontotalitarian, positive state should be a trustworthy protector of the rights of childhood. By reason of establishing and maintaining schools and by reason of compelling attendance thereat, the positive state must define what a school is, that is, lay down its minimum requirements. This minimum generally enhances the educational rights of the child and makes them much sturdier than in a *laissez faire* state, for the positive state is not content to educate a child to the mere level of his parents but claims the child has a right to a maximum of self-realization.[18] Moreover the positive state does not think that such a right of the child is incompatible with the right of the parents to educate him at home, if they wish, so long, of course, as the state reserves to itself the right to decide whether any particular home is an adequate school as measured against the state's minimum standards. Any public schools which the state sets up in addition, therefore, are to supplement the home, not to supplant it. They are not schools to which parents *must* send their offspring, but only places where they *may* send him to discharge the responsibility to educate him which every parent bears in a pluralistic society.

CHURCH AND STATE

The church, no less than the state, regards itself as a natural complement to the family when the latter reaches the limit of its educational resources in teaching the child. If the child had to depend exclusively on his parents and the state as his teachers, his education would inevitably suffer their limitations. Just as the father and mother, except in rare cases, are limited

---

[17] Charles N. Lischka, "Limitations of the Legislative Power to Compel Education," *Catholic Educational Review*, 27:22–23, January, 1929.
[18] *Supra*, pp. 102–103.

in their educational outlook by birth and training, so too the state, in spite of its larger and more diversified membership, is limited in educational outlook by its exclusively secular interests. If the young are to develop religious interests, therefore, if they are to develop interests in faith and morals, the church insists that it has no less right than the state to complement their education begun in the first instance by the family.

The independent right of both church and state to teach seems reasonable enough. The problem has been to keep them not only independent but separate. When asked about paying taxes, Jesus took a coin in which taxes were paid and, noting the imprint of Caesar's head thereon, enjoined his followers to render to Caesar the things that are Caesar's but to God the things that are God's. This separation of church and state was simple enough when the controversy was over taxes. But what to do when the controversy is over a child? Should the education of the child be surrendered to Caesar or to God? The fact is that both church and state want to be paramount in directing the child's educational destinies.

Patently there is an uneasy equilibrium existing here between church and state. In forming an attitude toward it, probably one's first step should be to understand the philosophical issue out of which it arises.[19] Catholics found the right of the church in educational matters in the supernatural order. The divine mission of the Catholic church to teach is derived by succession through Jesus' disciples, to whom he said, "All power is given to me in heaven and earth. Going therefore, teach ye all nations . . . teaching them to observe all things whatsoever I have commanded you."[20] Although, in the Catholic mind, this grant of power gives the church preeminence among all other educational institutions, it is not claimed to give the church exclusive jurisdiction over education. It is conceded that the family and the state have rights in education, too, but their rights are of the natural order. As the supernatural is higher than the natural, so it follows that the right of the church in educational matters is unqualifiedly superior to the title of the family and the state. Hence, any abridgement of the prerogatives of the church in education is palpably and deplorably unjust. And be it noted that the church is not less absolutely right on this point because the state may ignore her claim or even, through superior force, infringe upon her sacred precincts or, worse yet, suppress her activities.[21]

---

[19] William H. Kilpatrick, "Religion in Education: The Issues," *Progressive Education*, 26:98–102, February, 1949.

[20] Matthew 28:18–20 (Douay version of the Bible).

[21] Pius XI, "Christian Education of Youth," *Catholic Educational Review*, 28:138–147, March, 1930.

Normally this claim of the Catholic church to preeminence as an educational agency extends only to the church's proper end and object, instruction in faith and morals. In this field the divine origin of the church enables her to teach with immunity from error. Significantly enough, however, the church does not stop here in her claims. She also claims an independent right to decide, with regard to *every other* form of human learning and instruction, what will help or harm Christian education. This added claim is logical enough. If these other areas of instruction bear directly or indirectly on faith and morals, the church cannot carry out its primary function adequately unless it extends its educational jurisdiction over these incidental areas as well. Again, the church does not stop here but goes on to make the extremely broad claim that there is no form of instruction at all which in the last analysis is unconnected with man's last end or ultimate destiny and which therefore can be withdrawn from the jurisdiction of divine law of which the Catholic church is the infallible judge.[22]

This is an exceedingly strong statement. Stated more moderately but with no sacrifice of principle, it amounts to saying that the secular and religious curriculums are often very closely related. Where they are, the church will be concerned with secular instruction. But such a concern will be incidental and secondary, not an object proper of the church. For the state, on the other hand, this type of instruction is of primary importance. The church should teach in the secular realm only as an act of charity where the arts and sciences are insufficiently taught, or as an act of necessity where they are improperly taught. To teach that science and religion are contradictory to each other would be an instance where the church would feel it incumbent of necessity to teach science to correct what it would regard as a false impression. But to make this branch of education a main object and direct mission of the church is to make the church assume responsibility for the condition of the profane arts and sciences among Christian nations, an unnecessary responsibility.

However stated, this claim of the Catholic church to control over the education of the child not only rivals that of the state but actually overshadows it. It is no less overshadowing because the claim is the independent claim of Catholics just for Catholics. If the Catholic church really is infallible in its interpretation of the religious and secular curriculum, then its infallibility affects non-Catholics as well as Catholics. By entrenching itself behind metaphysical absolutes the church seems to have taken up an unassailable position,[23] which not only overshadows the state but which non-Catholic citizens of the state fear threatens their own religious abso-

---

[22] *Ibid.*, pp. 133–134. See also *infra*, pp. 193–195.   [23] *Supra*, Chap. 7.

lutes. Thinking that it takes a metaphysic to deny a metaphysic, they counter absolute with absolute. In this clash of metaphysical systems it would clearly be folly to allow any one of them to capture the state with its tremendous power of physical coercion. To allow the followers of one metaphysic to coerce the followers of another would lead to insurrection and the bloodiest and most senseless of all wars, religious war.

The paramountcy that the Catholic church claims in theory the state has asserted in fact. Thus communist and fascist regimes have arrogated to themselves the sole right to educate. Even a few of the states in the United States have done the same. But this totalitarian practice has been ruled inconsistent with the fundamental theory of liberty on which this nation rests. In the American philosophy of pluralism, the child is not a mere creature of the state, for parents may, if they wish, educate him elsewhere than in the public schools.[24] The real reason for the separation of church and state is not to divorce religion from politics but to guard against the tyranny of the state in religion and the orthodoxy of the church in politics.[25]

In spite of the need for the separation of church and state, these two powerful agencies seem constantly to find areas where their interests overlap. The Catholic church, for instance, wishes the state to give tax support to its parochial school system. Protestants and Jews, fearful of the advantage this would give Catholics, where they have no parochial systems of their own, have raised constitutional barriers against the proposal.[26]

If aiding the teaching of doctrine at public expense is forbidden, what about expenditures for nondoctrinal items such as school supplies and transportation? If the answer is no to the question, "Is it proper for the state to pay for these services for children attending private schools?," it would seem to follow logically that children attending a private school should have no claim to the services of a policeman stationed at a dangerous intersection on their way to school. This, of course, is absurd. On the other hand, if the answer is yes, then it seems difficult to determine where to stop in providing educational services at public expense. If the state provides transportation for private schools pupils, then why not buildings

---

[24] *Pierce v. Society of Sisters,* 268 U.S. 510.

[25] William T. Harris, "The Separation of the Church from the Tax-supported School," *Educational Review,* 26:222–235, October, 1903; George A. Coe, "Shall the State Teach Religion?" *School and Society,* 51:129–133, February, 1940. See also Second Conference on the Scientific Spirit and Democratic Faith, *The Authoritarian Attempt to Capture Education* (King's Crown Press, New York, 1945), pp. 138–139; and William K. Frankena, "Public Education and the Good Life," *Harvard Educational Review,* 31:413–426, Fall, 1961.

[26] Neil G. McCluskey, "Public Funds for Parochial Schools? Yes," *Teachers College Record,* 62:49–56, October, 1960; R. Freeman Butts, "Public Funds for Parochial Schools? No," *Teachers College Record,* 62:57–62, October, 1960.

and ultimately the payment of teachers' salaries? In formulating a philosophy on these and similar questions, the United States Supreme Court has played a prominent role. In the program of released time for religious instruction in public schools, the state has put school buildings with their staffs on school time and at public expense at the service of various church groups. But this goes too far in the direction of identifying the educational spheres of church and state,[27] just as the refusal of public transportation to private school pupils seems to go too far in divorcing these spheres.[28] The private school child must not become the stepchild of the state, and yet neither must his plight be made the excuse for the state's becoming involved in the interminable strife of irreconcilable metaphysical absolutes. In other words the principle of philosophy of the separation of church and state must not be pressed with too rigorous logic in either direction.

The state on its part finds it difficult not to encroach on church precincts. Take the patriotic observance of the hand salute to the flag practiced in many public schools. One religious sect, the Jehovah's Witnesses, claims the salute is a religious posture and therefore odious because it puts the nation-state as a deity in competition with their God. Who is to be paramount in such a clash of church and state?[29] Or take the case of the Amish who refuse to send their children to school beyond the elementary level or to have their teachers trained to meet state standards of certification, both statutory demands contrary to their religion.[30] Should state or church prevail? These are difficult cases. The expedient way to resolve these clashes is to allow dissent because these religious sects constitute so small a minority of the population. On principle, however, it seems that the larger welfare of the secular state should take precedence.

There is one final instance where, far from a clash of interests, the state thought its interests were identical with those of religion. In this case a state through its state board of regents endeavored to formulate a prayer which could be said in public schools wihout offending anyone. The United States Supreme Court, however, took exception to even such good intent, not because it infringed on religious liberty, but on the injunction against an establishment of religion.[31] Our philosophy, therefore, seems opposed not to the idea that God should have a prominent position in education but rather to the idea that the state should put Him there.

---

[27]*People ex rel. McCollum v. Board of Education*, 333 U.S. 203.
[28] *Everson v. Board of Education*, 330 U.S. 1.
[29] Cf. *Minersville School District v. Gobitis*, 310 U.S. 586, with *West Virginia State Board of Education v. Barnette*, 319 U.S. 624.
[30] *State v. Garber*, 197 Kans. 567.
[31] *Engle v. Vitale*, 370 U.S. 421.

NATIONALISM AND INTERNATIONALISM

The issue between an all-pervasive state control of education and liberty for the family, church, and other private agencies to supply educational opportunities has a final counterpart within the system of state educational administration itself. Ordinarily, the geographical limits of the state are too great to permit of a single administrative agency for education. Consequently the state is divided into smaller areas for the purpose of local educational administration. In some instances these local agencies are still further subdivided for more efficient management. The question now arises whether the central administration should dominate educational policy or whether a large measure of freedom should be left to the local authorities. Doubtless, much hinges on one's theory of the state. In the totalitarian state, centralization of educational administration with unitary control of educational policy seems a foregone conclusion. The spirit of the pluralistic state, with its toleration of private voluntary educational agencies, would seem to dictate the decentralization of educational administration in order to secure a large measure of initiative and experimentation from local educational authorities.[32] Decentralization also renders more difficult the introduction of any single item or scheme of propaganda into the schools of the nation as a whole and is thereby one effective way of guaranteeing academic freedom. Moreover, it seems logical to expect that political theory has some influence here. On the whole, one would surmise that rule by the one or few would be associated with centralization, rule by the many, with decentralization. In spite of this normal expectation, there are instances, especially in democracies, of highly centralized educational administration.

The issues under consideration here are particularly acute where national states are involved. The virus of nationalism gives a complexion to the role of the state in education which otherwise is quite lacking. Nationalism binds a people together in a sense of corporate life. It is not necessarily based on race, language, religion, political sovereignty, or geographical enclosure. Various combinations of these factors will make up the sense of nationalism, depending on the circumstances at hand. Running through all, however, is a sense of common interest, common destiny, common defeat, or common glory. When this corporate self-regard attaches itself to the state's interest in education, there are a number of possibilities which must be canvassed.

It should at once be obvious that here is an added influence in the

[32] John S. MacKenzie, *Outlines of Social Philosophy* (The Macmillan Company, New York, 1921), pp. 107–108.

direction of centralization of educational administration. No doubt there are definite educational benefits to be derived from such a centrifugal force. For one thing, loyalty to the broader cultural outlook of the nation makes possible a better type of manhood and womanhood than is often afforded where sectionalism bounds the school horizon. For another thing, through its personnel and greater financial resources the national educational administrative organization can become the instrument for making this higher type of personality possible. But social cooperation on a national scale to achieve this superior individual requires that every person shall contribute to the general homogeneity of language and ideals. If this is an outgrowth from the life of the people and not something forced on them by the government, it can be a great force for good.[33] Here, nationalism and democracy work toward common educational ends.

On the debit side several matters are to be noted. Nationalism is not always ready to be a humble means to the development of individuality as the end. All too frequently it becomes an educational end in itself, and the individual is turned into the means. Indeed, the individual may be completely engulfed and all but disappear in the nation.[34] Instead of developing free personality, it cultivates an enforced obedience and docility. Unfortunately, too, nationalism is easily turned into the channels of taking pride in the superiority of one's own nation and extending its influence in imperialistic fashion. Here it becomes the ready tool of the worst competitive features of capitalism. When nationalism becomes harnessed to such narrow and exclusive aims, broadly patriotic education gives way to jingoism and chauvinism.

At this point nationalism finds itself in opposition to democratic educational objectives. Democracy demands the sharing of culture not only within the group, but between groups.[35] To be democratic, therefore, nationalistic education should be internationalistic as well. But is the national state capable of such international cooperation? Could it sponsor a type of education for its citizens which would teach them to transcend mere national loyalties? Or is it necessary to establish some sort of world organization with its own educational counterpart to dispose the minds and hearts of men toward world-wide cooperation?[36] Again much will depend on what philosophical view we take toward such a world organization. Should it be

[33] John Dewey, "Toward a National System of Education," *Social Frontier,* 1:9–10, June, 1935.
[34] Giovanni Gentile, *The Reform of Education* (Harcourt, Brace & World, Inc., New York, 1922), p. 17.
[35] *Supra,* p. 67.
[36] Cf. George A. Coe, "The United Nations' Philosophy of Education," *School and Society,* 70:177–180, September, 1949.

cosmopolitan or international, a world state or cooperation among national states? There are sincere advocates of both positions. Those who favor the formation of a super-world state seem to trust the old notion that sovereignty is indivisible and therefore, to be effective on a world plane, must be lodged in some single political entity. Others who favor an international organization do so because they think of sovereignty as localized in a plurality of political entities which are capable of delegating limited sovereignty to some world organization for specific purposes.[37] It is this theory of internationalism which at present inspires UNESCO, but whether it is adequate to combat and restrain the beast of war remains to be seen.

SELECTED BIBLIOGRAPHY

Clarke, Fred: *Essays in the Politics of Education* (Oxford University Press, Fair Lawn, N.J., 1923), Chap. 2.

Coe, George A.: *Educating for Citizenship* (Charles Scribner's Sons, New York, 1938), Chaps. 8, 10.

Cohausz, Otto: *The Pope and Christian Education* (Benziger Bros., Inc., New York, 1933).

Deferrari, Roy J. (ed.): *Essays on Catholic Education in the United States* (The Catholic University of America Press, Washington, D.C., 1942), pp. 25–66.

Gentile, Giovanni: *The Reform of Education* (Harcourt, Brace & World, Inc., New York, 1922), Chap. 1.

Hans, Nicholas A.: *The Principles of Educational Policy* (P. S. King & Staples, Ltd., London, 1933), Chaps. 1–3.

Huxley, Julian: *UNESCO: Its Purpose and Philosophy* (Public Affairs Press, Washington, D.C., 1947).

International Institute: *Educational Yearbook, 1929* (Teachers College, Columbia University, New York, 1930).

Kallen, Horace M.: *The Education of Free Men* (Farrar, Straus & Cudahy, Inc., New York, 1949), Chaps. 12–13.

Meiklejohn, Alexander: *Education between Two Worlds* (Harper & Row, Publishers, Incorporated, New York, 1942), Chaps. 13, 20–21.

Sizer, Theodore R.: *Religion and Public Education* (Houghton Mifflin Company, Boston, 1967), Chaps. 1–3.

Smith, Houston: *The Purposes of Higher Education* (Harper & Row, Publishers, Incorporated, New York, 1955), Chap. 6.

---

[37] William Stanley, B. Othanel Smith, and Kenneth D. Benne, "Progressive Essentialism in Education," *Frontiers of Democracy*, 9:211, April, 1943; Bertrand Russell, *Education and the Modern World*, pp. 26–27.

PART TWO
Aims

CHAPTER FIVE

Educational Aims

Educational aims perform three important functions all of which are normative. In the first place they give direction to the educative process. Before one makes a change in the curriculum or plans a new school building or adds new personnel to the staff, he must ask himself what his objectives are. Unless he determines them, he will be overwhelmed by the number of options which confront him. Even without changes in the offing, it is worth while to be conscious of what direction custom and tradition are carrying the educative process. Otherwise education runs the risk of becoming humdrum, if not actually mechanical.

For education to slip into such a thoughtless pattern underscores the second function aims perform. Aims not only should give direction to education but should motivate it as well. Aims are values, and if they are valued, if they are wanted, they should induce the learner to release the energies necessary to accomplish them. Aims which direct but do not activate are only 50 per cent effective.

Finally, aims have the function of providing a criterion for evaluating the educational process. Whether one is examining students or accrediting high schools and colleges, he must have reference to initial objectives. To find students or institutions wanting in some achievement that had never been sought as a goal in the first place would be unjust indeed. There is the possibility, of course, that the aim, though held, is an unworthy one. Here more far-reaching aims—ultimate ones, if they can be established— may be necessary to evaluate narrow and more immediate ones.

THE DETERMINATION OF EDUCATIONAL AIMS

Our major interest at this point is in aims as giving direction to education.[1] From whence does this direction come? One might think the answer to this question is already foreshadowed in the preceding chapters. If education inevitably occurs in a social matrix, is it not logical to expect that the norms of society will and should set the aims of education? Indeed it is,

---

[1] For the treatment of aims as motivators and as standards of evaluation, see *infra*, pp. 253–255 and 268–269.

but that is only the beginning of the formulation of educational aims. For instance, the question has arisen whether or not education should form the man as well as the citizen. As already seen, this is not to affirm that the aim of the one is at odds with the other, but it is to suggest, at least, that they might differ in important respects. If so, one certainly cannot take the aims of education uncritically from the social matrix.

No doubt the school must be sensitive to the demands of lay society —the wishes of the Chamber of Commerce, the American Legion, the American Federation of Labor, the Congress of Industrial Organizations, the Parent-Teachers Association, and the like. Yet, in spite of such pressures the actual formulation of aims should be internal to the process of education itself. Part of education is learning to determine one's aims, what values are worthy to be pursued as ends. Hence the school must have some measure of autonomy in deciding its own direction just as it does in the selection of the curriculum and the method of instruction. To take the ends of education altogether ready-made from some source outside the educational process, therefore, would be false to the very nature of education itself.[2] External social conditions supply materials by which to judge the effect of the educational process but they do not supply the educational norm.

If one accepts society more or less as it is at any given time, the aim of bringing up children means to "bring" them "up" to the current level of adult competence. What is best in the conventions of adult society becomes the goal. Its achievement, we may be confident, will liquidate the ignorance and immaturity of the young. Naturally in such a case the aims of education are set externally by adults; children themselves have little to do but passively accept and conform to them.

On the other hand, if one finds himself dissatisfied with current social conditions, it is possible that the aims of education will take their origin in the defects of society and how they may be corrected. In such case youthful immaturity is not an empty lock in the scholastic canal the filling of which lifts the young to adult levels. Instead of a void, immaturity is viewed as a power to grow; instead of a liability, it is an asset.

There are several ways to determine what are the best patterns of adult life to follow. Some have tried to derive the aims of education from a historical analysis of social institutions. Others have derived them from a sociological analysis of current life. With an eye on the current scene they have made descriptive analyses, on the one hand, of children's activities and, on the other hand, of adult activities. Individuals in this group have recorded minutely the errors and mistakes of children which the

---

[2] John Dewey, *The Sources of a Science of Education* (Liveright Publishing Corporation, New York, 1929), pp. 73–75.

school should aim to correct, while others have made job analyses of various adult occupations for which the school should prepare. Somewhat different are those who have tried to predicate educational aims on a psychological study of the original nature of man.

There is one fault which tends to vitiate sociological approaches to the choice of educational aims. They are preoccupied with the *status quo.* They describe very well what values are in fact held by contemporary society, but they do not tell whether contemporary social values should be perpetuated or whether they should be amended or even supplanted. Sociology and history are fact-finding disciplines. They can tell what is desired, but they cannot tell what is desirable, that is, what ought to be desired. To let history and science arbitrate what is desirable too would be to enthrall the future to the present and the past.

While one should be cautious about scientists' setting the aims of education, one need not exclude them altogether, thus leaving the choice of aims strictly to philosophers. Although educators would not have to accept a scientist's aims on logical grounds, they might very well do so on psychological ones. The only protection necessary would be to insist that the scientist indicate his opinion as a philosophical rather than scientific one.[3]

The notorious difference of opinion among philosophers has disposed some to turn their backs on the effort to prescribe educational aims. Realizing that one cannot derive prescriptive statements of aims from descriptive statements of fact, they recommend that the determination of educational aims be transformed from a philosophical into a methodological problem. To do this, they find out what values are actually held in some particular social context and then make it their business to formulate the educational aims which would help this community realize its values.[4] This might suffice, as already indicated, where social conditions are relatively stable but hardly where educational aims are indeterminate because the social situation itself is indeterminate.

HOW AIMS FUNCTION

In considering the ways in which aims give direction to education, it is necessary at the outset to make two distinctions. In the first place, an aim or purpose is something more than a native impulse. It originates in impulse, to be sure, but it does not become an aim or purpose till some

[3] Charles L. Stevenson, "The Scientist's Role and the Aims of Education," *Harvard Educational Review*, 24:231–238, Fall, 1954.
[4] H. J. Perkinson, "The Methodological Determination of the Aims of Education," *Educational Theory*, 11:61–64, January, 1961.

endeavor has been made to predict the probable consequences of acting on the impulse. In the second place, educational outcomes will sometimes be a surprise, compared to what was anticipated or aimed at. For this reason, it is important to distinguish aims or objectives from outcomes or results. The former are a matter of foresight, while the latter are a matter of hindsight. The former are what one tries to learn or teach; the latter, what one actually succeeds in learning or teaching. Since time inexorably marches on, education is bound to have outcomes or results, whether or not they have been preceded by thought-out aims or objectives.

If intelligence is to be enlisted in the continual reformation of educational aims, as would be necessary in social reconstruction, it will perhaps be more graphic to speak of educational ends rather than educational aims. Not only does an aim try to foresee what the end or termination of present educative effort will or should be, but this vision, once gained, is an instrument in guiding both pupil and teacher to that end. In the first place it helps in sizing up the means which are available for reaching the end, and, in the second place, it suggests the order in which steps should be taken to get there. To have an aim, to act purposefully, to consider future events in the light of the past, is all one with acting intelligently.

The flexibility or rigidity of educational aims involves the further problem, whether educational aims should arise out of an ongoing experience or whether they should be conceived as external to it. Scholastic educational philosophy favors the latter conception. It thinks experience fluctuates too much to be a satisfactory source of educational aims. Aims arising out of such a flux could hardly be steady enough to give effective guidance to the educative process. What is needed is an aim which lies outside and above experience. It must lie outside, so that it may be fixed; it must lie above it, so that it may be perfect as an educational ideal.

The opposite view, that educational aims should emerge from experience, is almost a forced conclusion from the position that aims should be constantly reshaped to meet the needs of a dynamic environment. The advantage of this sort of aim to the teacher or learner is that he directly appreciates its relation to what is going on. It is of crucial importance that he is seeking an answer to his own problem, not someone else's. Educational aims are thus not only purposeful, but personal.

The crucial difference between these views seems to center on the mutual relation of ends and means.[5] The latter, or progressive, view holds that educational ends cannot be intelligently set forth without a considera-

[5] Lawrence G. Thomas, "The Meaning of 'Progress' in Progressive Education," *Educational Administration and Supervision*, 32:385–400, October, 1946. For a linguistic analysis of this relation, see C. J. B. Macmillan and James E. McClellan, "Can and Should Means-Ends Reasoning Be Used in Teaching?" *Studies in Philosophy of Education*, 5:375–406, Fall, 1967.

tion of the means that bring them within reach. Moreover, ends once achieved become resources or means in the quest for further ends. Stated differently, means refer to the immediate direction of learning while ends refer to its more remote direction. From the former, or essentialist, point of view, ends may remain trusted and worthy no matter how inaccessible they are, no matter how difficult it is to improvise means for their realization.

Sometimes, the externality of educational aims refers to their social origin rather than to their metaphysical character. The source of the aims which are to guide the learner is the teacher rather than the learner himself. Even the teacher's aims may not be his own but those of his superior administrative officer. Such a hierarchy of authority is generally based on the supposed incompetence of the one below, and the superior vision of the one above, in picking a suitable objective. Particularly is this the case where the objective itself is of the fixed external type and must therefore be insisted upon, in spite of the fact that its worth is not appreciated by those at the bottom of the hierarchical ladder. A number allege that the social philosophy antecedent to this view is undemocratic. The few pick the aims of the many. Yet what would be democratic in this situation is a moot point. Some hold that it is better for the many to be assured of specific good aims, even at the expense of not being consulted on their selection. Others question whether the judgment of the few is so superior as to warrant such responsibility. But, even granting that, and granting that the many would choose more bad aims than would the few, these others would prefer to have the many choose and learn from their mistakes, rather than never to choose at all.

The line of cleavage which so far has divided opinions on the way educational aims are to serve the educative process can be extended still further. In addition to the controversies over its other qualities, there also rages one on its temporal dimension. Should pupil and teacher aims have a present reference, or a more remote one in the future? Should school be life or a preparation for life?

In approaching a good answer to this question, there would probably be general assent to saying that the problem is not an either-or affair. Sober educational philosophy must take both periods into account. This is most easily done by recognizing no sharp razor-edged division between the present and the future, between childhood and adulthood. The future should be seen to grow imperceptibly out of the present, so that childhood and adulthood form one continuous development. With this point of departure, it is obvious that education disregards either period at its peril. Education must, therefore, be a judicious mixture of participation in present life and preparation for subsequent events.

But what proportion of ingredients shall go into this formula? Probably the answer to this question turns on the relative importance, in the educator's regard, of childhood and adulthood. In many quarters the conviction has prevailed that the latter is the more important. They depreciate children because they are only candidates for society, rather than full-fledged members of it. The aim of education, therefore, should properly put more stress on preparation for adulthood than on the present interests of childhood. If a man's years be threescore and ten, then the first fifteen or twenty years of education should be primarily concerned with getting ready for the last fifty. For many, moreover, even adulthood is but a stage on the way to life eternal. Hence, for them, education as preparation has an even more distant goal.

Over against this position can be pitted the opinions of those who underscore the claims of childhood and the present.[6] If education is growth, it must necessarily be directed toward the future. The mistake is not in emphasizing the future, therefore, but in making it the mainspring of present effort. Since growth occurs in the present, the constant aim and function of education is to get out of the present the kind of growth that is inherent in it. On this account, supporters of this view emphasize childhood's present interests and capacities. Preparation for the future, then, is but a by-product. Growing well in the present will be the best preparation for growing in the future. Consequently they are fearful of aims or values which are so deferred in time that, however sound, they may fail to enlist the native energies of the child because of their very remoteness. They do not mean to disregard long-standing values in the social heritage, but they would prefer to sacrifice a little steadiness of direction rather than a part of the efficiency with which the child's drives are geared to his present studies. Accordingly, school and college should aim at life, life here and now, not a preparation for it. In a contingent universe, the educator cannot bank too securely on deferred values, for they may be completely rescaled before they are achieved. Consequently, it is urged that learning focus its energies where the changes are now occurring, the present—always, of course, defining the present, not as a razor-thin slice of time, but as a span of time which constantly emerges from the past and imperceptibly merges with the future.

THE PROXIMATE AIMS OF EDUCATION

Some exception has been taken to the foregoing discussion of the aims of education. The basis for this exception is the contention that an abstract

6 John Dewey, *Human Nature and Conduct* (Holt, Rinehart and Winston, Inc., New York, 1922), p. 270; John Dewey, *Reconstruction in Philosophy* (Holt, Rinehart and Winston, Inc., New York, 1920), pp. 183–185.

idea like education cannot have any aims, that only people like pupils, teachers, and parents can have them. The point of this fine distinction is that aims arise out of concrete situations in which people are involved. Aims, therefore, must be tailor-made for the occasion; we cannot publish a list of them in advance. We do not know our aims till a situation arises and we project aims as means of guiding our observation and final selection of a plan for handling it. Consequently the number of immediate or proximate aims of education is legion.

What is needed in this welter of aims is some means of telling, on the one hand, whether the aims we have adopted are well balanced and, on the other, what priorities, if any, exist among them. On the point of balance, aims can be tested against such more inclusive or intermediate aims as that of a liberal education, especially where this time-honored concept stands for the well-rounded man, the man who is developed physically, morally, intellectually, and spiritually. Again, Herbert Spencer listed the specific ends of an education for "complete living" in his famous essay on *What Knowledge Is Most Worth?* There have been a number of attempts to improve upon him. Perhaps the most widely accepted design for complete living has been the "Cardinal Principles of Education" put forth by a commission of the National Education Association.[7] These principles were summarized under seven headings: (1) Health; (2) Command of the Fundamental Process, notably the three R's; (3) Worthy Home Membership; (4) Vocation; (5) Civic Functions; (6) Worthy Use of Leisure Time; and (7) Ethical Character. The most notable omission from this list is religion. It may be that its authors mistakenly thought this to be included in the item of ethical character, or it may be that the list was being recommended as a program for public schools from which religious instruction is ordinarily barred. In either event, with its inclusion, this enumeration of educational values should be fairly complete and satisfactory.

On the point of priorities it is necessary to commence by noting the close connection of aims and values. Suppose a student were to inquire whether he should aim or strive at excellence in his studies or in athletics. One ready response might be that it depends on some intermediate aim like a career aim. If the student is a good enough athlete to consider a career in professional sport, he might very well concentrate on sports and relegate his studies to second place. But if he plans on a career which will require further study in graduate or professional school, he had better aim

[7] National Education Association, Commission on the Reorganization of Secondary Education, "The Cardinal Principles of Education," *U.S. Bureau of Education Bulletin*, 35:11–15, 1918. For somewhat different statements, see National Education Association, Educational Policies Commission, *The Purposes of Education in American Democracy*, 1938; and American Federation of Teachers, Committee on Educational Reconstruction, *Goals of American Education*, 1948, Chap. 2.

at a high grade-point average in his studies. Obviously the approach to aims here is extrinsic or instrumental. The choice is extrinsic because it is contingent on aims or values lying outside or beyond the two between which the student is trying to establish a priority.

Another way to choose between these two aims would be to explore their intrinsic merits. Detaching himself from extrinsic considerations as disinterestedly as possible, the student might note that each aim, scholastic and athletic, is worth pursuing as an end in itself without further consequence. Now, is either one more worth while as an end in itself? Several criteria suggest themselves to arbitrate this choice. In the first place we might judge between the aims in terms of which one will be more enduring over the years. In the second place we might judge between the two on grounds of which is capable of the greater sophistication, which holds out the greater intellectual challenge? One advantage of this dimension of our criterion is that it seems to have no limit. And finally, we might inquire which aim relates itself to the widest area of other interests. By employing such criteria, we see that scholastic aims clearly take priority over athletic ones. Personal preference does not enter to make the final decision relativistic as where aims have an extrinsic or instrumental reference. Intrinsic aims, therefore, recommend themselves as having greater stability.

THE ULTIMATE AIMS OF EDUCATION

Yet another way to establish balance and priority among educational aims is to consider them—both proximate and intermediate—in the light of ultimate ones.[8] Various values have been put forth as constituting the ultimate aims of education. If one takes a religious view of the world, then the ultimate aim of education will most likely take its coloration from the ultimate end of human life. Consulting the penny catechism, we find that man was created to know, reverence, and serve God, thereby to earn eternal life with Him. If so, then the chief purpose of the school is to teach the child how to act so as not to disappoint this expectation. Fortunately for the child, he has the lives of Jesus and the saints to imitate as the concrete embodiment of this aim.[9] He will be particularly well advised to be mindful of Jesus' injunction, "Be ye therefore perfect, even as your Father which is in heaven is perfect."[10] Since nothing can be more perfect

---

[8] Cf. William J. Sanders, "Thomism, Instrumentalism, and Education," *Harvard Educational Review*, 10:98–101, January, 1940. For a further discussion of educational aims, see *infra*, p. 147.

[9] Thomas E. Shields, "The Ultimate Aim of Christian Education," *Catholic Education Review*, 12:308, November, 1916.

[10] Matthew 5:48.

than divine perfection itself, the ultimate quest for perfection is literally the last and final end of education.

Not unlike the religious statement of the final end of education is the view that the ultimate aim of education is self-realization. Here we should examine human nature, see what its potentialities are, and then set up an educational program which aims to actualize or realize them. Or, as some have expressed it, education should aim to perfect the individual in all his powers. The idea was well put by Rousseau when he stated that the object of education is not to make a soldier, magistrate, or priest, but to make a man. If such an education results in his becoming a better citizen or worker, such an outcome is to be considered a by-product of aiming at the improvement of his inner worth as an end in itself.[11]

Some have such confidence in the ultimacy of the aim of education which is rooted in human nature that they are ready to universalize it. Thus they claim that the aims of education should be the same for all men everywhere and always! Such a broad claim must mean that the ultimate aims of education are the same for oriental as well as occidental man, for man in the fourth century B.C. as well as man in the twentieth century A.D. Yet, how can such vast differences of time and place be reduced to identity? Simply by noting that the essential nature of man is the same today as it always has been within the memory of man. If such a sweeping statement seems to rule out the possible impact of evolution, suffice it to say, for the adherents of this view, that when there is convincing evidence that man has changed his species, it will be time enough to amend the ultimate aims of education.

The conflict on ultimate outlook here can be stated more broadly. Should educational aims in general have a fixed immutable quality, or should they be flexible and subject to continual reconstruction?[12] There are many who favor the former sort of aim. The metaphysic to which this group subscribes is obvious.[13] They feel no security or confidence in their educational endeavors unless they can strive toward a definite, unchanging ideal. If the ideal keeps constantly shifting, they feel a persistent, sidelong anxiety which saps their best efforts. Paradoxical though it may seem, an immutable goal liberates rather than inhibits their powers. Others, adopting the opposite metaphysic, find fixed aims not only inadequate, but al-

---

[11] For a similar vein in oriental philosophy of education, see Ratna Navaratnam, *New Frontiers in East-West Philosophies of Education* (Orient Longmans, Bombay, 1958), p. 113.

[12] William J. Sanders, "Fallacies Underlying Curriculum Theory," *Educational Administration and Supervision*, 25:161–181, March, 1939; William J. Sanders, "Thomism, Instrumentalism, and Education," *Harvard Educational Review*, 10:98–101, January, 1940.

[13] Cf. *infra*, pp. 138–139.

most a menace.[14] In a world composed of a mixture of the contingent and the recurrent, educational aims, to be realistic, must shift with the rest of the scenery. Instead of being final, they should be merely tentative. Thus, when an educational experience is evaluated at its conclusion, it may be found necessary to reconstruct its original aim as well as the procedure for gaining it. Not only does the environment change as one learns, but learning itself does something to the environment.

Self-realization, however, is not without its ambiguities. Can we reason, for instance, that what man determines, that he ought to become? In one sense, apparently we can. For instance, it is a waste of time to try to make a child into what he has no potentiality to become. If a pupil is tone deaf, it serves no useful purpose to try to make a musician out of him. In another sense, however, we should not make the mistake of thinking that, while man's natural capacities limit his range of fulfillment, they at the same time determine any specific fulfillment. Self-realization as embodied in the "unfoldment" theory of education makes exactly this mistake. It implies that the only proper self to be realized is already enfolded in the cell at birth. If we subscribe to self-realization as the ultimate aim of education, our view will be more consistent with psychological fact if we envision a wide range of possible selves the student might become.

Another ambiguity forms itself in the question: Does self-realization mean, for instance, the maximal development of all one's potentialities? If so, this is probably a physical impossibility. There is not time enough, in either formal or informal education, for each individual to become a poet and a plowman, a philosopher and a financier, a sinner and a saint, to say nothing of many other kinds of selves. Furthermore, there are some human potentialities like fear and anger which, useful as they may have been in the struggle for existence in the past, we might hope could be left to atrophy if ever law and order can come to regulate that struggle in the future. Stated somewhat differently, self-realization must not be confused with self-expression as the ultimate aim of education. To express the self he now is, the child might well disclose a very weak, bigoted, hateful self. The ultimate aim of self-realization is to realize, not so much the self one is as the self he ought to become. But this is just the issue: What kind of self should he become? What is the ultimate aim of education? Obviously self-realization without some further qualification is too ambiguous an aim.

Seizing upon rationality as man's peculiar excellence, some educational philosophers have tried to give self-realization a more definite character by declaring that the chief and ultimate end of education is the

---

14 *Ibid.*

cultivation of the intellect. Indeed, we have the authority of Aristotle for the assertion that of all human activities the intellectual is most akin to the activity of Deity. If Aristotle was right—and St. Thomas Aquinas tended to agree with him—then the pursuit of intellectual excellence and its by-product, knowledge for its own sake, can lay just claim to being the ultimate aim of education.[15] Even some who follow Darwin rather than Aristotle and who confine their educational philosophies to naturalism to the exclusion of supernaturalism come out with this same exaltation of intelligence as the principal aim of education.[16] In a dynamic culture the main business of society is to cultivate intelligence if ever it is to meet on even terms the uncertainties of a constantly changing social order. All of which is to say nothing of still others who think of formal discipline of the mind as the ultimate aim of education. In this case intellectual excellence does not so much consist in the pursuit of knowledge on its own account or in making adjustments to a contingent world, as in sharpening faculties so that the power developed in exercising them on one kind of subject matter will be easily transferable to any other.

Another way to qualify self-realization in more definite terms is to give it a social idealization. Man lives not to himself alone. On the contrary he lives among his fellows; in fact he would hardly be man without the benefit of the social structure. Hence self-realization is a matter of balanced participation in the institutions of society. It is a participation, as some add, not just in social institutions as they are but as they are becoming and as they ideally ought to become. The ultimate aim of education, therefore, takes its form from whatever the social stereotype may be. Naturally this stereotype will vary depending on whether society is organized along democratic, fascistic, or communistic lines.[17]

The foregoing is a necessary preface to saying that, if educators are to view the educative process as autonomous, then education is subordinate to nothing save more education. Or, as Dewey has stated it, "The educational process has no end beyond itself; it is its own end.[18] What does this mean? That knowledge is its own end? Not exactly. Perhaps the statement can best be understood in terms of Dewey's famous syllogism that education is all one with life, that life is growth, and therefore that education is growth. The ultimate aim of education, then, is to grow, not just physically,

[15] John Cardinal Newman, The Idea of a University, 6th ed. (Longmans, Green & Co., Ltd., London, 1886), pp. 103, 121. See also Walter B. Kolesnik, Mental Discipline in Modern Education (The University of Wisconsin Press, Madison, Wis., 1958).
[16] William H. Kilpatrick (ed.), The Educational Frontier (Appleton-Century-Crofts, Inc., New York, 1933), p. 108. Cf. infra, pp. 232–233, 241–242.
[17] Supra, Chap. 3.
[18] John Dewey, Democracy and Education (The Macmillan Company, New York, 1916), p. 59.

of course, but in greater insight into and control over one's environment. The growth that is thought of here must not be just the kind which grows toward perfection and upon reaching it necessarily stops. Rather is it the sort which leads to continued growing, to using current insights and controls to widen and deepen further insight and control.[19] It eschews growth which is made significant by any perfection it is approximating and holds that growth, to be a significant end of education, must be worth while on its own account.

To name growth as the ultimate aim of education seems confusing and vague to a number of educators. For one thing, it seems to confuse a consequence of education with its aim. All learning inescapably involves an increment of growth of some sort. But should not an aim specify which sort? For another thing, continual growth as the ultimate aim of education seems to confuse growth with progress. Certainly stepping up the tempo of growth is neither a guarantee nor a dependable index of progress. There is continued growth in cancer, but manifestly that is not the kind of growth we want. The pupil can grow in lazy and careless habits of study as well as in industrious and painstaking ones. For a last thing, there is apprehension that some educational activities will be content with mere commotion as an outcome of being guided by the concept of growth.[20] In sum, the chief indictment of growth as the ultimate aim of education is that it appears to fail to specify what is a desirable or right direction for growth to take.[21] It appears to have the alleged fatal weakness of instrumentalism, the lack of finality or decisiveness.

Adherents of the ultimate aim of education as growth have a rebuttal for these doubts and apparent confusions. Agreeing that change and progress are not to be confounded with each other, they still hold that the subtle and strategic significance of change and growth lies in further possibilities of change and growth. This does not mean a deference to the mere drift of the cosmic weather nor an almost superstitious reverence for the child's inner growth. Furthermore, they insist that one must be patient and take a long-range view of growth. From this perspective, it will be seen that baleful and obnoxious activities, though they may seem to flourish for a time, eventually sow the seeds of their own decay. Good and righteous

---

[19] Cf. E. M. White, "Bergson and Education," *Educational Review*, 47:431–443, May, 1914.

[20] George S. Counts, *Dare the School Build a New Social Order?* (The John Day Company, Inc., New York, 1932), pp. 6–7; John M. Mecklin, "Some Limitations of the Social Emphasis in Education," *School and Society*, 9:584–591, May, 1919.

[21] Cf. Boyd H. Bode, "Education as Growth: Some Confusions," *Progressive Education*, 14: 151–157, March, 1937; James H. O'Hara, *Limitations of the Educational Philosophy of John Dewey* (The Catholic University of America Press, Washington, D.C., 1929), p. 75.

habits, on the other hand, tend to lead to indefinite expansion. They increase and lead out into a variety of other activities, as well as grow in stature themselves. Cancerous growth undoubtedly leads on with increasing vigor—but to death. Some instructional methods also lead to growth, but only in school; after graduation the interests cultivated there, as in literature and public affairs, cease. The kind of teaching on which a high value can be placed is that which results in a permanent disposition to continue one's education, one's growth, as long as one lives.[22]

In all the foregoing discussion—whether of self-realization or growth —the ultimate goal of education has suggested the importance of "becoming." That every thing is in process seems an unmistakable characteristic of mortal life. Yet, while Western culture glorifies becoming, it is worth noting that some Eastern philosophies of education take a contrary view of the ultimate end of education. Since it is mortal to become, to be immortal we must put a stop to becoming. They think that education misdirected which pins its faith on trying to realize individuality with an identity which can survive not only from day to day but beyond life itself. On the contrary, the ultimate aim of education is for the individual to expand into the absolute. Yogi is the discipline whereby the individual achieves this unity.[23]

SELECTED BIBLIOGRAPHY

Barnett, George (ed.): *Philosophy and Educational Development* (Houghton Mifflin Company, Boston, 1966), Chap. 5.

Dewey, John: *Ethical Principles Underlying Education* (The University of Chicago Press, Chicago, 1903).

Hollins, T. H. B. (ed.): *Aims in Education: The Philosophic Approach* (Manchester University Press, Manchester, 1964).

Hook, Sidney: *Education for Modern Man* (The Dial Press, Inc., New York, 1963).

John Dewey Society: Seventh Yearbook, *The Public School and Spiritual Values* (Harper & Row, Publishers, Incorporated, New York, 1944).

New Educators Library: *Ideals, Aims, and Methods of Education* (Pitman Publishing Corporation, New York, 1922), Sec. 1.

O'Connor, Daniel J.: *The Philosophy of Education* (Philosophical Library, Inc., New York, 1957), Chap. 3.

Perry, Ralph B.: *Realms of Value* (Harvard University Press, Cambridge, Mass., 1954), Chap. 21.

[22] John Dewey, *Experience and Education* (The Macmillan Company, New York, 1938), pp. 28–29.

[23] Ratna Navaratnam, *op. cit.*, p. 52.

Peters, Richard S.: *Ethics and Education* (Scott, Foresman and Company, Chicago, 1967), Chaps. 4–5.

————: "Aims of Education—A Conceptual Inquiry," in Willard Brehaut (chmn.), *Philosophy of Education* (Ontario Institute for Studies in Education, Toronto, 1967), Chap. 1.

Phenix, Philip: *Realms of Meaning* (McGraw-Hill Book Company, New York, 1964), Chap. 17.

Smith, Huston: *The Purposes of Higher Education* (Harper & Row, Publishers, Incorporated, New York, 1955).

Whitehead, Alfred N.: *The Aims of Education and Other Essays* (The Macmillan Company, New York, 1929), Chap. 1.

CHAPTER SIX

Aims and Human Nature

Analysis of the aims of education has indicated at a number of points that they would be incomplete without a broader setting than the one already given. In one way or another, for instance, the preceding ultimate aims of education were predicated on a conception of human nature without giving any extended analysis of human nature itself. The ultimate aim of education, for instance, was said to be "self-realization" without much elucidation of the nature of the self to be realized. Again, some assigned a certain perennial quality to the ultimate aims of education because, it was claimed, human nature is essentially the same everywhere and always—the same east and west, north and south, and the same down the centuries. On account of this constancy of human nature many fastened with considerable confidence on intellectual excellence as the principal aim of education because intelligence has distinguished the nature of man from that of the brute since time out of mind. By contrast others have regarded the ultimate aims of education as much more flexible because, influenced by a theory of evolution, they have not discerned such a sharp difference between man and brute.

Obviously from the foregoing it is necessary to enlarge the discussion of educational aims by a more extended analysis of what kind of people we are, what is the nature of the human nature to be educated. It is an ancient question. "What is man that Thou art mindful of him?" cried the Hebrew psalmist to his God. The educator, like the priest and the physician, must earnestly ask himself this same question. He must ask it, not to make aims conform to this nature, for that would be to commit the naturalistic fallacy, but to be sure that they take into account and make compatible as many factors as seem to be relevant to giving education direction.

The educator runs into the question of "what is man" on a variety of occasions. Everywhere, for instance, there seems to be a struggle for the possession of men's minds. Prisoners of war are allegedly "brainwashed." Communists hope to contradict capitalist views of human nature by creating a "new Soviet man." In American schools a new educational technology is appearing with an increasing reliance on teaching machines, computerized instruction, and the like. All these events seem to imply a greatly increased control of man over man. Is this a threat to human nature, or is human nature quite capable of surmounting it? From another angle the forces struggling to capture men's minds are so diverse and highly organized that confusion results. Young people seem to be in the midst of an "identity" crisis. Not unlike the psalmist they cry out, "Who am I?" Never, consequently, has it seemed more necessary to follow the Socratic exhortation "know thyself."[1]

THE MIND-BODY PROBLEM

In helping the educator to formulate an answer to the question, "What is man?" we may as well start with the issue which historically and perhaps currently lies at the core of the whole problem. This is the metaphysical or ontological question: Of what is man made? It has long been the common-sense view of our culture that the nature of man is dualistic, that man is composed of mind and body, spirit and flesh. This division of man into mind and body is but a subdivision of the larger dichotomy of the world into animate and inanimate categories.[2] Matter is what we ordinarily refer to as having extension or occupying space. Furthermore, it is inert until pushed about by forces external to it. But there are exceptions to this definition. Man has a body which has extension in space too, but instead of being the inert butt of physical forces impinging on him from without, he can initiate activity himself. This ability to initiate action has led to the belief that there is more to reality than just matter. That man's self-activity takes the form of having purposes, making decisions, voluntarily executing them, and feeling responsibility for their consequence has led to the further conviction that there is another generic trait of reality in addition to matter, namely, mind or spirit.[3]

But for the aims of education, what more particularly is the nature of mind and spirit? Since it is in a different category from matter, we may conclude at once that mind is not matter, that it is immaterial. Being immaterial, it can think space even if it does not occupy it. Yet, though immaterial, mind is commonly referred to as an entity. This usage gives focus and a degree of permanence to the ephemeral flow of experiences through consciousness, such as our joys and sorrows, our perceptions and memories, our thoughts and feelings. In fact, this entity constitutes the central core of selfhood. The self, however, is not identical with any of the states of consciousness, nor with them all together. It is something more; it is the entity that has or entertains these states.

---

[1] C. A. Bowers, "Existentialism and Educational Theory," *Educational Theory*, 15:226, July, 1965.
[2] For a later reference to this problem, see *infra*, p. 156.
[3] Hence the quip: What is mind? It's no matter. What is matter? Never mind.

It is easier to make the common-sense distinction between matter and mind than it is to describe the mutual relation between the two. Ask the average teacher where the mind is located, and it is a better than average chance he will reply that it is located in the cerebrum. How an immaterial entity, which does not occupy space, can be located in a material one which encloses space is not explained. Indeed, the difficulty of location aside, it is still an unanswered question—at least to the satisfaction of all or even a majority—just how an immaterial entity like mind can operate on or interact with a material entity like the body. Yet, difficult as it is to comprehend how the dualism of mind and body is to be bridged, Catholic educational philosophy is confident that it can be. It holds that the school is neither a morgue nor a limbo of disembodied spirits but rather a place where learning cannot take place without the union of body and mind. St. Thomas Aquinas, as a matter of fact, found reason to think that after death the spirit or soul, when alienated from the body, is so incomplete as to be unable to learn new truths.

The educational consequences of adhering to a dualistic theory of the nature of man are not hard to surmise. They lead many to differentiate two kinds of educational psychology, rational for the explanation of mental phenomena and dynamic for the exposition of bodily ones. In either case, however, education is primarily a matter of training the mind, of exercising its faculties. The bodily senses have a part to play, to be sure, but since it is mind or spirit that activates the neuromuscular system of the body, it is the mind on which the educator lavishes his greatest solicitude. For the same reasons education is also primarily a matter of self-activity or self-development on the part of the pupil. Hence learning is anything but mechanistic. Matter may not change position till acted on by some external force, but man can change his position, that is, learn, without waiting for the teacher to act upon him. He can initiate responses without waiting for stimuli.

The educational consequences of a dualistic theory of human nature are not without their contradictions. One is the danger that mind and body, because they are so utterly different in kind, may travel along courses of action which ultimately run at cross purposes. The child, as has been pointed out, inescapably brings his body to school along with his mind. Since the body naturally has ends of its own, they are only too likely to become insurgent and intrude upon the child's attention at just the time when his mind ought to be occupied with his lessons. The teacher, consequently, has to spend much of his time restraining physical activities and insisting on order and quiet. Not only is this dualism a source of disciplinary problems, but it also poses the problem of how what the mind learns is to be translated into conduct of the body.

To avoid the theoretical and practical difficulties of a dualistic theory of human nature, a number of educational philosophers have turned to some form of monism. Instead of taking the common-sense view that human nature is composed of mind and body, each of which is an entirely different trait of reality, they try to simplify human nature by regarding it as all mind or all body. Thus some realists take the view that mental functions can be reduced to bodily ones, while certain idealists make matter a function of mind.

The idealists arrive at their monism by pointing out that it is mind that is central in understanding the world. To them nothing gives a greater sense of reality than the activity of mind engaged in trying to comprehend its world. For anything to give a greater sense of reality would be a contradiction in terms because to know anything more real than mind would itself have to be a conception of mind. Perhaps this reasoning does not exactly prove that the composition of matter is mental, but it does leave no doubt that education lives and moves and has its being in a world circumscribed by mind.

Many people who subscribe to this monistic point of view think of mind as an entity just as in the dualistic pattern and with similar educational results. But many others have come to opposite conclusions. The latter, starting with the notion that everything can be reduced to a concept of mind, come out with the conclusion, on further analysis, that there is nothing to the mind but a succession of concepts and percepts. When they try to inquire most intimately into what they call themselves, they always seem to stumble on some particular concept or percept which is occupying the forestage of their consciousness. In fact, try as they will, they never seem able to come upon their conscious selves without their being conscious of some particular thing or other—some time or place, some color or form, some hope or purpose. Unable to catch themselves so unoccupied, they have finally come to the conclusion that mind, instead of being an entity behind and entertaining ideas, is really a nonentity and therefore best to be described in terms of passing states of consciousness.

This view of mind leads to definitely different educational conclusions. Guided by a theory of mental states, the aim of educational psychology is to determine the structure of the mind by analyzing the complex affair of consciousness into its various elements. The whole is explained by its parts. On the side of learning, learning consists in putting parts together. It leans heavily on the psychological theory of associationism. Following this theory, the teacher organizes the lesson and presents it to the pupil so as to correlate and achieve the sequence of ideas or passing states of mind which will ensure understanding and retention in memory. This process is strongly reminiscent of Herbart and not a little mechanistic in spirit.

Quite different is the description of human nature which reduces the common-sense dualism of mind and body to the monism of body alone. Behaviorism is the best instance of this theory, where, as already noted, psychologist and educator base their knowledge of human nature strictly on an observation of overt physical behavior.[4] Mental phenomena have no standing except as they have muscular correlates. This theory is not only materialistic but mechanistic as well. Learning is fundamentally a matter of analysis of wholes into parts on the one hand and of association or forming connections between stimulus and response on the other. Connections are formed, habits stamped in, largely by mere repetition. Unlike the case where the mind is an entity and initiator of its responses, in behaviorism the response waits to go into action till it receives the appropriate stimulus. All human activity is reactivity. Purpose is just as mechanical as anything else.[5]

Going a step further, some behaviorists have taken as startling a view of human nature as Newton did of celestial bodies. In stating his first law of motion—that all objects tend to remain in constant velocity unless disturbed by some outside force—Newton gave up the ancient endeavor to account for the cause of motion. He confined himself to explaining changes in motion rather than motion itself. Similarly some behaviorists have given up the endeavor to account for the causes of human behavior, whether it is a push from behind in the form of tissue needs and endocrine ejections or a pull from ahead in the form of purpose or aim. Instead they have simply stated that man is an active organism learning from interaction with his environment. Thus, as Newton could confine himself to explaining changes in motion, behaviorist-educators concentrate on changes in the environment.[6]

Reaching a very similar result have been some linguistic analysts who have ascribed the mind-body problem to ambiguities arising from the use of language. They pay more attention to mental activity but do so as an aspect of behavior. Thus, when a student says that he is "thinking what he is doing," they regard it a mistake to hold he is doing two different

---

[4] For the relation between behaviorism and pragmatism, see John Dewey, *Essays in Experimental Logic* (Dover Publications, Inc., New York, 1953), p. 331.

[5] Edward L. Thorndike, *Human Learning* (Appleton-Century-Crofts, Inc., New York, 1931), p. 122.

[6] James E. McClellan, "B. F. Skinner's Philosophy of Human Nature: A Sympathetic Criticism," *Studies in Philosophy of Education*, 3:307–332, Spring, 1966. For a critique of McClellan, see George L. Newsome, "Philosophy of Human Nature vs. a Functional Analysis of Behavior," *ibid.*, 4:404–410, Summer, 1966.

things, that in tandem fashion he is first thinking and then doing. No doubt the student is both mentally and bodily active, but the two activities do not occur serially, not even synchronously; there is only one action. It is capable of two descriptions, to be sure, but it is still only one act. This view dispenses with trying to account for the cause of behavior through prior mental conditions. By eliminating this old idea it disposes of the outworn fiction of mind as a "ghost in the machine."[7]

Some realists and naturalists, too, think outright materialism and mechanism the only remedy for the confusion and division of opinion which reigns among those who continue to think in mentalistic terms. Human nature will remain an enigma as long as men insist on regarding it in such mentalistic terms as states of mind, consciousness, and the like. To them the only way to clarify the nature of human nature and reduce it to the rule of natural scientific law is to proceed on the theory that man is continuous with physical nature.

The materialism implied in this continuity between man and physical nature is not the old materialism where solid indivisible particles or atoms were supposed to be the essence of matter. On the contrary the materialism of the theory under consideration takes its meaning from modern physics, in which Einstein has given us the equation $E = MC^2$ where E stands for energy, M for mass, and C is a constant. In other words, matter is just a form of energy; the two are transposable. Gone now is matter as hard lumps or atoms, and in its place is a field theory of forces, matter being merely the place where there is the greatest concentration of forces. Accordingly the materialistically minded educator will hold that human nature is "essentially an electron-proton aggregate which is identical in nature with inorganic substances except for the presence of that unique process called life; and since the latter is seen only in connection with protoplasm, it is believed to be due to 'organizational properties' inherent in organic tissue."[8]

By studying these forces the modern materialistically minded realist hopes to invoke a strict cause-and-effect determinism and thus pave the way to a scientific control of human nature and behavior which should take a great deal of uncertainty out of teaching. Reduced to strictly mechanical terms, education would be translated into the physical impact of sound waves of the teacher's voice on the tympanum of the student's ear or the light waves from the printed page on the retina of the student's eye. Physiology interposes no difficulty to the transfer of such vibrations from

[7] James E. McClellan, op. cit., pp. 316–317.
[8] Louis P. Thorpe, Psychological Foundations of Personality (McGraw-Hill Book Company, New York, 1938), p. 92.

one medium to another without compromising their identity. Just as in the case of the telephone, vibrations can be transformed from atmospheric to electrical media and back again at the end of the line, so sound or light waves may be transposed into neural impulses without loss of character. This theory of human nature is all the more likely, think its sponsors, when we bear in mind the well-established fact of the electrical character of neural energy. Add to this fact the integrative action of the central nervous system, which, like an automatic telephone switchboard, is a device for receiving and organizing reactions to impulsions from without, and one has laid the basis for a thoroughly mechanistic theory of cognition and education.[9]

Bold as these materialistic and mechanistic theories of human nature are, they probably overreach themselves at least at present. Neither physiology nor neurology,[10] let alone physics or biochemistry, has been able as yet to propound a satisfactory mechanistic explanation of learning. There seems to be an "organizational" aspect of human nature, particularly of mind or the central nervous system, which they fully recognize, and which may in time yield itself to their interpretation, but which as yet remains undigested by them. Attempting to take this factor into account, some other educational psychologists and philosophers have made quite a different approach to the nature of human nature. Their approach is twofold. On the one hand they try to describe human nature not so much in terms of what it is as of what it does, and on the other hand they attach new significance to human nature as an integral whole. Hitherto human nature as a whole has seemed so complex to investigators that they have approached its understanding by analyzing it into parts and then putting these parts together to get a view of the whole. Believing that the whole is more than the sum of its parts, later theorists have started from the opposite end, the whole, and complex as it is, have kept relations to the whole constantly in mind while studying any of the parts. It is they in large part who have been responsible for urging the education of the "whole" child, that is, educating him both in regard to all the facets of his personality and in regard to these facets viewed in relation to each other as a whole.

As a basis for this approach these theorists too draw on field theory in physics but not so much for an exact explanation of human nature as for an analogy. Thus, in modern field theory the atom is no longer the unit of action. Since mass is transformable into energy, the atom is now con-

[9] Frederick S. Breed, in National Society for the Study of Education, Forty-first Yearbook, Part I, *Philosophies of Education* (Public School Publishing Company, Bloomington, Ill., 1942), pp. 107, 112.
[10] Clarence E. Ragsdale, *Modern Psychologies of Education* (The Macmillan Company, New York, 1932), p. 393.

tinuous with its field of forces. Any change in tension in part of the field will necessitate a redistribution of forces over the whole field. When forces are so redistributed, the result will be due to the resultant of all the forces entering therein. So, similarly, of child nature operating in its field, the school. Instead of assuming that the individual initiates his own responses, as where mind is conceived as an entity, or instead of responding to stimuli, as in the case of behaviorism, we should think of neither stimulus nor response as preceding the other but of both operating simultaneously. Thus the learner is already responding before the stimulus makes its impact upon him. In fact it is because of his motor set or attitude that he picks up the stimulus at all, say, the words of the teacher. If he were paying attention to something else, he might not even hear the teacher. If he forms the habit of paying attention to the teacher's directions when the teacher speaks, the resulting habit—the redistribution of energies—will be due or belong to the teacher as well as to the student. In other words, reorganization or redistribution of energies will be as much a reorganization of the environment as it is of the student.[11]

Learning, therefore, is as much a reorganization of the environment as it is of the self of the learner. Taking his cue from signs in the environment, the learner acts according to what he thinks the signs mean. If the consequences of acting show that the signs mean something else—if the dog that looked like an attractive playmate turns out to snarl and bite— then the child not only changes his own responses, but he changes the signs in his environment, in this case, what the dog means. From this it follows that habits about dogs are not stamped in but formed by constantly reorganizing and perfecting in detail one's responses to them. Mind, to sum up this position, is neither an entity, a nonentity, nor passing states of consciousness but rather "the power to understand things in terms of the use made of them."[12]

ORIGINAL NATURE

Whatever human nature is, to select suitable aims, we must now inquire what its various capacities are. It will be well to take inventory of these capacities before they have become overlaid with learning so that we can know as nearly as possible with just what educational capital the parent and teacher must begin. We must distinguish as nearly as we can between

---

[11] Edward B. Jordan, "Education and the Organization of Intelligence," *Journal of General Education*, 4:4, 8, October, 1949.

[12] John Dewey, *Democracy and Education* (The Macmillan Company, New York, 1916), p. 39.

heredity and environment, nature and nurture. It may appear to be emphasizing the obvious to state at the outset that human nature is, in the main, dynamic, active. What parent or teacher needs to be reminded of that? Yet in spite of this apparently obvious fact, there are some who think of youth as a rather passive recipient of the educative process.

The theory that the learner comes to school with a "vacant" sign hung on his mind and that it is the duty of the school to furnish the empty spaces is probably held more frequently by popular than by expert opinion. Nevertheless, some authorities still cling to the view first expounded by John Locke that the learner's mind at birth is like a clean slate on which the school, little by little, writes the accumulated heritage of race experience.[13] From a normative point of view, the practices which would follow from such a theory would be unacceptable. To hold that the mind is what it is taught unduly exalts the powers of teaching and demeans the priviliges of learning. There is further danger that teaching will become preoccupied with furnishing the mind with patterns of the past since these can be more readily cut and measured than those of a yet undetermined future. All this is to say nothing of the difficulty of translating knowledge into conduct. If teaching treats mind like an empty container to be filled, the problem arises how to empty it into action. Practice in filling is certainly not the equivalent of practice in pouring out.

It is not surprising, therefore, to find the weight of informed opinion holding to the theory that child nature is fundamentally dynamic. One has but to watch the child in the act of learning to become convinced of this. Take learning to write, for instance. Legs are employed as well as arms and hands, not to mention facial contortions. Even listening involves muscular coordination. A little further examination must also reveal that learning is not just a matter of perception but of apperception as well. The new is worked over by what is already familiar. The immaturity of the learner, far from being a void which needs to be filled, is a positive capacity or potentiality for growth.

The dynamic, growing, self-activating principle, which animates human nature and causes the human pattern to develop to maturity, has traditionally been known as the soul. While the soul is a single unitary principle, it possesses a number of faculties. A faculty, as its derivation from Latin facultas implies, is an "ability to do." Yet it must not be reified, that is, identified as a separate organic structure. The soul manifests two main kinds of faculties or abilities, the bodily and the mental. Through its bodily or somatic faculties the soul is able to sense, feel, and desire. Through

13 Cf. Ross Finney, Sociological Philosophy of Education (The Macmillan Company, New York, 1928), p. 64.

its mental or rational faculties the soul is able to remember, imagine, reason, and the like. Naturally there is a hierarchy of faculties in human nature, such that the bodily or somatic abilities are subordinate to the mental or rational. This is as it should be in order to check man's tumultuous appetites and give them profitable direction.

The educational corollary of this traditional conception of original nature is a traditional kind of education. Accordingly, the main aim of education is to exercise and develop the faculties, especially the mental or cognitive ones. There is some difference of opinion, however, as to what sort of curriculum is best suited to this end. The tradition of longest standing here is one extending from Aristotle to the present day. It seeks intellectual excellence as an end in itself by steeping the intellect in a curriculum as wide and rich as the liberal arts can afford.[14] Another tradition of long standing had its heyday in the nineteenth century but is still popular in some quarters. It strives for mental discipline through a formal training of the faculties on a narrow curriculum selected not so much for its rich breadth as for its being a medium of resistance, a whetstone for the mind. The expectation here is that the exercise of a faculty like memory results in an increment of improvement for that faculty which can be transferred at will to any field of mental endeavor.

Faculty psychology often recommends itself through an effective metaphor. People innocent of psychological theory as well as those versed in it often speak of a person as being dull- or sharp-witted. The obvious comparison is of the mind to some instrument with a cutting edge. When this edge is well honed it can be employed to cut any number of different materials. Striking as the metaphor is, however, it is no better than a half-truth and even as such has been roundly criticized. The weakness of the metaphor lies in the fact that it implies that the life of the mind may be postponed or held in abeyance till it is sharpened. But it cannot be so restrained. Life is urgent and moves inexorably forward. If the curriculum has significance, therefore, it is not as a whetstone to hone the mind for later use but as a nourishment to strengthen the learner's powers here and now.[15]

Another point of attack on the traditional theory of man alleges a top-heavy emphasis on his rational faculties. Descartes went so far as to assert, "I think, therefore I am." But there are many today who would transform that statement to read, "I choose, therefore I am." Some of them have had

---

[14] Cf. Raphael Demos, "Philosophical Aspects of the Recent Harvard Report on Education," *Philosophy and Phenomenological Research*, 7:203–208, December, 1946. Also cf. *infra*, p. 178.

[15] Alfred N. Whitehead, *The Aims of Education and Other Essays* (The Macmillan Company, New York, 1929), pp. 8–9.

their eyes opened by Freud. In making the transformation, they do not so much deny the rational component in human nature as try to understand the powerful role played by the irrational. Traditionalists were not unmindful of the irrational, but neither did they begin to comprehend the extent to which the explosive, turbulent passions, often inconsistent with one another, subconsciously determined choices. Indeed, what seemed rational control of the appetitive passions often turned out to be merely a psychological rationalization of their dominance.

Others, a shade different in opinion, have emphasized man as a goal-seeking animal because they see his predicament as the existentialists do.[16] The environment confronts him with ambiguities. He must decide what to do. Face to face with the awe-ful contingency of existence, it is small wonder that man feels apprehensive. In fact, his apprehension may mount to anguish if he feels, as the existentialist does, that man has to face the crises of life on his own and alone. Merely to understand his predicament is not enough. His "moment of truth," his sense of the starkly real, comes when he *chooses* how to confront the situation, when he makes a commitment.

A more modern inventory of human nature lists its original capacities under a quite different set of categories. These categories it draws chiefly from the biological approach to the study of man, raised to such importance by the theory of evolution. Treating man more as an organism continuous with nature than as a soul destined for heaven, it records his instincts and impulses rather than his faculties. There has been quite a variety of opinion on how wide a range of activities to include under instincts and impulses. This range runs all the way from two or three basic urges, such as hunger, sex, and fear, to a dozen or more, including such items as pugnacity, gregariousness, rivalry, imitation, curiosity, and play. The capital trait of them all, however, is that of modifiability; without this trait, of course, there would be no learning and no need for a philosophy of education.

Some of these urges can be identified with actual physical structures or organs of the body as, for example, when glandular secretions help condition fear or the cerebral center greatly conditions modifiability of behavior. But in spite of this identity, many who support these categories of original nature take care not to reify them. Even basic drives like sex and hunger have more than one channel of motor outlet and may vary in form of expression as the occasion for release varies. Hence terms like sex and hunger and even terms like intelligence or consciousness, should not be

16 Katherine N. Carroll, "Alienation, Existentialism, and Education," *Proceedings of the Philosophy of Education Society*, 1960, pp. 72–77.

used as nouns, for nouns are names of things and thus seem to designate entities, but rather as adverbs to describe ways in which the organism behaves.[17]

The chief difference which the more modern biological inventory of human nature makes in educational practice is that it directs greater attention to the forces which motivate human conduct. With a knowledge of what motives have been operating from the beginning in child nature, the adroit teacher can better learn how to harness them to draw varying curriculum loads. Some think these drives so important that they should guide the formulation of educational aims. School, they think, should provide for the release of the energies which are pent up in these native drives. But even if they cannot be given uninhibited expression, they are important for the teacher to bear in mind in trying to resolve pupil maladjustments arising out of conflicting drives or drives which conflict with deep-rooted social conventions.

MODIFIABILITY OF ORIGINAL NATURE

The discussion of the social basis of human nature has already required us to take note of an important difference of opinion about the modifiability of man's original nature.[18] Some think that there are definite limits beyond which human nature cannot be modified by membership in a social order, thus putting limits on the reconstruction of the social order itself. Others regard these limits as much more indefinite, if they exist at all, and are therefore much more optimistic about modifying human nature and remaking the social order as well. There is no disagreement between these two opinions on the fact of man's modifiability, only on how much of it affects nature, how much is due to nurture, and how independent nature and nurture are of each other. In fact adherents of both opinions would likely agree that modifiability is the principal item in any inventory of man's original nature and that no animal is so superbly equipped to learn as is man.

Central in this superb equipment is the human cerebrum. By virtue of it man can be matched by no other animal in flexibility and range of adaptation. Not all men, however, have the same range and flexibility of adaptation. Psychological tests show that men differ widely in intellectual capacity.[19] Intelligence quotients range up to 70 or more points above and

---

[17] William H. Kilpatrick, "The Nature of Human Nature," *Religious Education*, 35:3–12, January–March, 1940; Frank C. Wegener, "The Ten Basic Functions of Man," *School and Society*, 80:17–23, July, 1954.

[18] *Supra*, pp. 8–9.

[19] For further consideration of individual differences, see *infra*, pp. 265–268.

below 100, the norm. But what we want to know now is whether man can raise his intelligence quotient by improving his mental capacity. He can increase the content of his learning, no doubt, but can he add to his capacity to learn? The general opinion of psychologists is that he cannot. They do admit that if he is retested a second or a third time his quotient may be higher or lower but never by more than approximately fifteen points either way. And these points would be just an error due to differences in such accidental circumstances as the emotional disposition of the examinee and not at all to mental exertion taken with a view to adding cubits to his mental stature. In other words, human nature is modifiable in that it can learn but unmodifiable in that it cannot increase its inherent modifiability. There is a strict line separating nature and nurture.[20]

This doctrine of the constancy of the IQ has led to a kind of social determinism as a philosophy of education. The doctrine has afforded justification to some for the social-economic hierarchy of classes in our society. They believe that the individuals with higher IQs due to their superior abilities rise to the top of the social ladder, while those with lower IQs due to their more modest capacities settle to the bottom. Consequently the schools should guide the former into the higher intellectual studies and the latter toward vocational curriculums. Moreover, since like tends to beget like, the expectation is quite warranted that the children of families in the upper social-economic brackets will be more likely to profit by opportunities to stay in school longer than will those from the lower-income groups. All of which is to say nothing of using this logic to award superior educational opportunities to a dominant race and discriminate against an inferior one because the advanced culture of the dominant race is evidence of their superior native inventiveness and originality.

The doctrine of social determinism has aroused fierce resistance from those who believe it a dagger pointed at the very heart of democracy.[21] They counterattack by insisting that the constancy of the IQ is predicated on an unproved assumption. This assumption, as we have seen before, holds that mind is an entity external to and independent of its relations. Modifiability or learning, therefore, is purely a function of exercise which does not add to or subtract from the power of original nature but simply develops what is inherently and potentially present. Whatever its amount or extent, it is fixed from the beginning by one's genes.

To these critics there is another assumption just as warranted and more consistent with the pretensions of democracy. According to this assumption, mind is not so much unaffected by its relations as it is in

20 For an application of this view, see *infra*, pp. 265–266.
21 William C. Bagley, "Educational Determinism: Or Democracy and the IQ," *School and Society*, 15:373–384, April, 1922.

large part a product of them. Intelligence, therefore, is a quality of learned behavior. Every relation we enter into with our environment leaves its emotional or rational traces in us, and as a result we act differently when new relations are undertaken. In conserving the traces of former experiences our habits may vary in quality from being automatically routine and rigid to being sensitively resilient and adaptive. Which sort of habit is formed will depend on the social relations obtaining at the time, the kind of society in which education takes place. But the main point is that modifiability, far from being a biological constant, is in fact a social variant. The line between nature and nurture is not so clear-cut. If this is the case, then the superiority or inferiority of races and social classes is to be explained on the basis of their historical and cultural environment rather than their biological heredity.[22] Hence supposed limits to the modifiability of human nature in races and social classes should be a challenge to the educator to try to overcome them, and no limits should be tentatively or finally recognized till there have been unsuccessful attempts to exceed them.

It is revolutionary societies that tend to be most optimistic, and conservative ones most skeptical, about the modifiability of human nature. Revolutionary ones hope to overcome not only hereditary inequalities of ability but also hereditary ills in the social organism. Thus it has long been thought by capitalistic societies that the motive of private gain is so rooted in human nature that any attempt to motivate economic production in any other way is foredoomed to failure. Communistic societies, on the contrary, look on this trait as inherited through the social culture rather than through man's genes. Proceeding on this assumption, they see no reason why human nature cannot be changed by education and through it bring about fundamental changes in the social order itself. Consequently the communistic educational aim to produce a "new Soviet man" should catch no one by surprise.

Social determinism is not the only educational doctrine which finds its support in a theory of the constancy of human nature. Also starting with this theory or premise, another doctrine proposes that the aims of education should be the same for all men in all times and all places. This proposition is put forward in part as a denial of the theory of progressive education which holds that, since change is generic,[23] the aims of education must be progressively undergoing reconstruction all the time. One of

---

[22] George E. Axtelle, "Significance of the Inquiry into the Nature and Constancy of the IQ," *Educational Method,* 19:99–105, November, 1939. See also John T. Wahlquist, "Is the IQ Controversy Philosophical?" *School and Society,* 52:539–547, November, 1940.
[23] *Infra,* pp. 138–141.

the main premises of this theory, of course, is Darwinian evolution. If species are continually evolving, including *Homo sapiens*, then naturally the aims of education must take their cue from this fundamental fact. But the answer to such reasoning, according to those attacking it here, is not a denial of the theory of evolution but a claim that, if human nature should change radically, then we would have a new species.[24] When a new species appears other than *Homo sapiens*, it will be time enough to reconstruct the aims of education. In the meantime as long as man is man, as long as he continues to reproduce his present species—and what does species mean if not constancy of characteristics over and above mere accidental individual differences, which themselves have a limit of variability?—the aims of education should be constant, that is, the same for all men everywhere and always.

FREEDOM OF THE WILL

Granting that human nature is modifiable in some sense or other, we shall next want to know whether human nature can freely choose the aim, that is, the direction, its modification is to take or whether that direction is determined by forces beyond its control. The main issue in this age-old problem of "free will" is whether there is any incompatibility between causation and freedom.[25] The history of education is a progression of efforts in making the teacher a more effective agent in causing the child to learn. Does increasing predictive control of the educative process imply a corresponding decrease of the learner's freedom?

At the outset let us clarify this problem by distinguishing two kinds of freedom. One kind may be said to be social in character. Thus a parent or teacher may override or be permissive about a child's assertion of his individuality. It is an option with which we were concerned in discussing the democratic concept of education[26] and one which we shall consider later as part of the method of instruction.[27] A second kind of freedom is more subtle and more fundamental. It asks whether even the parent or teacher himself could freely choose to give more or less freedom to the child. Were forces operating on him through his own prior heredity and environment which really caused him to choose as he did? Is not his sense

---

[24] Mortimer J. Adler, "The Crisis in Contemporary Education," *Social Frontier*, 5:142, February, 1939.

[25] Cf. Israel Scheffler, "Science, Morals, and Educational Policy," *Harvard Educational Review*, 26:11–14, Winter, 1956.

[26] *Supra*, pp. 59–64.

[27] *Infra*, pp. 203–208.

of autonomy, of being the originator of his educational aims, a kind of self-deception? Indeed, in looking at the total field of forces operating past and present, is there any residue of freedom at all or is everything thoroughly determined?

In discussing the freedom of the will, it may be well first to say a word about the nature of the will itself. According to one doctrine, the will is a distinct faculty. It is not only to be distinguished from impulse, desire, and emotion, but it is to be elevated above all these as the sovereign faculty. Furthermore, will is not to be confused with intellect. It works closely in conjunction with the intellect but is separate from it. The way in which these two function is that the intellect apprehends the facts of any situation and presents them to the will for choice or decision. Nothing can be willed which is not first known. So conceived, will is a datum. Its training results in no intrinsic increase of the faculty itself. Strengthening the will merely affects its habits of execution as to whether they be deliberate and resolute or vacillating and weak.

An opposing school of thought rejects the view that will is a special faculty. For them it is not a power separate from the energy expressed in children's other activities.[28] It is to be found in every manifestation of motor energy either of original nature or of that nature as it has become overlaid with habit. Choice, preference, is the product of individuality. Indeed the individual cannot avoid making choices because it is of the very nature of individuality to be different from other individuals and therefore to prefer its own unique bias toward its environment. Choice may be delayed while the individual elaborates the consequences of alternate courses of conduct and until some preference becomes strong enough to dominate or integrate all conflicting preferences and so to command the channels of motor outlet. But in any event the focus of choice is on the outcome of this struggle, not on a faculty or entity of will sitting in judgment on the contending preferences. One wills, therefore, with everything that he has willed in the past. Consequently the training of the will is to be viewed genetically. The pattern of the will evoked at any time cannot be distinguished from the form of the culture which is coincidentally being transmitted.[29]

But now, whichever way we look at will and choice, we are anxious to know whether there is warrant for believing that we have some voluntary control over what we choose or aim to do. Common sense widely attests to the fact that we do. Yet the moment we systematically examine our

[28] William H. Kilpatrick, *Selfhood and Civilization* (The Macmillan Company, New York, 1941), pp. 30n, 176.
[29] William E. Hocking, *Human Nature and Its Remaking* (Yale University Press, New Haven, Conn., 1923), p. 258.

common-sense notion, doubts begin to arise in our minds. These doubts spring up from paying attention to the relation of cause and effect, or the so-called law of sufficient reason.[30] Take anything that a child does in or out of school. How did he come to do it? There must be definite reasons or causes in the past. The reasons or causes for the present situation, then, are to be found in the immediately preceding state of affairs. This, in turn, is the result of the circumstances which preceded it, and so on indefinitely. If a complete investigation of all these antecedent factors could be made, however remote their relevancy, no uncertainty whatever would be left in accounting for the child's deed under consideration. Far from having been free to select his own course of conduct, then, the pupil's choice will be seen to have been determined for him by the necessity of preceding events.

Nor need this view be depressing. A complete science of psychology, telling every fact past and present about every student, would enable the teacher to guide his student or the child psychiatrist his patient as unfailingly to a satisfying career and moral responsibility as the engineer is now able to direct the building of a bridge.[31] However far we are progressing toward making psychology and sociology exact sciences, the time of such control over human behavior is still far off. Nevertheless, the teacher will feel discouraged, even defeated, unless he can be assured that a large measure of determinism will attend repeated efforts to explain and motivate the lesson.

Even conceding the "ifs" in the determinist's case, the libertarian would doubtless still think the sacrifice of freedom too great a price to pay for the picture of educational efficiency offered. Yet again, where is there room for freedom in such an apparently common-sense account? Must not the events of this world seem at least that simple and complete to an omnipotent and omniscient deity? Nevertheless, various theories have been put forward to account for freedom and to secure the pupil and teacher from the ironclad determinism described. Some of these must now be considered.

Among those who hold that reality is already eternally realized and that change and novelty are merely appearance of reality so conceived, perhaps most popular is the theory that there is a transcendental freedom of the will. If every event in the past, present, and future is already accounted for in a changeless eternity, nothing less than a will able to transcend the ordinary chain of cause-and-effect relationships will be sufficient to assure freedom. According to this theory the individual is himself

[30] Edward L. Thorndike, "The Contribution of Psychology to Education," *Journal of Educational Psychology*, 1:6, January, 1910.
[31] *Ibid.* See also Burrhus F. Skinner, *Cumulative Record* (Appleton-Century-Crofts, Inc., New York, 1959), pp. 11–14.

an originating source of energy, an original cause. Because he is self-active, he is self-directive, self-determining. He is the author of his own deeds, the captain of his destiny. This enables him to modify the stream of causation which is operating upon him. He is free to coincide or interfere with it at will. Freedom is a primary quality of reality. It is God-given.

So stated, it would almost appear as if freedom of the will transcended all conditions, as if it were absolute, even indifferent. While some libertarians actually hold such an extreme position, others are inclined to set some limits to freedom. One count against absolute freedom of the will is that it might encroach on omnipotence itself. If man had such freedom, he might, by taking thought, add cubits to his mental stature, thus contradicting both science and scripture. A second count against it is the idea that the will acts without motivation—the so-called liberty of indifference. Motives very definitely do bear on the will. As has been noted, there cannot be willing without knowing facts or motives for a decision. Hence, there is no freedom from motivation, but rather freedom to pick among the different motivations presented. Yet, though conditioned by motives, the will is not limited to respond to the strongest motive. It is not free, indeed, unless it can also choose the initially weaker motive or cause.[32]

Yet even with such conditions, a transcendental freedom of the will presents the educator with knotty problems. If the pupil is free to choose among the aims of education, is he not also free to accept or reject the instruction of the teacher? How, in other words, can the teacher make his teaching stick? If he is quite frank, the teacher will probably admit that he cannot assure that learning will follow teaching. To be consistent, the libertarian teacher will probably say that in the last analysis the pupil is self-educated. Neither the teacher nor anyone else can educate him; an education is something he must choose for himself. He can no more be constrained to learn than the proverbial horse can be made to drink. So if, in the day of the visitation of the teacher, the pupil willfully refuses the teacher's ministrations, it is unfortunate, but the responsibility is the pupil's.

Another problem may be set by inquiring what this freedom of self-activity is for? A good transcendentalist would probably reply that only in freedom can the pupil achieve self-realization, that is, develop his individuality. In the language of the unfoldment theory of education, he must be free to unfold properly. Freedom consists in voluntarily becoming what one was intended to become. The addition of this condition further circumscribes the concept of freedom. In a sense it almost seems to cut it off. But there is an all-important choice still left for the child: he is free

32 For later reference to this theory, see *infra*, pp. 198, 282, 357.

to choose between his destiny and the privation of failing to realize it. With the choice stated in this fashion, great pressure is brought upon the child to exercise his freedom of will as he "ought" to. His freedom of choice lies between duty and fault.

Quite a different theory of freedom occurs to those who are committed in the first instance to viewing novelty, time, and change as basic realities. The alternative to determinism or mechanism here is found in predicating freedom on the indeterminism which such realities entail. Freedom, instead of being an original datum transcending determinism, is something to be wrought out in a contingent, precarious universe. It occurs principally when opposing or conflicting pulls on the individual from his environment are about equally balanced. In this case he becomes the agent for determining which pull will govern the subsequent course of events. Through the medium of his imagination he anticipates and elaborates the consequences of each pull of the environment. If he is self-conscious at all he must be aware that he—that is, the dramatic rehearsal in his mind of future events struggling to see which shall be born—is a real determinant of the course of events. This realization not only gives him a sense of agency but also a sense of responsibility.[33] The thrill in this experience lies not in the sense that he can freely declare his independence from the past but in the sense of challenge and adventure which remains even after the past has fully exerted itself to predict and control the precarious future. Hence any stimulating sense of personal autonomy is due to the outcropping of cosmic novelty, to an emergent evolution. Freedom of the will is the human phase of this creative process.[34] Here one's range of freedom of choice is not just between good and bad, between great happiness or abject misery, but between alternative goods.

Some think unpredictability, and hence freedom, is but a cover for human ignorance of the underlying determinism really at work. To one with complete knowledge of all the factors, they say nothing is unpredictable or new. There are two reasons, however, one theoretical and one practical, why it is inadvisable to discuss educational policy in these terms. In the first place, it can only make nonsense for the educator to say what he would do if he knew what he does not and cannot know. To ground educational aims on such unverifiable premises serves no rational end. In the second place, predictability is impossible practically. To obtain an exact account of the complete configuration of forces playing on any stu-

[33] Lawrence G. Thomas, "What Metaphysics for Modern Education?" *Educational Forum,* 6:120, January, 1942.
[34] William C. Bagley, *Education and Emergent Man* (Thomas Nelson & Sons, New York, 1934), pp. 65–66, 68; *Education, Crime, and Social Progress* (The Macmillan Company, New York, 1931), pp. 121–122.

dent at a given time would require that the educational researcher, like Joshua, make time stand still. Unless he does, by the time he gets around to summarizing his data, further changes will have occurred with regard to factors earlier measured. But obviously the educational researcher can no more make time stand still than King Canute could forbid the tide to rise. The ceaseless flow of time, with its accompanying change and novelty, therefore, continually outmodes the teacher and prevents him from ever acting in the light of all the circumstances. In fact it may be that the more one aims to get complete control of the educational situation, the more he increases the contingent elements and hence the number of permutations and combinations possible.[35] Consequently the teacher's ignorance of the total configuration of forces is the product, not of an undisclosed determinism, but of a contingent indeterminism. The fact is that the fruit of intelligence and knowledge is not freedom but power, and power is no liberator. On the contrary, the exercise of power, to be maximally effective, must occur according to set conditions.

Accordingly, much of the anxiety over too much determinism or mechanism in education is unwarranted. By and large, the teacher should welcome every device that the educational psychologist or educational sociologist offers as a means of more certainly controlling the outcomes of instruction. A world in which the precarious and contingent are not just figments of the human mind but genuine traits of the cosmos will always baffle any complete educational determinism. Consequently computerized and programmed instruction, often feared as mechanizing education, should be viewed, not as threats to the child's becoming the captain of his destiny, but rather as assets in more economically giving him the power to achieve his ultimate goal of autonomy.

The chief caution the instructor needs to observe is to remember to select aims and to adjust method and curriculum so that his pupils will learn the lifelong thrill of matching their wits against nature in an attempt to anticipate and control her outcomes. In this matching of wits the learner will frequently make agonizing mistakes, tempting the teacher to intervene. Often it will be wise for the learner to become aware of his freedom through his mistakes, thus emphasizing the solitariness of decision making and the anguish of its uncertainty as to outcome, both of which existentialists associate with their belief that man is "condemned to freedom." Inescapable as freedom may be, it must be recognized that too much of it and too soon may overwhelm the uninitiated and sometimes cause him to abandon freedom for the security of authority.

[35] John Dewey, *The Public and Its Problems* (Holt, Rinehart and Winston, Inc., New York, 1927).

INTEGRATION

Any way one approaches human nature it would appear to be possessed of a diversity of traits, whether of faculties, instincts, or habits. Yet, in spite of this diversity of traits, the individual gives every appearance of being an integer. He maintains unity and order among his attributes. Or, should we say, he is a more or less integrated individual. Although his feelings and thoughts change from moment to moment, it always seems to be the same self that is doing the feeling and thinking. Although the child grows older from day to day and although he learns new habits and attitudes at home and at play, the teacher has no difficulty in identifying him on his return to school the next day. Furthermore, one of the earliest things the child learns is to be aware of his own identity—of the difference between I, me, and mine, you and yours, they and theirs. Whence this identity, whence this idea of unity or integration? Is integration an original datum which the child brings to the educational situation, or is it a subsequent acquisition which is gained in the social or educational process? Obviously the answer to this question will have a strategic bearing on the aims of education.

This paradox of identity in the midst of change raises again one of the most difficult issues in educational philosophy.[36] Some think of unity as an addition to or imposition on human nature which commences at birth as a big, buzzing confusion. Unity emerges from this chaos by organizing the sequence of passing states of mind or through building up aggregates of stimulus-response bonds. It is a rather mechanical putting together of parts to make a whole, a gluing together of boards to make trees. According to this view, the learner achieves integration in school through having subject matter presented to him in well-organized fashion by the teacher. If his personality is in danger of disintegration because of the diverse and conflicting loyalties in the community—the family, the gang, the school, the church—then the therapy is to organize the community so that it presents a more unified aspect to youth. In both instances, integration is an acquisition; it is added on. The learner is integrated from without.

Others incline to the view that integration is an original datum, that it is a native tendency of the child to maintain his identity throughout the flow of his learning experiences. He is always integrating, but never integrated—save in death. They gain their chief support from biology with its conviction that organisms tend to act as wholes. From them, also, comes much of the emphasis on the education of "the whole child."[37]

---

[36] See *infra*, pp. 138–141.

[37] Robert M. Hutchins, in his article "Education and Social Improvement," *Educational Trends,* 6:7, June–July, 1938, completely misunderstands the technical meaning of the "whole child." He erroneously identifies the phrase with making the school responsible for the whole education of the child.

In this they are careful to point out that they do not mean that the whole armory of a child's impulses, habits, skills, and attitudes are simultaneously involved in learning. Such a coincidence of forces might rather result in confusion. The emphasis on wholeness here should rather be on integration, wherein each resource for action comes into play at a time and in an amount measured to some dominating design, some thoughtful purpose.

To hold that the child is an organic unity does not go far enough to satisfy others. They agree with the organic theory that the child is something "more" than an agglomeration, something "more" than the sum of his parts. Yet it is still not enough that selfhood is a biological emergent. That far, the "more" is but an empirical fact. The "whole" child is not yet a complete whole. Nor can he be, until there is some vital principle, a spiritual soul, which, as mentioned earlier, provides the underlying unity of the faculties, orders them in a hierarchy, and saves the behavior of the self from being a mere stream of states of consciousness, wherein each state virtually becomes the thinker and actor.

In whatever manner the self precedes or emerges from the educational process, there at least seems unanimity of opinion on the point that the selves of pupils, young and old, are in an incomplete state of development. How shall this deficiency be accounted for, and whither shall one look for its repair? According to one view of Christian teaching, perfect selfhood is something which, once possessed, has since been lost and now must be regained. In the original state of justice man's being is supposed to have been in order. Because of his initial fall from grace, however, the perfect equilibrium of his hierarchy of powers has been lost. Original sin—man's fallen nature, his disorderly inclinations, his lack of integration—thus naturally orients education to antecedent goals. From the outlook of the experimentalist, education is pointed the opposite way. Integration is something ahead, something yet to be attained for the first time.

SELECTED BIBLIOGRAPHY

American Catholic Philosophical Association: Proceedings of the Western Division: The Philosophy of Christian Education, 1941, pp. 7–19, 38–48.

Bagley, William C.: Education, Crime, and Social Progress (The Macmillan Company, New York, 1931), Chap. 7.

Brown, L. M.: General Philosophy in Education (McGraw-Hill Book Company, New York, 1966), Chap. 7.

Dewey, John: Human Nature and Conduct (Holt, Rinehart and Winston, Inc., New York, 1922).

Hardie, Charles D.: Truth and Fallacy in Education (Cambridge University Press, New York, 1942), Chap. 1.

Hocking, William E.: *Human Nature and Its Remaking* (Yale University Press, New Haven, Conn., 1923).
Hook, Sidney: *Education for Modern Man* (The Dial Press, Inc., New York, 1963), Chap. 2.
Kallen, Horace M.: *The Education of Free Men* (Farrar, Straus & Cudahy, Inc., New York, 1949), Chap. 10.
Kelly, William A.: *Educational Psychology* (The Bruce Publishing Company, Milwaukee, 1946), Chaps. 2, 14.
Kneller, George F.: *Existentialism and Education* (Philosophical Library, Inc., New York, 1958).
Kolesnik, Walter: *Mental Discipline in Modern Education* (The University of Wisconsin Press, Madison, Wis., 1958).
Krishnamurti, Jiddu: *Education and the Significance of Life* (Harper & Row, Publishers, Incorporated, New York, 1953).
Lindworsky, Johannes: *The Training of the Will* (The Bruce Publishing Company, Milwaukee, 1929).
Nash, Paul: *Authority and Freedom in Education* (John Wiley & Sons, Inc., New York, 1965), Chap. 6.
Organ, Troy: "Philosophical Bases for Integration," in National Society for the Study of Education, Fifty-seventh Yearbook, Part III, *The Integration of Educational Experiences* (The University of Chicago Press, Chicago, 1958), Chap. 2.
Ragsdale, Clarence E.: *Modern Psychologies of Education* (The Macmillan Company, New York, 1932), Chap. 2.
Reid, Louis A.: *Philosophy and Education* (William Heinemann, Ltd., London, 1962), Chap. 8.
Scheffler, Israel (ed.): *Philosophy and Education* (Allyn and Bacon, Inc., Boston, 1966), Chaps. 8–9.
Smith, Philip: *Philosophy of Education* (Harper & Row, Publishers, Incorporated, New York, 1965), Chap. 8.

CHAPTER SEVEN

Aims and Cosmology

Since the day of Aristotle, as we have seen, and probably from a time much earlier, there has been perennial disagreement on the question how education should be designed. If we try to resolve this disagreement we shall find that it stems from various sources. One of the principal sources has been disagreement over the real nature of the world or cosmos in which education takes place. Virtually all shades of educational philosophy are unanimous in their agreement that the design of education should take the realities of this world into account. But this unanimity is shattered into fragments on the rocky question of just precisely what kind of world confronts the learner.

Progressive educators, for instance, are wont to think of the cosmos as continually undergoing change. Therefore they do not feel called upon to accept any educational aims as fixed or final. They define education as the constant reconstruction of experience and hold that educational growth is subordinate to nothing save more growth. Growth, they hope, will be creative and progressive by their cultivation of individual differences among their pupils. Uncertain, however, about the outcome of the future, they lay heavy stress on the problem-solving method of teaching and learning. Consequently they confine their attention to education for the here and now of the world of nature and eschew preparation for a supernatural hereafter.

Critics and opponents of progressive education, on the other hand, find themselves confronted with quite a different sort of cosmos. Recognizing change in the world, they also discern much in the world that does not change. Attaching greater significance to the enduring and changeless, they do not hesitate to accept some educational aims as perennially fixed. Consequently education, though inescapably involving the alteration of existing habits, has some definite pattern which it is seeking to realize. Individual differences, too, while important, will give way to a cultivation of what is universal in man's nature. Sure of their aims and of what is universal in nature, the opponents of progressive education feel much more free to teach authoritatively and even dogmatically. Much of their confidence in doing so arises from the fact that they do not confine their educational attentions to the ephemeral world of nature but have a constant educational eye on the supernatural world of eternity.

THE NEED FOR METAPHYSICS

The perennial attempt to orient the aims of education by a synoptic map of the terrain of ultimate reality is, technically speaking, a problem of metaphysics. There are some who think it a waste of time, if not positively misleading, to try to sketch such a map. Indeed, as we have already seen, they think the enterprise so highly speculative that the distinctions among various metaphysics of education are largely verbal and without practical differences.[1] The professed metaphysician tries to meet this objection by admitting at once that his speculations are no substitute for the factual inquiries of scientists. Yet, in spite of this necessary limitation, he realizes the fact that the educator must be as synoptic as possible as he embarks on the educational program. He must act in the light of all the relevant data, which more often than not are incomplete and incongruous. Consequently the metaphysician offers an over-all mosaic, where the connections among factual data are inconclusive and, on occasion, actually missing.

Some even claim that to deny a metaphysics implies a metaphysics. Thus many who take a traditional Christian view of the world hold that education should prepare for the life hereafter as well as for the life here and now. There are not a few progressive educators, on the other hand, who think educators will do well to confine their professional efforts to the phenomena of this world. In rejecting the idea that the world has a supernatural dimension which the architects of educational policy must take into account, these progressive educators think they are rejecting the need for metaphysics and for ontology as well. What they are doing is, in effect, to assert that the world of education has only one dimension, that of nature. Yet what is this assertion but a statement of metaphysics, the metaphysic of naturalism?[2] In other words, it seems to take a metaphysic or ontology to reject a metaphysic or ontology. If this be so, it will certainly be in the interests of clarity and frankness to make metaphysical considerations explicit rather than to allow them implictly and unwittingly to control educational policy.

At the very least, one should try to avoid a careless eclecticism. Of course there is nothing wrong with being eclectic about one's philosophy so long as it does not incorporate incompatible or inconsistent items. The best instance of such eclecticism is the case of teachers who profess al-

[1] Cf. Frederick C. Neff, "Education—Yes, Metaphysics—No," *Educational Theory*, 13:59–64, January, 1963; and Van Cleve Morris, "Is There a Metaphysics of Education?" *ibid.*, 17:141–146, April, 1967.
[2] Cf. John L. Childs, *Education and the Philosophy of Experimentalism* (The Macmillan Company, New York, 1931), pp. 43–46; and Herman H. Horne, *The Democratic Philosophy of Education* (The Macmillan Company, New York, 1935), pp. 471–472.

legiance to progressive education which underwrites no aims of education as final or beyond revision, but who at the same time subscribe to a theory of the cosmos in which certain ends or patterns are fixed and unalterable. They see no deep inconsistency in making temporal revisions of their approach to eternal ends. What else can the wisest finite man do with ends that are infinite? While this attitude may satisfy the uncritical, it is difficult to justify on close examination.[3]

APPEARANCE AND REALITY

In proceeding on the conviction that the educator should be sensitive to metaphysical considerations, the instructor and student find that their first and perhaps most important problem is to reconnoiter the realities of the educational terrain. Certain realities obtrude themselves at once. One is that instructor and student are constantly facing changing conditions, changing physical circumstances as well as a changing social situation. Learning, in fact, is a kind of change which tries to keep abreast of change. As the environment changes, novelties appear as a further aspect of reality. Indeed, if there were no novelties, what cause would there be for learning at all? Not only is there novelty in the learning situation, but novelty appears in the unique individuality of students, no two of them being altogether alike, not even identical twins. Still another reality is the matrix of time, which envelops education. It takes time for changes to occur and for learning to take effect.

While change, novelty, and time are undisputed realities conditioning educational aims, the question arises whether they are its ultimate realities. Some think not. Some think that change, novelty, and time are only apparent realities. The really real lies beyond or behind them. Change and time, particularly, have a too transitory quality. A reality which abides, which transcends change, would certainly be of a higher order, and one that did not change at all would be the final word, ultimate. In an educational situation continually beset with contingent modifications of aim, method, and curriculum, there is little if any empirical evidence of such an ultimate unchanging order. Nonetheless, many educators can conceive of such an order. Indeed, so logical does their conception seem that they are more than half-convinced it actually does exist. If unable to prove its existence in fact, except possibly with the aid of revelation, they make it an article of belief.

[3] Lawrence G. Thomas, "What Metaphysics for Modern Education?" *Educational Forum*, 6:127–131, January, 1942.

If change, novelty, and time are characteristics of the environment which are only apparent, what about other aspects of the educational environment? What about school buildings, laboratory equipment, and textbooks? What about facts and values incorporated in texts or the social culture generally? Do these entities exist *extra mentem*, external to the human mind? Or are they just appearances, figments of the imagination? Is there a *Ding an sich*, a thing in itself, an external reality, from which our aims take their direction? Common sense generally answers these questions affirmatively. The more recondite mind will be inclined to hedge. Scientists, unable to prove the existence of an external world independent of a human observer, generally make its existence one of their major assumptions. Not a few educational philosophers follow suit and just take the reality of appearances for granted.[4] Other educational philosophers, overcome by their inability to get satisfactory proof of the existence of anything *extra mentem*, the *Ding an sich* which Kant made famous, prefer to regard their feelings or ideas, to which the world gives rise, as the only sure reality. Their argument is that anything more real than thoughts and feelings would itself be a conception of thought or feeling.[5] Whatever warrant there is for holding any of these positions is an epistemological question to be taken up later,[6] but whatever stance is taken, it clearly sets metaphysical bounds to one's educational philosophy.

There is a broader issue here than just whether things exist independently of their apparent relation to a human learner. This broader issue is the nature of relations in general. Are relations between things themselves external or internal? Does the nature of a thing change when its relations to other things change, or does it retain its characteristic properties despite any alteration in its relations? If a change in its relations does not affect the thing itself, then a thing is independent of its relations and the relations can be said to be external to the thing concerned.

If, on the other hand, a change in a thing's relations also alters the thing itself, then relations may be said to be internal; they are a part of the very constitution of the thing itself. Perhaps the best illustration of internal relations is to be found in the "field" theory first popularized by physics and subsequently borrowed by psychology and other disciplines. It is a

4 Frederick S. Breed, in National Society for the Study of Education, Forty-first Yearbook, *Philosophies of Education* (Public School Publishing Company, Bloomington, Ill., 1942), pp. 93, 105; John Dewey also seems to take the same view in *Logic: The Theory of Inquiry* (Holt, Rinehart and Winston, Inc., New York, 1938), p. 521. For a further instance of this theory see *infra*, p. 167.

5 Herman H. Horne, in National Society for the Study of Education, Forty-first Yearbook, *Philosophies of Education* (Public School Publishing Company, Bloomington, Ill., 1942), p. 142.

6 *Infra*, pp. 163–168.

familiar figure that as a magnet exerts a field of electric force, so analogously, does a person and so does a culture. The total field of forces operating at any given time and place is obviously very complex. Nevertheless, vary any of these in direction or intensity, and it will inescapably involve a redistribution of the remaining forces. This is true whether we are speaking of the person or of his environment. Indeed, so internal are relations between the two that a new habit learned may as well be said to belong to the environment as to the person.

The externality or internality of relations leads to two quite different views of the world. The externality of relations leads to an atomistic view of reality. The irreducible components of reality are atoms in physical phenomena and individuals in social phenomena. It is noteworthy that the Greek root of the word "atom" and the Latin root of the word "individual" have the same meaning—uncuttable, undividable, indivisible. In other words, while atoms and individuals assume a variety of configurations, they are always the same old atoms and individuals. Since they are the irreducible core of all relations, their relations must be external. Furthermore, since atoms and individuals are many and diverse, many think reality to be pluralistic and the universe really a multiverse. Internality of relations leads to a more organic view of the nature of reality. Since the nature of any one thing is contingent on its relation to everything else, there may be an over-all interrelatedness or ultimate unity of all things. If so, it follows that reality is monistic and the world truly a universe instead of a multiverse.[7]

All these considerations come to an educational focus in such questions as how the teacher is to conceive the relation of the learner to the world, the child to the curriculum. If relations are external and therefore the world exists independently of a human knower, then the teacher may well take the view that there are physical facts and social customs which constitute the brute realities of life to be included in the curriculum and learned—with the relish of interest if possible but without it if necessary. Learning in such a case will be largely a matter of discovery of antecedent truth. The accuracy of what is learned or discovered will turn on how closely it corresponds to external reality. This will hold as the measure of truth, whether it is the learning of students in the classroom or the learning of the investigator in the laboratory. If, on the other hand, relations are internal, then the nature of the world to be learned will depend somewhat on the relations or reactions of the learner to it. Truth will not be just a matter of accurate correspondence between reality and what is learned but will depend in part on how the learner's reactions or activities turn out.

[7] For another instance, see *infra*, p. 5.

Starting with such premises, the instructor will probably pay more attention to the student's feelings and interests and permit him greater freedom to express his own individual outlook.

CHANGE AND THE CHANGELESS

The trait of our cosmos which has stirred up the greatest amount of controversy in educational objectives is that of change. Change is a familiar term. At the very outset we note that learning is itself an active process of change. For that matter, so too is life——to be alive is to be constantly active and changing. Change is not only a main trait of our world psychologically and biologically, but it is a chief characteristic of our social world as well. The social milieu of the school is constantly undergoing political and economic changes to which the learner must make adaptations.[8]

So far, probably no one will be so rash as to deny change as a generic trait of reality which besets educational objectives, early and late. Probably no one will be so rash, either, as to refuse to acknowledge that there is often a uniform pattern according to which change takes place. Indeed without some degree of uniformity of recurrence there could be no prediction, no setting up of norms. Without predictability of what the student will do and norms of what he should do, the task of education would be well-nigh impossible. So it may be taken for granted that some kind of stability is also a generic trait of reality. The acute philosophical quarrel starts brewing, however, when we try to assess more precisely just what the character of this stability is. Is it predicated on uniformities which themselves are anchored in static traits of reality? Or is it predicated on uniformities which are statistical statements, based on past performance, of the probability with which changes will recur?

Traditionally man has sought stability in the faith that there are permanent traits in reality. Confronted with the hazards of change on every hand, he has sought security in the changeless. In spite of daily activities and the changes consequent upon them, the basic culture patterns of prehistoric man must have changed almost imperceptibly if at all for centuries at a stretch. Under such circumstances the education of each generation so nearly repeated that of the preceding that it was not difficult to conclude that there was a certain immutability in the aims and content of instruction.

During the period of classical antiquity this traditional outlook re-

---

[8] Cf. William H. Kilpatrick, *Education for a Changing Civilization* (The Macmillan Company, New York, 1927).

ceived a brilliant rationalization by Aristotle, which for many Catholics and Protestants still provides a satisfying philosophy. For the basis of this rationalization Aristotle went to botany and biology. In these life sciences growth is one of the most obvious facts, and growth, of course, implies change. But the changes incident to growth occur according to very well-defined patterns. Thus an acorn falls to the ground, becomes embedded in the earth, germinates under proper conditions of moisture and warmth, puts a shoot above the ground, and grows into a sapling and later into a mature oak, which bears acorns, which fall to the ground, thus completing the cycle of growth and preparing to repeat it. The notable feature about this cycle is that there is change from its beginning to its end but no change in the pattern of the cycle itself. The organism maintains its identity throughout its various stages of growth. Since there is this constancy during change, it is the constant that is viewed as the truly real. Being is more real than becoming and the changeless more real than the changing. The changeless is a sign of perfection, while "change and decay" are associated with each other as in the appealing old hymn "Abide with me."

With few exceptions, no one seriously questioned Aristotle's subordination of change to the changeless till the nineteenth century when Charles Darwin published his *Origin of Species*. Down to the time of this famous book, it was common opinion that each species with its unique, unchanging cycle of growth came into being through a supernatural act of creation. By putting forward his theory of evolution, that species come into existence quite naturally, Darwin shook the thought structure of the world to its very foundations. He observed that offspring are seldom exactly like their parents but rather exhibit individual differences marking them off from their parents as well as from one another. In nature's struggle for existence some of these differences are better adapted for survival than are others. The differences that survive perpetuate their kind. By compounding these differences over many generations, new species arise. The startling philosophical inference from this epitome of Darwin's work is the fact that species change. There is not only change within the cycle of growth, but the cycle itself can change. If this is so, then change is no longer to be subordinated to the changeless. Change is now an ultimate trait of reality.[9]

If one decides to support the conclusion that change is a generic trait of reality, he may yet wish to inquire its direction. According to the Aristotelian view, change had an orbit or cycle to contain it. Nothing could

---

[9] In defense of this view, see John Dewey, "The Influence of Darwin on Philosophy," *Popular Science Monthly*, 75:90–98, July, 1909; and, critical of it, see E. B. Jordan, "The Proper Attitude of the Catholic Scientist toward Evolution," *Catholic Educational Review*, 23:321–335, June, 1925.

evolve which was not already involved. Education aimed at actualization of potentialities found in the child at birth. Indeed children grow educationally like plants in a garden. Nothing can unfold from seed or cell which was not enfolded at inception. This is the lesson of Froebel's *Kinder-garten.* In the Christian story also, the changes aimed at by education conform to a definite course. Here there had been a primordial state, a golden age, in which every thing proceeded according to plan. This divine order, unfortunately, was disrupted by Adam's disobedience and his expulsion from the Garden of Eden. Since that time the development of education has been magnetized by the goal of a restoration of the primordial state of bliss.

The direction of Darwinian evolution, however, is not so clear. If it has any ultimate purpose, it has not yet been disclosed. Perhaps the most accurate description is that evolution is headed toward indefinite increase in variety of organisms and individuals. If so, the most distinctive product of evolution is novelty itself. Closer examination reveals a world characterized by uncertainty, plasticity, process—a world whose very contingency invites adventure. In such a world it is the future rather than the past that dominates the present.

At first glance it may appear as if this evolutionary philosophy reduces things to a state of flux and relativity, conditions which are the very denial of what is necessary for some degree of stability in an educational philosophy. As a matter of fact the situation is not quite that ominous. On the point of complete flux, it is well to note that not everything changes at the same rate. Some principles of the psychology of learning, for instance, are more firmly established than others which are currently still under investigation. Consequently, in a flux where some things alter more slowly than others, one can achieve a not inconsiderable measure of stability by viewing the flux from the standpoint of those things having a low probability of changing either soon or often.

On the point of relativity, it is well to note that adoption of the evolutionary concept need not necessarily cause one to slip the stability of his philosophical moorings. Change does not become uncontrolled merely because it is relative. What one needs now is to study the order of change which is consequent on a shift in relations. Aristotle took the view that relations were external. He thought that things changed or functioned according to their structure but that this structure was antecedent to and unaffected by relations with other things into which functioning brought it. In the evolutionary concept these relations are internal and therefore play a much more vital role. In this view structure not only functions variously according to its relations but may in fact actually be altered by these relations. Thus subtle changes in circumstances may cause emergent mutations or sports in acorns, ultimately resulting in a different kind of species of oak from its parent. Such relativity does not render stability impossible, though it does, of course, render it more complicated.

Brief as the foregoing excursion into morphology has been, it requires little imagination now to appreciate more fully the profound disagreements in educational aim and purpose which the twentieth century has witnessed. Obviously the controversy which has hovered over "progressive" education is more than an issue of whether to keep abreast of the latest educational reforms. However much progressive education may have commenced merely as a protest against the formalism of the education inherited from the nineteenth century, it has become in the twentieth century a system of education predicated on a theory of reform or reconstruction. It hardly needs pointing out that this theory rests squarely on the notion of a dynamic world order. Progressives conceive of education as the constant reconstruction of experience because in a continually evolving world experience is always more or less in need of revision. Furthermore, revision is not in terms of some fixed goal. Progress is not successive stages in the advance toward some perfect immutable standard. On the contrary, in a dynamic and relativistic world the goal of the educative process will be found not outside, but inside the process itself. The process of growth will be its own end. Thus growth becomes a goal; it is subordinate to nothing save more growth.

There are many thoughtful educators—and laymen too—who are sincerely anxious for the schools to be in the forward ranks of progress but who are frankly alarmed at the theory of progress put forward by the so-called progressive educators. They accept the theory of evolution as good science but not as good philosophy. The fluidity and relativity of this theory they think a threat to the ultimate security of the family, state, and church. From their viewpoint these institutions represent a funded capital of social experience which, though subject to amendment in detail, stand in need of no essential or major revision. The fundamental tenets of this culture root deep in an immutable structure of reality and human nature. Placing abiding faith in such unchanging traits of reality, they do not hesitate to affirm that there are absolute and universal objectives which should govern education.[10] Education is progressive merely in the sense that it is striving toward the fulfillment of a cycle of personal development, the ends of which are absolute and immutable.[11]

---

[10] Mortimer J. Adler, "Are There Absolute and Universal Principles on Which Education Should Be Founded?" *Educational Trends*, 9:11–18, July–August, 1941.
[11] For another instance of change and the changeless, see *infra*, pp. 120–123.

THE NOVEL AND THE PRIMORDIAL

First cousins to change and the changeless as generic traits of reality conditioning the outcomes of educational theory and practice are two further
traits, the novel and the primordial. One of the most inescapable impressions we derive from our changing environment is the fact that there is
uncertainty as to how the changing current scene will turn out. The future
is fraught with contingency.[12] Events seem to be constantly taking a novel
turn. But how seriously should the educational philosopher take novelty and
contingency as generic traits of reality on which to predicate his educational goals? It is an old adage that there is nothing new under the sun.
Omar Khayyam stated it not very differently when he observed:

> Yea, the first morning of creation wrote
> What the last day of reckoning shall read.

Although the truth of this poetic insight is not easily apparent on the face
of events, yet, if it states the underlying reality, then it will certainly
behoove the educator not to be a victim of first impressions about novelty
and contingency but rather to rest his educational purposes on the
foundations of the familiar and the primordial.

Logically, it would seem as if there could be no genuine novelty or
contingency. The emergence of genuine novelty would violate the ancient
axiom, *ex nihilo nihil fit*—it is impossible to make something out of nothing. Stated differently, every effect must have a cause. Not only that, but
the cause must be sufficient to produce the effect. Therefore an effect
cannot be greater than its cause, the creature greater than its creator. On
the other hand, if this reasoning is accepted, then there can be nothing
new under the sun; there must have been latent in the first moment of
creation everything which has emerged since that time. There is no more
possibility of novelty in evolution than of pulling from a ball yarn which
was not originally wound on it. Hence novelty is apparent only; what seems
novel is just a semblance due to human ignorance. But this conclusion is
so repellent, again, that many who take the view of emergent evolution are
inclined to overthrow ancient axioms. Unable to find a satisfactory explana-

---

[12] There has been some tendency to invoke support for this view from physics, where
Heisenberg has announced that a principle of indeterminacy reigns in the subatomic
world. The full significance of this random element in the constitution of the universe,
however, has not yet been fully established. For an educational reference to it, see Frederick S. Breed, *Education and the New Realism* (The Macmillan Company, New York,
1939), p. 45.

tion of the future in the womb of the past, they accept the partial uniqueness of the present as a new axiom.

Cogent as this argument appears, it is no stronger than the assumption on which it is based. As a matter of fact, the assumption that every event has a sufficient cause, useful as it is, cannot be established beyond reasonable doubt. And even if it could be, the lack of novelty would only be apparent retrospectively. Prospectively, an emerging event might still give every evidence of being novel and unpredictable on the basis of the causes known to have been operating. Consequently it is far from an altogether unreasonable view of the world to conclude that the future is not merely the unfolding of a reality already antecedently complete. On the contrary, it may well be that reality itself is incomplete. Novelty, instead of having occurred just once at the beginning of the world, may be constantly recurring in the evolutionary process. In this case the last instances of novelty are just as truly novel as the first ones. The universe is not a closed but an open one—open at the end marked "future." It is William James's world with the "lid off," a world in which the book of Genesis is still being written.

The consequences for educational aims of these two attitudes toward reality—whether or not it has a streak of contingency running through it—are plain to see. The progressive education movement has proceeded on the assumption that novelty is genuine. Naturally, therefore, when progressive educators encourage children to be creative in poetry or prose, painting or music, they regard the product as unique and not something the children have created merely because they have found what already existed. They plan just as much, however, for creativity in the class in "problems of democracy" or inventiveness in shopwork as they do for the class in art. Furthermore, when they introduce controversial issues into the curriculum of the social sciences, they regard the issues as controversial because their outcome or solution is genuinely in doubt. Issues are not controversial because benighted pupils or adults quarrel over a truth or a good which is merely awaiting discovery. Progressive educators, moreover, frankly confess to such a real contingency abroad in the universe that they cannot accurately predict the kind of difficulties which their children will meet when they grow up.[13] As a result, instead of merely transmitting to them solutions for past or future problems, they concentrate especially on cultivating in their pupils a problem-solving attitude of mind as the best preparation for meeting future problems.

---

[13] Attacking this view, see Isaac L. Kandel, *The Cult of Uncertainty* (The Macmillan Company, New York, 1943).

The educators who guide their practice by objectives grounded in the primordial teach with greater assurance and authority. They confront pupils with problems, too, but are more likely to keep a finger in the back of the book because, relying on the primordial, they are more likely to think they have the right answers. Often this confidence has been predicated on an analogy between education and plant life. The theory that children are to be likened to plants and the school to a garden has principally achieved a prominent place in educational vocabularies through the German-derived "kindergarten." Just as the full-grown plant already blooms in the seed, so too the pupil's mind already has latently concealed within it all the powers it can ever hope to develop. Neither plant nor child has potentialities for becoming anything which is not already foreshadowed in the germ. Education thus becomes a process of unfolding what was primordially enfolded. It cannot endow a child with capacity that he does not have; it can only develop what he already is. The process of education is, then, indeed well named from the Latin e-ducere, to lead forth, to bring out. What was potentially implicit it makes actually explicit.

So stated, this theory of educational development may seem to neglect the influence of environment. It is, however, not so intended. Neglect of the environment can stunt the finest potentialities of both plant and child. Just as the gardener must cultivate, fertilize, and water a plant to get the best results, so too the parent and teacher must be diligent if they would cultivate in the child the right habits of manhood. And the same doubtless applies to the training of teachers. Whether or not teachers are born, not made, there can be no doubt but that the professional study of education will be necessary to bring into full play whatever genius a person has.

There is some danger in revering every activity of the child as a manifestation of primordial purpose. To do this would probably put too high a price on his nuisance value. Consequently it is necessary to have some standard by which to judge whether he is unfolding properly. Naturally this must be his state of complete unfoldedness. The culture-epoch and recapitulation theories of education, perhaps, offer the best insight into complete unfoldedness. The thought here is that the child becomes adapted to life by passing through all the stages of culture that the race has already passed through. Thus he should learn the culture of the nomadic, pastoral, agrarian, and industrial epochs. By recapitulating these, the child proceeds from being a little savage to becoming a civilized man. Nor is this pattern of development an offhand suggestion, for it is rooted in the very constitution of the universe itself. It is the way history itself has unfolded. And what is history but the unfolding of the mind of God Himself, a dramatization of the ultimate nature of things on the world as a stage.

THE INDIVIDUAL AND THE UNIVERSAL

A novelly developing cosmos, if such we have, or a cosmos developing according to some primordial design, if that be nearer the truth, calls attention to two other possible traits of reality to which educational aims or goals should undoubtedly be sensitive. These are the traits of individuality and universality. The problem which they present is that of the relation of the part to the whole or, in Plato's phrase, the problem of "the one and the many."

On the whole, it needs little or perhaps no argument to convince us that the school is surrounded by a multivariety of people, things, and events. One might say that such diversity is a self-evident trait of existence. If further proof were required, we would need go no further than to the scientist—to the physicist for a catalogue of the variety of physical phenomena, to the biologist for a list of the various forms of life, to the educational psychologist for an inventory of ways in which children and adults differ in their intellectual capacities and emotional dispositions, or to the sociologist for an inventory of the diversity of conventions under which people live. The accumulation of such differences is what one would expect, no doubt, if change and novelty have been genuinely operating for any length of time in this world.

By themselves these differences are harmless enough. But taken together—for they cannot be kept separated from each other—these differences, especially the personal and social ones, give rise to problems. Instead of always supplementing or complementing one another they often contradict one another. The individualities of parent and child, teacher and pupil, to say nothing of the individual interests of pressure groups like the chamber of commerce or labor unions, frequently cross purposes on what is best to do educationally. Are such conflicts inescapable because of the variegated nature of reality, or is there some unity or harmony as a generic trait of ultimate reality, according to which they can be reconciled?

The classic view here is that there is an ultimate unity to which the diversities of existence are finally subject.[14] Differences there are, to be sure, but these differences are accidental variations within the essential or generic. Children, for instance, differ widely as to sex, height, weight, mental capacity, and the like, and yet are all numerators of the common denominator childhood. Childhood, thus, is a generic or universal concept which sums up a whole variety of particulars. It gives us unity in the midst of diversity. Childhood in turn is part of the larger unity of humanity, which

[14] For a later reference to this point, see *infra*, p. 171. Cf. also, p. 247.

in turn has its place in an ascending hierarchy of unity, wherein finally all parts are related to all other parts in a final universal whole and all parts are in "preestablished harmony."

Some have believed the concept of the universal to antedate in time the individual or particular and therefore to be more truly a generic trait of reality than the individual or particular. The universal, thus, is a primordial quality of the world. It is not the product of the human mind but has been discovered by it. To illustrate the significance of this conclusion, the school as an ideal must antedate any particular school of brick or mortar. So too, the "normal" school, if it is to set the model for teacher training, must have its birth in conception before a single step can be taken toward its actualization. Indeed, should some terrible cataclysm, such as atomic war, leave not a single school standing, the universal idea of school would still persist and provide the causative energy to raise up new edifices.

Without passing judgment on these claims for the universal, let us make clear what their educational import is. An educational philosophy, exalting the importance of the universal, aims at an education which stresses what is common or essential to all human nature.[15] Without neglecting individual differences, it puts individual differences where they ought to be, in a subordinate position. Instead of teaching children how to adapt themselves to the particular environment in which they live, a too narrow objective, education will teach them to adjust to any clime or epoch. For the same reason, what is universally applicable will justify a prescribed rather than an elective curriculum. Hence the curriculum will give large place to the classics of our culture, whose universal value has been attested by all men the world over. Finally, educational innovations will probably be suspect as "fads and frills" because, more than likely, they are mere accidental particulars of some already existent universal.

Universals, however appealing, are, in the last analysis, only concepts, while individual particulars are percepts. Since the concept is so abstract and the percept so concrete, it will occasion little suprise that many have a greater sense of reality when dealing with particular students than when dealing with students in general. Consequently many are inclined to regard individuality rather than universality, conflict rather than harmony, as more truly generic traits of reality. If this gives reality a rather untidy aspect, they do not deplore it but count it a gain, since the novelty of individuality and the uncertainty of conflict are what make life more zestful. The manifold variety of pluralism of such a world demands not only wide latitude for, but a generous toleration of, individual expression.

15 Robert M. Hutchins, *The Higher Learning in America* (Yale University Press, New Haven, Conn., 1936), p. 66.

Moreover, following the medieval nominalists, some think universals are mere words or names for classes of things. Others, not unmindful of the importance of universals, look upon them as merely a statistical summary of human experience with particulars to date. The summary neither exhausts the individuality of particular things, people, or events yet to be met, nor makes it impossible to deal with a single child apart from his relations to childhood in general or his relations to reality as a whole, the sum total of all relations. Instead of being a final statement of primordial reality which governs education, universals are rather points of departure for attacking and resolving the confusions and conflicts of tomorrow with its set of unique experiences.

An educational philosophy constructed from this point of view will leave its own distinctive impress on educational purpose. In place of making the school a Procrustean bed for the child, it will bend every energy toward individualizing instruction both as to curriculum and as to method. The indigenous experience of the child rather than the universality of reason will become the measure of educational practice. The formation of broad policy must be for a particular kind of political economy, in a particular country, and for a particular time in history.[16] Of course the child will try to reconcile the various conflicting demands of his environment in terms of some larger whole of experience. He will try to achieve integration. But integration will be a result of his efforts, not an initial datum.

TIME AND ETERNITY

So far, in discussing the generic traits of reality, we have already had the dimension of time either openly or covertly forced on our attention at a number of points. Our educational objectives have the impress of time upon them either because it requires time to encompass the change and emergent novelty which they admire or because what they emphasize remains the same in spite of the passage of time. Some educational philosophers, however, are not content with traits of reality which stand uncorroded by the lapse of time but want to escape from the transitoriness of time as well. Unable to think of time as anything but finite, these philosophers try to project their thinking beyond the finite limits of time into the infinite, which is timeless and eternal.[17] To other educational philosophers this projection is an idle speculation without any verification of

[16] American Historical Association, *Report of the Commission on Social Studies: Conclusions and Recommendations* (Charles Scribner's Sons, New York, 1934), p. 31.
[17] For further treatment of this point, see *infra*, p. 147.

fact. They, on the contrary, take time rather than the timeless as the basic trait of reality.

Those who consider time as a generic trait of existence realize that time is past and future as well as present. The flow of time not only affects the stream of learning now, but learning has the quality it has now because of the circumstances which conditioned it a moment or hours or even years ago. History, therefore, and the history of education particularly, is an inescapable dimension of the educational process. But if this is true of past time, it is equally true of future time, still others claim. They regard a utopian view of what education should become an important condition in determining what it could be like if proper steps are taken now. If the educator is to consider the past and future as current dimensions of the educative process, it will be necessary to regard the present not just as a razor-edged slice of time that is constantly being replaced but as an accordionlike span, which expands and contracts with variable portions of the past and future to suit the occasion.

If a world of eternity is speculative at best and if a world of time is all that we can surely count on, then must we aim to conform to all its temporal vagaries? With the passage of time comes change, and with the occurrence of change come novelties. To be prepared for both, the educator must keep his attention riveted on the present, for it is there that change is at work producing novelty. For this reason education, instead of preparing children for the sort of life they will live as adults, must prepare them for their contemporary life as children. Similarly, instead of preparing them for an uncertain life hereafter, education must prepare them for life here and now. Education for adulthood or for a life beyond the grave puts too much of a premium on past time, relies too much on the assumption that for all essential purposes the future will be a repetition of the past, of a primordial cycle. It forgets that "time makes ancient good uncouth." If one believes that changes occurring at the present time are progressively turning out genuine novelties, then the more distant the future for which the educator prepares, the more uncertain his plans. Therefore he best prepares youth for the future by preparing them for the living present.

There are many who feel very insecure and uncomfortable at this emphasis on "presentism" in education. For themselves they prefer an educational philosophy which steers its course not only by the changeless and the primordial but by the eternal as well. They draw great comfort from the words of the liturgy, "As it was in the beginning, is now, and ever shall be." With such a view it goes without saying that the aims of education may well be unwavering, the method of instruction authoritarian, and the curriculum composed of the "great books" of undying worth which are contemporaneous with any period. While during life those with this inclination cannot escape time, they do, nonetheless, regard education as a process whereby the child "becomes in time what he eternally is."[18] This is a fitting educational corollary to the interpretation of evolution that nothing can evolve which was not previously involved. But life, like time, is finite. Its threescore years and ten are an insufficient span for education to enable the child to achieve a fulfillment of his potentialities. The failure to reach a full perfection of these powers argues speculatively to some that there must be immortality, an eternity of life after death, in which to accomplish what was left undone.[19]

NATURAL AND SUPERNATURAL

Reference to the possibility of an eternal as well as a temporal dimension to reality raises the inquiry whether all the generic traits of existence which educational aims and goals must take into account are to be found in the natural order or whether some derive from a supernatural realm. Until mention of the eternal, our exposition proceeded on the assumption that we were trying to get a better understanding of the natural order when we were inquiring whether the world was characterized better by change or the changeless, by the novel or the primordial, by the individual or the universal. We proceeded as if nature, the world about us, contained within itself all the answers for which we were looking. Now the mention of the eternal casts doubt on this assumption. The natural order is a temporal order. If there is a nontemporal order, it must lie outside or beyond the natural order. If there is a supranatural order, perhaps some of the answers we have been looking for are to be found there. At least a further inquiry must be made in that direction.

Before pressing that inquiry it may be well first to improve our understanding of the natural. When we try to conduct education according to nature, whether the nature of the child or the nature of his physical and social environment, what do we mean? Unfortunately we do not all mean the same thing. Progressive educators, when they claim to make nature their norm, seem to give primary attention to dimensions of time, change, novelty, and individuality. Following these specifications, as already seen, they build an educational program which permits of continual adjustment and readjustment of one's talents and aptitudes in terms of the constantly changing demands of time and place. And carrying this preoccupation to an

---

[18] Herman H. Horne, *Philosophy of Education,* rev. ed. (The Macmillan Company, New York, 1927), p. 286.
[19] *Ibid.,* p. 283.

extreme, some progressives have such a strong tendency to revere the unique and novelly developing in nature that they advise wide and almost complete freedom for the child. They warn parents and teachers to interfere only at their peril with nature's processes.

There are notable critics of progressive education who think that its conception of naturalism is a false naturalism. According to the critics, a true understanding of nature would bring out in bold relief, not what is variant in the physical and social world about us, but that which is invariant and uniform. If this is the case, then the principal dimensions for the house of knowledge are those which are changeless and universal. Certainly this is the norm of nature against which the scientists, closest students of nature, measure their efforts and results. The naturalistic educator will therefore do well to be content with a no less exacting standard. He will find it good pedagogy, to be sure, to pay attention to the individual differences of his pupils or to the prevailing opinions and conventions of the day in which his students come to school, but he will even more surely not fail to pass from these accidental and transitory matters to those of universal validity. Thus the instructor will be following a naturalistic educational philosophy of sorts if he permits the student freedom to express his individuality, but he will fall short of what a truly naturalistic philosophy demands if he fails to show the pupil that the greatest freedom comes, not from the uninhibited expression of mere whim, but from ruling himself by principles of natural law.[20]

Is there any clue, now, as to which of these views of nature stands closer to nature as she really is? Apparently nature reveals none herself since equally sincere and competent spokesmen for her make such different representations. At this point there are many who think we must look beyond nature to the supernatural for further dimensions and specifications of educational aims and purposes.

In arguing that reality is not characterized by emergent novelty, we saw that the case was made plausible by alluding to the so-called law of cause and effect. It was stated that for anything to occur there must have been a preceding cause capable of bringing it forth. Proceeding on this law, or perhaps better, assumption, we saw how many conclude that educational objectives should be guided by the old and familiar rather than by the new and unique. Pressing back in time for the causes of later effects, an inquiring mind is more likely to search for the even earlier cause

---

[20] For a rebuttal of an education governed by natural law, see Richard B. Morland, "The Doctrine of Natural Law: Its Implications for Education," *Educational Theory*, 11:168–173, 185, July, 1961.

which produced the cause which produce the effect with which he started out. In fact he can keep on pressing back for prior causes of later causes till he finds their traces lost in the imperfect or nonexistent records of history and geology. Undaunted by such obstacles, he may continue to press his search logically if not empirically. He may speculate whether logically there must have been a first cause not caused by any antecedent cause. Was there a beginning of time and a prime order, which set the primordial pattern of all that was to follow?

Those who find it impossible to refrain from assuming the relation of cause and effect find no difficulty in answering these questions in the affirmative. They have no hesitation in affirming that nature had a beginning and that the prime mover of nature was a God omniscient and omnipotent, in fact, perfect in respect to every attribute ascribed to Him. Being the author of man as well as of nature, God must be a personal God since the creator must be at least the equal of His creatures in order to bring them forth.[21] Prepotent as the supernatural is, however, it should not be thought of as superseding nature or as standing in opposition to it. Rather should the supernatural be regarded as complementing and completing nature.

If a supernatural God is the maker and ruler of nature, then the teacher will do well to let His will be done in the classroom as it is in heaven. The educational philosopher, seeking to formulate the aim of education, should hasten to find out the purpose for which God made man so that he may fashion a program which will enable man to meet his creator's expectations. Of course this will not be easy to do; there will be problems to solve. Yet, if nature seems problematical, it is because the Deity has arranged it so. Likewise, if He has provided perplexities, He has not provided them in such a manner that they completely baffle the expectation of solution. On the contrary He has, in the opinion of many, given indications of the proper solutions through divinely inspired teachers and supernaturally inspired writings. From these indications it will be of decisive importance for the dignity of teaching that teachers regard children, not just as organisms behaving according to nature, but as "images of their Great Original and children of eternity."

It is only fair to add in conclusion that many naturalists find the appeal to the supernatural distasteful and unnecessary. Confining themselves to the natural order, they find no reason, not even the law of sufficient

---

[21] For a critique of a philosophy of education predicated on this view, see H. E. Langan, *The Philosophy of Personalism and Its Educational Applications* (The Catholic University of America Press, Washington, D.C., 1935).

reason, the law of cause and effect, for undergirding the natural order with a principle or spirit more real than its own product.[22] The supernatural to them is at best so speculative that they prefer to conserve and improve their time by attending to education in the natural order, where experimental methods permit of more reliable and objective conclusions.

SELECTED BIBLIOGRAPHY

Burnett, Joe R.: "Whitehead's Concept of Creativity and Some of its Educational Implications," *Harvard Educational Review*, 27:220–234, Summer, 1957.

Dame, John F.: *Naturalism in Education: Its Meaning and Influence* (Temple University, Philadelphia, 1938), Chaps. 7–8.

Fleshman, Arthur C.: *The Metaphysics of Education* (Mayhew Publishing Company, Boston, 1914).

Hutchins, Robert M.: "The Philosophy of Education," in Robert N. Montgomery (ed.), *William Rainey Harper Memorial Conference* (The University of Chicago Press, Chicago, 1938), pp. 35–50.

O'Connell, Geoffrey: *Naturalism in American Education* (The Catholic University of America Press, Washington, D.C., 1936).

Pollock, Robert: "Process and Experience," in John Blewett (ed.), *John Dewey: His Thought and Influence* (Fordham University Press, New York, 1960), Chap. 7.

Singh, Tara: *An Outline of the Philosophy of Creative Education* (Orient Publishers, Jullundur City, India).

Taba, Hilda: *The Dynamics of Education* (Routledge & Kegan Paul, Ltd., London, 1932), Chap. 2.

---

[22] John L. Childs, "Whither Progressive Education?" *Progressive Education*, 13:584, December, 1936.

PART THREE
Curriculum

CHAPTER EIGHT

Curriculum

With the aim or direction of the educative process once determined, the next step is obviously one of ways and means. Among these, the curriculum demands first attention. According to its Latin origin, a curriculum is a "runway," a course which one runs to reach a goal, as in a race. This figure has been carried over into educational parlance, where it is sometimes called a curriculum, sometimes a course of study. Whatever its name, it describes the ground which pupil and teacher cover to reach the goal or objective of education. For this reason, it almost goes without saying that one will run a different course for different goals or aims. The curriculum being so dependent on the goal set, it is hardly surprising to find that learning the curriculum will be virtually equivalent to achieving one's objectives. In fact, so close is the relation between aim and curriculum that, as already mentioned, one may well say that the curriculum is nothing more than aims or values writ large in expanded form.

The critical importance of aim for curriculum can be seen in the careless or uncritical analogy of likening the process of education to building a house. A house, it has been said, cannot be properly built till all the materials for its construction—bricks, lumber, and the like—have been brought together in one place. Analogously the student should not strive to solve social problems till he has stocked his mind with a wide assortment of curriculum materials such as history, mathematics, science, and similar subjects. The analogy fails, however, when one stops to realize that a contractor does not assemble a general collection of materials but only those suitable for the kind of edifice the blueprints specify. This is how curriculum materials should be assembled, not in general, but to realize a clearly defined end.

The philosophical issues underlying the curriculum can, perhaps, be best summarized under the well-known trinity of the true, the good, and the beautiful. While we might grant at once that a curriculum composed of the true, the good, and the beautiful is well proportioned, we must not stumble into overlooking the difficulties which divide men on the nature of the true, the good, and the beautiful. Treating the rubric of truth broadly, we must inquire into the nature of knowledge, into whether it is ruled by a dualism, and into when it is true. Treating the rubric of the good broadly, we must inquire into value theory, into the values which rule the curriculum, and also into the possibility of a hierarchy of value. Similarly, with the category of the beautiful, we must inquire into the scope of aesthetics, since it will also have a marked bearing on what is to be included in the curriculum.

THE CHILD AND THE CURRICULUM

The fundamental ingredients of the educative process consist of a learner and something to be learned. But, now, shall this second ingredient, the curriculum, be conceived from the point of view of the first, the learner? Or shall it be conceived to have a more or less objective, independent status? The latter alternative seems to establish a dualism between the terms. The former finds an essential continuity between them.

The traditional treatment of the curriculum has been definitely dualistic. The basic dualism has been that between mind and matter.[1] This has been matched with another, that between mind and subject matter, child and curriculum. The child represents the particular, the curriculum the general or universal. The one represents the individual, the other society. Of the two, it is the universal or the social that is favored in determining the nature of the curriculum. Any resulting conflicts between learner and curriculum, therefore, are generally resolved in favor of the curriculum. The curriculum, representing the social culture, becomes a sort of Procrustean bed for the learner. Instead of fitting the curriculum to the student need, the educator fits the student to the curriculum. Since a youth's nature is ordinarily impulsive and narrowly self-centered, since his experience is crude, vague, and uncertain, it follows that it is incumbent on the school to prescribe a curriculum which will broaden him out and introduce him to the law and order of the universe.

The alternative to such a curriculum theory is to conceive of the curriculum more in terms of the nature of the learner. In order to do this, one must cease thinking of subject matter as something fixed and ready-made in advance. In like manner, one must give up thinking of the curriculum as something outside the child's experience, as something that can be poured into the child from without. On the contrary, it is necessary to see that the content of student experience and the content of race experience—the curriculum—differ in degree rather than in kind. The content of the former already contains elements of the same sort as those to be found in the latter. The student's experience and his studies in school are but the initial and terminal aspects of a single reality or process—education, life. The one flows into the other, is continuous with it. It is one of the functions of method to discover the steps which intervene between the child's present

---

[1] *Supra,* pp. 110–116.

experiences and their richer maturity in the social heritage. The curriculum is the social stuff out of which the self realizes itself. To think of these two as opposed to each other would produce the unnatural result of putting the nature and destiny of the child at war with each other.

Our initial problem, whether to state the curriculum in terms of dualism or continuity, has yet a further angle, whether to state the curriculum in terms of traditional subject-matter divisions or of children's activities.[2] In the traditional view of the curriculum, the basic units are facts or skills which have been homogeneously grouped into various subject fields, like arithmetic and history. Such a classification is not only inevitable but highly useful. Since the mind cannot grasp the race experience in its totality, by analysis it breaks it up into different clusters of related interests. What makes the curriculum traditional is the fact that the particular organization and specialization of knowledge which obtains at present has been inherited largely from centuries past. Each epoch has organized its experiences as they would best serve its own characteristic struggles and interests. These patterns have come down through the schools almost like geological strata. Each new subject, representing new life interests, is added on often without reorganizing what preceded. It is not surprising, therefore, that in the course of time the subdivisions in which the curriculum has been inherited tend to be studied as final and unalterable.

As a consequence, the curriculum comes to be prescribed without much regard to the interests and point of view of the learner. It is enough that the curriculum is backed by the authority of the teacher, who is backed by the authority of the centuries. The subjects of the time-honored divisions are learned one by one. Portions of each constitute the assignment of facts and skills to be learned from day to day. Unless one is very careful to insist that subjects be correlated on the idealistic assumption of the wholeness of knowledge, a certain atomism settles down on the curriculum. Facts and skills are learned one at a time. Credits—and the subjects they represent—are accumulated like coupons and presented for diplomas. Attitudes, if important at all, are also learned separately, and their concomitant significance is neglected or minimized. Finally, the curriculum so learned remains stored away in memory till one assembles enough to be able to use it or is asked to bring it forth on demand in the recitation or examination.

On the other hand, one has the more student-centered type of curriculum. Since the student is living now, the curriculum becomes all the student's life for which the school or college is responsible. It includes

---

[2] William H. Kilpatrick, "Subject Matter and the Educative Process," *Educational Method*, 2:94–101, 230–237, 367–376, November, February, May, 1923.

emotional attitudes and moral ideals, as well as the usual sorts of informa-tion. The curriculum concerns itself with the whole person. The instructor remembers that the verb "teach" takes a double accusative; it governs John and Mary as well as language and science. Indeed, in the modern grammar of pedagogy, John and Mary have become direct objectives of teaching rather than indirect ones as in the grammar of yesterday. The unit element in such a curriculum is neither facts and skills nor subjects of instruction, but a novelly developing life situation. Experience is cen-tral.[3] The curriculum uses subject matter, but it does not wholly consist of it, nor are its conventional divisions allowed to become barriers against meeting new needs. Subject matter is called in to help in the recovery of the continuity of action which has been interrupted by some problematic situation.

This view rejects the idea that subject matter is something that can be put in cold storage against some contingent day of use. It refuses to treat the curriculum like a deposit which is to be handed down from one gen-eration to another or as an object which can be wrapped up in package form to be handed to students. Such conceptions are too static. Rather is the curriculum to be thought of as dynamic. From this view, such things as facts, knowledge, information, subject matter all become plans of action, ways of responding or reacting. Consistent with this interpretation is the recommendation that the names of the different subjects be cast as par-ticipial rather than as substantive nouns. Thus, for instance, reading, writ-ing, and reckoning, to mention but the three R's, more truly portray the character of the curriculum than do literature, penmanship, and arithmetic. All subjects are arts or skills, patterns of behavior.

Here a word must be interpolated with regard to conceiving the nature of the curriculum as composed of activities.[4] To many, activity tends to mean physical activity on the part of the student, such as field trips or construction work. Those who have accepted this view generally take this position in protest against the sort of curriculum which is learned at desks, where quietness is a school virtue. It would, however, probably be an un-warranted inference to think no physical activity at all is involved in the latter type of curriculum. Even so passive a type of learning as listening involves a very definite physical coordination for attentiveness. The signifi-cance of the activity curriculum, therefore, if any, lies in the kind of activity rather than in its contrast with no activity at all.

[3] Reginald D. Archambault, "The Philosophical Bases of the Experience Curriculum," *Har-vard Educational Review*, 26:263–275, Summer, 1956.
[4] *Infra*, pp. 224–226.

For purposes of curriculum theory two kinds of activity may be distinguished. On the one hand, there is the kind of activity inherited as a legacy from the empiricism of Locke and Pestalozzi. Here, learning is a matter of sense impression. The senses are supposed to be active in absorbing impressions of the world round about the learner. Education seems to be something that is done to the child from without. He undergoes it. Even if the content of the curriculum is made to appeal to the mind rather than the senses, any learning activity goes on chiefly inside the learner. The mind is preoccupied with mirroring the universe of knowledge and value. There is a minimum of overt behavior by way of trying to reconstruct it.

On the other hand, there is a more aggressive kind of activity. This sort does not wait for meanings to appear; it seeks them out. Such activity, ever reaching outward, forms an active curiosity which constantly forces new meanings to appear. Here, instead of learning through passive response, the pupil learns from noting the results which occur when he takes the initiative in physically manipulating his environment. In this view, one gets better impressions coincident to active expression. In accepting this more vigorous and energetic conception of activity, one must beware of just activity in general or of activity for its own sake, as in the case of mere "busy work." In the abstract, activity may be boisterous and random as well as guided and purposeful. If the activity curriculum is to be known preferably by the more overt sort of activities, the justification therefore must be found in their greater promise of educational growth.

There are various educational activities which give this promise. Physical exercise for promoting health is one instance; emotional outlet through the dance is another. Of outstanding importance are work and play. Both of these afford unique opportunities for an activity curriculum since they initiate acquaintance with things and processes, and work, at least, provides some terminal opportunity to test out one's knowledge of them.[5] While most people seem agreed on the educational significance of work activities, some think that play has no proper place in the curriculum. The younger generation will have plenty of opportunity to play outside of school, they say, and therefore there is no use wasting schooltime with such a duplication of activity. This misgiving might have some point in a frontier society, but in the modern industrial community quite the opposite seems to carry weight.[6]

[5] John Dewey, *Democracy and Education* (The Macmillan Company, New York, 1916), p. 229.
[6] *Supra*, pp. 37–38.

THE CURRICULUM AND THEORY OF KNOWLEDGE

Whether a dualism reigns between child and curriculum, between a pre-scribed and an elective curriculum, between a conception of the curriculum as static or dynamic, echoes problems of a theory of knowledge. For curriculum purposes, knowledge seems to fall into two categories, knowledge about things and knowledge of how to do things. The former may be called propositional knowledge and the latter, cognitive action. Those paying attention to linguistic analysis factor the word "knowledge" at the very outset into "knowing that" and "knowing how." The distinction is important to correct the age-long tendency of schools to regard all knowledge to be of the former variety. The distinction is also important to make the educational point that "knowing how," that is, learning skills, need not be preceded by "knowing that," that is, a set of rules. Men knew, for instance, how to reason correctly before Aristotle formulated his *Organon*, the rules of correct reasoning. Moreover, "knowing that" is no guarantee of "knowing how," as is abundantly clear in physical education where one might know the rules of a sport without being able to play it.[7]

Although it is true that the problem of curriculum construction, simply stated, is one of selecting propositional knowledge for cognitive action, it will make considerable difference with which category one starts.[8] If the curriculum maker starts with propositional knowledge, two alternatives confront him. On the one hand, he may try to derive the curriculum from a knowledge of first principles. Here he will be guided by an ascending hierarchy of subject matter from physical science through mathematics and logic to metaphysics. The symmetry of such a curriculum confessedly has an aesthetic quality but, quite as obviously, no counterpart in practice. On the other hand, he may organize propositional knowledge in the curriculum around questions which we put ourselves. To meet the question, for instance, how to express ourselves appealingly in both the written and spoken word, we have over the ages organized the famous trivium of grammar, logic, and rhetoric. But if the curriculum builder takes this tack, he may find that his increasing power to organize propositional materials outruns his power to describe them.

At this point he may turn and try to commence curriculum construction from the starting point of knowledge as cognitive action. Here, too,

[7] For one educational application of these ideas, see Thomas F. Green, "Teaching, Acting, and Behaving," *Harvard Educational Review*, 34:507–524, Fall, 1964.
[8] James E. McClellan, "Knowledge and the Curriculum," *Teachers College Record*, 57:410–418, March, 1956. See also Arno A. Bellack, "The Structure of Knowledge and the Structure of the Curriculum," in Dwayne E. Huebner (ed.), *A Reassessment of the Curriculum* (Teachers College Press, Columbia University, New York, 1964), Chap. 3.

he has two alternatives. Following one, he may approach his task empirically. He may find out in what activities a person engages and arrange to give the learner cognitive experience in each of them. Since the number of such activities could well be legion, this approach is, to say the least, too audacious. The better alternative is to economize the student's time and increase the scope of effective cognitive action by emphasizing theory, that is, by grouping these activities under conceptual heads.

We may next take the question whether to treat subject matter in the curriculum as knowledge that is already known before the lesson starts. For some it has already been found out, collected, systematized, and tucked away in textbooks, cyclopedias, dictionaries, and other academic paraphernalia. The curriculum thus has a tailor-made, ready-to-wear aspect, so that all the teacher has to do is to make an appropriate selection of it in advance from the wardrobe of knowledge and to assign it for the student to acquire and don as his own. Other teachers plan their lessons in terms of pupil problems, the answers to which they may suspect but do not specifically know in advance. Consequently they feel unable to give precise formulation to the curriculum in advance of the emergence of the problem. Rather does the curriculum unfold as they make selections from the storehouse of culture which give promise of advancing the problem to a solution. Instead of being ready-to-wear, the curriculum is custom-made out of selections from the social culture chosen for their promise in advancing this particular problem to a solution. But even so, they will deign to label any selections knowledge only in the form finally adapted for use and only then to the extent warranted by its outcome in use.

The most commonly accepted view of subject matter in the curriculum is that it already has the status of knowledge. Subject matter is the funded capital of social experience which has met the test of life. It is the truth. At least it is the truth tempered and hammered on the anvil of experience to as near perfect shape as human effort can bring it. The great repository of known truths is the library. There, arranged shelf after shelf, tome upon tome, is the systematized knowledge of the race. What better can the teacher do than go to this storehouse of knowledge before school opens and carefully choose select portions of its contents to be included in the curriculum of the school! And what better can the pupil do after reaching school than to appropriate unto himself his daily assignment of knowledge of the great truths of the past!

It is best that these truths be stated in the curriculum in theoretical form because it is a prime function of the school for those dedicated to this view of truth to teach pure theory. The reason for organizing the curriculum in this fashion is to release the student from the demands of the immediate situation. If all he learns is what to do *ad hoc* in a particular concrete situation, his education will be narrow and limited. Neither the school day nor the school year will be long enough for him to learn all the specific things he will need to know. Worse yet, he will be deprived of both the broad- and the long-range view of his situation which theory would provide him. To regard this kind of theoretical education as impractical is a serious mistake. Besides, not all situations are practical; some are strictly theoretical. Investigating and discovering may be ends in themselves, hence not to be identified with the scheming and plotting which go into solving a practical problem.

Perhaps two cautions are in order at this point, one concerning the purity of theory and the other concerning teaching theory as an end in itself. As to pure theory there can be no doubt about its importance in principles of order or conceptual frames of reference by which to organize the particulars of experience. But the proponents of a school curriculum devoted to pure theory must be careful to avoid implying that theory is to be taught apart from example.[9] To let that implication stand is tantamount to treating principles of order and conceptualizations as if they could themselves be objects of knowledge. That ideas will remain ideas after being detached from reality or use is a very dubious assumption. An assumption more in accord with usage would seem to demand that theories be regarded rather as ways of knowing and organizing reality.

Even if one watches his step in the use of pure theory he may still trip over it in worshiping theory in the form of knowledge for its own sake. The caution is not that knowledge is not worthy as an aesthetic end but that knowledge as an aesthetic having and contemplating may be exaggerated. This obstructs or severs intelligence from action and volition, knowledge from the everyday concerns of life. Moreover, the content of the curriculum too easily becomes largely verbal, to say nothing of being stated largely in other men's words. Vicarious experience gets to be substituted for that which is firsthand, and children become victims of a regime of memorizing mere facts and words. In sum, man is taken captive by his own cultural spoils.

A more recent view regards subject matter in the curriculum more in the nature of data or information. The fact that this subject matter is the verified knowledge resulting from previous problematic inquiry is no guarantee to those who hold this view that it should be learned in exactly the form in which it emerged from that inquiry. In a changing, precarious world they maintain that it is premature to assume that the next problem for inquiry will so closely resemble the former one that knowledge gleaned

9 Charner Perry, "Education: Ideas or Knowledge," *Journal of International Ethics*, 47:355–357, April, 1937.

from it can be carried over to the new without verification. Consequently they prefer to regard knowledge from previous inquiries merely as the data for solving subsequent ones. In this view of the matter the curriculum cannot be selected in advance of the opening of school. To be sure, a course of study can be drawn up of possible and even probable things to learn during the year. But what goes into the ongoing curriculum from day to day will be determined largely by what problems come up. There will be subject matter in this curriculum, but it will not be learned exactly in the form in which it emerged from previous inquiry. Rather will it be learned as it is adapted to the unique problem at hand. Only as the modification is successful will the materials of the curriculum be transformed from the status of subject matter, data, information, into that of knowledge.

This view of the curriculum also deserves a caution. It is the caution, already mentioned in another connection, of considering no subject matter unless it is related to some practical situation. Some students have aesthetic and scientific interests in subject matter quite apart from employing it to solve their personal problems. They enjoy exploring the grove of knowledge on its own account. Another limitation of too exclusive preoccupation with the practical situation is that, if school or college sticks too closely to what chance presents this way, it may omit or overlook some important areas included in the course of study. Neither, moreover, must become so absorbed in the informal character of the curriculum that it forgets the function of the more formal course of study. The latter, planned in advance, affords perspective from which the instructor can judge whether his protégé is getting sufficient scope and sequence in his curriculum which is made somewhat extempore.

KNOWLEDGE AS TRUTH

Reference has already been made to the curriculum as the funded capital of truth taken from the respository of the social heritage. But we cannot rest the matter there. In addition we must have a yardstick by which to judge whether knowledge in the curriculum is really true. We must decide whether truth is a matter of external or internal relations. Will studying the curriculum affect its truth, or is the truth independent of study?

Seemingly, selecting a criterion of truth should be a comparatively easy task. It should be just a matter of comparing any bit of information, fact, or opinion with reality. If it squares with reality, then it is true. This is the "correspondence" theory of truth. It obviously proceeds on the metaphysical or ontological theory that there is an objective world independent of a human knower. The pupil has learned the truth when his ideas or impressions correspond to this external reality. Hence correspondence is a matter of external rather than internal relations.[10] On this basis truth is objective. It is preexistent to the learning of it. Therefore the person engaged in educational research literally "finds" the truth; he dis-covers it in the sense of removing or cutting through the cover of ignorance or misunderstanding which obscured its location during the period of search. Hence truth is not temporal; rather is it eternal, immutable.[11] Any variability or ambiguity about it is apparent only, the result of human error in comprehending it.

This is almost undoubtedly the conception of truth with which the young come to school. Thus a major part of their moral upbringing at home has been always to tell the truth. What does this moral injunction mean but that the child should make his statements of events correspond to fact. He must learn the difference between telling a story which grows out of his imagination and a story which unimpeachably corresponds to events as they happened.

There are some philosophers of the curriculum who think truth is not just occasionally infected with human errors but always suffers from being refracted through the prism of the human mind. Furthermore, they inquire, how can we be sure that our ideas or impressions really correspond to actuality? Successive contacts with the same object often lead to widely different reactions. Moreover, our ideas or impressions of reality frequently do not correspond to those of others. How shall we tell, then, who is closer to the truth, whose reaction is closer to reality? Whichever way we judge, we must realize that any judgment is but still another idea. Obviously to those who interpose these embarrassing questions the criterion of truth must be something more than correspondence to reality. Their own answer is that truth as correspondence to naked reality lies beyond the curriculum maker's grasp. Hence the best we can do is to seek truth as the consistency between our ideas or impressions about reality. This is the "consistency" theory of truth.

Consistency rather than correspondence is the usual test of most of those engaged in educational research or educational measurement. It undergirds their quest for "objectivity" and "reliability." To them experimental or test results are reliable if successive impressions of a single investigator tend to be consistent with each other and objective if they are consistent with the impressions of other investigators operating under the same experimental conditions. Scientific knowledge of education, therefore, is true in so far as it achieves this sort of consistency among observations.

---

[10] *Supra*, pp. 137–138.   [11] For a further reference, see *infra*, pp. 239–240.

Perhaps it needs pointing out here that the consistency theory of truth need not radically supplant the correspondence theory. The two views may not be so much opposed as supplementary to each other. The correspondence theory is a statement of the meaning of truth, while the coherence theory is a statement of the test of truth. Both posit an external objective reality and probably also an eternal immutable order of truth. They differ only on how close they can bring reality and truth within the reach of curriculum design. Thus the consistency theory despairs of defining the objectivity of our knowledge of external reality except in human terms, while the correspondence theory expects to leap over human barriers and come face to face with objective naked reality.

On second thought, as well as at first glance, it is difficult to see any way to break the impasse between the advocates of the corespondence and consistency theories of truth, respectively, the realist and the idealist. In place of meeting this deadlock head on, another group of educational philosophers, the pragmatists—also known as instrumentalists or experimentalists—endeavor to bypass it. Instead of trying to gain truth by attacking reality frontally, as in the case of the correspondence theory, or from the flank, as in the case of the consistency theory, they propose to test the truth of ideas (opinions, facts, theories, or what have you) by inquiring what would be the practical consequences of acting on them? Ideas by themselves are neither true nor false. They only become true or false when employed to clear up some confusion or ambiguity which has occurred to obstruct educational practice. If they clear it up and restore the continuity of instruction, then they are true; if not, then they are false. As the pragmatist says, truth is what "works."[12] Truth, thus, does not exist; it happens. Truth is literally veri-fication, truth-making. It is never perfect, immutable, eternal but always in the making.

The pragmatic test of truth as workability will perhaps be most familiar to educators in the project or problem curriculum. The project is ordinarily a problem arising in a real-life situation. After thorough analysis of the problem and mobilization of data to solve it, there may appear to be one or more possible solutions. Which is the true one? The one that appears most logically consistent in view of all the data? Probably but not certainly. Pupil and teacher will not know for sure until they have tried it out to see if it works. A hypothesis will be said to work, its truth will be established, if the consequences of acting on it corroborate the expectations it has aroused.

In assaying truth in the crucible of a problem or project curriculum

---

[12] Cf. *infra*, pp. 230 and 233–234, where differences in theory that do not make a difference in practice are ruled out as trivial or neglegible.

we must be careful what ingredients enter in and what conclusions are drawn forth. The pupil and teacher, for instance, generally have a purpose which motivates their efforts to find a solution for their project. For this reason some pragmatic progressive educators have slipped into thinking that a solution works if it helps to realize this purpose. If so, then the search for truth is in danger of being conditioned by the interests or values motivating the educational program.[13] If truth is subject to expediency, how can we escape the cynical attitude of Pilate when he asked, "What is truth?"

Critics of pragmatism have been quick to pounce on this confusion of truth with value. The curriculum theorists under criticism, however, can appeal for support to no less an advocate of pragmatism than William James. James took the view that any good which flows from acting on an idea or belief proves the truth of that idea "in so far forth." He acted on this rule in religious quandaries. Let us apply it in an educational situation. In giving an intelligence test, a teacher may tell a timid child he is doing well in order to instill confidence in him so that he may put forth his very best effort; and yet the teacher may know all the time that the child is doing poorly. The motivating ruse may work, and if it does, it is true in so far as the child scores higher as a result of it.

Other pragmatists, like John Dewey, have been careful to avoid this confusion of truth and value. Dewey treats an idea or proposed solution of a problem or project as a hypothesis. In acting on the hypothesis, he looks to see whether the consequences of action corroborate the original hypothesis, whether the outcome is what the hypothesis led him to anticipate. Corroboration, even where the problem concerns values, is just a question of fact. That a theory or hypothesis works when it is corroborated by its consequences suggests that possibly Dewey's theory of truth is, in a sense, a further development of the consistency theory. For him consistency is not just the relation which holds between ideas but also the relation which holds between ideas and their consequences. Yet, although there is this similarity, Dewey would still be a thoroughgoing pragmatist in holding that truth is no already completed logical pattern of consistency but rather something which is constantly and indefinitely in the making.

At this point it will be well to meet an important criticism which has

---

[13] Cf. George S. Counts, School and Society in Chicago (Harcourt, Brace & World, Inc., New York, 1928), p. 344, "Toward truth in any abstract sense, social groups have no inclination; rather do they seek effective instruments for the winning of battles. If truth, however it may be defined, serves them, well and good; but if it does not, so much the worse for truth." Note how political philosophies like those of the Nazis and communists have claimed that truth is not academic but conditioned by the interests of the state. Cf. Harry S. Broudy, "Implications of Classical Realism for Philosophy of Education," Proceedings of the Association for Realistic Philosophy, 1949, pp. 13–14. See also infra, p. 282.

been leveled at Dewey's pragmatism. If not subject to the kind of criticism leveled at James and his brand of pragmatism, Dewey has not escaped criticism from other directions. The claim is that since Dewey thinks of truth as veri-fication, truth-making, he thinks of the pupil as "making" the world.[14] This is clearly a misconception. Dewey holds to the existence of an externally real world just as do those who espouse the correspondence and consistency theories.[15] He differs on this point principally in how the learner gets to know the world. Instead of trying to learn to know objects directly in and of themselves (the correspondence theory) or indirectly through impressions of them (the consistency theory), Dewey holds that the student learns about them incidentally by using them to solve problems. Acquiring is subordinate to inquiring. In the course of inquiry the learner may alter the existing state of affairs, but he does not make it.

Another criticism of the pragmatist's position implies that he has got the cart before the horse. The question arises at the outset, why does any educational theory "work"? Is it an arbitrary, accidental happening? Or is there some inherent quality or interconnection of the factors at work which makes them "work"? If the latter, then educational theories are not true because they "work" but, conversely, they "work" because they are true.[16]

The difference between pragmatism and its critics at this point is one of metaphysics or ontology. Is the curriculum studied in a world in which ultimate reality is already complete, in which change is insignificant, in which there is no genuine novelty, and in which time is but a vestibule to eternity?[17] If so, then the conditions of truth are already preexistent so that naturally any hypothesis would work because it is already true. But if the opposite metaphysic holds, if genuine novelties are still emerging, then some conditions of truth are yet to be determined by the way man's decisions work out, and the pragmatist has the horse and the cart in the right order. Nevertheless, this idea that truth may change is very uncongenial to many. If truth is not a fixed star in the educational firmament, they cannot steer a steady course of study. Others do not feel uncom-

---

[14] Frederick S. Breed, in National Society for the Study of Education, Forty-first Yearbook, Part I, *Philosophies of Education* (Public School Publishing Company, Bloomington, Ill., 1942), pp. 108, 117.

[15] John Dewey, *Logic: The Theory of Inquiry* (Holt, Rinehart and Winston, Inc., New York, 1938), p. 521; Paul A. Schilpp (ed.), *The Philosophy of John Dewey* (Northwestern University, Evanston, Ill., 1939), p. 113.

[16] Herman H. Horne, *The Democratic Philosophy of Education* (The Macmillan Company, New York, 1935), pp. 500–503. In his *Philosophy of Education*, rev. ed. (The Macmillan Company, New York, 1927), p. 303, Horne qualifies this statement by saying, ". . . or will work when conditions are better." This seems like a vital concession to those who contend that truth is temporal and contingent on circumstances. See also *The Democratic Philosophy of Education*, pp. 420–421, where the author states that truth does not have to wait to become true.

[17] *Supra*, Chap. 7.

fortable at all in such a world. They prefer to stake everything on their experimental method of ascertaining the truth rather than on any completed statement of it in any given syllabus.

Reliance on method is very important, as anyone would admit; yet two complaints arise against its use by the educational pragmatist. One is that it leads to relativism and the other that it leads to skepticism. In either event the curriculum maker's role is undermined. As to the former complaint, the incomplete and changing character of truth would seem bound to compel the educational pragmatist to regard any statement about truth as relative to a particular time and place. But is this really upsetting? Much depends on the nature assigned to the theories which man uses to describe and explain his world. Formerly scientists thought that these theories described the actual external order of the universe; today scientists realize they describe only a conceptual order on which man chooses to act. Man's theories read an order into the universe rather than describe one that is actually there. His theories are based not on *data* but on *capta*, not on what is "given" but on what is "taken" in the universe to act on. We do not know whether there *actually* are neutrons, protons, and electrons, but we carry on research in physics as if there were. We do not know whether there *really* are S-R bonds in educational psychology, but we can teach as if there were. Truth thus is relative to the particular concepts which we have the imagination to formulate and to the consequences which flow therefrom. A strict regard for truth, therefore, requires us to be meticulous in stating the particular conceptions or conditions on which we act. Such a relativity, far from undermining the course of study is a prerequisite to clarity in what he thinks he is doing.

As to the complaint of skepticism, many think pragmatic curriculum experts suffer from a "methodomania." Some educational theorists certainly think so. Employing systematic methodical doubt, the pragmatist is constantly in the pursuit of truth, but he never catches up with it. His critics for the most part do not catch up with it either, but they think it would be theoretically possible to do so if they were only smart enough. The pragmatists do not even grant themselves this theoretical chance. The conclusions they reach are never final, only more or less doubtful. This persistent undercurrent of doubt leads many to charge that pragmatism is ultimately based on skepticism. This charge may be admitted, but only in part. Doubt is cultivated but not as an end in itself as by the ancient skeptics. Skeptical doubting paralyzes action. The educational pragmatist, as already stated, employs doubt to clarify action, to clear up ambiguity. Yet even with this qualification the critics are only half convinced his methodomania is cured.

NORMATIVE ASPECTS OF THE CURRICULUM

We have just seen the need for distinguishing the true from the good as separate categories in the curriculum. After confining ourselves to the true, we must now singly examine the role of values in the curriculum. Our first question is whether the curriculum should be shaped by the social culture and the requirements of society or by the needs of the individual. Since, as already seen,[18] education inescapably occurs in a social matrix, there are many who think that the curriculum should take its specifications from the social culture. The best of that culture, of course, is contained in tradition. Hence tradition—whether through history, literature, or science—takes top priority in any course of study.

Paired against this theory is one where the curriculum derives its value from the way it serves the needs of the learner. But this idea of a curriculum is not unambiguous. There seem to be two meanings of the word "needs," one prescriptive and the other motivational. Thus it makes some difference whether needs stem from a social requirement or whether they are "felt" needs of the student himself. Prescriptive needs will further vary depending on whether "needs" means necessity or mere deficiency, and they will vary much further if one raises the question "need for what?"[19]

At this point the "needs" curriculum merges with one which takes its value from pupil purposes. On this basis, the past has no significance of its own which is worth studying. It is significant only as it enters into and illuminates present purposes. To study the past, as the past, makes the past a rival of the present and the present a futile imitation of what is past. Where such a curriculum theory obtains, culture is in danger of becoming an ornament and a solace, if not a refuge and an asylum as well. In contrast to such a result is a curriculum which, far from being indifferent to the past, draws heavily on it but always as a resource for learning the way out of some contemporary perplexity. In this theory, the culture of the past does not belong to another almost disconnected world—the dualistic view—but is continuous with the present. But, even accepting this instrumentalistic curricular hypothesis, some anxious educators think that the question must still be raised whether some things are not so useful that they must be learned, even though no immediate occasion presents itself in which learning can occur through use. The probable answer to this

[18] *Supra*, p. 4.
[19] Cf. R. F. Deardon, " 'Needs' in Education," *British Journal of Educational Studies*, 14:5–17, November, 1966. See also Reginald D. Archambault, "The Concept of Needs and Its Relation to Certain Aspects of Educational Theory," *Harvard Educational Review*, 27:38–62, Winter, 1957.

question is that material so important will not long want an occasion for revealing its necessity. Failing such an opportune opening, the farseeing teacher will adroitly maneuver the children into a situation where they will themselves demand it.

This consideration of the element of time in curriculum construction naturally leads to another moot problem, whether the curriculum can be made out in advance. In time-honored practice, it has been customary to lay out the curriculum in advance of either the year or day of its use. The more sure the teacher is of his objectives, of the intrinsic worth of studies, of their enduring quality, the more assurance can he have in preparing his course in advance of meeting his class. Contrariwise, if subject matter is learned to meet the needs of the learner, and if educational aims represented by these needs constantly vary, then one's advance planning becomes by so much less precise. The curriculum then must be made as life and learning develop.

This, however, does not necessarily mean that the curriculum is always to be improvised extempore. Instead of rejecting planning, this theory requires an even more difficult kind of planning, the kind that is so broad and flexible that it is prepared for a variety of contingencies. When unexpected events occur, it will be well to depart from prior plans and to squeeze every educational value one can from the instant situation. But, in doing so, there is the ever-present danger that in retrospect the curriculum will appear fragmentary, discontinuous, and unrelated. The chief remedy for guarding against such a misadventure is the selection of relatively large units of work requiring a relatively long time to accomplish. In that event there will have to be year-by-year cooperation among the different teachers. But, even then, unity is best found in the integrity of the pupil's purpose rather than in any external organization of the curriculum by the teacher.

Because of his more mature experience, the teacher should be able to do much to guide this continuity of experience, to anticipate within limits what problems are most likely to press for solution in the child's life. To this extent, surely, he must be prepared with information and sources for its further procurement. Some prefer to call this general plan the course of study, or program of studies, in contradistinction to the curriculum. The term curriculum they reserve for what actually occurs in the specific ongoing process of the learning situation. The curriculum can thus vary with the values of the moment and yet have as a steadying keel the course of instruction.

If the curriculum must be flexible in point of time, then, there are others who think that it must also be flexible enough to meet the individual differences of students. Not only is the nature of the curriculum to be conceived in terms of their nature but, since that nature is infinitely variegated, the curriculum must be individualized. Since individuality is of the ultimate nature of reality,[20] no educational authorities can make a uniform curriculum for a multitude of youngsters. Accordingly, each one must have his own curriculum. Perhaps not going quite so far in their individualism are those who reserve an important place for it, nevertheless, through the elective curriculum. Here, chiefly for democratic reasons,[21] they would insist on a curriculum broad enough so that some element in it will strike a sympathetic chord in the capacity of every youth. It must not be forgotten, however, that the elective system is akin to the policy of *laissez faire.*[22] For eduational authorities to hold back from prescribing curriculum values is to run much the same risks as the state does when it adopts a hands-off policy toward schools. The more the educational staff fails to take a hand, the more the children are left to the mercy of the opinions of their parents, the attitudes of fellow students, and the popularity of certain instructors.

The multiplication of studies, whether encouraged by *laissez faire* or otherwise, leads to the constant danger of congestion, confusion, superficiality, and dispersiveness unless, as some say, there is some unifying tendency. But how to obtain the value of unity or integration in the curriculum?[23] Many think that unity or integration is to be found in the inherent logical unity of knowledge. Accordingly, though we find it necessary to break down the total scope of knowledge into subject-matter divisions like mathematics, language, and the various sciences, many believe that there is an essential relatedness of all these fields of knowledge. Thus, chemistry and biology are related through biochemistry, biology and psychology through psychobiology, psychology and sociology through social psychology, and so on. It would be a grave mistake, many feel, if students should complete their education without some appreciation of how all knowledge tends to hang together according to the logical nature of the universe. A number of other educators seek integration in a different direction. Instead of finding it ready-made in the logic of the universe, they form it around specific problems or centers of interest. Each new problem demands its own unique selection of subject matter, which must receive its own unique organization or integration to ensure solution. The organization or integration achieved will be useful for the next problem, but to the extent to which that problem has unique features there will have to be

---

[20] *Supra,* pp. 145–147.

[21] Cf. *supra,* pp. 57–64.

[22] William P. Montague, *Ways of Knowing* (The Macmillan Company, New York, 1925), p. 147; cf. *supra,* pp. 146–147.

[23] Howard Hong, *Integration in the Christian Liberal Arts College* (St. Olaf's College Press, Northfield, Minn., 1956), pp. 128–147; and Henry Margenau, "Integrative Education in the Sciences," in Sixth Yearbook of the American Association of College Teachers of Education, 1953, p. 134. See also *supra,* pp. 129–130 and 145–147.

some reorganization, a new integration. Whichever way we approach integration of the curriculum, of course, leads ultimately to a fresh realization that unity or integration is the heart of the philosophic viewpoint in education.[24]

It but remains to accord consideration to the proper parties to be entrusted with the selection of the curriculum. Not infrequently laymen through legislatures and boards of education like to think of themselves as competent to state which subjects should be included. No doubt it is quite proper for the lay public to set the general direction of the schools, but the task of determining the particular materials appropriate to moving in that direction should be left in charge of the professionally competent. But even when such decisions are left in the hands of professional experts, philosophical difficulties pursue the educator. Should the superintendent of schools or some curriculum expert draw up the curriculum and then pass it on to the teacher to be passed on in turn to the children? Or should the teacher participate in the first instance with the superintendent or expert consultant in curriculum making, inviting the children later on to participate to the extent of their abilities? Obviously a question of social philosophy stands out here. Of the two suggested practices, the former is more autocratic and the latter more democratic. The democratic practice, let it be noted in answer to some of its critics, does not expect the teacher to abdicate his responsibilities in curriculum formation in favor of immature children. Rather he consults the interests of children to see what they desire in the curriculum but later pools this data with what the adult group holds socially desirable in arriving at the final statement of the curriculum.

THE CURRICULUM AND VALUE THEORY

It is obvious now that the curriculum can be viewed either from the angle of knowledge or from the angle of value. As we found it necessary to undergird the curriculum with a theory of knowledge, so we must now undergird it with a theory of value. First we must note the nature of value and then how values may be compared. Lord Bacon took all knowledge to be his province, but such is the extent of knowledge today that there is not time enough in the years of schooling to include it all. Hence we need a criterion to tell not only what knowledge is good but what knowledge is better and best to save time by establishing priorities.

Do values inhere in the curriculum independently of the valuer, or do

---

[24] *Infra*, pp. 313–314.

they find their origin in a valuing organism? This is one of the first questions to answer in forming a conscious theory of educational values. The question will be recognized at once as another form of our old problem of whether to regard relations as internal or external.[25] As might be expected, some educators take the view that values are internal and subjective. They are biological and psychological in origin. The only claim, for example, which textbooks, curriculums, or laboratories have to value is that they satisfy wants or fulfill needs of the student. Possessed of no inherent value of their own, these academic paraphernalia are merely valuable, that is, capable of being valued. In ascribing value to any of them, the student or teacher is merely projecting his feelings into them. Hence the environment is educationally neither worthy nor worthless unless the organism is involved. But upset the human organism's equilibrium, confront him with a problem, and instinct, emotion, and intellect will at once combine to express an individual preference. Value is then realized in the efforts put forth to restore equilibrium.

Other educators are inclined to regard values resident in the curriculum as external and objective. They deny that value is just a private inner experience. To them there is an ontology of value, in which values have as real an existence as any of the so-called laws of nature.[26] One description of their conviction is that everything has some form or purpose. For instance, the skilled artisan takes wood and steel and fashions them into schoolroom seats and desks. That is, he gives form to these raw materials. This form lends purpose or value to the product. Value, thus, is incorporated into the object; it is objectively and inherently part of it. Adherents of this view do not doubt that personal desire is an important element of educational value; but they do claim that value is independent of desire. It antedates and arouses desire. Indeed they are ready to defend the thesis that, unless value inheres in the form of the universe as a whole, it can scarcely be said to abide in a fragment thereof, such as man. Consequently, there must be more to educational value than the mere wishful behavior of persons engaged in constructing curricula.

A third view of educational value rejects both the preceding views for their exclusiveness. Instead of locating the wellspring of value in either the subject or the object of the educational process, it describes valuation as the product of a relation between them. As it takes a combination of hydrogen and oxygen to make water, so it takes the interaction of both organism and environment to distill value. The nature of the interaction

[25] Supra, pp. 136–137.
[26] J. Donald Butler, "The Role of Value Theory in Education," Educational Theory, 4:70, January, 1954.

is well brought out by the word "interest." Etymologically, interest means "to be between" and carries the connotation that it is a value relation which lies between the poles of interest—child and curriculum, for instance.[27] So interrelated are the poles that, were the reaction to become habitual, the resulting habit could as well be said to belong to the environment as to the organism, to the curriculum as well as to the student. In any event, little interest or little value will be distilled from the interaction if the transaction is largely cognitive. To put it somewhat clumsily, values are rarely known by being "known about." On the contrary, they must be felt. Thus it is all too easy to teach the truth about value without teaching value itself. Yet in the course of instruction teachers can hardly be expected to prove values; about all they can do is to report them to their disciples with the authority of personal enthusiasm.

Lest this difference of opinion on the subjectivity or objectivity of values seem a hairsplitting distinction, it may be well to point out the significant differences to which it leads in school practice. The problem of whether Latin, or any subject for that matter, should be included in the curriculum against the wishes of those studying it will illustrate the importance of the distinction. If the curriculum maker follows the subjective theory of value, it will be difficult for him to insist on the continued inclusion of Latin in the face of the fact that adolescents are not *interested* in it or that parents do not see the *need* of it. But if, on the contrary, the curriculum maker follows the objective theory of value and holds that Latin has values regardless of whether pupils or parents recognize them, he will feel justified in requiring Latin in spite of the disinclination of its patrons.

On the other hand, to insist that youth study only when and what they like seems to make all values relative. If all values are relative to individual taste, what is to become of social stability? What will happen to moral education if there is no settled curriculum of what is right and what is wrong? According to this view there is no common rule of good and evil, no standard of value that is simply and absolutely so. On the contrary, this view seems to assert with a vengeance Hamlet's judgment that "there is nothing either good or bad, but thinking makes it so."

Omnious as the charge against the subjectivity and relativity of educational values sounds, one fact must not be overlooked: that the charge does not bother some educators at all. Quite the opposite, they welcome the prospect of teaching where values are constantly subject to examination relative to each school and each of its denizens. For them, indeed, only those values which retain the sap of flexibility have sufficient vitality to

27 Cf. *infra*, pp. 253–254.

survive in a constantly evolving world. They take seriously the poet's dictum, "New occasions teach new duties; time makes ancient good uncouth."

It is worth noting in passing that the subjectivist has his own way of dealing with social values so that youth will not be reared to disregard them. He holds that the juvenile will and must inevitably learn that he lives with adults who are as interested in asserting and maintaining their values as he is in his. If he expects adults to concede him the opportunity of realizing his values, he too must behave so they can realize theirs. For the young to conform to adult social values without personally accepting or endorsing them may seem, perhaps, to differ little if at all from the situation where values are regarded as objective. But if they are objective here too, it is a different kind of objectivity. It is a situation in which values are objective, not in the metaphysical sense of being independent of human valuers, but in the social sense of being confirmed by others.

As we come to closer grips with the values in the curriculum it will be well to distinguish several kinds of value. At the outset two major categories develop from two meanings which attach to the infinitive "to value." A moment's reflection will reveal that this infinitive means both to value and to evaluate. The same difference appears in to prize and to appraise, to esteem and to estimate. The difference also comes out in the distinction between what is desired and what is desirable. It is a commonplace that not everything that a child desires is in fact desirable. Desires are simple expressions of biological urges or bodily appetites. They become elevated to the level of the desirable only when, after taking other things into account, they have been judged desirable.[28] Educational values, therefore, cover both likings and intelligent likings. Like knowledge, they are both immediate and mediate.[29]

Values in the curriculum involving simple or immediate likings, prizings, or desirings are consummatory values. As such they are ineffable, *sui generis*. They satisfy a unique craving or want which cannot be satisfied by any other thing. If a student has a bent for the fine arts, then work in painting, modeling, music, or dancing is the only thing which will adequately give realization to his values. There is no use prescribing chemistry, history, or trigonometry for they will not carry the same sense of consummation, self-fulfillment. Similarly, if one has a bent for chemicals or antiquity, then there is no use trying to substitute work in the fine arts. Only chemistry or history will satisfy these unique inclinations. At the initial level of desire, then, every school activity has its own invaluable value. The stu-

---

[28] Cf. Boyd H. Bode, "The Concept of Needs in Education," *Progressive Education*, 15:7–9, January, 1938.
[29] *Supra*, p. 230.

dent should learn to appreciate each of these activities in some measure on its own account, just for the simple fulfillment of the desire it satisfies.

Yet, valuable as it is to squeeze each curricular activity to as complete fulfillment of desire as it is possible, it is even more valuable to be intelligent in the choice of the desires which one seeks to fulfill. Not all desires are of equal worth. Moreover there frequently is not time enough to realize even every worthy desire. Hence we must choose between desires; we must use our heads as well as our hearts to get the most value out of school and out of life. Our values must undergo evaluation and appraisal. In the process of mediating or intelligently selecting values we should note two further kinds of educational values, extrinsic and intrinsic.

Extrinsic or instrumental values are values that are judged good because they are good *for* something. Their value depends on their consequences when used to achieve some other value. In drawing up a course of study for a student to pursue, for example, what subjects or values should be included? Much will depend on what career the student has set for himself. If he has decided to become an engineer, then studies like mathematics and science will have first call on his adviser's attention. Because they are the indispensable means or tools for the student's future career, their value is clearly instrumental. They are good *for* such a career. But they might not be good at all for some other career, such as that of a lawyer or actor. Instrumental values, thus, are clearly subjective in character and relative to people and situations.

Intrinsic values are values which are judged good, not for something else, but *in* and *of* themselves. Their value is not contingent on other values outside and beyond themselves but is inherent, self-contained. They stand on their own pretensions and are sufficient unto themselves without sequel. The idea of knowledge for knowledge's sake is not to be confused with the kind of curriculum where schools have assigned fact after fact to be learned merely because the task was something that could be learned. Too much learning, it may be confessed, is merely for school purposes, for marks and promotions. It is almost of the order of incantation. The curriculum as properly conceived here is to be learned, not because it can be learned, but because it contains values which are coincident with the very humanity of man.

Can anything have both instrumental and objective value at the same time? Instrumentalists, because they regard all values as subjective and relative, feel that they would be contradicting themselves were they to hold that values could be instrumental and objective or inherent as well. But those who subscribe to inherent value are quite willing to admit that anything, such as a school desk, might have instrumental as well as intrinsic value. Thus, the teacher might strike an informal pose by sitting on his desk as he explains some problem. Although not designed to be a seat, a desk can be used for one. It can have that instrumental subjective value assigned to it by use. But whatever its use, it still retains its original objective, inherent value.

HIERARCHIES OF VALUE

After recognizing the existence of different kinds of value and the need for judging among them, it is but logical to inquire whether there is any hierarchy of values which the educator can use as a yardstick or norm to evaluate subjects in the curriculum. On this point educational philosophers differ. Those holding that educational values are objective and intrinsic are most likely to be the ones to think it possible to erect a hierarchy of value. Lowest in their scale are the values arising from simple unmediated desire or animal appetite. Such are the child's spontaneous joy in play, in color, or in rhythm. While all such consummatory values are good, some are better than others. This suggests a second or higher level of values, those rationally judged valuable. By general consent values thoughtfully chosen in the light of their consequences, values thoughtfully conceived in harmony with cosmic design, take precedence over unreflected desires.

Even curriculum values thoughtfully chosen are capable of organization into a further order of preference. To make this arrangement we may begin by ranking intrinsic values above instrumental ones. Instrumental values, because they are subject to individual purpose and circumstance, have much greater variability than do intrinsic ones which remain settled by the form or purpose originally impressed on or embodied in the thing valued. From this we may conclude more generally that the values which are more durable are on the whole superior to those with less lasting qualities. Temporal values must give way to eternal. Similarly those values which are more inclusive or more many-sided take priority over those which are exclusive and less variegated. Much the same can be said for values marked by greater productivity, greater creativity.[30]

A hierarchy of values may also be securely grounded in the metaphysical principle that the more being an item has, the more value it has also. For instance, man as a human being has various potentialities. The more fully he succeeds through the curriculum to actualize these poten-

---

[30] Some try to organize thoughtfully chosen values in a hierarchy based on the frequency of their occurrence in daily life. To an extent this is possible, but there are some educational values, like knowing how to swim, which the child may not need often, but when he does, in a rare emergency, the value has a cruciality which outweighs its frequency of occurrence.

tialities, the more of a human being he will be. The more he realizes him-self—the more he makes of himself—the more valuable a person he becomes. The measure of his value is not in his contribution to society but in his self-fulfillment.

In grounding a hierarchy of studies in human nature, we must note that man has many faculties for potential development. Does a hierarchy reign among these faculties? Yes, it does, and the way to come at it is by noting a further metaphysical principle that everything in nature has its own unique excellence. Man's unique excellence is his rationality. Somatic faculties he shares with the brute. They both take nourishment, get angry, move about, and succumb to sleep. But over and above this common heritage man possesses one faculty not shared with any other animal, the faculty of reason. True, other animals can learn to adapt themselves to unusual situations; yet, in spite of this ability, there still remains a vast gap between rational man and the most adaptable animal.

Man's unique excellence of intelligence provides a further criterion by which to establish a hierarchy of value. The more he actualizes his rational faculty, the more uniquely human he becomes. Therefore the more that studies have intellectual content, the more valuable they are. Consequently liberal studies such as mathematics, science, and the humanities are su-perior to physical education and vocational studies such as shop and agri-culture. If any doubt remains about the principle of such a hierarchy, it should be laid at rest by Aristotle. We have his word for it that the highest form of happiness is to be found in sheer intellectual contemplation; indeed such activity is most like the divine occupation of God Himself. If studies have the intrinsic hierarchy of worth indicated, then we can further lay it down that the order of studies in the curriculum is prescriptive and not elective. The order of worth being inherent in the nature of things, it is not subject to the preference of the individual student.

The instrumentalist cannot help but look askance at so elaborate an attempt to set up a hierarchy of educational values. To the instrumentalist, it will be remembered, values are good *for* something. Which of two values, therefore, outranks the other will depend on which one is the better in-strument for achieving some given educational objective or policy. A standard hierarchy, thus, cannot be established in advance or once for all. The order of value will rather depend on each particular education situation, each particular person, at some particular time, at some particular place. Such a relativity of standard is maddening to the critics of instrumental-ism but utterly necessary for the instrumentalist if standards are to grow experimentally in the light of a dynamic universe.[31]

---

[31] Ernest E. Bayles, "Are Values Verifiable?" *Educational Theory*, 10:71–77, January, 1960.

For example, which of several textbooks put out by competing pub-lishers most adequately achieves curriculum objectives? If the policy of the board of education is to emphasize economy, then perhaps the book with the sturdiest binding or the one with the lowest sale price will be chosen. If cost is not a factor and the policy of the board is to look for educational advantages, then the book with print most suited to the age of the pupil, the clearest exposition, and the most attractive illustrations will be selected as the best means of instrumenting the board's policy.

It goes without saying, of course, that deciding which of several books is the best instrument for giving effect to curriculum policy is in the first instance a matter for intellectual deliberation. But the instrumental com-parison of values does not end there. Comparison is not finally validated until choice has been put to the test. Valuation is as much a matter of inquiry as knowledge is. Just as the pragmatist verifies knowledge by acting on his hypothesis and checking the consequences back against it, so too his cousin, the instrumentalist, ultimately chooses values on the basis of how they work out in practice. In other words, does one textbook wear longer than another; do children *actually* find one book easier to read and to comprehend than another? That is, do these instrumental values ac-complish the consummation of values anticipated? If so, then preference can be substantially grounded.

A more difficult case for the instrumental comparison of values arises where the teacher must choose, not just between subjects in the curriculum which are means or instruments for achieving some educational aim or policy, but between several educational policies themselves. Everything de-pends here on the role assigned reason in adjudicating the dispute, that is, on whether values are cognitive. Some claim that values are noncognitive, that is, nonverifiable, and that values are just emotive expressions. They are a case of *de gustibus non disputandum est.* If that is the case, the disagreement can only be resolved by force, compromise, or majority vote. Others take the view that values have cognitive qualities just as well as facts. If so, it should be possible to test experimentally not only which means are best to effectuate policy, but also which policy or normative principle is best.[32]

But even putting the norm to an experimental test is no simple affair. Setting one policy over against another will involve comparing it to some

[32] William T. Blackstone, "Metaphysics and Value Conflicts in Education," *Proceedings of the Philosophy of Education Society,* 1963, pp. 9–16. See also Gail Kennedy, "The Role of Value Theory in Dewey's Philosophy of Education, *ibid.,* 1965, pp. 25–40; and Martin Levit, "Non-cognitive Ethics, Scientific Method, and Education," *Studies in Philosophy and Education,* 2:304–330, Winter, 1963. Finally, note National Society of College Teach-ers of Education, Twenty-eighth Yearbook, *The Discipline of Practical Judgment in a Democratic Society* (The University of Chicago Press, Chicago, 1942).

broader or more general educational policy or value. For instance, should the board of education govern with an eye to fiscal economy or with an eye to enrichment of the curriculum? Much will depend, no doubt, on whether the need for determining policy comes up during a period of economic depression or a period of economic prosperity. But even if it is the former, should the board practice economy at the expense of effective texts for the younger generation or at the expense of building repairs? Which is more valuable, people or buildings? Yet granted that people are more important than things, a contract for building repairs might relieve the ranks of the unemployed. How, from that angle, shall we balance the interests of growing minds against the interests of the adult unemployed? And even if relief from unemployment has first claim on our values, is it better to seek a solution of our economic woes by educating the next generation more effectively or by salvaging the economic wrecks of the preceding generation?

This analysis, basic to choosing educational policy, can obviously be carried much further. The difficulty lurking in this analysis is that it might be carried indefinitely further. Each level of policy analysis seems to depend for determination on some other value, which depends on still some other value, which depends on some more remote value, and so on ad infinitum. At each level of analysis choice depends on the acceptance of some common denominator of value from the next level into which the values of the lower level are divisible. But one never arrives at a final level or denominator of value which is accepted on its own cognizance as finally backing all preceding values and not on its instrumentality in achieving further values. Refusing recourse to some fixed value a priori, the instrumentalist educator seems confronted with the dilemma either of never acting, because his mental elaboration of what instrumental values are good for leads on and on into an infinite regress,[33] or of acting before he has thought his values through to a final conclusion.

If the educator is a good instrumentalist, he knows he cannot expect complete and final intellectual assurance in advance for values which can only be validated in the future by noting the consequences of acting on them. Therefore he has no great difficulty in resolving the above dilemma. Being a good pragmatist or experimentalist, he mentally anticipates as carefully as possible which value is most likely to be the best means of attaining some end and then acts on it. But the question persists, how does he ar-

[33] Lawrence G. Thomas, "The Meaning of 'Progress' in Progressive Education," *Educational Administration and Supervision*, 32:395–396, October, 1946; Raymond Bachetti, "Experimentalist Value Theory in American Culture," *Proceedings of the Philosophy of Education Society*, 1961, pp. 76–81.

rive at the preference of a value on which to act? He does so by treating some end, not as a potential means to another end, but as an end in itself. That is, he anchors his preference on this end value, not as a final or objective value, as the advocate of an intrinsic hierarchy of values might do, but as an ineffable or consummatory value. The advantage of doing this is that consummatory values are, somewhat paradoxically, good without being good *for* anything. They are, it will be remembered, unique, *sui generis*. Being what they uniquely are, they are not only irreplaceable but incomparable. There is no appeal from them. They can serve at once as a dependable criterion to select what appears to be the greater instrumental value upon which to act and by which to judge the consequences of action. Thus this invocation of consummatory values puts an effective, if not final, stop to any tendency to string out a series of instrumental values into an infinite regress.

This elaborate analysis seems to confirm rather than to dispose of the repeated criticism that instrumental values are infected with a relativism which renders standards meaningless. If educational values are relative, they will fluctuate like a weather vane, veering in the direction of the strongest pressure. This instability is dangerous, for the public schools will then take their direction from whatever power group is able to capture the government. Under such circumstances there can be no measuring stick by which to criticize fascist, communist, or even democratic control of the schools. To assert that we can guard against such an outcome by regarding values as objective presents not an antidote but the other horn of a dilemma. The moment we assert value as objective rather than relative we are sure to have more than one candidate for the good. Obviously it is no relief to escape from the horn of relativity only to be impaled on the horn of an ambiguous objectivity.[34]

It but remains to deal with those who jump from the uniqueness of consummatory educational values to the conclusion that consummatory values are all of equal worth. In evaluating courses for college admission, for instance, they claim that every subject is of equal value with every other one if pursued for an equal length of time under equally competent instruction. Now there is no doubt that each school subject has its own unique consummatory value which it alone satisfies. If a student is interested in the past, then history is the one and only study which will satisfy that interest. Neither physics nor mathematics nor any other nonhistorical study can do it. Similarly, if one desires to study the atom, physics and mathematics and not history are the uniquely valuable subject matters. One can-

---

[34] Harry Broudy, "Implications of Classical Realism for Philosophy of Education," *Proceedings of the Association for Realistic Philosophy*, 1949, pp. 13–14.

not transpose history and physics or mathematics and history. But these subjects are not therefore equal. They are rather incommensurable. If they are incommensurable, then they are neither equal with each other nor greater nor less than each other.

AESTHETIC DIMENSION OF THE CURRICULUM

The true and the good have well-established positions in the curriculum. The beautiful has been much less secure. As the arts occupy the leisure part of life so, Herbert Spencer said, they must occupy the leisure part of education. For many, ever since, the arts have been a frill, an icing on the curriculum. This position seems to be justified by the further assertion that the arts are noncognitive, nonverifiable—another case of *de gustibus non disputandum est*. Since the arts are affective and education on the whole is intellective, it seems that the arts quite justifiably hold a peripheral position in the curriculum. Even where the arts have been seen as useful in problem solving—as where novels are read to understand social problems—they nonetheless enjoy only an ancillary position and consequently tend to languish where they are.

More recently, however, the assumptions which underly the foregoing conclusions have been challenged. Adherents of the arts claim that an aesthetic component in the curriculum is quite capable of enriching aims, making them better understood, and increasing the potentiality of deliberately choosing them. Such people consider it not at all impossible to develop connoisseurs in setting up intellectual standards to adjudicate questions of taste. Indeed, they regard no class of subjects as exclusively aesthetic. On the contrary, questions of aesthetics are intricately intertwined with cognitive, ethical, and moral ones. The arts, therefore, have a well-deserved place in the curriculum because they are the chief agencies for enhancing appreciation and fixing standards of later experience.[35]

We may define the aesthetic component in the curriculum by noting that even though a subject has instrumental value, there is also a sense in which it is satisfying on its own account. Thus one may master fundamental operations in arithmetic preparatory to their use in commerce or industry, but it is quite possible to enjoy the process, itself, without ever a thought of its use. In addition, a subject has aesthetic quality if its study is marked by arousal of an affective state in the learner. It is this emotional state which enhances and intensifies appreciation of the learning

[35] Donald Arnstine, "Shaping the Emotions: The Sources of Standards for Aesthetic Education," *School Review*, 72:241–271, Autumn, 1964.

experience. This result is achieved by pointing up its unity and coherence, its closure and culmination.

There is a tendency in education to limit aesthetic values to a restricted range of subject matter in the school, notably the fine arts of music, dancing, painting, modeling, and perhaps literature, especially poetry. Yet there are a number of educators who think this much too narrow a range.[36] They think that pupils can have intensified appreciation of geography and shopwork just as well as of music and drawing, that pupils can enjoy beauty in mathematics as well as in poetry. They would regard all the arts as offering fulfillment to young people's aesthetic yearnings, the useful arts along with the fine ones. When the young actually perceive the possibility of intensified values in the arts, it is nothing short of extraordinary what tasks they will lay on themselves in order to achieve the enhanced values of perfected performance. In this sense the aesthetic emphasis on schoolwork is not a luxury but an emphatic expression and final embodiment of what makes education important and valuable.[37]

To cultivate a more intense appreciation of the subject matters or arts included in the school curriculum is no easy matter. The instructor cannot simply assign values and tell his students to appreciate them, much less to appreciate them deeply. There seems to be general agreement that the approach to this problem has both emotional and intellectual components. If there is difference of opinion, it is on the amount of each of these ingredients.[38] Some seem to think that the appreciative or creative mood is dominated by an inward orientation; it is propelled by an inner desire to objectify one's emotional mood. Of course there must be intellectual guidance, but yet that can be effective only when surcharged with emotion. Others, recognizing the importance of emotion in enhanced appreciation, nevertheless put more stress on the intellectual, problem-solving aspect of aesthetic creation and aesthetic appreciation. Perhaps the balance of these forces is different for different individuals.

In any event the educator will do well not to confuse aesthetic values with other kinds of value in the curriculum. Studies are capable of aesthetic enjoyment quite apart from the support or criticism they afford of existing

---

[36] John Dewey, *Democracy and Education* (The Macmillan Company, New York, 1916), pp. 278, 281; John Dewey, "Appreciation and Cultivation," *Harvard Teachers Record*, 1:73, April, 1931.

[37] Alfred N. Whitehead, *The Aims of Education* (Williams & Norgate, Ltd., London, 1929), pp. 62–63; Max Black, "Education as Art and Discipline," *Ethics*, 54:290–294, July, 1944.

[38] Harold O. Rugg, *Culture and Education in America* (Harcourt, Brace & World, Inc., New York, 1931), pp. 364–370. See also Herman H. Horne, *Philosophy of Education*, rev. ed., (The Macmillan Company, New York, 1927), pp. 221, 307–310; and Sr. Joseph M. Raby, *A Critical Study of the New Education* (Catholic Education Press, Washington, D.C., 1932), pp. 53–54, 100.

institutions. The fine, industrial, or liberal arts can be intensively prized by pupils quite apart from whether they pull their own weight in the economic boat, whether they make the pupil a more patriotic American, or whether they coincide with Christian morals. Yet while aesthetic values are capable of standing independently on their own feet, nevertheless they should not stand apart from the activities of daily life. On the contrary they should lend a quality of enrichment to every decision that the pupil has to make.[39]

It should not be overlooked that an aesthetic quality can attach to teaching itself.[40] It has its own rhetoric and its own poetics. As teaching is an art, so it is capable of artistic execution. Both student and teacher can take joy in a polished performance. The fact that a performance is polished may well indicate that the teacher has worked his materials over again and again to bring them to a fine point of perfection. Not unlike artists in other fields—music, painting, and drama—the instructor may over the years lavish incredible labors on his art in order to get precisely the results he is looking for. With infinite pains he has trimmed the irrelevant from the course of study, simplified the complex, pointed up the obtuse, and inspired the commonplace.

The great enemy of artistic teaching, of course, is routine. Going over their materials again and again, some teachers, unfortunately, leave a humdrum impression. The line between painstaking preparation which results in perfunctory routine and that which results in artistic elegance may be very thin, but yet it is of the utmost importance. The heart of the distinction, to which the teacher should attend, lies in treating each lesson as the actor treats each performance, no matter how many times repeated, as a unique experience. There are various ways to bring out uniqueness in the familiar. Perhaps the teacher has added to his fund of knowledge since last he taught the lesson; perhaps he has achieved greater insight into his field as a whole; perhaps he has devised a novel nuance of exposition; almost certainly he has a new class to teach, new personalities to introduce to the memorable truths of the past. To rest the success of one's teaching on the perennial values of our lustrous heritage and fail to capitalize on the uniqueness of the moment for teaching them can easily jeopardize artistic results. Not only that, but to teach and never experience the joy of creativity which springs from grasping the significance of the unique is to miss one of the keenest satisfactions won in the course of an educational career.

[39] Kenneth D. Benne, "Art Education as the Development of Human Resources," *Art Education Today*, pp. 1–8, 1948.
[40] Clyde E. Curran, "Artistry in Teaching," *Educational Theory*, 3:134–149, April, 1953. See also Royce W. Van Norman, Jr., "In Search of an Aesthetics of Education," *Educational Theory*, 13:155–160, April, 1963.

SELECTED BIBLIOGRAPHY

Arnstine, Donald: *Philosophy of Education,* (Harper & Row, Publishers, Incorporated, New York, 1967), Chaps. 6–7, 10.

Bandman, Bertram: *The Place of Reason in Education* (Ohio State University Press, Columbus, Ohio, 1967).

Brown, L. M.: *General Philosophy in Education* (McGraw-Hill Book Company, New York, 1966), Chap. 5.

Dewey, John: *Child and Curriculum* (The University of Chicago Press, Chicago, 1902).

Elam, Stanley (ed.): *Education and the Structure of Knowledge* (Rand McNally & Company, Chicago, 1964).

Ford, G. W., and Lawrence Pugno (eds.): *The Structure of Knowledge and the Curriculum* (Rand McNally & Company, Chicago, 1964).

Guzie, Tad W.: *The Analogy of Learning* (Sheed & Ward, Inc., New York, 1960).

John Dewey Society: Third Yearbook, *Democracy and the Curriculum* (Appleton-Century-Crofts, New York, 1939), Chap. 13.

————: Seventh Yearbook, *The Public School and Spiritual Values* (Harper & Row, Publishers, Incorporated, New York, 1944), Chap. 9.

Kilpatrick, William H.: *Remaking the Curriculum* (Newson and Company, New York, 1936), Chaps. 6, 8.

King, Arthur R., and John A. Brownell: *The Curriculum and the Discipline of Knowledge* (John Wiley & Sons, Inc., New York, 1966).

Martin, Oliver: *The Order and Integration of Knowledge* (The University of Michigan Press, Ann Arbor, Mich., 1957).

O'Connor, Daniel J.: *The Philosophy of Education* (Philosophical Library, Inc., New York, 1957), Chap. 3.

Peters, Richard S.: *Ethics and Education* (Scott, Foresman and Company, Chicago, 1967), Chap. 4.

Phenix, Philip: *Realms of Meaning* (McGraw-Hill Book Company, New York, 1964).

Scheffler, Israel: *Conditions of Knowledge* (Scott, Foresman and Company, Chicago, 1965), Chap. 2.

Smith, B. Othanel, and Robert H. Ennis (eds.): *Language and Concepts in Education* (Rand McNally & Company, Chicago, 1961), Chaps. 2–4.

CHAPTER NINE

Religious Education

So far we have discussed the philosophical principles underlying education as if they were the same for all subjects in the curriculum. We have assumed that theories of knowledge and value were the same whether the teacher was teaching science, history, or geography. We have taken for granted that principles of selection and organization of the curriculum would hold irrespective of whether the teacher was teaching grammar or mathematics. The question now arises whether we can continue to hold this point of view as we pass from secular to religious and moral education. Will principles of educational philosophy worked out for a secular and profane curriculum hold equally for a religious and moral one?

Let us concentrate first on religious education. If the same philosophy of education were to hold for religious instruction as for secular instruction, for the Sunday school as well as for the weekday school, there would be no need for this further exposition. As a matter of fact, however, there is a sharp difference of opinion on this very point. While some educators make no change in their philosophical habits of mind as they pass from secular to religious education or in the reverse direction, other educators, particularly among some sections of the clergy, find it necessary to make clear distinction between these two fields. Since they insist on making a distinction, it will be necessary now to examine their position and compare it with what has preceded.[1]

Anyone will recognize at the outset that the area of religion offers a peculiarly fertile field to stimulate the growth of diverse theories of truth, reality, and value. Certainly secular subjects like the three R's would fall far behind in proliferating the philosophic subtleties of which religion and morals are capable. Yet, in undertaking this exposition of the philosophy of religious education, we must constantly remember that our primary concern is not with these philosophic subtleties as such but with their educational implications.[2]

---

[1] William H. Kilpatrick, "Religion in Education: The Issues," *Progressive Education*, 26:96–102, February, 1949.

[2] It will not be possible to note the educational philosophy of each religious sect. For some of this detail, see George A. Coe, *A Social Theory of Religious Education* (Charles Scribner's Sons, New York, 1917), Chaps. 20–24; P. H. Lotz and L. W. Crawford, *Studies in Religious Education* (Abingdon Press, Nashville, Tenn., 1931), Chaps. 20–22; William C. Bower, "The Church as Educator," *Religious Education*, 22:368–416, April, 1927; Lewis G. James, "Religious Instruction in State Schools: An Agnostic View," *Educational Review*, 4:117–128, September, 1892; and William W. Brickman, "Education for Eternal Existence: The Philosophy of Jewish Education," *School and Society*, 57:554–560, May, 1943.

Concrete evidence of educational difficulties, only hinted at so far, lie about on every hand. Most obvious, perhaps, is the fact that the secular public school offers no direct instruction in religion. As everyone knows, this glaring omission has resulted from an inability of the friends of religion to compose their differences sufficiently to agree on either a prescribed or an elective course of study in religion. In spite of this exclusion the public school continues to be solicitous over the moral education of its charges. If it does not teach morals directly, it does give much attention to teaching them indirectly and incidentally. Yet even so, a sharp difference of opinion arises as to whether morals can be satisfactorily taught apart from religion. Those who think it cannot and who want religion taught over and beyond morals are forced to provide religious and moral instruction privately either in the home, at the church, or in a private or parochial school. And even among this select group marked differences of opinion remain on the nature of religion. As with different theories in politics and economics, different theories of religion lead to distinctly different educational practices. Some think of religion in broad humanistic terms, while others can understand it only in terms of the supernatural. The one group motivates children to be moral because it leads to more satisfactory social adjustments. The other group enjoins the moral life on its children because the moral law is the will of God, to whom all mankind owes strict obedience.

SECULARISM

Perhaps the whole problem of the philosophy of religious education will stand out most clearly if silhouetted not against just a philosophy of secular education but against a philosophy of education which limits itself to secularism, which even exalts secularism as an all-inclusive view of life. There is no gainsaying the fact that the omission of religion from the curriculum of the public school has encouraged or at least coincided with the rise of a strongly secular temper of mind. Unreminded of religious ties, many people have learned to get along with few or no religious observances at all. In fact, when their attention is called to religion, they are inclined to turn deliberately away from it. They seem to regard their children as well adjusted when they have learned to meet the principal social and scientific demands of the everyday world about them.

In confining his attention to the world here and now the secularist frankly admits and boldly faces the fact that his continued adjustment is contingent on an uncertain and precarious future. However, though he is as anxious as the religious person for security, he is inclined to seek it, not in the worship of supernatural or what he gravely suspects are superstitious powers, but in obedience to natural law. Instead of bringing up his children in liturgical exercises, he instructs them in scientific method. Concerning any meaning of the world beyond what the natural and social sciences reveal, he is agnostic or at least holds himself in a state of suspended judgment. If the secularist has any religion at all, it is likely that scientific doctrines constitute the presuppositions of that religion and that scientists are its high priests. Moreover, democracy, if it is to give full scope to its emphasis on the common man, demands a secular religion and morals which rest on the self-sufficiency of man's own natural powers to direct his own destiny.[3]

The fact that the secularist confines himself to the world of natural forces should not mislead anyone into thinking that the secularist does not believe the school should dispense spiritual values. Far from it. As a matter of fact he is quite convinced that the school is and should be deeply spiritual. In addition to teaching respect for, and emotional attachment to, scientific methods he would, among other spiritual values, have high regard for teaching loyalty to academic freedom and its cousin, civil liberty, for recognizing the dignity of utilitarian occupations in the school's curriculum, and for placing ultimate confidence in the ability of man to be captain of his social destiny. Indeed he feels that such a secular approach to spiritual values is peculiarly akin to the spiritual values represented by democracy. If democracy stands for the essential dignity and equality of man, whatever his race, sex, or cultural origin, and for government by the free consent of the governed, then all should have equal access to spiritual values. Since the churches are in disagreement on their own values, the only spiritual values which the public school, democracy's principal educational agency, can bring within reach of all are secular views.[4] This is not a total loss for religion for, it has been said, the public schools are performing an infinitely significant religious work in bringing together children of diverse racial, national, and creedal backgrounds and, in promoting their assimilation into some sort of social unity, they are laying the basis on which any ultimate brotherhood of man must rest.[5]

[3] Boyd H. Bode, "Religion and the Public Schools," School and Society, 67:225–229, March, 1948. Directly criticizing this view is S. Raymond, "The Principles of Pragmatism and the Teaching of Religion in the Public School," Catholic Educational Review, 47:365–379, June, 1949. More recently, see Harvey Cox, "Secularization and the Secular Mentality: A New Challenge to Christian Education," Religious Education, 61:83–87, March–April, 1966. The rest of this issue is devoted to critiques of Cox's thesis and a final rejoinder by him.
[4] For an attempt to state values held in common by all religions but letting each sect supply its own supporting reasons for them, see William C. Trow, "A Valuistic Approach to Religious Education," Religious Education, 43:169–174, May–June, 1948.
[5] John Dewey, "Religion and Our Schools," Hibbert Journal, 6:806–807, July, 1908. For some of the impact of Vatican II, see Randolph C. Miller, "The Challenge of the Ecumenical Movement to Church Education," Religious Education, 61:369–376, September–October, 1966.

If the secular public school can hold forth such promise of religious unity, it may not be beyond imagination that education itself has some characteristics of a secular religion.[6] In religion's long history many things have been declared to be God. At a time when race, nationality, and the state have each been raised up as objects of worship, one could certainly do worse than to make education a religion. The fundamental principle of faith of such a religion would be belief in the possibility of human achievement. Education would then become at once the symbol of humanity's as yet unrealized potentialities and the means of its salvation. Such a religion, however, would have the drawback of the political religions already mentioned. It would be only fragmentary; it would be worshiping the part for the whole. This might be a misdirection of religious endeavor if religion be taken, as it generally is, to denote inclusiveness of viewpoint. On the other hand, at least one outstanding advantage could be claimed for such a religion. It would not be in conflict with science. On the contrary, it would be based on science. Without the invigorating vitality of science, such a religion would be in danger of lapsing into the dogmas of pedagogy and the rituals of educational administration. At all events, in view of man's innumerable previous mistakes and discouraging backslidings, it takes courage, if nothing else, to hold to a faith in education as a religion.

HUMANISTIC RELIGIOUS EDUCATION

Many teachers, though profoundly influenced by a philosophy of the secular or profane branches of education, would be quite unwilling to erect secularism into a philosophy of life or, what is more to the point here, a philosophy of religious education. They go a long way with the secular point of view in secular education, but they do not stop there; they do not say that secularism is all there is, that it is the whole story. To them, religious education builds on the base of secular education, but it adds a certain "plus." While science has enabled them to see that this "plus" no longer consists of demons, witches, sorcery, or magic, they nonetheless still find that scientific progress has made the world more rather than less mysterious. The "why" of life is still the top mystery question for them. Consequently they do not shrink from speculating on a meaning of life and education which lies beyond purely secular explanations.

For most educators this quest for "plus" values beyond secularism centers in some conception of God. In giving further direction to this quest, the question immediately arises, does God lie beyond human experience?

---

6 John Dewey, "Education as a Religion," *New Republic*, 32:64–65, August, 1922.

Does He transcend it? Or is God to be found within human experience? Is He immanent? Both ways seem beset with difficulties. If God is transcendent, then how is the child to learn about Him, how is he to communicate with Him through prayer and worship and have fellowship with Him? If God is immanent in human experience, then how is religious education to be distinguished from mere ethical education, indeed, from a secularist point of view?[7] In either event the "plus" values of religious education stem from something more than the fact that it is given on a separate day of the week, Sunday, or that it is based on a unique book, the Bible.[8]

The humanistic religious educator is inclined to make his approach to God through the agency of human experience. A firm believer in God, he tests his knowledge and understanding of Him by his own experiences of Him. While formerly men recognized only a narrow range of experience as constituting God's revelation of Himself, the humanist has now quite enlarged the scope of such experience. Formerly finding God only through mystical visions and reading of His holy scriptures, the humanist now makes His acquaintance through science[9] and social relationships[10] as well. Indeed, so confident is he now of his newer resources of knowledge that he is frequently skeptical of any knowledge based on a faith which leaps beyond the evidence of human experience.[11] Furthermore, he regards the church as a community and religious education as participation therein. Since he believes that the community having the highest regard for human personality is the democratic one, he believes that the rising generation should learn to think of the Christian community in modern democratic rather than in traditional monarchistic terms.[12] They may still learn to pray "Thy kingdom come," but the content of contemporary social experience will lead them to think of God more as a kind father and loving guide than as an austere lord and forbidding monarch.

The educational corollaries of the humanist's conception of God and religion are not far to seek. Clearly the humanist believes in a social theory of religious education. Learning the two great commandments—to love

---

[7] Nevin C. Harner, "Three Ways to Think of God," *Religious Education*, 34:216–221, October–December, 1939. Cf. Luther A. Weigle, "What Makes Education Religious?" *Religious Education*, 18:90–92, April, 1923.

[8] George Betts, "What Makes Education Religious?" *Religious Education*, 18:84–87, April, 1923.

[9] William C. Bower, "The Significance for Religious Education of Trends in the Psychology of Religion," *Religious Education*, 23:7–19, January, 1928.

[10] Edward S. Ames, "Can Religion Be Taught?" *Religious Education*, 25:42–50, January, 1930.

[11] Albert M. Carmichael, "Are Church and Public School Indispensable for Character Education?" *Religious Education*, 27:408–412, May, 1932; and I. A. Morton, "Religious Motive in Education," *Religious Education*, 40:23–26, January–February, 1945.

[12] Cf. John P. Williams, "The Schoolman and Religion," *School and Society*, 70:97–100, August, 1949.

God and to love one's neighbor—turns out to be pretty much one and the same thing. Both are learned not so much directly as incidentally to a social situation.[13] To learn these two commandments of religion, the humanist depends more on education than on evangelism, more on human than on divine initiative.

Placing dependence on human initiative and human experience happily coincides with the tendency of the progressive philosophy of education to emphasize the importance of pupil activity in learning. But it is significant that this dependence of the humanist on experience runs well beyond its usefulness as an improved method of instruction. As a matter of fact, this dependence on experience affords a critique of religion itself. A youth not only comes to a religious understanding of God through experience, but he constantly reconstructs his notions about God and religion in the light of the consequences of this experience. In other words, to teach and to learn religion is a creative experience.[14]

To trust human experience this far indicates that the humanistic educator's tests of religious and secular truth differ little if at all. Indeed, he is inclined to regard the division of the curriculum into sacred and secular truth as a grave misfortune since it distracts attention from the religious character of much of the secular curriculum. Properly conceived, he would argue, all education has religious overtones and implications. Since religion is nothing if it is not an all-inclusive, all-commanding attitude, it follows that religious education is simply education in the most complete sense of the term. On this account, the humanistic religious educator claims that progressive education with its emphasis on the "whole" child and on learning by "wholes" has much that is implicitly if not intentionally religious in emphasis.

At this point, a possibly suppressed question may come to the surface. Is the humanist's confidence in man and his experience warranted? Is human nature sound and strong enough to carry the educational burden the humanist places on it? Is it not unbridled pride and an abysmal want of humility on the part of man to assume that God is what pupil and teacher creatively learn that He is? Does not their anthropomorphism cause them to forget that it is God who made them and not they themselves? To all these questions the humanistic religious educator has but one answer, and that is that the only approach he has to religion is through human experience. Until something more dependable than human experience ap-

---

[13] Victor E. Marriott, "New Flowers of the Spirit," *Religious Education*, 24:250–262, March, 1929.
[14] Cf. *infra*, p. 267. See also Martin Buber, *Between Man and Man* (Routledge & Kegan Paul, Ltd., London, 1947), Chap. 3.

pears, it would be folly for religious education to depreciate it, much less discard it.

THEOLOGY OF EDUCATION

Humanistic religious education is a step beyond secularism but is still short of what many think religion properly demands of education. They suspect that the failure of humanism to go further is due to the fact that humanism is infected with the virus of secularism. The dependence of humanism on human experience and its reluctance to distinguish between secular and sacred truth in the curriculum confirm their suspicion. To them religion is nothing if its object, God, does not transcend human experience. Religious education is inadequate for them if it does not involve a theology of education over and above a philosophy of education.[15] Whether they start from the historical authenticity of the Judeo-Christian tradition or permit themselves to speculate freely, they found their religious conceptions on a supernatural, personal God, who is not only author and sustainer of the universe but its supreme lawgiver as well.

Author of the universe, God is naturally Father of mankind. In view of such august lineage, it becomes man to order himself lowly and humbly before his God and Maker. If he does, he will hardly be inclined to put too great reliance on the powers of human experience to penetrate the mysteries of religious truth. Born with only natural gifts of mind and these weakened by the loss of such added gifts of understanding as Adam may have had and lost through his disobedience, man is desperately in need of divine assistance and guidance in his religious education.[16] Without God as Redeemer as well as Creator of mankind, man's educational plight is not a happy one. To forget this fact, to think that man by his human experience can possess himself of the divine content of religion, is a pretension which leads to a false and misleading pedagogical naturalism.[17]

In his educational thinking, therefore, the theologian-educator starts, not with autonomous man, but with divine thought about man. To see what this may mean, take the educational principle that man should grow and develop according to the laws of his own being.[18] The question may

---

[15] Elmer G. Homrighausen, "The Real Problem of Religious Education," *Religious Education,* 34:10–17, January–March, 1939. See also Will Herberg, "Toward a Theology of Education," *Christian Scholar,* 36:259–272, December, 1953, and Paul Van Buren, "Christian Education *Post Mortem Dei*," *Religious Education,* 60:4–10, January–February, 1965.

[16] Thomas E. Shields, "Principles in the Teaching of Religion," *Catholic Educational Review,* 1:341, April, 1911.

[17] Pius XI, "The Christian Education of Youth," *Catholic Educational Review,* 28:149, March, 1930.

[18] For a further discussion of this aim of education, see *supra,* pp. 103–104.

arise, how do we know what the laws of his being are? Can we determine the nature of human nature by what man thinks about himself? Or must the educator's estimate of man come from beyond man, that is, from God himself? For the theologian it is God, of course, who is the light which, too bright to see, is nonetheless the light by which all else is seen. It is necessary, therefore, to supplement the child's natural reason with divine revelation. In dealing with such dazzling and unimpeachable truth as revelation, it will not be surprising if an infallible church claims to be the principal sponsor of education.[19] Backed by such unerring sponsorship, the teacher's method can well afford to be dogmatic and authoritarian.

Exalted as revealed truths are, there is no intent that they should supplant secular ones. To be sure, sacred truth is distinct from secular, but the two are to be taught concurrently in the same curriculum. Yet one may wonder how supernatural truths like beatification are to be taught in a mundane classroom. Several quite mundane ways are possible. The teacher can inform the student about revealed truths, hold them up to him as a motive for his conduct, explain to him the imperative need for attaining them, and last, but not least, show him by example how to deserve them.

It is the theologian's view of religion which, much more than the humanist's, introduces educational implications not hitherto met in a philosophy of secular education. Before following out these implications in greater detail, however, it may be well to pause briefly to compare the theological and humanistic approaches to religious education. The theological approach seems based on a political analogy, while the humanistic seems based on a biological one.[20] The former expresses itself in terms of the sovereignty of God, while the latter expresses itself in terms of growth and interaction of organisms. If God is sovereign and mankind perversely rebels against His law, the courts of heaven must mete out punishment just as in any case where a subject disobeys his king. This punishment can be mitigated only if a Savior can be found to intercede on behalf of mankind and redeem it. Reverting to the more naturalistic biological analogy, the humanist is not so likely to regard deviations from the law as rebellion but as the natural outcome of encouraging initiative and responsibility in the development of individuality. From this angle the role of Jesus is not so much that of Savior and Redeemer as peerless teacher and reformer. Finally, the theologian-educator stands in need of an unequivocal guide to determine God's law or will. Some supernaturalists find this in the church as a divinely appointed teaching agency, others in the Bible as a divinely

---

[19] For a further discussion of this point, see *supra*, pp. 85–86.
[20] Stuart G. Cole, "Where Religious Education and Theology Meet," *Religious Education*, 35:18–25, January–March, 1940.

inspired text for the curriculum. Humanists, on the other hand, while they highly esteem church and Bible, recognize no social agency and no book that can hold univocal command over the approaches to religious education.

FALLEN AND SUPERNATURAL NATURE

Reference has just been made to man's perversity. What educational account shall we give this trait? Some theologians think perversity is due to a moral handicap which man suffers in his nature. Humanists and secularists are more likely to regard human deviation not as a handicap but as the positive promise of growth which immaturity holds forth. Which view should we take? Is human nature essentially good or essentially bad? This is an age-old question and as important for the teacher to answer as for the clergyman. If the child is active by nature and if learning, therefore, is a process of self-activity, then, if in addition human nature is essentially good, the teacher must regard the child's native tendencies as essentially good. He will have to make the aims of education a projection of these tendencies and select the curriculum as a means of releasing and promoting them. In his method the teacher will have to pay due respect to the pupil's freedom for fear of impairing the goodness of nature manifested in his originality.

If, one the contrary, the teacher detects shortcomings and perversities in human nature, then his educational procedures will take on a different complexion. He will aim to teach the child to like the good things he ought to like, not merely to follow the aims toward which his propensities incline him. He will select the curriculum from the great treasure-trove of the race, not just in terms of the individual's personal proclivities. In his method he will be glad to utilize the learner's native drives to accomplish the school's task, but he will not hesitate to run counter to those drives in order to arrive at his chosen objective.

What are the reasons, now, for choosing either of these views of human nature and the educational practices predicated on it? The traditional Christian line takes a rather dim view of human nature; it holds to the familiar doctrine of original sin. This doctrine has been variously expounded, but since it is the Catholics who give it principal place in their educational philosophy, it is the Catholic view which will receive major consideration here.[21] According to this view, when God created Adam, He endowed him with a human nature to which He added for good measure a supernature as well. When Adam sinned by rebelling against God in the

[21] C. Vollert, "Original Sin and Education," *Review for Religious*, 5:217–228, July, 1946.

Garden of Eden, God punished him by depriving him of the benefits of this supernature. The effect of Adam's fall from grace was not, as is often thought, to wound human nature. On the contrary, it left human nature with its powers of will and intellect just as they had been originally constituted. In other words, Adam's descendants, the children in school today, are no worse off in regard to their strictly human nature than they would have been had God never vested Adam with a supernature.

The respect in which contemporary man is worse off, however, is in the loss of the supernature which Adam forfeited. Now what were the added gifts of this supernature? They were notably two, the gift of integrity, whereby all man's faculties were perfectly subordinated to his reason and will, and the gift of immortality, whereby man's body was subjected to his soul, so that it was freed from falling into corruption and death. It is in respect to the loss of these priceless gifts, then, that human nature is worse off today as a result of original sin than it would have been had Adam freely chosen to obey God's commandment. Any darkening of understanding or weakening of will as a result of original sin, therefore, is a deterioration, not from human nature, but from the state of perfect justice in Eden when Adam possessed the attributes of supernature as well as of human nature.

The educational damage of Adam's sinful act is almost incalculable. His descendants in the modern classroom will certainly not thank him for the immeasurably more difficult task he has made of acquiring an education. Thus if their first ancestor had not sinned, he would have passed on to them his special gift of infused knowledge. Through this they might have had minds equipped with a unique aptitude for higher truths. Furthermore, if they now possessed the supernatural gift of integrity—having all their faculties perfectly subordinated to will and intellect—they would not suffer the distractions from their studies provided by unruly appetites, bodies lacking robust health, or the need to spend most of their daylight hours chained to toil to care for their bodily needs at the expense of time that might otherwise be spent on spiritual development.

If one subscribes to a Calvinistic view of human nature, the situation is even worse. According to Calvin, human nature was not just deprived of the special gifts of supernature, but it became depraved as a result of the expulsion from Eden. Scholasticism teaches that human nature though fallen can rise again; it can learn and be redeemed. But Calvinism maintains that human nature is so cast down that it cannot lift itself up again without divine aid. It is, furthermore, predestined to iniquity or salvation so that education can affect the final outcome little if at all.

In contrast to the Scholastic and Calvinistic views of human nature is that of Rousseau. According to Rousseau, human nature as it came from the hands of its Maker was essentially good. To be sure, it was immature and had weaknesses that needed correcting through education, but even so the material the parent and teacher had to work with was basically good. Consequently Rousseau and his followers have been optimistic about the possibilities of education, not pessimistic like Calvin. As one may infer, Scholastics also are optimistic about the possibilities of education, but Rousseau in the eighteenth century and the more romantic progressive educators of the twentieth century have been even more so. The optimism of the Scholastic labors under the heavy burden of original sin. The optimism of the progressive educators is not so weighted down. They reject the doctrine of original sin, that man once had a superior nature which he is trying to regain through education. On the contrary, they take the view that his human nature is the only nature he has. Taking this basically sound capital free from Adam's debts, they naturally enjoy a more buoyant optimism as they boldly build the school of the future.

With the rise of modern studies like sociology and anthropology, still another approach to the moral quality of human nature has recommended itself to some educators. This is the view that original nature is neither good nor bad. The moral quality of original tendencies of human nature is not resident in the impulse to act but rather in the manner in which it reaches fulfillment, the consequences it entails in its environment, particularly its social environment. Following this theory, the educator cannot take human nature as a blueprint for his instructional plans as some more romantic progressives have done. Instead, human nature will be seen to have both strengths and weaknesses, but just which they are will depend on the environmental context or field of forces.

SIN, REGENERATION, AND GRACE

These three terms as well as any, perhaps, illustrate the salient differences which theology introduces into a philosophy of education. They describe the principal facets of learning, where the curriculum is religious rather than secular.[22] The need for changing the terms in which one describes learning when the curriculum shifts from secular to religious materials grows out of the theologian's conception of man and his relation to God. Since human nature still suffers from the punishment visited on Adam as a result of his defiance of God's command, the question initially

---

[22] For a statement of secular theories of learning, see *infra*, pp. 221–226. See also Rachel Henderlite, "Toward a Learning Theory for Ecumenical Education," *Religious Education*, 61:386–393, September–October, 1966.

arises whether there is anything that can be done to improve the disposition of human nature to learn what is necessary for its salvation.

The first step to be taken in this direction is the religious rite of baptism. The purpose of this sacrament is to repair the damage done to human nature by the head of the human line, its first progenitor, Adam. Neither parent nor teacher, however, should confuse the sacrament of baptism with the process of education or think that the consummation of this sacrament renders further education unnecessary. Baptism does not completely purge human nature of its weaknesses; it merely marks a point at which a new effort begins. There will still be a lifelong struggle between the child's good and bad inclinations, for which he will need every resource which divine authority and the wisdom of the race can supply him. Obviously the secularist would put baptism in the garret as outworn hocus-pocus; but for the theologian who accepts Holy Writ as his guide, it is an indispensable aspect of religious education.

At best, as indicated, baptism merely disposes human nature to the right educational influences. As an act of free will[23] the child may still choose to turn his back on the road to his salvation. He may still sin and sin repeatedly. Now what is the educational nature of sin? Is it essentially different from error, its counterpart in secular educational theory? Error is generally the outgrowth of ignorance. The secular educator assumes, like Socrates, that if the child had known better he would not have erred. To know better in this instance, moreover, means more than intellectually cognizing the better; it means impelling the better to issue forth in motor conduct. If it does not, then more learning is still in order. Is sin any different? It seems so. It seems that when the child sins, he knows better but does the worse. Knowing and doing, intellect and will, are set over against each other. If man's will remains insubordinate to his intellect or reason, he will have to do penance.[24]

When child or adult is committed to the life of sin, how does he break away from it? How does he find his way to the straight and narrow path? If the religious educator follows the Bible—and the theologian generally does—he will hold it necessary for the wayward one to undergo a certain regeneration. As Jesus said to Nicodemus, we must be born again if we expect to be admitted to the kingdom of God in good standing. Naturally the Christian conception of regeneration here is not a physical rebirth but

---

[23] For extended discussion of this concept, see supra, pp. 123–128.

[24] For a psychiatric redefinition of sin as social maladaptation, see Anton T. Boisen, "Religious Education and Human Nature," Religious Education, 35:13–18, January–March, 1940. For a further clarification of religious terms in education, see Randolph C. Miller, "Linguistic Models for Religious Education," Religious Education, 61:269–278, July–August, 1966.

a spiritual one. But how does spiritual reorientation come about? Does a person learn it as in secular education he might learn to adopt a new political train of thought? Or is spiritual rebirth in a class by itself?

Some, especially those who take an evangelical point of view, seem to look upon regeneration as a unique experience. They think it the function of the Sunday school, for instance, first to lead the offspring of Adam to religion and *then* to train them in their new way of life.[25] Education appears to be something which follows regeneration but is not involved in it. Perhaps a more familiar term for the about-face wrought in individuals by regeneration is conversion. We frequently speak of a person as being converted to religion or from one religious sect to another. But the same question still arises: Is conversion an educational experience or something other? Again, most people regard it as something other. Conversion seems to be associated with mystical flashes of insight. The experience of St. Paul on the road to Damascus sets the pattern. The core of this experience is obviously mystical rather than educational.

It needs pointing out that some religious educators have come to regard regeneration and conversion as in no way different from conventional or secular descriptions of the learning process. Becoming convinced of the worthwhileness of the religious point of view for them is composed of not one but many turning points. Thus there will be many decisions for the child to make as the countless situations of life roll up. It is even possible that one of these decisions may overtop and influence all the rest as *the* decision. But what appears to be an instantaneous conversion, a mystical rebirth, they would prefer to interpret as the accumulated effect of prior, if perhaps submerged and unnoted, decisions. Learning to dedicate one's life to God's way becomes a matter of process rather than crisis. With this comes the full realization that it takes duration rather than just an instant of time to build stable religious character.

The mysticism already mentioned has also led to another type of learning experience, which may distinguish religious instruction from that in lay subjects.[26] This is learning through worship. The theory underlying this sort of learning is that, by putting the learner in an attitude of contemplation in a fitting environment, the windows of his soul will be opened to divine truths which otherwise he might never learn to know. Public religious worship may even have the effect of creating a spiritual bond in the school and community of considerable social significance. Learning, in such instances, is peculiarly direct, intuitive, aesthetic. As a type, however,

25 George A. Coe, *op. cit.*, p. 310. Cf. Elmer O. Homrighausen, "Christian Theology and Christian Education," *Religious Education*, 44:360–362, November–December, 1949.
26 For a further discussion of mysticism in learning, see *infra*, pp. 229–230.

it is not altogether unlike the approach to art and music in the lay curriculum.

Furthermore, there seems to be definite objection to any theory that religious experience comes by way of an inner illumination, independent from the ordinary channels of learning. The prime difficulty with this theory is that it may render religion incapable of being taught to some people. According to such a pattern, there may be emotionally stolid people, who can no more sense a religious experience than color-blind people can recognize color, or tone-deaf ones, music. It seems preferable to many, therefore, to state the curriculum in psychological terms, that is, as a mode of child experience and growth, for only so can its significance for religious conduct be realized.

Of course, not every wayward child or adult finds his way to the straight and narrow path or stays on it when he has found it. Not everyone is converted; not everyone sees the need for reorienting his life. Why are some more fortunate than others in coming on a reorienting or regenerating experience, such as being blessed with an understanding parent, studying under a sympathetic teacher, playing for a great coach, or reading an inspiring book at just the right time? In part, it is a matter of God's grace, as the theologian would put it. Changes in a person's life are not always the result of his own efforts. There is also a divine initiative operating on occasion. As St. Paul wrote to the Ephesians, "By grace are ye saved through faith; and that not of yourselves: it is the gift of God."[27] The secularist, too, recognizes that education occurs under contingent and precarious circumstances.[28] Sometimes these circumstances hinder the education of the young, and sometimes they further it. But, like "breaks of the game" in sports, they seem to defy planned anticipation. The theologian, however, is unwilling to view these unusual circumstances as merely chance affairs. Where an omniscient and omnipotent deity rules the universe, it is unlikely that anything happens by chance. Hence God's grace is not, as some Christians seem to have thought, like the wind which "bloweth where it listeth, and thou hearest the sound thereof, but canst not tell whence it cometh and whither it goeth."[29] While it is a gift to which man has no right, it does not altogether baffle expectation. Man can put himself in the way of grace by participation in the sacraments and thus, as we have already noted in the discussion of baptism, improve his educational prospects. Conversely, education, if properly directed, can be an excellent

[27] Ephesians 2:8:
[28] *Supra*, pp. 142–143. Cf. Gerald Kreyche, "The Impact of Existentialism on Christian Thought," *Religious Education*, 60:423–426, November–December, 1965.
[29] John 3:8.

preparation for receiving grace should it come the student's way. But grace, though it may be offered, will in no way coerce the student's will.

SELECTED BIBLIOGRAPHY

American Catholic Philosophical Association: *Proceedings of the Western Division: The Philosophy of Christian Education*, 1941, pp. 63–73.

Bower, William C.: *The Curriculum of Religious Education* (Charles Scribner's Sons, New York, 1925), Chaps. 14, 15.

Brunner, Emil: *The Divine Imperative* (Lutterworth Press, London, 1937), Chap. 41.

Coe, George A.: *A Social Theory of Religious Education* (Charles Scribner's Sons, New York, 1918).

————: *What Is Christian Education?* (Charles Scribner's Sons, New York, 1930).

Donlan, Thomas C.: *Theology and Education* (William C. Brown Co., DuBuque, 1952).

Elliott, Harrison S.: *Can Religious Education Be Christian?* (The Macmillan Company, New York, 1940).

Fitzpatrick, Edward C.: *Exploring a Theology of Education* (The Bruce Publishing Company, Milwaukee, 1950).

Maritain, Jacques: "Some Typical Aspects of Christian Education," in Donald Gallagher and Idella Gallagher (eds.), *The Education of Man* (Doubleday & Company, Inc., Garden City, N.Y., 1962), Chap. 6.

Mueller, Gustav E.: *Education Limited* (University of Oklahoma Press, Norman, Okla., 1949), Chaps. 5, 7.

Rugh, Charles E.: *The Essential Place of Religion in Education*, National Education Association Monograph, 1916.

Soares, Theodore G.: *Religious Education* (The University of Chicago Press, Chicago, 1928).

"Theological Foundations of the Christian College," *Christian Scholar*, 41:273–285, Autumn, 1958.

Van Grueningen, John P.: *Toward a Christian Philosophy of Higher Education* (The Westminster Press, Philadelphia, 1957), Chaps. 2–3.

CHAPTER TEN

Moral Education

The clash of secular and religious influences already noted immediately above is also to be found in the philosophy of moral education. Some assign a relatively narrow scope to moral education. For them it involves chiefly such questions as honesty, loyalty, courage, sex purity, and the like. Others see moral issues in a wider range of educational happenings. It has already been implied in such issues as posed by the discussion of freedom in education. Whether we are free or determined in the choice of educational aims has obvious moral undertones.[1] Even if we are free, the question remains—and a moral one at that—whether the adult community should exercise liberty or constraint in inviting the younger generation to aid in deciding their educational objectives. Again, the effective exercise of freedom necessitates school rules and the submission to their discipline. Maintenance of discipline has been a moral problem since time immemorial. Important as are the moral issues at these and similar levels, we must press even deeper to inquire into the nature of the moral enterprise itself. With Socrates we must still fundamentally inquire, "Can virtue be taught?" If so, in what sense? How does parent or teacher develop a sense of responsibility? And lastly, how does one motivate a sense of obligation?

FREEDOM AND AUTHORITY

Democracy lays great store by the individual. Inasmuch as this is the case, the teacher's method must so organize the social environment of the school that pupil individuality will have an opportunity to be and express itself. Many definitions of freedom have accrued to the educative process.[2] Their essence, however, seems to simmer down to the conclusion that freedom is a function of individuality.[3] If pupils had no individual differences, there would be no demand for freedom. Everyone would act alike. No one could even want to be different, that is, free. But in identifying freedom with

---

[1] *Supra*, pp. 123–128.
[2] W. J. McCallister, *The Growth of Freedom in Education* (The Richard R. Smith Co., Inc., Peterborough, N.H., 1931), p. 543; Ernest Horn, "Educating for Freedom and Responsibility," *Religious Education*, 25:631, September, 1930.
[3] *Infra*, p. 59.

difference, there is an implied social reference. Children not only differ from one another, but they are sufficiently like one another to be able to live together agreeably. Homogeneity, therefore, is as important as heterogeneity. A sound social group needs both these qualities. But just how much homogeneity and heterogeneity should there be? How much freedom and how much control should there be in the classroom? Obviously, to anyone who stops to think, there is no single answer to this question. Any position is a matter of moral emphasis, based on one's attitude to a multiplicity of other phases of educational philosophy.

However widespread the notion of freedom in democracy—even in fascism and communism—it is often surprising how little it is countenanced toward the young in the classroom. Long-standing tradition rather supports the notion that the child should early learn unquestioning obedience to the authority of the parent or to the teacher *in loco parentis.* Since the mature adult unquestionably knows better what to do than the immature child, implicit trust in the authority of the parent or teacher promises the quickest and most direct route to solid knowledge and sound morals. So confident were our forebears of this pedagogical economy that they claimed it was better for a child to go right in chains than wrong in freedom.

The educators who lean farthest in the opposite direction of pupil freedom in the classroom are the more romantic of the progressive educators. They lean so far in this direction because they regard individual differences among children as fixed features on the face of nature. Worshiping nature in reverend awe, they obdurately defend the freedom of the individual to assert the unique differences which mark his individuality. Consequently they enjoin parents, teachers, and adults generally to adopt a *laissez faire* attitude toward children.[4] Their rule is to keep out of nature's way so that it may fulfill itself according to its own inherent laws.

As the young are often disinclined to restraint, the *laissez faire,* or permissive, attitude is expectably quite welcome to them. Presumably they rejoice in a school or home where they are left to do what they want to do. But this is not always true. One of the standing jibes at progressive education concerns the child who paradoxically asked his teacher, "Do we have to do what we want to do today?" Actually this question is not entirely a joking matter. Resentment at being left to one's own devices often occurs in so-called "nondirective" teaching.[5] A chief purpose of this method is,

---

4 *Supra,* pp. 78–79.
5 Nathaniel Cantor, *The Teaching-Learning Process* (The Dryden Press, Inc., New York, 1953), p. 241. See also Earl C. Kelley and Marie I. Rasey, *Education and the Nature of Man* (Harper & Row, Publishers, Incorporated, New York, 1952). *Contra,* see Fred N. Kerlinger, "The Implications of the Permissiveness Doctrine in American Education," *Educational Theory,* 10:120–127, April, 1960.

paradoxically, to force the student to use his own initiative. Older students, especially, get so accustomed to waiting on the instructor's initiative that they fail to develop any enterprise of their own. By refusing to give initial direction to the lesson the instructor confronts the student with the necessity of exerting his own initiative as the only alternative to boredom. The *laissez faire*, or permissive, attitude, therefore, is not altogether negative; nondirective teaching is its positive variant.

Other educators do not find the moral reason for freedom in a romantic adoration of nature at all. Far from basing freedom on the inherent goodness of child nature, they favor it because of the evil consequences which they observe flowing from its opposite, authoritarianism. Vesting absolute authority in the teacher, they contend, is bad for both the teacher and the pupil. It more than likely will corrupt the teacher into becoming a tyrant, and it will more than likely make children either too rebellious or too submissive. The danger in making them rebellious is that they come to think that opposition to any authority is meritorious, and the danger in making them submissive is that they lose all sense of initiative. Worse yet, constant frustration of the pupil's self-assertiveness may well render him a bully in his own relations with still younger and weaker children and thus perpetuate the vice of tyranny in the next generation of teachers and parents.[6]

There are still other educators who, in rejecting the extravagant claims of a romantic, *laissez faire* conception of freedom, do not at the same time take a hostile view of authority.[7] Instead of looking on freedom and authority as antagonistic to each other, they make a synthesis of them of such a nature that freedom becomes the legitimate offspring of authority. To let a child act without restriction in the classroom as his individuality dictates invites chaos. When chaos reigns there can be no genuine freedom because everybody will be getting in everybody else's way, and the resulting confusion will deprive all but the most powerful of freedom to accomplish anything. To secure moral freedom there must be some rule of law according to which children and adults regulate their conduct and to the authority of which they submit. Genuine freedom, then, must mean freedom to do what the rule of authority states we ought to do, in other words, to do what the law permits.[8] Thus the child learns freedom under the discipline

[6] Bertrand Russell, "Education and Civilization," *The New Statesman and Nation*, 7:667, May, 1934.

[7] William H. Kilpatrick, "Social Factors Influencing Educational Method in 1930," *Journal of Educational Sociology*, 4:485–486, April, 1931; and Frederick S. Breed, "Good-bye Laissez-faire in Education," *Elementary School Journal*, 38:365–372, January, 1938.

[8] Mortimer J. Adler, "Freedom through Discipline," *Vital Speeches*, 10:380–382, April, 1944. Henry W. Wieman, "Purpose and Discipline in Education," *Educational Forum*, 27:279–295, March, 1963. See also Sidney Hook, "Thirteen Arrows against Progressive Liberal Education," *Humanist*, 4:1–10, Spring, 1944.

of the law; he does not learn it by being uninhibited in his conduct. The parent or teacher, of course, is the personification of this authority. To avoid abuses of authority and to ensure that it results in freedom rather than tyranny, the teacher will do well not to carry his mantle of authority in an imperious manner but to wear it with a tempered dignity and humanity.[9]

Recognizing the indispensable role of authority in freedom are yet other educators who insist that moral freedom must also mean freedom from the law as well as freedom within or under the law, especially where the law is anachronistic, worn out, and out of date.[10] Students young and old must be free to assert their individuality against benumbing restrictings of convention, from enslavement to routine prejudice and fear. The purpose of such freedom is not romantically to capitalize on the natural goodness of individual child nature as an end in itself, but to capitalize on the individual differences of the younger generation as a means of progressively reforming the social culture. This view, of course, implies that the social culture is not a chain to bind the younger generation but a ladder on which it may climb. In other words, that child is learning moral freedom who can see more than one alternative in a problem confronting him and who, after dramatizing these alternatives in imagination, intelligently selects one to act upon.[11]

With this conception of educational freedom freshly in mind, the moment is appropriate to glance at the position of those who think of freedom chiefly in terms of freedom of physical movement for the child. This identification is too narrow. Physical freedom which is in no way connected with, or guided by, the intellect becomes irresponsible. It tends to become destructive of shared cooperative activities, which are the usual source of order. The antidote prescribes that we do not isolate physical freedom from the inner freedom of the mind. Conversely, freedom of thought must have an opportunity to test its own consequences through overt behavior. The proper place of physical freedom, therefore, is as a means and not as an end.

But even an instructional method which incorporates freedom as intelligent choosing between conventional and unconventional alternatives is not without its difficulties. How can the pupil or teacher tell whether the case at hand is one where it is morally better to follow the tried experience of convention or one where some innovation would be an improvement

---

9 V. M. Michael, "The Rule of Authority," *Catholic Educational Review*, 22:267–271, May, 1924.

10 A. E. Murphy, "Education for Freedom: Which Way?" *Humanist*, 5:26–29, April, 1945.

11 John L. Childs, "A Way of Dealing with Experience," *Progressive Education*, 8:695–698, December, 1931; and Pickens E. Harris, "What Is the Newer Meaning of School Discipline?" *Education*, 52:466–471, April, 1932.

on convention? It is perhaps a good principle to lay down here that command of race experience is an indispensable condition precedent to freedom to experiment with that race experience.[12] No person should be free, for instance, to enter the chemistry laboratory of his school who does not know some chemistry. The same is true of departures from time-tested standards of moral education. Even if a youth knows his social culture pretty well, there still should be some advance assurance that any deviation or nonconformity on his part will not risk irreparable harm either to himself or to his social group. Indeed there should be some prospect that his unconventional conduct will redound to their mutual benefit. Yet in weighing the risk the parent and teacher must bear in mind that there can be neither freedom nor progress without some jeopardy both individual and social.

The intimate relation between freedom and authority will perhaps help to explain the kind of freedom known as training in self-control. As we have already seen, some kind of control or regulation is a prerequisite to effective freedom. During a child's younger years, the locus of this control is usually in some agent external to the child, such as the parent, policeman, or teacher. The aim of most ethical systems in educational philosophy is to transform this external control into internal control, that is, to transfer it gradually from the external agent to the child himself, so that he may learn to exercise the moral autonomy of self-control. Ascetic educational philosophies regard the inhibitions incident to self-control as worthy ends in themselves. Other educational philosophies usually justify such inhibitions merely as means to ends. They are a moral warning to "stop and think." Thinking is a stoppage of activity in its impulsive stage until its probable consequences have been connected up with other meanings and a more comprehensive plan of action is formed. The larger the store of meanings and the more disposed a youth is to think of them before he acts, the less external restraint he need be under and the more internal freedom or self-control he is entitled to.

So far the focus of the discussion has been on freedom for the pupil. What of freedom for the teacher? What of his individuality? Some would make a colossus out of it, while others would reduce it to near the vanishing point. The former would constitute the teacher a final authority and require direct personal obedience from the pupil. The latter would have a social situation in the school bordering on anarchy, wherein the pupil's individuality would never be subordinated to that of the teacher. Both of these extremes seem predicated on the theory that the total amount of

---

[12] Frank N. Freeman, "Education as a Prerequisite to Freedom," *School and Society*, 45:593–596, May, 1937.

freedom in the school situation is so limited that the more the pupil or the teacher enjoys, the less the other possesses. As a matter of fact, this is not necessarily true. It may well be that the more freedom the teacher has, the more the child will enjoy also.

Indeed, there can be no genuine freedom for the pupil unless the teacher is free to make his greater experience available for his pupils. Since education is a social process, a process of sharing, nothing could be more absurd than to exclude from the group or reduce the significance in the group of the person who has the most to share, the teacher.[13] On the contrary, children can grow in moral freedom only if the teacher is free to advise how the capacities of individuals can be brought to richer fruition. But it is equally absurd to assume that the teacher is the only one who has anything to share. Children too have significant experience. The teacher will exercise his freedom preferably, therefore, not as an overbearing dictator but rather as a sympathetic counselor.

Proceeding on such principles, the wise teacher will not allow himself to be maneuvered into a social relation with his class where the sole initiative for planning the work of the school has passed over to his charges. He will adroitly avoid being committed in advance to such answers as he may get from directly putting the question to them, "What do you want to do today?" The reason for this is that the child, more than likely unacquainted with what are the enduring phases of his own underlying interests, will respond by snatching at some passing trifle or purely accidental affair. The teacher can best avoid this artificial consulting of interest by being so close a student of children's interests that he will often know them better than the children do themselves. Children will then not so much do what they want to, as want to do what they do. Instead of leading to freedom, to do as one pleases may actually lead into a new bondage, the bondage of impulse or ignorance.

SCHOOLROOM DISCIPLINE

A special instance of the social and moral infrastructure of the school that deserves separate mention is discipline. Whether one's educational philosophy calls for much or little freedom, certain optimum social conditions must obtain in the school if effective learning is to take place. These are the conditions of law and order. Law and order are as necessary for the carrying on of instruction as they are for the ordinary pursuits of everyday life outside school. This much may be taken for granted. The main ques-

[13] Cf. *supra*, pp. 67–69.

tion, however, is how discipline, this law and order, is to be maintained in the school.

One method makes discipline a condition precedent to instruction. There must be a certain amount of order and quiet before instruction can begin. Indeed, maintaining order and giving instruction are almost two different functions of the teacher. Under such conditions, codes of discipline usually state the rules. In these, prompt obedience to the will of the teacher is the first and great commandment.[14] The parent or teacher may give reasons for his request, but he need not. Children should obey simply because the parent—or the teacher *in loco parentis*—wills it. In doing so, they are really obedient to the moral law itself. If anything, the discipline of the school should be even more strict than that of the home.

A second method makes discipline coincident to interesting instruction. Here the teacher, whose enthusiasm for his field of specialization should be so contagious that it spreads to his pupils, need not bother about discipline as a separate concern. Children will be so engrossed in the curriculum that their interest will afford a self-discipline. According to this theory, there is such a moral and spiritual unity between pupil and teacher that the docility of the former as a condition precedent to instruction never arises. The happy schoolroom is like the happy society. Children, as well as adults, who have significant work to do are seldom the source of disciplinary problems for either the teacher or the policeman.

A third method goes even beyond utilizing interest to transfer the locus of authority for maintaining discipline from the teacher alone to the class as a whole. Here rule by the one gives way to rule by the many. Social order in the school becomes a function of a group purpose. If children are cooperatively engaged with the teacher in a joint project, pursuit of the common end will enforce its own order.[15] The children will discipline themselves in order to gain their accepted objective. Here, each member of the group exercises moral compulsion on every other and in turn submits to moral compulsion from him. Under such a regime, there may not be the same kind of quiet and order as where the teacher alone "keeps order," but it will be nonetheless effective.

Whatever one's basis for maintaining discipline, suppose, now, that after the teacher has done the best he can within the limits of his capacities, some individual child still remains recalcitrant. Should the parent or

---

[14] George Partridge, *Genetic Philosophy of Education* (Sturgis and Walton, New York, 1912); Felix Pécaut, "The Philosophy Underlying the National System of Education in France," International Institute, *Educational Yearbook*, 1929 (Teachers College, Columbia University, New York, 1930), pp. 169–171.

[15] John Dewey, *School and Society* (The University of Chicago Press, Chicago, 1899), pp. 30–31.

teacher ever punish such a child? Some are frankly skeptical whether punishment should ever be resorted to. And if there are such occasions, they are very skeptical of the results that are achieved. Others are by no means prepared to eschew punishment entirely.[16] As a last resort, they would probably employ some form of coercion proportioned to the circumstances of the case in order to achieve the ends of the family or the class. Certainly they would not have the teacher's authority completely shorn of the weapon of coercion.

Where punishment is necessary, the ethical theory on which it is meted out may be variously stated. We may first pay attention to the theory of retribution or retaliation. According to this view, punishment is a sort of revenge. Harm done to others can be wiped out or compensated only by a harm done to the offender. It is the age-old moral law of an eye for an eye and a tooth for a tooth. Added support for this theory is found where it can be proved that infractions are "willfully" perpetrated.[17] The child knew his intended act was wrong, but did it in spite of his knowledge; he did it with malice aforethought. For such a flaunting of the moral law, many think, only punishment will suffice as expiation.

Another theory is that punishment is administered to protect the class by making an example of the offender. The emphasis, in this instance, is not on cleansing the individual of his fault so much as ensuring the group against similar infractions of its peace and security. Antisocial behavior is a threat to the very existence of the power and prestige of the classroom group and through it of the school or even society itself. The social group must therefore be protected. The chief danger in deterrence as a motive for punishment is that it may be too severe and therefore create a feeling of resentment rather than warning.

A final theory of punishment is educative.[18] The shortcomings of the previous theories of punishment are that they are so largely negative and that they do not positively point the way to rehabilitate the recalcitrant child. The point of this third theory is that no punishment should be administered which does not reconstruct or reeducate him. In this sense, punishment is a moral expression of social hope. The offender is given a chance to see himself as others see him. But if he fails to see and accept

16 William D. Hyde, *The Teacher's Philosophy* (Houghton Mifflin Company, Boston, 1910), pp. 10–11; Pius XI, "The Christian Education of Youth," *Catholic Mind*, 28:78, February, 1930; S. A. Courtis, "The Problem of Immaturity," *Progressive Education*, 8:703–705, June, 1931.

17 Cf. Clarence E. Ragsdale, *Modern Psychologies of Education* (The Macmillan Company, New York, 1932), pp. 39–40.

18 Boyd H. Bode, *Democracy as a Way of Life* (The Macmillan Company, New York, 1937), pp. 80–82; William E. Hocking, *Human Nature and Its Remaking* (Yale University Press, New Haven, Conn., 1923), pp. 284–285; Clarence E. Ragsdale, *op. cit.*, p. 40.

the principle at stake, then even punishment has failed. We can then only commend him to our prayers.

MORAL PRINCIPLES AND THE CURRICULUM

Thus far we have noted social aspects of education that have incidental moral undertones. It remains to discuss moral principles as the direct object of instruction. There are two main issues.[19] How shall we conceive of morals as subject matter, and how can we ensure, not just moral knowledge, but moral conduct as well?

At the outset, perhaps, we should address ourselves to the distinction between moral and ethical instruction. Some would teach young people morals but not ethics. To them morals emphasize performance; ethics stress knowledge. What they prize in the young are prompt and sure moral responses. If the young stop to be rationally ethical, there is reason to fear that their goodness will become demoralized into a calculated expediency. Teaching ethics prematurely can hinder moral development just as premature emphasis on grammar by the teacher may impede rather than accelerate good habits of speech. If ethical instruction is to be given—and of course it cannot be postponed indefinitely—it should be reserved for the student's more mature years.

The intellectualization of moral education raises the allied question of how closely to relate moral education with other intellectual studies. Some are inclined to look on moral knowledge as essentially different from other kinds of knowledge. Particularly is this true where morality needs the support of supernatural religion. Others take the view that intellectual and moral studies should go along hand in hand. Atomic fission is a case in point. Before its discovery many thought that physics and politics were separate courses in the curriculum. With the construction of the super-destructive atomic bomb, however, the separation no longer exists. Atomic fission now has not only scientific but moral significance. Intellectual and moral studies, therefore, should be taught in conjunction with each other. Short of this correlation, moral education runs the imminent risk of being no more than instruction about morals, in which pupils learn abstract virtues without learning to be virtuous in the affairs of life.

The proper place of morals in the curriculum is rendered further ambiguous by differences of opinion about the nature of morals themselves.[20]

---

[19] William K. Frankena, "Toward a Philosophy of Moral Education," *Harvard Educational Review*, 28:300–313, Fall, 1958.

[20] Alan Montefiore "Moral Philosophy and the Teaching of Morality," *Harvard Educational Review*, 35:435–449, Fall, 1965.

One side to this difference holds that morals have an objective quality capable of authoritative adjudication.[21] The other side holds that the individual must determine for himself what is right and wrong. If one tries to resolve this impasse by an analysis of moral discourse, he will reject objective moral values because moral values are noncognitive and nonverifiable. Since, on the contrary, such values are only emotive, all the teacher can do is paint pictures of different modes of moral life and let the learner choose according to his own passion.[22] Objectivists, of course, hold that this kind of moral education would result in an unwarranted relativism. Whichever point of view is espoused, the outcome for developing moral autonomy is fraught with grave consequences.

Involvement of the autonomy of the student raises the issue of his moral responsibility. It is generally held that without some sort of freedom there can be no responsibility. Thus, if a rigid determinism obtains, the child can hardly be held accountable for what he does. Accountability must be predicated upon choice. But even so, there are many who incline to lay the blame for past acts at the door of early training. If training is to blame, then responsibility is not merely individual but social as well. The teacher, parent, and community are jointly accountable with the child. Others would ground responsibility, not on what has already happened, but in the anticipation of future consequences. The student is responsible, then, only as he can be taught to become responsible, to act in the light of the reasonably foreseeable consequences of his acts. Some think that this function has been performed when the educand has been educated to know better. Others insist that he does not truly become accountable till he does better as well. This does not mean that ignorance is an excuse before the law. Public liability may attach to one's acts in spite of one's ignorance. But moral responsibility must be based on anticipation of consequences, on education.

We may stop at this point to ask whether a youth has a moral obligation to develop his talents. Undoubtedly he has the historically hard-won right to an education. If he is remiss in exercising it, society may correct the lapse by compelling his attendance at school up to a certain age. But it may be that he has talents which warrant development well beyond the compulsory age limit. Now, to repeat, does youth have a moral obligation

---

21 Cf. *supra*, pp. 86–87.

22 For a general review of linguistic analysis as a background for moral education, see Henry D. Aiken, "Moral Philosophy and Education," *Harvard Educational Review*, 25:39–59, Winter, 1955. For a critique of this position, see Martin Levit, "Non-cognitivist Ethics, Scientific Method, and Education," *Studies in Philosophy and Education*, 2:304–330, Winter, 1963.

to develop his powers to as near their maximum as possible? Or, since it is his own life, may he waste his opportunities if he wishes? At its best, the moral life is autonomous. Consequently, if a youth has fulfilled statutory requirements, any further obligation must be of his own choosing. Ordinarily he will choose to recognize further claims, but if he does not, the loss is part of the price we must pay for autonomy.

It is a well-known fact that to teach moral knowledge is one thing, but to ensure that that knowledge issue forth in moral conduct is quite another. Some think one reason for this lies in the fact that the conventional learning curve in secular education, to which psychologists have introduced us, does not apply to cases of learning religious and moral education.[23] The reason for this is rather subtle. In secular subjects such as the three R's, there is a clearly defined subject matter to be learned. The target to be aimed at is unmistakable. But, in spite of the best intent to strike it, a degree of failure is almost certain to attend the beginner's efforts. Obstacles of imperfect organization and control will interfere. He will have to practice to become perfect. In the moral situation, all this is declared to be different. One's effort to do the right does not fall short for want of habits of organization and control, for it is of the very nature of right always to be within reach. If it were not within reach, it could exert no moral obligation on the individual. Failure to do what is within reach, therefore, must be due to a lack of will to reach for the right. Thus sin results, not from falling short of a morality organically beyond the learner's reach, but out of a defection from what was admittedly definitely within his power. If the individual is under obligation to do right, then he ought to do it the first time. He should need no practice. Hence, there is no law or curve in learning for morality, as there is in the secular branches.

Another difficulty may lie in the fact that even if the student succeeds, with or without a learning curve for morals, in perfecting himself in the most approved virtues, he may still fall short of being a moral, virtuous man. Some educators have never stopped to realize how they can include a list of the finest virtues in the curriculum and yet fail to have the pupil become virtuous. Take from the moral catalogue such virtues as industry, patience, courage, perseverance, fidelity. A young person could learn to excel in all these and yet not be moral or virtuous. The reason is that criminals as well as law-abiding citizens cultivate these virtues. Really the virtues listed are the marks of an efficient rather than a good will. That is,

---

[23] William E. Hocking, *Human Nature and Its Remaking* (Yale University Press, New Haven, Conn., 1923), pp. 151–152. But see Hugh Hartshorne, "A Few Principles of Character Education," *Religious Education*, 24:808–815, November, 1929, who says one learns to resist temptation by grading and increasing the difficulty of it.

the child can practice these virtues while pursuing bad ends. Consequently it is not so much specific virtues which should govern the curriculum in moral education as it is some central ethical purpose.[24]

Presumably such an overarching ethical purpose will be its own incentive, its own reward, and thus give sanction to the moral life. But when the parent or teacher says the child ought to pursue such a purpose, what is the basis for the obligation? Paying attention to the mode of moral discourse, what does it mean when a teacher says to his class, "We all don't like to cheat on examinations, do we?" Two meanings appear possible from such a statement.[25] The teacher may be simply stating a fact. Or, knowing full well that the contrary is the fact, he may be taking this form of exhorting his students to make it the fact. Obviously the impact of the two meanings of the same words is quite different. The class may be quick to perceive just what this impact is. So too in a theory of educational values we must be alert to make the same distinction. We must distinguish what in fact *is* held valuable from what *ought* to be held valuable.

Again, suppose the teacher says, "This school has an honor code; therefore we ought to obey it." Does such an obligation follow from a mere indicative statement of fact? Not at all, think a number. One can easily take note of a factual situation without necessarily putting himself under a resulting obligation. For the teacher to try to carry the moral day with reasons in the form of more facts—for example, that the proposed conduct is in harmony with human nature, natural law, or divine ordinance—adds not one iota of obligation. As a matter of linguistic analysis, the teacher's statement comes down to "I approve of the school code, and I wish you would likewise." A sense of oughtness arises only if the student addressed accepts the same basic value as the teacher. Even if the teacher changes his tone from persuasion to command, the student will still feel a duty to obey only if he accepts the authority of the teacher as one of his motivating ideals.

Rejecting the results of linguistic analysis are those who think that moral obligation can be established on more objective grounds. Thus, recall the three-cornered contrast in religion between secularism, humanism, and theology.[26] The primary question here is whether the school can teach morals successfully without placing them in a religious context. The secular public school has long taught moral character without mention of religion. The theoretical implication of this practice is that morals have a naturalistic origin in the folkways and mores of the community. The social and moral

---

[24] George A. Coe, "Virtue and the Virtues," *Religious Education*, 6:485–492, January, 1912.
[25] Charles D. Hardie, *Truth and Fallacy in Educational Theory* (Cambridge University Press, New York, 1942), p. 123. Cf. *infra*, pp. 319–320.
[26] *Supra*, pp. 188–195.

are one and the same. While the humanist tends to coincide with the secularist on this point, the theologian differs quite fundamentally. To him the moral law is not just customary but divinely ordained. It is God, not man, who legislates the moral law. Consequently the endeavor to teach morals apart from religion, good as far as it goes, is doomed to fall far short of its objective.[27]

Obviously it makes a profound difference which of these two theories of morals underlies the motivation employed in the formation of moral character. In secular moral education the pressure to lead the good life comes from the social group—the class, the school, the home, and the like. These groups conform to or remold codes for very practical considerations. Motivation is quite pragmatic.[28] In theological moral education, social pressure and the individual habituation it represents are good but insufficient by themselves. There must be in addition a religious sanction.[29] The theologian has no confidence in moral education unless the child is taught that the oughtness of moral duty rests in his obligation to obey divine command. It is God as supreme lawgiver and perhaps even more as eternal judge, therefore, who ultimately guarantees moral conduct.

Those who look upon conversion and regeneration in mystical rather than educational terms tend to reflect the subjectivity of their mysticism in their absorption with inner motivation in moral education. In character education they are more concerned with what a young person is than with what he does. In a sense morality becomes an internal affair depending on good intention. If a child does wrong but has a good will, if he means well, then they relieve him in a measure from responsibility for the consequences of his conduct. They calculate the goodness of his act, not by its results, but by the quality of the impulse which prompted it.

Those who regard conversion and regeneration as aspects of education are likely to find fault with moral and character education so dependent on the child's internal disposition to do good, because then character becomes too inaccessible to methods of the teacher or parent. The antidote they recommend is to look for the development of a young person's character in what he does more than in what he is. What they seek is not only inner character but force of character, that is, efficiency in the active and overt execution of ideals.

The basic difference which has divided moral and character education so far continues to divide it in the matter of method. If moral duty binds

[27] Cf. Rachel M. Goodrich, "Moral Education: A Thomist Contribution," *British Journal of Educational Studies*, 14:5–17, November, 1966.

[28] For a more complete discussion of educational motivation, see *infra*, pp. 253–261. See also R. Bruce Raup, "Moral Authority and Religious Sanction," *Teachers College Record*, 54:299–306, March, 1953.

[29] Regis Canevin, "Religion First in Catholic Schools," *Catholic Educational Review*, 4:97–109, September, 1912.

the conscience of man because it is the obligation he owes to obey the will of a sovereign Lord, then the teacher's method may well take on the authoritarian manner of indoctrination. If, on the other hand, the moral law is just the outgrowth of social custom, which is constantly being remade in the light of further social experience, then an experimental, problem-solving method is more apropos. We often think of the moral situation as represented by a forked road. Which fork to take, that is the moral dilemma. If God's will has been vouchsafed to us, the teacher can tell his class in advance the right fork from the wrong one. If, on the contrary, the forked road represents a genuinely novel situation in which it is not clear in advance which is the better fork, then teacher and class will have to approach the matter problematically.[30] Instead of presenting his pupils with a choice between right and wrong, he will have to present them with a choice between two possible rights, in which the wrong becomes the alternative that is ultimately rejected in the light of the consequences of experience.

Such moral instruction more or less contemplates a direct attack on the problem of educating for moral character. Not a few think this the best way of handling the matter;[31] others, however, favor an indirect approach.[32] They see young people all the time learning moral attitudes incidental to whatever activities are mainly occupying their attention. Incidental to work, study, and play, they see children constantly and inescapably learning attitudes of perseverance, kindness, frankness, loyalty, and the like. Recognizing that all learning has this multiple character, the wise teacher, they think, will have a constant eye out for calling attention to moral values though seldom making them the main object of the lesson.

Whether moral education should be the direct or the indirect object of any lesson, no doubt most educators of whatever philosophy would agree that efforts at moral education will prove abortive unless there is opportunity for the child to practice what the school or church preaches. We cannot teach the oncoming generation to be good simply by teaching them to be wise.[33] They must have plenty of opportunity to habituate themselves to moral ideals. In other words, the only way to learn fair play is to play fair. Instead of learning lessons in school apart from life, school must incorporate into itself a social context of shops, laboratories, and play-

---

30 For a further discussion of this method, see *infra*, pp. 240–246. For a caution in its employment, see W. A. Squires, "Idealism, Mechanism, and the Project Principle," *Religious Education*, 21:458–466, October, 1926.

31 For example, Frederick S. Breed, "A Preface to Moral Training," *School and Society*, 32: 275, August, 1930.

32 For example, Preston W. Search, "The Ethics of the Public Schools," *Educational Review*, 11:134–145, February, 1896.

33 Cf. Robert M. Hutchins, *Morals, Religion, and Higher Education* (The University of Chicago Press, Chicago, 1950). For a linguistic analysis of this problem, see James McClellan, "Two Questions about the Teaching of Moral Values," *Educational Theory*, 11:1–14, January, 1961.

grounds. Not only that, but moral learning in school and college must be continuous with moral learning outside through field trips, community activities, and the like. If school fulfills this larger function, we may be assured that anything learned in an enterprise having an aim and in cooperation with others will be inescapably moral.[34]

SELECTED BIBLIOGRAPHY

Benne, Kenneth D.: *A Conception of Authority* (Teachers College, Columbia University, New York, 1943), Chap. 5.

Brown, L. M.: *General Philosophy in Education* (McGraw-Hill Book Company, New York, 1966), Chap. 8.

Childs, John L.: *Education and Morals* (Appleton-Century-Crofts, Inc., New York, 1950).

Coe, George A.: Educating for Citizenship (Charles Scribner's Sons, New York, 1932), Chap. 3.

————: *Law and Freedom in the School* (The University of Chicago Press, Chicago, 1924), Chaps. 2, 5–7.

Dewey, John: *Moral Principles in Education* (Houghton Mifflin Company, Boston, 1909).

Hartshorne, Hugh: *Character and Human Relations* (Charles Scribner's Sons, New York, 1932), Chaps. 21–24.

John Dewey Society: Seventh Yearbook, *The Public School and Spiritual Values* (Harper & Row, Publishers, Incorporated, New York, 1944).

McCallister, W. J.: *The Growth of Freedom in Education* (The Richard R. Smith Co., Inc., Peterborough, N.H., 1931), Chaps. 28, 30–32.

Maritain, Jacques: "Moral and Spiritual Values in Education" and "Moral Education," in Donald Gallagher and Idella Gallagher (eds.), *The Education of Man* (Doubleday & Company, Inc., Garden City, N.Y., 1962), Chaps. 4–5.

Nash, Paul: *Authority and Freedom in Education* (John Wiley & Sons, Inc., New York, 1966), Chap. 3.

O'Connor, D. J.: *The Philosophy of Education* (Philosophical Library, Inc., New York, 1957), Chap. 3.

Palmer, George H.: *Ethical and Moral Instruction in the Schools* (Houghton Mifflin Company, Boston, 1909).

Peters, Richard S.: *Ethics and Education* (Scott Foresman and Company, Chicago, 1967), Chap. 9.

Phenix, Philip H.: *Education and the Common Good* (Harper & Row, Publishers, Incorporated, New York, 1961).

Romein, Tunis: *Education and Responsibility* (University of Kentucky Press, Lexington, Ky., 1955).

Scheffler, Israel (ed.): *Philosophy and Education* (Allyn and Bacon, Inc., Boston, 1966), Chaps. 10–13.

Sizer, Theodore R. (ed.): *Religion and Public Education* (Houghton Mifflin Company, Boston, 1967) Chaps. 8, 10.

[34] Cf. Reginald D. Archambault, "Criterion for Success in Moral Education," *Harvard Educational Review*, 33:472–491, Fall, 1963.

PART FOUR
Method

CHAPTER ELEVEN

Epistemological Aspects of Method

With the aims of education set and with the curriculum appropriate to the aim determined, we must next ponder how to teach that curriculum to ensure achieving our objectives as effectively as possible. Ordinarily one thinks of method of instruction as concerned with what the teacher does. If the pupil were made of quite malleable stuff, perhaps that is all there would be to it. But if one regards the pupil as an energy system wound up to go its own direction, it behooves us to regard philosophy of method as much a matter of what the pupil does as what the teacher does. Our examination of method, therefore, must involve both teaching and learning.

Under the rubric of what the teacher does, we must ask what design the teacher should employ in arranging the lesson. Should it be authoritarian or problematic? Whichever it is, in what sequence should materials be presented, logical or psychological? This is an epistemological question. Under the rubric of learning we must ask further such questions as "How does learning occur?" "How is learning related to knowing?" And in both, what is the role of intelligence? Of these two, teaching and learning, it will probably serve our purposes best to commence with the category of learning.

LEARNING

Perhaps the major epistemological question in learning is the same today as it was more than two thousand years ago when the Greeks first asked it—how can anything new enter the mind? The Greeks had doubts on this point which they expressed in a famous dilemma. Either you know or you do not know some new item, they said. If you know it, then you are wasting your time learning it again, and if you do not know it, how will you recognize it should you come upon it? Of course the Greeks did not allow for "getting to know." But if they had, what is the subtle alchemy by which one "gets to know," by which one learns the novel? How can the teacher help in advancing this metamorphosis of the new into the old? There is a metabolism of learning just as surely as there is a metabolism of nourishment. Yet, what is the transmutation?

In addressing ourselves to the question how anything new can enter the mind, much turns on how one conceives the mind. We shall note several theories and subtheories. First and oldest is a theory which we may term "vitalism." According to this theory, mind is an invisible entity within the learner. This inner core of self is autoactivating and is sometimes known as the soul. If this latter term is preferred, it will be well to employ it in its psychological rather than its theological sense.[1] Vitalists regard the mind as not just more complex than its correlate in other animals but as uniquely different. According to this theory, learning is a profound personal experience, a self-actualizing, a coming to know oneself by his own efforts. One learns, gets to know, what one is. On this view, as existentialists might say, learning is not about existence; it is existence.

Perhaps the question still persists how can anything new enter this vitalistic citadel of the mind. For some the problem is really insuperable. If there is anything new, it must come from within. It must have been resident in original nature from birth.[2] Learning thus becomes an actualization of what was potentially present from conception. The environment of the home or the school may be necessary to tip off the actualization of this potentiality, but the important thing to remember is that any novelty in the learning process stems from child nature, not the environment. Learning thus is an unfolding of what was originally enfolded. It is developmental, a kind of growth.

Other students have been as equally impressed with the fact that the source of novelty in learning is in the environment outside the child. Some of this school of thought hold that human nature is rather colorless, malleable stuff. Hence practically everything it learns takes its origin in the environment. Learning the novel is largely a matter of mechanical impact from the outside world. It is a matter of making an impression on the plastic mind of the child.[3]

A more recent theory is that of behaviorism. If exponents of this view do not ridicule the mind as a kind of a "ghost in the machine" or "black box," at least they give it little credence. Unimpressed with an entity they cannot see, they confine their conclusions about learning to what they can physically see by way of changes in the learner's behavior. According to

---

[1] Note that our word "psychology" stems from the Greek ψυχή, or psyche, which is often translated as soul.

[2] Cf. James L. Mursell, "The Miracle of Learning," Atlantic Monthly, 155:735, June, 1935.

[3] Cf. Ross L. Finney, A Sociological Philosophy of Education (Appleton-Century-Crofts, Inc., New York, 1950), pp. 57–60.

this theory, learning is the acquisition of new behavior patterns through either simple or complex conditioning and reinforcement.

There are many who are dissatisfied with the behaviorists' elimination of mind and yet unhappy with the vitalists' mind as an invisible and probably immaterial entity. Their remedy for this unsatisfactory situation is to stop regarding mind as one thing and environment as another in the learning process. On the contrary, take the teacher's injunction to his pupils, "Mind your p's and q's." "Mind" is actually being careful to distinguish these very similar letters of the alphabet. "Mind" is adverbial; it is behaving discriminatingly, meaningfully, purposefully. Learning occurs, then, when there is a change of mind because the environment changes, that is, becomes problematical.

This view of learning permits a more emergent or creative view of learning. Confronted with a novel situation for which the individual has no response in his repertoire—a situation which is cosmically indeterminate, not just indeterminate to the individual—the individual contrives a way out by reorganizing both the environment and his own experience. According to this view, the novel situation has upset a total field of forces. Hence learning is not just the simple impact of these disturbed forces on the mind of the learner, the second view above. Neither is it merely a modification of the learner internally, the first view. On the contrary, learning is a reorganization of the whole field of forces including both the environment and the learner. Hence the subsequent pattern of behavior is as much a function of the one as of the other. As a result of such a reorganization of forces or relations the individual is a different person. Novel functioning leads to a modification of human nature. Indeed, learning is the actual building of new structure.[4]

To prove that this is not just a theoretical problem, take such an item in the science curriculum as the Heisenberg principle of indeterminacy. If the student in the laboratory tries to measure precisely both the velocity and position of a sub-atomic particle at a given moment, he will find that he can get either one of the two dimensions accurately but not both. Indeed, no matter how sophisticated the student becomes in his observations this indeterminacy is confirmed again and again. Now, how to interpret this result in the context of education? Does it mean that reality is actually indeterminate or that reality is determinate enough but that the student is

4 Robert M. Ogden, "The Gestalt Theory of Learning," School and Society, 41:529, April, 1935; William H. Kilpatrick, A Reconstructed Theory of the Educative Process (Teachers College, Columbia University, New York, 1935), p. 4. These sources document the last view, which is that of progressive educators generally. The preceding view is that of behaviorists and associationists, while the first view will be recognized as that of Froebel and other early educators.

not smart enough to figure it out? If we take the latter view, then learner and curriculum must be separate entities. The learner only "interacts" with his environment because the environment stubbornly remains what it is in spite of the endeavor to learn it. If we take the former view, then learner and curriculum are on a continuum. Learning is a "transaction" with the environment instead of an interaction because the learning experience actually shapes and transforms reality.[5] Hence reality (curriculum) is not a "given" in the learning process but rather an emergent of it.

It is very easy to make the mistake of thinking that knowing or learning is just a matter of intellection, just a matter of using one's head. This mistake is doubly unfortunate if it begets the further mistake of thinking that learning is something principally done while the pupil is seated at his desk in a state of relative physical inactivity. Indeed the conclusion that learning is a relatively inactive affair is not infrequently reinforced by the theory that mind is passive, that it is some sort of tablet on which impressions are registered by the teacher or environment.[6] In any event this position has offered stubborn resistance to progressive education with its theory that acquiring knowledge is an active rather than passive affair.

Those who have advocated the view that getting to know is an essentially active affair have by no means been unanimous in their supporting reasons. Of longest standing is the ontological view that the principle of life which animates man is fundamentally active.[7] Therefore when the psyche or soul, which embodies this principle of life, engages in learning, it must be an active process. This was essentially the view of St. Thomas Aquinas. He made this very clear in the analogy he drew between the offices of the doctor and the teacher. Getting well, he pointed out, is something which the patient has to do for himself. By prescribing a regimen of medicine or exercise the doctor can only aid the potentialities of the natural processes of the body to heal themselves. Similarly with education and getting to know. The student must do it himself; the teacher cannot do it for him. The teacher can teach him but, to put it ungrammatically, he cannot "learn" him. Education, accordingly, is not so much an imparting of knowledge as it is a soliciting or prompting of the student to exert his native potentialities for knowing or learning.

Many who rally to the support of "activity" schools, "activity" curriculums, learning by "doing," and the like, are attracted to this educa-

[5] Lawrence G. Thomas, "Implications of Transaction Theory," *Educational Forum*, 32:145–155, January, 1968. See also Henry Miller, "Transaction: Dewey's Last Contribution to the Theory of Learning," *Educational Theory*, 13:13–28, January, 1963.
[6] *Supra*, p. 117.
[7] *Ibid.*

tional device because it suggests, in particular, physical activities. When they employ this idea, they have in mind the activities of the gymnasium, the shop, and field excursions, to say nothing of freedom to move about the regular classroom. Activities of this sort they regard as a belated recognition of the student's biological nature. Generations of adults on end have tried to curb the restless and boundless energies of youth with only indifferent success. What is more sensible, therefore, than to go along with nature rather than against it, to build education upon the enlistment of activity rather than its suppression!

Pursuing this theory, its advocates hold that students must move about if they are to have an adequate chance to learn. They must actually go to the farm or the factory, for instance, if their knowledge of these places is to rise above vicarious impressions. Pictures and books are good as far as they go, but at best they are only symbols. They merely denote, point to, kinds of richer experience which may be had. They do not convey the actual hum of machines or the smell of new-mown hay. Such firsthand knowledge can be had only through an activity program.

Moreover it is no accident, as someone has said, that "ken" and "can" are allied words. Hence it will no longer suffice to say, for example, that we know the Ten Commandments though we have failed to act on them. Knowing does not have an exclusive locus inside the head. Learning occurs not just from the neck up; it involves habituation of the muscles from the neck down as well. Not only that, but knowledge of the participator must be seen to entail genuinely different results from that of the mere spectator. We cannot learn to play a sport or a musical instrument by merely watching someone else or by reading the directions. We must step forth and produce real strokes of the tennis racket or the violin bow ourselves if we are to learn these accomplishments.

To pragmatists progressive education's emphasis on activity suggests still another justification. With them, it will be remembered, activity is an all-important step in the method of knowing. Confronted with a problem and alternate solutions which might turn out in various ways, the pragmatic pupil or teacher will not know which is the best way till he acts on one or more of them. He must translate his hypotheses into a series of activities, activities in fact which result in physical changes in the environment, and note their consequences before he can conclude what he knows or has learned.[8] Hence learning is akin to verification; it is essentially experimental. The process is the same whether carried on in the classroom or the

[8] John Dewey, *Democracy and Education* (The Macmillan Company, New York, 1916), pp. 181, 321–322, 393.

laboratory. The paramount reason for the activity program, then, is not ontological nor biological, but epistemological.

Although the activity theories of learning and knowing seem to coincide, it should not be overlooked that they do not always do so. It is quite possible that a student may not know what he has learned. Thus, he may only "believe" or "think" he knows what he has learned. Or he may not know what he has learned in the sense of understanding it. He can repeat a formula in mathematics without knowing or understanding when and how to use it.[9]

Considerable exception is taken to the pragmatist's theory of activity learning. The chief resistance centers in certain kinds of learning in which, so his opponents allege, no activity of the learner could possibly alter the relations of the subject matter under study. Take the case of astronomy as an instance. Certainly no activities engaged in by the learner are going to alter astronomical relations. Again take the case of history. Surely no study activities of the pupil or even of the graduate student of historical research can change the course of past history. He may amplify or amend the historical record but not the historical fact. In slightly different vein look at moral education. Need one engage in vice in order to learn to eschew it? Merely to ask the question is to discredit it. Finally, may it not be possible that some people will delight in the acquisition of impractical knowledge, knowledge which solves no problems? Thus, should there not be a place in school for viewing great art, hearing edifying music, and witnessing inspiring drama?

These are pointed questions. They do not, however, want for a rejoinder.[10] The pragmatic educator does not contend that all relations are internal, only that some are. Yet, even if learning cannot alter history and astronomy, it nevertheless is still true that one cannot learn history or astronomy without undertaking definite physical activities, such as examining documents or peering through telescopes. Again, the pragmatic educator would probably grant that not all knowledge involves practical activities, for obviously there is much knowledge that is pursued for purely aesthetic and scientific ends. But one fact needs pointing out even in this case— that scientific and aesthetic knowledge have usually been distilled by intelligence from what originally were practical activities. And even in the scientific and aesthetic pursuit of knowledge for its own sake learning must ultimately involve activity if it is to be verified.

[9] Marcus Brown, "Knowing and Learning," Harvard Educational Review, 31:1–20, Winter, 1961.
[10] Cf. William P. Montague, Ways of Knowing (The Macmillan Company, New York, 1925), pp. 134–135n.

WAYS OF KNOWING

As the explication of learning theory almost imperceptibly merges with theory of knowledge, it would seem logical next to add ways of knowing to the scope of method of instruction. Just as there are different theories of truth in the curriculum, just so there are also different ways of getting to know the truth. Indeed, each conception of truth[11] has its own peculiar theory of how truth is acquired and how learning, therefore, is conditioned. We may start with the correspondence theory, whose adherents think that truth results from the direct apprehension of naked reality. To some of them this apprehension is a very simple affair. In fact it is so simple that they are almost disinclined to propose a theory of how it occurs. They naïvely trust their experience. Reality is what their senses tell them it is. For the urban school child who makes a field trip to the farm, the making of butter is just what it appears to be. He needs no recondite epistemological theory to explain it. It is just a fact, something he knows.

Other adherents of the correspondence theory of truth do not place such naïve confidence in their senses as a way of knowing reality. The variability of sense information is too notorious for that. They depend more on theory. To them knowing is a direct participation by the learner in the nature of the object under study. Any such object generally has a number of facets by which it may be apprehended. Some of them are accidental and some are indispensable to its essential nature. The watch by which the child gets to school on time may be a pocket watch or a wrist watch, may have Arabic or Roman numerals, may or may not have a second hand, or other features, but if it is a watch it certainly does have some mechanism which measures the passage of time. Knowing the watch consists of prescinding its accidental qualities and seizing upon its essential form, its "watchness." It is the essential form of the human mind that it can select out and lay hold of the essential form in the objects presented to it. When the form of the mind operates on the form of the object, even if in the indirect form of symbols of physicomathematical science, it knows the object. Knowing is dianoetic; it participates in the very being of that object.[12] It is for this reason that the advocates of this theory are convinced that they know reality and that they know it directly and in its protean nakedness.

---

[11] *Supra*, pp. 163–168.

[12] As Jacques Maritain is quoted, "In the act of knowledge, the thing and the thought are not only united, they are strictly one." See the American Catholic Philosophical Association, *Proceedings of the Western Division: The Philosophy of Christian Education*, 1941, p. 51. See also Gerard Esser, "The Meaning of Intelligence and Its Value for Education," *Catholic Educational Review*, 33:257–270, May, 1935.

To be more specific on the way in which this sort of knowing occurs it is necessary to distinguish five steps. The first is a report from the senses of the apprehension of some object, say, the pupil's watch just mentioned. Second, memory holds the image or phantasm of the watch in mind together with other similar images or phantasms so that, third, the active intellect can distinguish between the accidental and the essential qualities of the watch. The essence of the watch, fourth, is presented to the cognitive intellect which, fifth, conceptualizes this essence in terms of what is common to all watches.[13] But of course the learner should not stop with this morphology of knowledge. From a knowledge of things he should go on to an understanding of the relation of one known thing to another. The true scholar, thus, is the one who seeks to know the totality of all things defined and organized in their proper hierarchical relationship to one another.

It is well to note here that the learner is not empty-handed as he starts the process of learning or acquiring knowledge. He comes to his task already possessed of certain potentialities for knowledge beyond sense data. His mind is already equipped with such primary ideas or first principles as "being," "contradiction," and "cause and effect." Such principles as these are not learned through experience; neither do they require demonstration. Rather are they self-evident. Although they do not antedate all experience, they are applied on the occasion of the first experience and are indispensable to all subsequent experience.[14]

Yet, in spite of this superb equipment, the faculties of human nature lack the perfect coordination which might enable them unerringly to strike straight to the heart of knowledge in every attempt at learning. This defect of man's nature can be compensated by extraordinary aids to the learning process. In the first place, it is an old article of Catholic faith that one must have faith in order to understand. The weaknesses of human nature's equipment for learning, however, can be further strengthened by divine grace and revelation. This does not argue the neglect of man's animal nature, but merely its need for help beyond its own powers. Yet no single one of the three—faith, grace, or revelation—is sufficient by itself to help intellect to the deeper vision of truth; it is necessary that all three be employed. Moreover, not even conceiving intelligence as a possession held in common by the race will make up for the shortcomings of individual intelligence. There will still be need for divine authority. Only later, as learning

[13] William J. Sanders, "Thomism, Instrumentalism, and Education," *Harvard Educational Review*, 10:103–105, January, 1940.

[14] Pierre J. Marique, *Philosophy of Christian Education* (Prentice-Hall, Inc., Englewood Cliffs, N.J., 1939), pp. 209–210.

expands, is it expected that authoritarianism as a crutch can be discarded. By that time, it is hoped, the intellect will be so strengthened that it will be able to record the truth from a distillate of intrinsic evidence alone.

A principal criticism of this way of knowing is that it is limited to the discovery of truth. There seems to be little room for invention, for creative learning. As a form of discovery, learning is always moving toward a limit fixed in advance, that is, the apprehension of the form or species resident in objects perceived by the senses. When the teacher presents the curriculum in the shape of problems, the pupil's only thrill is the discovery of what is already known by the teacher or textbook. Even invention, whether by the great man or the pupil, is taught as the discovery of what was antecedently true or possible.[15]

To return now to the second theory of truth, the consistency theory, we find a very similar and yet quite dissimilar conception of how knowledge is acquired. Here too knowledge takes its point of departure from the senses. Sense impressions in this theory, however, are not the first step toward an unobstructed view of objective external reality. Advocates of the consistency theory, as already seen, doubt that anyone can ever come into naked contact with reality as it actually is. Like Immanuel Kant, they have no hope of getting to know any object in itself, *das Ding an sich*. Hence they view their sense impressions as merely copies of reality, copies, at that, which take much of their character from the a priori nature of the human mind. Indeed mind tends to make knowledge in terms of its own categories of time, space, causation, and the like. Consequently this so-called "copy" theory of acquiring knowledge is as much a building forth from within as it is a taking in from without. In operating on its sense data the mind checks them for internal consistency. The more consistent they are, the more nearly they approximate the universal law and order which is characteristic of the rationality of the world wherein all knowledge subsists as an interrelated whole.

Perhaps here is the place to refer to another way of knowing, one which claims to penetrate to the very core of reality and yet one which at the same time is the highly private internal product of the knower or learner. This is learning one's world through an intuitive or mystical experience.[16] Here knowledge seems to come in sudden flashes or sharp insights.

---

[15] John Dewey, *op. cit.*, pp. 87–88.

[16] Jacques Maritain, *Education at the Crossroads* (Yale University Press, New Haven, Conn., 1943), pp. 42–43. See also Herman H. Horne, "The Application of Ontologies to Education," *Educational Administration and Supervision*, 2:557, November, 1916; and Howard H. Brinton, *Quaker Education in Theory and Practice* (Pendle Hill, Wallingford, Pa., 1940), p. 63. For further reference, see *supra*, pp. 190–191.

Often it is as difficult to state precisely what these intuitions are as to state systematically and objectively how they come about. They are inscrutable, ineffable, *sui generis*. Perhaps self-validating knowledge of this sort is merely an expression of the uniqueness of a person's individuality. Yet, whether it is or not, obviously the weakness of mystical or intuitive learning is its ineffable character. Incommunicable knowledge—granting there is such—can be taught only with the greatest difficulty if it can be taught at all. The teacher can indicate things to do which *may* lead the pupil to have a particular intuition. But, since intuition is ineffable, there is no checking to see whether he has had it. There is more than a little risk, therefore, that intuition and mysticism as ways of knowing will be educationally sterile.[17]

The pragmatic way of knowing leads to different results. This is to be expected since the pragmatic conception of truth aims not so much to come at the reality of the external world as to try to solve the problems it presents. Learning is not just cognitive. To get to know, rather, is to participate in what is known. Consequently learning does not start, as do the preceding theories, with sensations or intuitions of the world. Rather does it start with a student or organism interacting with his environment. For some reason, unforeseen contingencies arise which interrupt the continuity of this interaction. The interruption poses a problem for inquiry. Again, search for a solution is not just a cranial exercise. The search will not terminate till the learner acts on his physical environment to see what consequences flow from his manipulations. Whatever the outcome, positive or negative, that is precisely what the learner can say he knows.

It is important to note at the outset that not all interaction with the environment terminates in knowledge. Much of the child's interaction with his environment will be just a being or a having, a doing or an undergoing. Such direct immediate acquaintance with his environment, as in the case of color, sound, or rhythm in his study of fine art, is just *sui generis*. As sensation or intuition it is ineffable. Of such experiences it is futile to try to say anything to himself and impossible to say anything to anyone else. They fall short of knowledge, however, not because they enshroud themselves in a veil impenetrable to the human mind, but because by themselves they do not call for judgment, criticism, or interpretation. Jeopardize such experiences by interrupting their smooth-flowing continuity, and then one will have to decide what conditions will restore it. If invoking these con-

---

17 George A. Coe, *What Is Christian Education?* (Charles Scribner's Sons, New York, 1930), pp. 276–281.

ditions actually does restore it, then that much we know. But the knowledge we have learned is not immediate but mediate. It is mediated through intelligence which adjudged its instrumental usefulness.

Finally a word should be said about authority as a path of knowledge. There are many occasions when the pupil has not the time, training, or inclination to make a personal investigation of the truth, however conceived, about some proposition important in his life. On such occasions he not infrequently accepts the word of authority, that is, the word of some book like an encyclopedia, a textbook, the Bible, or the word of some expert, such as the parent, teacher, or scientist. But how far is the student warranted in taking this way to knowledge?

Some find warrant for depending on authority in the prestige of the source from which it emanates. There is no better example of such a source than the Catholic church. Particularly as a teacher of faith and morals it enjoys tremendous prestige. Much of this prestige is owing to the fact that its authority has a centuries-old tradition. But principally it is owing to the fact that the fount of its authority is vouchsafed by divine revelation. Of all ways of knowing, divine revelation—if such there be—provides the most impeccable approach to truth. It is beyond the tests of correspondence, consistency, and workability for it is the very standard of criticism itself. It is unassailable; it is, indeed, infallible.[18]

On the whole, the modern temper has been averse to accepting authority based on some unique insight which transcends the ordinary processes of public scrutiny. Authority, indeed, which rests on private rather than public sources, is rather called authoritarianism. Yet, while suspicious of authority with unquestioned credentials, many modern educators teach their students to accept the kind of authority which is questioned and to accept it just because it can be questioned. That is, the student learns to accept conclusions he does not otherwise understand simply because they have been tempered by a method of questioning or knowing which he accepts, although in this particular instance he has neither the training nor the time to apply the method himself personally.[19] Without the acceptance of this kind of authority, the individual would have to learn everything slowly and painfully through personal experience. He could never take short cuts around other people's mistakes or get a better view of the future by standing on the shoulders of experience of his forebears.

---

[18] See also *supra*, p. 86.
[19] Cf. Charles D. Hardie, *Truth and Fallacy in Educational Theory* (Cambridge University Press, New York, 1942), pp. 22–23. See also Lloyd P. Williams, "The Experimentalist's Conception of Authority," *Educational Theory*, 3:208–211, July, 1953.

THE ROLE OF INTELLIGENCE

The different notions of truth and the different ways of knowing already suggest that there are different views with regard to the critical role which intelligence should play in education.[20] The traditional humanistic view holds that, since the world is intelligible and can be known directly, the role of intelligence is to know. To know most fully and thoroughly is, indeed, to achieve intellectual excellence. In these terms it is easy to understand why knowledge was long thought to be the proper aim of education. Not only was knowledge thought to be power, but it was thought to be worth while on its own acount. Therefore the best employment the student can give his intellect is to acquire knowledge, that is, to master the knowledge already in conceptualized form, to formulate new concepts of the essential nature of true being of things in areas yet untouched, and to bring the whole to a new high level of organization and systematization. To pursue knowledge in this fashion without thought of further sequel is to achieve the cultivation of intellect par excellence.[21]

The educational norm, that the role of the intellect is to know, is also held by those who have no expectation of knowing their world directly. Although they have no hope that mind can penetrate the true nature of being, nevertheless they hold that the main business of education is to enable the mind to know as fully as its natural limitations will permit. So, as their way of knowing results in a "copy" of reality, just so intelligence in their conception is cast as a "spectator" of reality. Mind is a sort of intricate photostatic or picture-taking device. Knowledge recorded in the mind will, of course, reflect the mind's own finite limitations just as any picture suffers the defects of the lens and film which record it. Furthermore, mind does not mirror the world impartially like a film. Earlier views of the mind bias and help to organize subsequent ones. But in spite of these limitations the main aim of education is to perfect mental development. This mental development takes the direction of working incessantly toward that perfection or consistency of knowledge represented in concepts of universal law and order. Again to pursue the perfection of knowledge without sequel on its own account sets the highest aim of intellectual education.

The pragmatic teacher conceives the role of intelligence quite differently. Concerned with solving practical problems rather than wondering about the true nature of reality or obtaining as near perfect facsimiles of

---

20 Frederick C. Neff, "Six Theories of Intellectual Discipline," *Educational Theory*, 7:161–172, July, 1957.
21 Cf. *supra*, pp. 104–105.

it as possible, he conceives of intelligence in the role of an instrument in formulating and testing hypothetical solutions to his difficulties. Following Darwin, he regards mind as a relatively late comer in the evolutionary process rather than as a force primordially present throughout all history as do the preceding two theories. Instead of regarding mind as designed from all eternity to be preoccupied in beholding knowledge in all its disciplines, the pragmatist thinks of intelligence as appearing to facilitate the superior organic adaptation of man to his physical and social environment. Consequently the pragmatist in the school is not given to cultivating intellectual excellence on its own account but rather to refining it as the instrument of human adaptation to a precarious world. Adaptation leads but to continuous readaptation. No intellectual task of the school could be more absorbing than the continual solving of problems.

In taking an instrumental view of intelligence, the pragmatic teacher finds that a question arises as to the locus of the problem to be solved. Does the confusion which is delaying action lie just in the learner's mind? Is the situation determinate but the learner ignorant of the fact? If so, then education is a matter of informing the mind—of liquidating ignorance, as some one has said. Or is the learner in doubt because the situation itself is indeterminate? If this is the fact, then learning is not just a matter of drawing aside the veil of ignorance but a matter of acting on the indeterminate situation to force it to become determinate, that is, to disclose its meaning.[22]

Whether to consider the cultivation of intellectual excellence as an end in itself in education or to regard it as a means of adaptation tells something further about the relations of intelligence to the world. Where the role of intelligence is principally to behold and know reality, the relations of intelligence to the world are largely external.[23] That is, knowing the world does nothing to the world. It does not disturb its existing relations in any essential way either among themselves or involving the intellect doing the knowing. This conclusion definitely holds for the correspondence theory of truth and probably for the consistency one as well, for though in the latter case knowledge is largely subjective, it still does not alter reality, *das Ding an sich.* The situation is otherwise, however, where intellect is regarded as an agent of adaptation. Here the relations of intelligence to its

---

[22] For a presentation of the contention that the role of intelligence is not exclusively one or the other of these functions, see John W. Donohue, "From a Philosophy of Man: Reflections on Intelligence as a Dyadic Function," *Proceedings of the Philosophy of Education Society,* 1958, pp. 13–26. See also George R. Geiger, "An Experimentalist Approach to Education," 54th Yearbook of the National Society for the Study of Education, Part I, *Modern Philosophies and Education* (Published by the Society, Chicago, 1955), p. 156.

[23] *Supra,* pp. 136–137.

world are at least to an extent internal. Given a situation in the present whose outcome is uncertain and precarious, it becomes the function of intelligence to anticipate the future. Where there are alternate routes to completing in the future what is going on in the present, intelligence will have to choose which one is to be the future. In performing this role, intellect does not merely discover a foreordained, eternally completed set of relations in the world, but on the contrary it is instrumental in directing or readapting them. In other words, intelligence makes a difference in the course of events; it is truly creative.

It may occasion some surprise that pragmatic teachers are sometimes called "anti-intellectuals" by their critics. Much of this indictment grows out of the pragmatists' identification with the "life-adjustment" curriculum. Adjustment, critics fear, too often emphasizes emotional factors at the expense of intellectual ones. Too often, also, the curriculum is chosen for sentimental and humanitarian rather than noetic reasons.[24] These adjustments not only suggest relativism, already discussed, but a rejection of a strong subject-matter curriculum, which, when given systematic, logical organization, is a sure guarantee of intellectual structure.[25]

In considering the indictment of pragmatists for anti-intellectualism, it would be a mistake to read the charge as one delivered by the friends of theory (most frequently humanists) against opponents of theory (presumably pragmatists). As a matter of fact, pragmatists are deeply interested in theory.[26] Properly stated, therefore, the real charge against them is the kind of theory they support, particularly their theory of the role of intelligence in education, which runs so contrary to tradition. The theory that the world is intelligible and can be known by the mind in a one-to-one correspondence is entrenched behind centuries of belief and conviction. For Dewey to say now that the proper role of thinking is to solve problems rather than to plumb the depths of reality naturally seems to his critics to demean intelligence, to be, therefore, anti-intellectual. It demotes intelligence from the exalted role of an educational end to the menial role of a mere means. It reduces thinking from man's nearest approach to divine reason to a mode of natural adaptation just a little above the brute.

Obviously it will make no little difference which view of intelligence the teacher employs in planning the instructional program. In the one case, he is likely to assign work as if the child's mind was a storehouse of

---

24 Cf. Paul K. Crosser, *The Nihilism of John Dewey* (Philosophical Library, Inc., New York, 1955), Chaps. 7–8.
25 Harry Broudy, "An Analysis of Anti-intellectualism," *Educational Theory*, 4:187–199, July, 1954.
26 E.g., note that John Dewey, the leading educational pragmatist, entitled one of his principal works *How We Think*, rev. ed. (D. C. Heath and Company, Boston, 1933).

information about the world, some gleaned from books, some from laboratories, and some from field trips or life outside the school. At examination time the teacher makes demand for the delivery of goods stored, hoping against hope that they will be returned in at least as good condition as when first deposited by lecture or demonstration. In the other case, he will challenge the student's mind with problems for which he must exercise ingenuity in digging up data and inventing hypothetical solutions. If as a result of overcoming the obstacles in the problem some knowledge clings to the pupil's mind, it will be an incidental result rather than the main objective of education.

TEACHING

Often teaching and learning are thought to be correlative terms like selling and buying. One term implies the other. Close analysis of the educational pair of terms, however, casts some doubt on this conclusion. Though a buyer may imply a seller, a learner does not necessarily imply a teacher. Valuable as a teacher may be, it is quite possible, as almost anyone knows from experience, to learn all by oneself without the aid of a teacher. Again, though selling may imply buying, teaching does not necessarily imply learning. Consider the sentence "The teacher taught the student for a month, but he didn't learn a thing." A statement such as this shows at once that we must recognize two different phases of the verb "to teach." On the one hand the verb may denote intention and on the other it may denote achievement. The distinction is not trivial because, however intertwined teaching and learning may become, it will justify our pulling them apart when necessary for separate examination.[27]

To teach intentionally, of course, implies some kind of plan or structure of the lesson. The problem of structure primarily concerns the shape and form in which the curriculum should be cast in order to accomplish chosen educational aims most suitably. How one conceives structure, or more commonly method, borders immediately on, and perhaps even overlaps, the way in which one conceives the nature of the curriculum.[28] Indeed, it has not been uncommon at times to treat method as but a phase of the major curriculum problem. But with equal cogency it can be argued

---

[27] B. Othanel Smith, "The Anatomy of Teaching," *Journal of Teacher Education*, 7:339–346, December, 1956. Cf. William O. Martin, "A Phenomenological Analysis of the Teaching-Learning Activity," *Proceedings of the Philosophy of Education Society*, 1966, pp. 82–86. For an even more detailed anatomy, see Abraham Kaufman, "Teaching as an Intentional Serial Performance," *Studies in Philosophy and Education*, 4:361–389, Summer, 1966.
[28] *Supra*, Chap. 8.

that the curriculum is subordinate to the primacy of method. As a matter of fact, structure and material, method and curriculum are correlative words. Each can be transformed into the other. Thus the arts of reading and writing may be methods of communication or material for methods of communication, that is, methods of instruction. Which is which and when can be determined by reference to the two aspects of experience already mentioned, doing and undergoing.[29] The active, contriving phase of experience corresponds to method, while experience as something undergone in consequence of striving is akin to the curriculum.

Even with this distinction we must be discriminating in the extent to which we pursue it. Some educators go so far as to contend that method exists separately from content. Such a separation is clearly implied in the remark that one can teach the identical subject matter by several different methods, or that the same principles of method prevail whether teaching a sinner or a saint. Setting method off from or even over against curriculum is a product of the ancient dualism supposed to exist between mind and the world it inhabits. If the dualism is sound, then the function of method is to see how subject matter is to be presented to the mind. Yet since many teachers, especially university professors, have acquired and dispense their vast learning entirely innocent of pedagogical method, there exists a strong tendency to depreciate methods of instruction, if not the whole field of pedagogy.

Other educators claim that the educative process is not the interaction of two independent factors such as curriculum and method. They contend that method is never something outside the materials of instruction. The art or method of swimming cannot be learned outside the medium of water. For them, the distinction between method and curriculum is not a separation in existence but merely a distinction of thought within experience itself. Experience is a single process, in which the individual perceives the connection between something he attempts to do and the consequences which flow from this attempt. Apart from the effort to control the course of this process, there is no noticeable difference between method and subject matter. To change the method alters the content, and to change the content inevitably results in the need for a readjustment in method.

Given, then, a child interacting with an environment, there are conceivably two ways in which this interaction might be organized or controlled for educative purposes. The first would be to operate in the field of eugenics and thus attempt directly to improve the stuff of which children are made, their heredity. The second would be to effect a control of the

[29] *Supra*, p. 230.

environment. Since the scientific exploration of eugenics is but in its infancy, and since social taboos prevent the use of what is known, it is with this second area of endeavor that educational method will be preoccupied. The teacher's method, therefore, will be to vary the environment in the hope that modification of the stimuli will produce modification of the pupil's intellectual and emotional responses.

This may immediately sound as if teaching is to be regarded as mechanistic. Such, however, is not the case. The intent is rather to locate the emphasis of teaching in the proper quarter. Indeed, the possibility of the external and mechanical direction of the child is gravely doubted.[30] The most that the teacher's method could possibly do is to redirect the student, for his existing instincts and habits are doubtless already holding him in tension in some direction or other well before the teacher starts to apply his art. And, even here, one must be careful to distinguish the physical and moral results of redirection. If in redirecting the learner's activities the teacher fails to enlist the latter's voluntary participation, fails to get his will on the side of the new course, we may well question whether there has been any worthwhile educative effect of the teacher's method at all. A response cannot be compelled, it can only be educed. The main peril in the educative process, then, is not that the learner's will may be overborne by the teacher's method, but that he will not be exposed to a sufficiently enriched environment of stimuli to suggest what is most noble and generous in his own responses.[31]

If this be so, it is probably well, at this point, to canvass the scope of the environment, the medium in which the teacher plies his techniques. The chief thing to remember is that the environment is something more than the objective surroundings which encompass the student. More exactly, it is made up of everything which concerns him, which is continuous with his own interests and purposes. The advantage of such a definition of environment is that it can include things that are remote both in time and place, as for instance, history and geography. Hence the remark that the things with which a student varies constitute his most genuine environment. With the environment so broadly defined, the teacher should acutely realize how manifold are the resources which he can mobilize for gaining the aims of the educative process. The old environment consisted of pencils, paper, and books. Subsequently it expanded to include shops and laboratories. But, even so, it still remained a pretty academic environment. More recently it has expanded to include much of life outside the school

---

[30] William E. Hocking, *Human Nature and Its Remaking* (Yale University Press, New Haven, Conn., 1923), pp. 258–260. Cf. *supra*, pp. 115, 127–128.
[31] *Infra*, p. 257.

as well, the home and the church, radio and the press, industry and recreation, to mention but a few general things.

THE METHOD OF AUTHORITATIVE EXPOSITION

In controlling the educative environment, the teacher may organize the lesson according to a number of pedagogical structures or methods.[32] Perhaps the most familiar is some form of authoritative, more or less dogmatic, expository teaching. This method implies or invokes authority as a mode of knowing and may even be predicated on the "copy" theory of intelligence and the correspondence theory of truth. It may take the impersonal form of reliance on a textbook or the more personal form of oral instruction. In the latter instance the teacher may deliver a lecture or give a closely supervised exposition through recitation. In either event the Herbartian "five steps" will suggest themselves as the most effective way to organize instruction. Knowing precisely what he wants to teach during the lesson, the teacher's first step is one of "preparation," that is, he prepares the child's mind by helping him recollect familiar material he already knows which will make the new material more comprehensible. At the second step of "presentation," the teacher presents the new material which goes beyond the child's present ken. With the old and new material before him, the teacher proceeds through the third step of "comparison" to point out differences and likenesses between the old and the new. After assimilating the differences to the likenesses the next step is one of "generalization" in which other instances of the new material are noted and a general rule of handling is suggested. The last step is one of "assignment" or "testing," in which the child sees if he can apply the rule to still other instances of the novel material.[33]

Where one person is in possession of well authenticated knowledge which another lacks—whether the relation be one of teacher and pupil, lawyer and jury, or president and board of directors—there is probably no better method of exposition or teaching than the Herbartian. If the teacher knows precisely what he wants to teach, a more admirable method could hardly be designed to give the teacher effective control to direct the pupil logically step by step to the clearly seen end or aim of the lesson.

[32] E.g., Israel Scheffler, "Philosophical Models of Teaching," *Harvard Educational Review*, 35:363–367, Fall, 1965.

[33] For a more complete reference to the Herbartian method, see John S. Brubacher, *A History of the Problems of Education* (McGraw-Hill Book Company, New York, 1966), pp. 212–214.

Indeed, this is basically the method of the so-called teaching machine. The teacher's first duty is to gain firm ground by having something to communicate which he is convinced is sound and true. From this high ground he needs only *persuade* the student of the curriculum's truth and worth. The art of communication thus employs not only the skills of the logician but the wiles of the rhetorician as well.

With sympathetic understanding between pupil and teacher such that the pupil wholeheartedly submits to the sway of the teacher, authoritative teaching puts the experience of the race at the disposition of the pupil quickly and without floundering experimentation. The teacher cites and the pupil *recites*. The experience of the learner is utilized as deductive proof of the lesson taught rather than for inductive discovery. While the latter function of pupil experience is not to be ignored, neither should it be the preponderating emphasis in the arrangement of the educative environment. There is but a very slight amount of the social heritage that the beginner could possibly rediscover for himself and only an outside chance that through an experimental method of teaching he will add to it. To be sure, the method here recommended is the method of authority, but if the authority is wholesome and reasonable, many think it should have a first claim on the attention of the teacher.

A sophisticated teaching machine can be designed to function in this fashion. This mechanization of instruction has frightened some. They fear the control which it lodges in the hands of those who program the machines, particularly if machines are ultimately to supplant live teachers. If that were to happen, the lay and professional public might well take alarm. But no sober-minded person who understands this new "hardware" or educational technology has proposed such an educational philosophy.[34] The output of the teaching machine is strictly limited to its input, the "software"; it can only teach what it has been programmed to teach. Therefore it can teach what is known but will hardly be an instrument for teaching where genuine novelties are encountered. Employed as just one resource among others, like audio-visual aids, it can be very effective, but installed as an exclusive device, it would fail miserably.[35]

This method fits in very consistently with other aspects of the philosophy of education already discussed. A method based on the authority

---

[34] Yet see B. F. Skinner, *Walden II* (The Macmillan Company, New York, 1948).

[35] Elizabeth Maccia, "Epistemological Considerations in Relation to the Use of Teaching Machines," *Educational Theory*, 12:234–240, October, 1962; David Epperson and Richard A. Schmuck, "An Experimentalist's Critique of Programmed Instruction," *ibid.*, pp. 247–254. See also Nathaniel Lawrence, "Whitehead's Educational Philosophy and Mechanized Teaching," *Proceedings of the Philosophy of Education Society*, 1967, pp. 199–215.

of the teacher, backed by the authority of the social heritage, may imply relatively fixed educational aims. It probably also assumes the kind of curriculum which is ready-made in advance and which, therefore, has a character independent of the learner. Not only that, but authority is at its best when the materials dealt with are part of a fixed undeviating truth and its values are thought to be intrinsic and ultimate. Such underlying theories, in turn, find support in such metaphysical assumptions as the immutable and eternal character of reality.

Justification for this method can also be framed in more psychological and sociological terms. If one falls back on a philosophy of mind as relatively passive or, if active, a mind which is chiefly cognitive in function, the teacher finds himself confronted with the necessity of forming the pupil's mind from without. He must instruct the pupil, that is, he must almost literally build structure into him. Naturally, such a method of *instruction* must rely heavily upon the authority of the teacher.

On the other hand, if one prefers the social approach, there seem to be several presuppositions which might well support the method of authority. One thing to mention is the way in which the social process may operate through social suggestion. In learning through this means, the mores are acquired by a process of habituation rather than ratiocination. The authority for the suggested mores may be vague, but it is nevertheless always omnipresent. Certainly, there can be little doubt of the momentum and efficiency with which people learn to conform under this method. Further social support for the theory of this method is also to be found in authoritarian political philosophies, such as fascism and communism, for instance. Both of these tend to favor indoctrination, which is definitely authoritarian in the theory of its method.

THE PROBLEM METHOD OF INQUIRY

Quite another method and quite another underlying theory obtains where the learning situation is more indeterminate and where a large measure of contingency enters in. Here, the structural form of the lesson materials follows one of the various forms of a problem. To some, the perplexity implied here is problematical only to the student, the teacher already knowing the answer. So conceived, the problem method easily lends itself to authoritative uses and so requires no further theoretical exposition. Others conceive of this method as presenting something of the problematical to the teacher as well. Here, uncertainty is not merely something artificially injected into the educative process, but arises out of the very nature of the universe itself. Problems are not just school problems, but the enigmatical riddles of life itself. Instead of studying subjects, the student puzzles over projects and life situations.[36]

It is Dewey who has given classic formulation to the structure of the problem method of teaching. The problem, Dewey says, should not start with some school subject like arithmetic or history, but rather with some life experience, some handling of materials in either work or play which runs into perplexities provocative of thinking on the part of the student. Preferably, the problem should be the pupil's rather than simply the teacher's or the textbook's. The next step is to locate and define the perplexity which is holding up or baffling the further prosecution of work or play. The third stage demands a search for data suggesting possible ways of solving the problem. To obtain the full benefit of this step, the teacher will do well not to let the student depend too much on ready-made solutions for his problem, for only by personally contriving to adapt means to ends will he learn the discipline of hard thinking. The fourth stage, then, is one in which he finally constructs his own hypothetical solution to his problem, and the fifth stage one in which he tests it out in practice. In this last stage he sets in motion a chain of physical circumstances to see what the consequences will be and whether they corroborate his initial hypothesis.[37] The "feedback" from early consequences may indicate a need for modifying the hypothesis even before it is fully tested. This "feedback" and the ultimate consequences of the test will constitute what he learns. Learning thus is a product of the lesson rather than its main objective.

There are several phases of the problem method which deserve comment. To begin with, it is to be noted that the problem approach is based on a pragmatic epistemology. Pupil and teacher make a joint investigation of the problem. Both attack its solution experimentally—even where moral and religious principles are involved. Learning the truth will be no different in school from in the laboratory; the same criteria will apply. A school employing this method, therefore, will naturally need a library to hunt up data but especially laboratories, field excursions, and shops whereby these consequences may be traced out.

To proceed further, the role which the problem method gives to intelligence must be pointed out.[38] There is a strong conviction here that a student's thinking is aroused only by the dubious and contingent in experience. So long as experience flows smoothly, habit will take the place of

[36] William H. Kilpatrick, "The Project Method," *Teachers College Record*, 19:319–335, September, 1918.

[37] Cf. Philip G. Smith, "How We Think: A Reexamination," *Educational Forum*, 31:411–420, May, 1967.

[38] Cf. Robert H. Ennis, "A Concept of Critical Thinking," *Harvard Educational Review*, 32: 81–111, Winter, 1962.

thought. The teacher, then, will most succeed in stimulating thinking by interrupting the pupil's complacency. The teacher's method will be to show that the possibility of continued complacency is doubtful, problematical. He will endeavor to show, for example, that this present interest is incompatible with other interests of the pupil. The discrepancy between the two will stir the latter to think. Instead of using thinking to apprehend ready-made subject matter, the problem method employs it as an instrument for trying to control the baffling in experience.

In selecting problems, the teacher should exercise caution as to the degree of difficulty. If reality is a mixture of the precarious and the familiar, the teacher must arrange the problem so that the mixture is neither too thin nor too heavy for the student. If it is weighted too predominantly toward the precarious and baffling, the student will be likely to fail and become discouraged. If it is weighted too heavily toward the familiar and habitual, the student's full powers will not be brought into play and he may fall to fooling or lose interest because of the vain repetition.

Another caution is in order for those instances where the instructor confronts the student with a problem and then tells him to figure it out for himself. This may be proper for developing initiative and self-reliance, but it is only fair that at the same time the student be supplied with the sort of environment necessary for initiating and guiding thought. Independent thinking is a very commendable outcome of education, but it is more than likely to be fruitless if unfertilized by, or done independently of, the social heritage or suggestions from the instructor.[39] Such an environment having been provided, however, the instructor's obligation should end. He should have no responsibility for a specific outcome. If the problem involves genuine novelty or risk so that even the instructor does not know the answer in advance, it should be attacked by student and instructor as a joint adventure. Faith in democracy requires at least this much.

Moreover, thinking should be carried on under the supervision of those who are more skilled in the art of thinking.[40] But this is one of the most difficult tasks in the whole theory of the problem of method. It is difficult because it presents parents and teachers with a delicate dilemma. On the one hand, there is the danger that if the pupil does all his own thinking, he may make decisions seriously hurtful to himself. On the other

---

[39] John Dewey, "Progressive Education and the Science of Education," *Progressive Education*, 5:197–202, August, 1928.

[40] The criticism of the problem approach in Herman H. Horne, *Philosophy of Education*, rev. ed. (The Macmillan Company, New York, 1927), p. 307, seems misconceived. The teacher does not prefer impersonal relations with the pupil in confronting him with a problem. The teacher retires from the problem only to build self-reliance and independence in the pupil.

hand, there is the risk that if the parent or teacher steps in on occasion and does the thinking for him, the child will come to depend on them instead of himself. Which horn of the dilemma to seize at the moment will depend on circumstances. As a general principle, it may be laid down that instead of trying, as formerly, to "break the child's will," compelling him to subordinate his thinking to adult patterns, parents and teachers will do well to make their help progressively less and less necessary as children grow up. This is the only way to prepare for the time when ultimately adults must unreservedly yield the sovereignty of thinking to the rising generation.

In emphasizing the habit of thinking in the problem-solving method, one often hears the advice that the learner should be taught *how* to think rather than *what* to think. In a changing world, it is said, there can be no enduring subject matter, and therefore it is agility of method that is most important. A little reflection, however, should reveal that the *what* and the *how* are inextricably interwoven.[41] The *how* apart from the *what* becomes abstract and formal. Indeed, if one does not have a good store of previous facts and experience with which to supplement his techniques of thinking, he will have to proceed at once to get them before he can attack the problem in hand. If too much of this preliminary work has to be done, it will greatly retard the efficiency of thinking as the heart of the problem method.

It would be a great mistake to believe that thinking is all there is to the problem-solving method. It is important, also, that there be other experience as well. The learner must not only be skillful in manipulation of the symbols of thought, but he must be directly exposed to the sorts of experience which they denote. Language is only a pointer; it takes firsthand experience to clinch its meaning. But one must take care not to confuse this intuitive learning with the raw empiricism of sense impressions derived from Pestalozzian "object lessons."[42] This gymnastic of the senses was carried on in relative isolation. Thinking was not coincidentally involved. That was something done later, after the sense impressions had been gathered together. And the thinking which did follow later was merely a matter of separating and arranging sensory units of experience. Or, if thinking did precede, sense impressions were employed merely to lend interest to learning its bare symbols.

Such a view, some assert, has severe limitations. In the first place, it overlooks the primary role of the motor organs, of active response. Because the child is an individual, he is from the start organically biased; he has preferences. When disturbances in the environment upset him, these pref-

---

[41] Ben D. Wood and Fred S. Beers, "Knowledge vs. Thinking?" *Teachers College Record*, 37: 487–499, March, 1936.

[42] John S. Brubacher, *op. cit.*, pp. 207–211.

erences go to work to attempt the restoration of the previous equilibrium. In this striving and activity, mind is intimately involved in contriving to solve the problem presented by the disturbance. But note that mind responds to meanings, not just physical stimuli. So, in the second place, mere sensationalism would hardly be adequate for the constructive tasks of solving learning problems through experimentation. The experimentalist fails to learn about things adequately, merely through his sense impressions of them. He must also do something to the objects about which he would learn.[43] He must alter their conditions and then note the consequences which flow therefrom. Knowledge cannot remain celibate; it must mate with action.

There are many teachers who recognize the educational significance of active experience in the thinking engendered by the problem method, but who, at the same time, think that such experience on the part of the student may be assumed. Once it is assumed, the tendency of such teachers is to concentrate on inner or mental activity with a minimum of overt action. Indeed, if one be an Aristotelian, he will aim at an educational activity which is exclusively mental as being the nearest approach to pure activity. While the experimentalist would admit that there are occasions when learning through symbols requires little perceptible overt action, nevertheless he would still insist that physical activity cannot be omitted from the complete cycle of thought. Consequently, he will never be content merely to assume experience but will demand that some actual empirical situation be the initiating and the concluding phases of the educative process.

There is some dispute about when to start the problem method. The point at issue is when would subject matter be best acquired. Some say as a result of problem solving—hunting data and then acting on one's hypothesis. Others think the acquisition of subject matter is a condition precedent to problem solving. Indeed, the latter think that a disgraceful amount of time can be wasted in problem solving without first stashing away a goodly store of subject matter. Hence the early years of schooling they would devote to this end and only the latter, more mature years to problem solving.

This method of teaching will be recognized as quite appropriate to the aim of education as preparation. Appropriate though it is, it runs several risks. For one thing, there is the risk that by the time the facts and information taught are taken out of storage they will be out of date. For another, having learned these things in isolation from a specific prob-

---

[43] Cf. *supra*, p. 165.

lem, the pupil may not appreciate their relevancy when an actual problem does turn up. Without a problem to direct the educator's efforts, a youth might accumulate mathematics when he should have been accumulating history, or history when he should have been accumulating physics. Consequently, the experimentalist would hold that thought and experience should go along hand in hand, contemporaneously, each guiding the other.

There is one kind of activity which deserves special mention and that is drill. The conventional view here is that the lesson must sometimes be organized for drill purposes because repetition is necessary to fix learning in the mind. Some hold that just mere repetition is all that is necessary. Others contend that to manage the lesson in this fashion reduces drill to so repellent a feature of school that it often becomes almost meaningless. The antidote for this situation, they contend, is to connect drill with thought. This may be done in two ways. In the first place, the student will do well to reflect on each repetition of the subject of drill to see to what extent he is improving and wherein he needs further improvement. Almost any athletic skill is a good illustration as, for instance, a golf swing, a swimming stroke, or target practice. In the second place, if repetition is still boring, he may overcome his distaste by concentrating on the connection of the drill with the purpose for which it is done, properly a purpose well worth the drudgery of achieving it. Again, athletics is an excellent example. To participate effectively in the "big game" is worth many an hour of toilsome drill.

Organization of the learning environment in the form of problems is not without its critics, even among pragmatists themselves.[44] It is well enough to point out the vital similarity between learning in the classroom and in the research laboratory, but is there not also an important difference? However novel it may be to the student, much of the material in the curriculum is not only already well known to the teacher but so stable in our culture that there is only an outside chance that learning it will have novel outcomes necessitating its reconstruction. It is a question, therefore, whether this material can be arranged problematically in any vital sense. The question is the more pointed if one expects all these well-known stable components of the culture to be taught "incidentally" to some ongoing life situation in which the learner has an interest for its own sake.

All these considerations point to the fact that the problem method can hardly be an exclusive method. There are still times when it is most efficient to learn through the systematic exposition of well-grounded subject matter. In fact, trial-and-error learning can be very wasteful of the student's time,

[44] John L. Childs, *American Pragmatism and Education* (Holt, Rinehart and Winston, Inc., New York, 1956), pp. 353–358.

especially if he is allowed to repeat errors the race has long since learned to avoid. There is even danger that in this process the student will forgo sound solutions in exchange for a mere problem-solving attitude of mind.

These objections undoubtedly suggest valuable cautions for the teacher to bear in mind. Yet it should be a mistake to think that the methods of authoritative exposition and problematic inquiry necessarily stand in opposition to each other. As a matter of fact, they should rather supplement each other. There is an appropriate time for each, and the teacher should be facile in recognizing both. In the very midst of a problem, for example, the pupil may ask to have explained to him some technique which he may need to complete the attack on his problem. Having acquired it on good authority, he can return to his problem solving. Antagonism between the two methods arises only where the teacher invokes the wrong method for the wrong occasion, as, when engaged in teaching controversial social issues, he employs an authoritarian rather than a problem-solving approach.

LOGICAL ORDER OF THE LESSON

Whether one invokes the problem method or the method of authority, it is necessary to arrange the curriculum in some temporal sequence. Should that sequence be logical or psychological? The curriculum or lesson may be said to be organized logically when the order is determined by the nature of the subject or discipline being studied. Ordinarily this means that the subject matter is organized deductively or that the order follows the hierarchy by which one idea explains another. The subject matter is organized psychologically when the order is determined by regard for the individuality of the student, that is, his level of physiological maturity or his dominant interests.

Some strongly prefer the logical arrangement of subject matter. Perhaps the chief reason for this preference is that the student will then be able to relate ideas in the discipline to each other and to other disciplines more quickly and effectively if he comes directly to grips with the fundamental concepts of the discipline in their simple austerity.[45] A supporting conviction among the advocates of this view claims that nothing in learning theory stands in the way of students' of varying ages mastering basic ideas in their ascending order of explanatory power.

[45] Jerome Bruner, *The Process of Education* (Harvard University Press, Cambridge, Mass., 1960), pp. 6–9.

Just as a single discipline has its own ascending order of explanatory ideas, so too it is thought that the various disciplines can similarly be organized in the order in which they are useful in explaining each other.[46] Obviously, such an order, if it can be established, should be very useful in deciding the sequence in which subjects appear in the curriculum. One such sequence starts basically with mathematics, which is seen as necessary to a study of physics. Both of these in turn are necessary to understand chemistry, which is a condition precedent to understanding biology. And a comprehension of biology certainly precedes the social sciences.

Another more metaphysical sequence of studies is based on a theory of knowledge as a graded penetration into the very nature of being. These grades they measure by the degree of abstraction they achieve, that is, the degree of being to which they penetrate. The first degree is a knowledge of physical nature, animate and inanimate. Here the pupil studies physical objects or physical organisms, analyzed and conceptualized according to the form or species of each. This level includes all physical sciences such as physics, chemistry, biology, and geology. The next degree of knowledge is that of mathematics. Physical objects and organisms all exist in some quantity or number. Yet, while things must have number, number itself can be abstracted from things and can be given a logical development of its own. Indeed the validity of the logic of mathematics depends on its own self-consistency rather than on any empirical verification. The final degree of knowledge is metaphysics. Here the pupil deals with pure being. Here he reaches a level of abstraction of his knowledge which is quite free from any material specification, as is so preeminently the case in the first degree and to a limited extent in the second. Of course the well-balanced curriculum will include all three degrees of knowledge, but even so there will be no doubt as to the hierarchical order of their importance. Metaphysics is clearly the queen of all disciplines in the curriculum.

Some go so far as to think the logical order is ingrained in nature. As the grain of a piece of wood, this structure of knowledge is simply a stubborn fact of existence. In selecting curriculum material, the logical grain which it has by nature is an inexorable item which the teacher must incorporate into his lesson plan. Logical order, thus, is not simply the longing of the human mind for system but an invincible quality of the world about which the school endeavors to teach. The minds of both pupil and teacher must conform to and obey this objective order. On the whole, this is the view which modern science has encouraged.

[46] Joseph J. Schwab, "The Concept of the Structure of a Discipline." *Educational Record*, 43:197–205, July, 1962.

Another approach to the conclusion that the logic of the lesson is relatively rigid is based on the assumption that mind itself has no predisposition toward logical form. This being the case, it becomes necessary to import logical order into the mind from without. The importer is naturally the teacher, who has the material already organized in systematic form. Being an expert in the field, he has been able to survey the whole area and give it its proper definition and classification. This done, it but remains to transfer this perfected order bodily into the child's mind, which, according to assumption, has no native organizing tendencies of its own. In this way the learner can not only be saved time and energy, but he can be protected from needless errors because he can start where previous investigators in the field have left off.

Both these approaches to the logic of the lesson have been the butt of considerable criticism. One criticism arises out of the social consequences of such a doctrine. Such a logic, some fear, would be too powerful a weapon in the hands of an authoritarian regime and would, indeed, invite such a regime. To assume that logical organization exists independently of and prior to the act of learning would enable an authoritarian state to indoctrinate a preconceived social order in the learner's mind, almost secure from the attack of criticism.

A further criticism takes exception to the idea that mind is alogical. Far from being indifferent to logical activity, mind's earliest manifestation, many hold, is positively in that direction. The native curiosity of the child is obviously predisposed to exploration, inference, and testing. Yet, while of a logical turn of mind, the child fortunately is not necessarily predisposed to learn either in the chronological order of history or in the scientific order of proof. Although the student may be capable of logical thought, it does not necessarily follow that he learns logically or even that he ought to learn logically.

It is imperative, accordingly, to distinguish the logical and psychological aspects of learning. They are not different aspects of the same process. Psychology describes how children actually do learn but logic provides a yardstick by which the precision or cogency of learning may be assessed.[47] Such terms as thinking, perceiving, conceiving, and judging are used to denote psychological processes, and such terms as defining, explaining, proving, and justifying denote logical ones. The distinction is of critical importance because the advancing role of psychology in the education of teachers has almost eclipsed that of logic. A great deal of the teacher's time is spent in the classroom in such operations as defining, explaining,

---

[47] B. Othanel Smith, *loc. cit.*

and classifying without the teacher's ever having studied what these logical terms connote and entail.[48]

Perhaps the most frequent objection, however, is that logic, rigidly construed, renders accommodation to the problem of motivation very difficult. The order of the lesson, based on the external grain of the universe or made up from the point of view of the person who already knows, neglects the point of view of the person who is about to learn. By failing to start with the present powers of the child, the teacher will probably encounter a lack of interest in study, and may find that whatever is learned of the logical organization presented will be mechanically memorized with a minimum of understanding of what it is all about. Indeed, the teacher will be fortunate if the child does not develop a positive aversion to intellectual application.

PSYCHOLOGICAL ORDER OF THE LESSON

The cure proposed for these objections is to base the logical organization of the curriculum on a different premise. This premise is that there is no final order of experience, that order is always relative to aims or values. Logic, like one pragmatic conception of truth, is influenced by interest. Instead of commencing with subject matter, organization should take its point of departure from the interests and purposes of the child. Because purposes are many and diverse, the logical order in which to learn will differ from child to child, depending on the present point of his knowledge and interests. There will be many logical orders. None will be "the" logical order. This kind of presentation may take longer, but, because it maintains continuity with the nature of the student, there is greater earnest that what he learns he will at least understand.

Some push these conclusions even a step further. Since the minds of individual students are not to be made to fit any single one logical order, they conclude that logical order is of slight importance in the education of the young. To them, mind is more than just lacking in a predisposition toward logical order; it is by nature positively averse to it. In schools based on this theory, one finds free rein given to individuality, spontaneity, uninhibited self-expression, and natural growth.

Such a management of the educative process may well be convicted on its own testimony of being illogical rather than logical. But those who think that the purpose of the student is irrelevant in the logical organiza-

---

[48] B. Othanel Smith, "Logic, Thinking, and Teaching," *Educational Theory*, 7:225–233, October, 1957. See also Kenneth B. Henderson, "A Logical Model for Conceptualizing and Other Related Activities," *Educational Theory*, 13:277–284, October, 1963.

tion of subject matter more than likely would hold that a logic biased by purpose is also distorted and therefore, in the end, illogical. And those who follow the lead of purpose think that those who disregard it are illogical. What is logical and what is illogical at this point is on the way to becoming very confusing. This ambiguity can be dispelled only by being clear about one's initial definitions. Consequently, to avoid misunderstanding, some call the logic based on purpose the "psychological" organization of the educative process in contradistinction to the logic based on the grain of the universe.[49]

It may be well to pause, at this point, and examine more in detail the exact order of events entailed by both the logical and psychological arrangements of the lesson. It is often said that the logical order in which to teach is from the simple to the complex. Here, too, everything turns on the definition of terms. "Simple to whom?" is the strategic question. If one takes the view of the teacher or research scholar, he will probably define the simple in terms of fundamental elements and proceed from the simple to the complex by building these elements up into wholes. Again, this invokes the order of nature, the grain of the universe. In teaching science, for example, one finds electrons, protons, and neutrons the basic units. Put together, these constitute atoms. Atoms in turn make up molecules, and so on into the most complex studies of physics and chemistry. Since this is the organization the child is bound to come to in the end, it seems only sensible to economize by starting with it.

On the other hand, if one takes the point of view of the beginner, the foregoing may not commence with what is simple to the learner at all. As a matter of fact, atomic structure to him might be exceedingly complex. To the learner, the simplest thing is some present purpose he wishes to fulfill. In accomplishing purposes, the order of events may be either deductive or inductive in character, but more likely it will be a combination of both. If the instructor takes off from where the student is—indeed, where this particular student with his unique background of heredity and environmental influences is situated historically and geographically—and if the instructor has a due regard for unexpected contingencies as they may arise during the pursuit of the learner's initial purpose, the order of instruction may seem quite haphazard. But it really is not, not even where pupil and teacher need to modify their original purpose in the light of subsequent

---

[49] Cf. Mortimer J. Adler, "The Order of Learning," *Proceedings of the Western Division of the American Catholic Philosophical Association,* 1941, pp. 117–122. The author refers to these two logics as "the order of learning" and "the order of knowledge." See also the same author's "Tradition and Communication," *Proceedings of the Western Division of the American Catholic Philosophical Association,* 1937, pp. 110–119.

or intermediate events, for to keep purpose firmly in mind is to give integration and order to experience.

It is at the conclusion of the pursuit of a purpose that the psychological organization of a learning experience makes the closest approach to the logical. In reviewing the frequently tortuous, roundabout course which the psychological organization of learning takes, it is often possible to see short cuts that could have been made, also further interconnections not previously seen. The more one analyzes his experience this way and the more he generalizes and simplifies it, the more nearly he approaches the so-called logical organization of subject matter of the savant or scholar.

If this is the case, then the logical and psychological methods of organizing the educative process need not be opposed to each other at all. Rather, they will be seen to represent appropriate kinds of organization for different stages in the process. On the one hand, there is a logic of investigation for finding out, for learning. On the other hand, there is a logic for organizing matters which have already been found out, which have already been learned. Both will be necessary for any rounded approach to the educative process. Bearing this out, is the interesting note that those favoring psychological organization go out of their way to counteract the impression that their method has no place at all for the logical organization of subject matter.

It is worth while to conclude this phase of educational philosophy by pointing out that a considerable amount of the instructor's information must be organized in logical fashion. The more information he has and the more logically interrelated it is, the more flexible and sensitive he should be to perceive the uses for which it can be invoked in further developing the present interests of the child. The instructor must have logically organized subject matter at his fingertips, not as a show of scholarship, but so that he can free his immediate attention for observing the way in which the curriculum is interacting with the student's present attitudes and needs. Yet he must constantly remind himself that this scholarly method of organization is not that of the beginner. The logic of teaching and of learning have notable differences, because the teacher represents in achievement and maturity what the pupil only potentially is in his immaturity.

SELECTED BIBLIOGRAPHY

American Catholic Philosophical Association: *Proceedings of the Western Division: The Philosophy of Christian Education*, 1941, pp. 49–62.

Arnstine, Donald: *Philosophy of Education* (Harper & Row, Publishers, Incorporated, New York, 1967), Chaps. 2–5, 9.

Barnett, George (ed.): *Philosophy and Educational Development* (Houghton Mifflin Company, Boston, 1966) Chap. 1.

Bode, Boyd: *How We Learn* (D. C. Heath and Company, Boston, 1940).

Castell, Alburey: *Philosophy and the Teacher's World* (Bureau of Educational Research, University of Oregon, Eugene, 1967), Chap. 2.

Dewey, John: *Child and Curriculum* (The University of Chicago Press, Chicago, 1903), pp. 25–34.

————: *Experience and Education* (The Macmillan Company, New York, 1938), Chaps. 2–3.

————: *How We Think* (D. C. Heath and Company, Boston, 1933).

Guzie, Tad W.: *The Analogy of Learning* (Sheed & Ward, Inc., New York, 1960).

Hardie, Charles D.: *Truth and Fallacy in Educational Theory* (Cambridge University Press, New York, 1942), Chap. 3.

Hullfish, Gordon H., and Philip G. Smith: *Reflective Thinking* (Dodd, Mead & Company, Inc., New York, 1961).

Kneller, George F.: *Logic and Language of Education* (John Wiley & Sons, Inc., New York, 1966), Chaps. 3–5.

O'Connor, Daniel J.: *An Introduction to the Philosophy of Education* (Philosophical Library, Inc., New York, 1957), Chap. 4.

Scheffler, Israel (ed.): *Philosophy and Education* (Allyn and Bacon Inc., Boston, 1966), Chaps. 6–9.

Smith, B. Othanel, and Robert H. Ennis (eds.): *Language and Concepts in Education* (Rand McNally & Company, Chicago, 1961), Chaps. 1, 6, 8, 10, 12.

Smith, Philip G.: "Philosophy and the Teaching-Learning Process," in Willard Brehaut (Chmn.), *Philosophy of Education* (Ontario Institute for Studies in Education, Toronto, 1967), Chap. 2.

CHAPTER TWELVE

Axiological Aspects of Method

The preceding chapter has approached the philosophy of method largely in epistemological terms. But as we made the transition from a logical to a psychological order of the lesson, epistemological considerations began to give way to axiological ones. The structure of knowledge began to have a value component. Let us use this transition as a bridge to the present chapter where we shall restrict ourselves as singly as possible to problems of method as viewed from the angle of value theory. Here we must ask, "What is the proper social setting for the lesson?" "What steps should the teacher take to motivate it and at the end to measure or evaluate its outcome?"

INTEREST

We come most quickly on issues of value in examining the motivation of the lesson. Our best point of departure here will be to return to our initial analysis of educational aims. There, it will be remembered, aims were seen to provide not only direction for instruction, but also its motivation. If aims are the values sought, the energy with which they are sought will be directly proportional to the degree these values are actually accepted to act upon. The fact that educational aims are desirable does not ensure that they will be desired. The basic problem of what methods to pursue to enlist the student's interest, therefore, is how to make the desirable desired.

With our initial emphasis on aim perhaps our first clue to interest is that it is essentially purposeful. The spontaneity of purpose, however, is more than just random spontaneity. In purpose both interest and intent are closely akin. The pupil is under tension not only to act but to act toward some end. When the continuity of his present experience is interrupted by some perplexity, he sees a connection between his predicament and the way some object or activity will reduce the disturbance and restore the even tenor of his life again. While interest frequently begins with a question or problem, the instructor will do well to remember that it may also cease with too early an answer or solution. This turn of the discussion casts interest in the role of means or instrument. Given a child attracted toward some aim, those things which lie "between" him and his objective become middle conditions, things that have to be done before he can achieve the consummation of his quest. These intermediate conditions are of interest precisely because, without their fulfillment, present activities cannot develop into the pupil's foreseen and desired end. Thus, to be between the pupil and his goal, to be the means for achieving that goal, to be of interest, are all ways of saying the same thing.

Interest as a mediating force seems to be borne out by its etymology. *Inter-est* is Latin for that which "is between." It is a word which establishes a relationship between things otherwise unrelated, as for instance, child and curriculum. But just what is it that lies between these poles of the educative process? From one quarter, it has been described as a kind of tension, a tension, however, which involves something more than is usually covered by attention. Indeed, one must be very much on his guard against the fallacy that attention bespeaks interest. To think that when a student accedes to the wishes of an instructor he necessarily does so for the same purpose that is in the mind of the teacher may often turn out to be a sad delusion. From another quarter, interest is characterized as an emotional attachment or fascination which is self-active and propulsive. Accompanying this emotion, it is generally agreed, is a feeling of worth and approval. Thus human nature, being what it is, prefers to find its motivation in the agreeable rather than in the painful. Furthermore, interest, when felt, is spontaneous, wholeheartedly stirring; it is freely willed.

In a sense this bipolar conception of interest means that the learner identifies himself with the kind of activity which his environment invites. It means that he wants to be that kind of self, that he "accepts" for himself the pattern of life presented. It literally becomes part of himself. He learns it all over and through and through. He lives it. In this sense, interest originates in individuality. Individuality is inescapably biased, and therefore to assert this bias, that is, to be oneself, is to be interested. In fact, the efficiency of learning increases directly in proportion to the extent to which the learner is wholly bound up in his task. If he is united in a singleness of purpose, if he is absorbed and engrossed in his occupation, he begins to possess a mental integrity which is invaluable for learning.

Some think that interest should be an end as well as a means of the educational process. Thus, the fascinating attraction of some activities does not arise out of their being mediate to some more remote aim or value. Rather does mere engagement in them suffice as the source of interest. Here, interest approaches an aesthetic quality. Moreover, interest begets interest. One cannot hope to get interest on the part of the pupil unless the latter already has an interest. This will be recognized as the old doctrine of apperception. Interest depends on knowledge, and knowledge is the outgrowth of prior instruction. The interesting instructor, therefore, is the one who can make new things seem old. It is notable, in this view, that the pupil is thought of as "having" interests rather than of "being" interested.

Perhaps these points with regard to the function of interest in the dynamics of learning can be further sharpened by approaching the problem from the side of instruction that is uninteresting. Instruction is usually dull and mechanical just in the proportion that the curriculum, as presented, lacks connection with present reservoirs of pupil energy, or that the connection, if there is any, is not perceived. The loss in learning efficiency under such circumstances very much resembles the way in which a slipping clutch fails to deliver the full power of a motor to its load of work. And let no one think that he can teach without tapping and applying the pupil's powers. No activity, no learning. Somehow, sometime, motive must be enlisted. It is merely a question of source. If it does not grow out of the natural continuity between child nature and the curriculum, then the lesson must be *made* interesting. But to have to *make* it interesting is at once a tacit admission that genuine interest is lacking. Consequently, resort must be had to external inducements. Artificial and fictitious stimuli must be applied, such as marks and examinations, or even rewards and punishments. This is virtually motivational bankruptcy.

If the handle to gaining interest is the student's present activities, then many think the obvious conclusion to be that curriculum materials should be taken from the real-life situations which surround him. Indeed, they regard incentives drawn from local industry, agriculture, home, and community life so real and compelling that they almost make interest pale into an artificial doctrine employed only in schools. But there is real danger of a wrong emphasis here, too. It is quite possible for some people to be blasé even when plunged into the very midst of some of the starkest realities of life. Or sometimes these realities themselves are altogether barren and colorless. And conversely, it is not at all infrequent that the fantastic—fairy tales, for instance—may stir to a high pitch of interest. Real as life situations may often be, then, they are only a starting point. Interest is not to be defined or guaranteed in terms of any particular curriculum. Interest and value, it is reiterated, depend on what has significance and worth to the child.[1]

EFFORT AND DISCIPLINE

Solid learning is rarely going to be a pushover for the learner, even when he is armed with a driving interest. He must also put forth effort. The mention of effort, however, brings forward an old controversy, that between interest and effort. Several positions may be distinguished here.

[1] Edwin Reeder, "What Are Life Situations?" *Teachers College Record*, 29:409–416, February, 1928; R. Bruce Raup, "Realistic Education," *Progressive Education*, 11:40–44, January, 1934; Boyd H. Bode, "Education and Social Change," *Progressive Education*, 11:45–48, January, 1934.

One position holds to what is probably the popular notion of effort. It holds that effort is an exercise of the will. It represents the strain one feels in doing distasteful tasks.[2] At such moments, one seems to need to make an extra exertion of voluntary attention to keep steadfastly at his task. Viewed in this light, effort seems to be the antithesis of interest. The latter furnishes the motivation for the agreeable, while effort is relied upon when the going is disagreeable. If a child does not put forth effort in his studies, the strategy is to make a direct frontal appeal to his volition.

A variation of this view finds the foregoing opposition of interest and effort a bit too rigid. It would probably recognize an area in which interest and effort overlap and mutually aid each other. It would reject both the extreme of exerting effort without interest, because that would make education wearisome, and the extreme of being interested without the need of putting forth effort, for that would merely make education entertaining. Yet this view stops short of making interest and effort identical. Interest and effort can go a long way in tandem style, but it may still not be far enough. Situations arise in which duty and obligation are binding on conduct even though interest points in another direction. Here effort must be on the side of the sense of oughtness. If it is, it will many times ultimately beget interest. In fact, the depth of interest so begotten is often in proportion to the difficulty of the challenge. But effort must be on this side, even without interest, where obedience to conscience or moral law is involved.

Yet a third view treats interest and effort as unopposed to each other at any point. Instead of interest being sometimes an outgrowth of effort, here effort is made the henchman of interest. When obstacles slow down the learner's progress and almost distract him from the accomplishment of his project, it is purpose or interest that recruits the necessary extra exertion or effort to remain steadfastly at his task. He does distasteful things because reference to his purpose shows that he cannot otherwise continue along his chosen line of self-development. So viewed, it is purpose or interest rather than a sense of the disagreeable that stimulates effort. Indeed, it is often claimed that young people will put forth much more effort in proportion to interest than they will in proportion to irksomeness. Moreover, it is also claimed that greater moral value attaches where effort is put forth on the side of an accepted purpose than where effort is an isolated exertion of volition. We always run the risk of insincerity where we look for moral worth in the learner's assumption of some required ex-

[2] Sr. Joseph M. Raby, in her *Critical Study of the New Education* (Catholic Education Press, Washington, 1932), pp. 88–92, specifically repudiates the opposition of interest and effort as the basis for asceticism in Catholic education.

ternal posture. A better gauge of the moral significance of effort is to be found in the inner spirit with which the agent acts.

Finally, suppose the student is uninterested in his studies in spite of the most artful maneuvering on the part of the teacher, or suppose that he will not put forth effort in spite of the most challenging appeal to his will and self-respect. Is it justifiable, under these circumstances, to use compulsion to motivate learning? The usual answer seems to lend approval, but only as an emergency measure. Where objectives outside the school are vital, and harm is otherwise likely to result, society itself will not hesitate to employ coercion as a last resort to gain its ends. Under similar circumstances, it seems that the school is justified in falling back on like expedients.

If it does so, however, it must be under no illusion as to the results obtained. The mere fact that a student is obedient in doing what he is put under duress to do should by no means lead to the inference that he is moved by the same purpose that moves the teacher or parent. As a matter of fact, the student may only be leaning to respect superior might. Some people are doubtful that education even results from such a display of force.[3] Their point is that no one can be forced to be good, that one can be good only if he himself resolves to be good. But even here consent, while it may be an ultimate condition of learning, is not necessarily held to be a condition precedent thereto. While one may not be able to make a child drink from the fountain of knowledge, to expand an old adage, it will often happen that after one gets him there he will be thirsty enough to drink.

Although the discussion so far has pretty largely centered on the nature of interest and how it is to be induced, there has been a strong implication that interest is a condition precedent to good instruction and learning. Many, however, take exception to this conclusion. On the one hand, they feel that this implication leads to distinctly soft pedagogy. If one teaches only at the level where he can obtain the interest of the student, they have a sizable fear that much of the social heritage will be neglected and that education will result in a sort of sentimental indulgence of child whims. Furthermore, they take added fear that the oncoming generation will form habits of selecting the path of least resistance and most comfort, that it will confuse the respective attitudes of work and play to the detriment of solid industry.[4] The critics would not deny that at times work will

[3] William E. Hocking, *Human Nature and Its Remaking* (Yale University Press, New Haven, Conn., 1923), pp. 258–259.
[4] Frank M. McMurry, "Interest: Some Objections to It," *Educational Review*, 11:146–156, February, 1896.

be interesting, but neither would they have the teacher "humbug" himself into thinking that every time must be such an experience. Such a thoroughgoing insistence on interest will make education wholly hedonistic.[5] To make everything bow to the doctrine of child need or interest reduces truth and goodness to the level of expediency. On the other hand, it also is felt to be bad policy to compromise with interest by sugarcoating the more exacting parts of the curriculum to make them palatable. To offer children prizes to stimulate learning effort is thought in some quarters to be no better than a bribe. Such an appeal to extraneous sources of motivation, however, does not totally lack apologists. Extraneous motivation operates, the apologists claim, like scaffolding in erecting a building: when the building is up, the scaffolding can be taken down. So too in school. Sugarcoating and prizes are a scaffolding to build genuine interest which, when and if built, can be withdrawn and discarded. If the building cannot stand without the scaffolding or if the scaffolding has become important independently of the building, there is something radically wrong with the educational engineering.

The antidote demanded to preserve education from such excuses and degeneracies is training in duty and discipline.[6] The duty and discipline thought to be imperative here are such as result from controlling conduct in the light of relatively long-range interests and well-established standards. Learning prosecuted from this point of view will override immediate interest whenever it is inconsistent with the ideals in question. In consequence will come a renewed emphasis on hard work, doing things that are irksome under the duress of social pressure. To omit such a spirit from the school is to make the school unlike the social process and to work an unnecessary cruelty upon children. While the discipline projected here will probably have to be initiated through external control by teachers and parents, the ultimate objective will be to reach the point where the child will be free because he can discipline himself.

Interestingly enough, the defenders of the doctrine of interest are also severe in their condemnation of the abuses of interest. They agree that it is spoiling a child to indulge him at his present level of interest. Their therapy, however, is not to discard interest but to treat it aright. The value of interest, they insist, lies in the leverage it affords to gain the next level of experience. It is neither play, amusement, ease, nor following the line of

---

[5] William T. Harris, "Professor John Dewey's Doctrine of Interest as Related to Will," *Educational Review*, 11:486–493, May, 1896.
[6] William C. Bagley, *Education, Crime, and Social Progress* (The Macmillan Company, New York, 1931), pp. 104–108; William J. McGucken, *The Catholic Way in Education* (The Bruce Publishing Company, Milwaukee, 1934), p. 55.

least resistance. Rather is it the inviting activity of engrossing occupation and attractive work. They therefore concur that it is a mistake to think of children's interests as accomplishments, as something finally significant.

Similarly, the advocates of interest are insistent on the need for discipline, but they see no occasion for gaining it at the expense of interest. They define discipline much as do the disciplinarians, as the power to choose a course of action and to persist at it in the face of obstacles and distractions till its deferred values have been realized. What carries one through discouragement and distraction is not loyalty to duty or principle in the abstract, but interest in the personally accepted values of his job. The bare overcoming of difficulties has no more isolated value in and of itself than has the mere satisfaction of interest. In fact, it is possible to view duty as just another though probably deeper and more remote interest. Thus duty is not opposed to interest but is itself a competing interest which, when clearly seen, the child would not want to miss or fail to realize.[7]

KINDS OF MOTIVATION

The problems of interest, effort, and discipline but reflect deeper problems of value or axiology. This becomes clear if one rehearses for a moment the questions already raised about the locus of values.[8] Do educational values have an objective status? Are studies valuable independently of their being valued by student or teacher? Obviously, if they do, adults can insist that the younger generation apply themselves to their studies whether or not they are interested in them. Other things equal, of course, adults would prefer study to be accompanied by interest, but if it is not, they will not hesitate to insist that youth resolutely bend themselves to the curriculum because its worth is objectively there. Students will surely discover it if they will but persist digging into their studies, if they will only discipline themselves by putting forth the requisite effort.

If, on the contrary, value originates in the valuer, adults can hardly ignore the factor of student interest. It is the only dynamics available. Either the teacher will have to exercise his ingenuity to organize the curriculum so as to release youthful energies, or he will have to change to another part of it which is not only desirable but also desired.

Both theories of educational values, plausible as they may be, are not

[7] For an interesting balance of the arguments on interest and discipline, see Ignace Feuer-licht, "Discipline and Freedom," *Educational Forum*, 11:359–365, March, 1947.
[8] *Supra*, pp. 172–174.

(margin handwriting: MOTIVATION VS BEHAVIORISM)

without their difficulties. On the one hand, to insist that adolescents keep at Latin, the piano, or anything else on the theory that it is good for them even if they do not recognize the subject's value places a great strain on motivation, almost contradicting it. If it does not deny motivation, it at least results in a severe dislocation of it. Instead of locating motive in the relation of the pupil to the curriculum, it locates it in his relation to the adults supervising his instruction. Instead of pleasing himself, he seeks to please others. If he has to put forth uncongenial efforts in this direction, the result will still be justified to him as having great value, the value of discipline, of learning to do things one does not like to do.

It is one thing intellectually to recognize an obligation to act on the values which he accepts; it may be quite another to mobilize the physical energies necessary to actualize these values.[9] Some educational philosophers have thought that intellectual recognition of educational values is sufficient to motivate the student to learn his lessons. If he has difficulty in rising to the demand of his homework or his piano practice, when his friends are out playing, then he must lift himself up to it by loyalty to sheer abstract duty. Similarly, if he finds it an effort to live the ideal of good manners and morals taught him at home and in church, he must nonetheless attach himself disinterestedly to principle, for any appeal to personal desire could not escape being selfishly expedient.

Other educational philosophers take the view that motivation must originate and be sustained by the physical, biological drives of the human organism. It is unfulfilled desire or coiled up native energies seeking release, they claim, which galvanize values and make them come alive. What carries the student over a period of flagging enthusiasm, therefore, is not loyalty to abstract duty but intensity of commitment to the larger, more remote, the more inclusive ends he is pursuing. So, it is the enjoyment of eating off clean plates that gets the drudgery of dishwashing done. So too with the dishwashing in any vocation. It is the game on Saturday that makes the routine drill of daily football practice palatable or the ambition to become an engineer that motivates the dreary stretches of solving mathematical riddles in college.

Another way value theory brings out this contrast can be seen in the comparison of instrumental and intrinsic values. Thus it is fairly easy to motivate a student if he sees that mastery of the subject matter selected is a sure means of achieving something else he very much wants. For example, it is usually not difficult to motivate professional students. It is crystal clear to them that academic success in legal or medical studies will

---

[9] Kenneth D. Benne, "Toward a Grammar of Educational Motives," *Educational Forum*, 11: 233–239, January, 1947.

generally lead to subsequent success in practice. Since there is little doubt what these courses are good for, the student freely releases energies for their mastery.

All this is not so clear in the case of studies with intrinsic values. Thus, liberal arts are undoubtedly good, but good for what? Instead of being good for earning a living, they are just good in and of themselves; they are intrinsically good. Such an appeal is not likely to unlock spontaneously student energies except among the scholarly inclined. Hence it is much easier to justify instrumental values than intrinsic ones. Intrinsic values are the kind that are ruled by the well-known Latin proverb, de gustibus non disputandum est.

Whether motivation is external or internal, it is preferable that youth have direct rather than vicarious experience of the values involved. Values actually experienced are much more positive energizers of conduct. Conversely this is why the motivation of moral conduct is often weak. Too frequently we can only warn youth vicariously, since to have them learn the wages of sin by actual experience might lead to devastating consequences.

SOCIAL STRUCTURE AS METHOD

Another dimension of method influenced by values is the social structure that envelops it. Most learning occurs in a social context. Of course a person can teach himself, but he would learn very little if he had to depend exclusively on his own resources. Without the social experience capitalized in libraries and artifacts, those who take pride in being self-taught would have relatively little to show for their efforts. The social context not only provides a content for learning but indicates a method of learning and instruction as well. If individuals are what they are largely by virtue of their social relationships,[10] it follows that a most effective method of instruction is to be found in the manipulation of social relationships. Change the social context, and change the individual. Moreover, where social problems of one sort or another pose the content of instruction, it may well be doubted whether an individual can learn their solution short of being involved in the actual process of social reconstruction which solutions suggest. Certainly the individual cannot solve these problems just within the academic walls of the school. To check his solution and to motivate his work he must have a sense of involvement in a vitally real social situation. Otherwise there is danger that the subject materials of his curriculum will become largely technical and abstract.

[10] Supra, pp. 4–9.

If we accept this social dimension of method, we may have to add some qualifications to our use of the problem method. This method meets little opposition when applied to learning how to deal with perplexities of fact—even when values are treated as facts. When the problem is stated in the indicative mood, solutions can be subjected to tests of reliability and objectivity to the satisfaction of nearly any competent learner-investigator. Consensus is possible because personal preference and subconscious bias can be reduced in this way to a minimum. But change the statement of the problem to the optative mood, as is likely to be done where social norms are involved, and the possibility of eliminating preference and bias at once becomes much more difficult, if not impossible. Indeed, probably no one wants to eliminate it, since some value judgment may well be the principal issue in a social problem. To inhibit the investigator's scheme of values, his moral character, as a factor in the solution, would emasculate the problem.[11]

So different are problems in the optative mood from those in the indicative, that some educators would prescribe a special "discipline of practical judgment."[12] There are four steps in this proposed discipline. The first is a clarification of common purpose, which is followed by the second step—a survey and assessment of the existing state of affairs. Next comes an effort to suit the ideas employed to the claims of the situation as a whole; and the final step is an attempted fusion of the ideal and the existing program. Others see no need for a new discipline, holding that a better recognition of the moral factors in the conventional scientific discipline is enough.[13] They call attention to the fact that the learner or investigator is not just an observer or spectator. On the contrary, he is personally involved. Inquiry starts in doubt, and doubt is personal. Doubt creates tension, and tension involves emotional influences even where the situation is factual. Intellectual conviction, in fact, may be as emotionally charged as moral attitudes. An excellent illustration of this view is the inability of some students to reconstruct their religious and moral outlooks when they learn the facts of evolution.

Taken seriously on the economic side, the social dimension of method would require that every young person have an opportunity to participate in the production of wealth as an important part of his education. Obviously

---

[11] Cf. B. Othanel Smith, "What Is a Social Problem?" *Progressive Education*, 26:165–168, April, 1949; and William O. Stanley, "What We Learn by Problem Solving," *Progressive Education*, 26:173–179.

[12] R. Bruce Raup et al., *The Improvement of Practical Intelligence* (Harper & Row, Publishers, Incorporated, New York, 1950).

[13] John L. Childs, *American Pragmatism and Education* (Holt, Rinehart and Winston, Inc., New York, 1956), pp. 305–309.

this means something more than mere cooperative labor in the school. What is really meant is the kind of participation in economic endeavor which formerly was possible under the old domestic system of handicrafts. If it be said that this is impossible in an era of machino-facture, the more is the pity if industry cannot correct its distorted and narrow absorption in its own processes. Industry is part of a social whole. Viewed in its larger proportions, its educational significance must be recovered and a happy place for children found in it.

Much the same might be said in behalf of winning for the younger generation the unhampered opportunity to study and learn at firsthand the workings of the political institutions under which they live. Several obstacles impede the realization of this objective. Peculiarly enough, there is a fear shared by small minds that the condition of public affairs is such that their close inspection by the school would be healthy neither for the morals of the young nor for the nerves of the body politic. But quite apart from such a consideration of expediency, the law itself presents an odd hurdle. Statutes and constitutions defining the franchise draw an arbitrary age line, on one side of which the young adult can exercise the rights of citizenship and on the other side of which he cannot. Achieving one's majority, thus, results in a rather abrupt induction into its rights and responsibilities. The failure of the fundamental law to recognize degrees of civic capacity is obviously out of harmony with educational theory, which definitely recognizes that the learning curve rises through graduated levels of difficulty. This being the case, it is a pertinent inquiry how rearing or ruling adolescents autocratically without representation on the one side of the age line can be considered a good preparation for self-government on the other. Perhaps it is this inefficient articulation of educational and political philosophy which all too frequently results in civic irresponsibility among the electorate.[14]

To a certain extent, the disadvantages of this anomalous situation can be offset by organizing the social environment of the school so as to permit the students to participate with the faculty in forming and administering school policies. From one angle, this too is but an artificial school device and thus a poor substitute for what might be learned at firsthand in the community. But from another angle, it partakes of genuine sovereign power. The authority exercised by teachers and administrators derives directly from the sovereign state. Consequently, it is possible for pupils to have preliminary training in citizenship if the "establishment" will but share its sovereign power with them.[15]

[14] George A. Coe, "The Nature of Discipline for Democracy," *Religious Education,* 14:136–146, June, 1919.
[15] *Supra,* pp. 67–68.

Roughly, there are two philosophies of managing this. One is to set up a frame of student government where on the surface there is every appearance of responsible government by the pupils themselves, but where, underneath, real and effective government is still in the hands of the faculty and administration. To be sure, the adult hand of power is to be kept gloved and out of sight as much as possible, but no doubt is left of its existence and the willingness of the school authorities to exercise it with irresistible force if necessary—in the sphere both of lessons and of school decorum.

The other philosophy of student government is to make the sharing of power the sort of enterprise which it actually purports to be. Here, it is fundamental principle that such an adventure be not undertaken in a spirit of play.[16] Youngsters will soon tire of that. It is also fundamental principle that self-government cannot be effectively learned where power is dangled before the young as a toy or where it is given them merely on loan. Authority and responsibility must be real. Yet, they must not be thrust on the young; they must be the expression of a common will. Moreover, their weight must be shifted to younger shoulders gradually, for it will take time to make over a juvenile's caprice—his former sport of taunting the teacher's authority—into the law and order of society.

Yet, though real, should the total authority and responsibility of the school or college staff be shared with the students? Some seem to have the confidence to go far in this direction.[17] It no more worries them to put young and old on a par in the government of school and college than it does to contemplate the inequalities of ability which exist in any electorate. If democracy is applied seriously and wholeheartedly in institutions of learning, they feel every assurance that the youth will rise worthily to their responsibilities. Others stop somewhere short of such an extension of authority and responsibility to the younger generation. There are some aspects of the sovereignty delegated to the "establishment" by the state which they think cannot be shifted to the young. This they would frankly admit at the earliest possible moment to the students themselves. Afer all, they point out, the schools are a part of the total social enterprise in which adults have a stake as well as the oncoming generation, and a more important stake at that.

Learning citizenship, especially democratic principles of citizenship, need not be confined to student government or to civic projects in the

16 Beryl Pring, *Education, Capitalist and Socialist* (Methuen & Co., Lt., London, 1937), pp. 237–238; Albert Pinkevitch, *The New Education in the Soviet Republic* (The John Day Company, Inc., New York, 1929), pp. 213–214.
17 Beryl Pring, *op. cit.*, pp. 237–241.

economic and political life of the community. There are a number of faculty who advocate incorporating these principles into their classroom methods of teaching as well. Accordingly, they would invite their pupils to share to the extent of their abilities in selecting the projects to be studied. They would consult them in regard to ways and means of prosecuting these projects to a successful conclusion. And in the end they would encourage their students to participate in the evaluation of their achievements.[18] Learning the ways of democracy, these teachers are confident, will be sterile and barren if restricted to learning the definitions and slogans of democracy. To learn democracy effectively, the next generation must learn it operationally.

INDIVIDUAL DIFFERENCES

Another direction from which the social structure of the learning environment needs to be reorganized is not so much concerned with securing a social context for learning as it is with the place of pupil individuality in that situation.[19] But first, as to the nature of individuality as a factor in the educative process. There are several aspects which are worthy of note. For one thing, it should be observed that individuality emphasizes a certain intuitive quality of learning.[20] Learning is personal to the individual who does the learning. Only he can do it, no one can do it for him. Instruction can be neither "given" nor "received." It must be experienced. It is just as personal an operation as the digestion of food. For another thing, individuality points to the respects in which any particular child is different from other children. It is such unique variations as these that generally make difficult the application of any uniform educative procedures.

The rigidity of these differences is a matter of some dispute. Some are inclined to organize the educative environment with these differences as a relatively fixed point of departure. Naturally, therefore, they accord pupil individuality a preeminent position.[21] To them, individuality represents nature as over against the school, which at its best is but an artificial development of a social convention. They pride themselves on following nature. Not what should child nature be, but what is it, is the question

[18] Ernest Horn, "Educating for Freedom and Responsibility," *Religious Education*, 25:635–636, September, 1930.
[19] For a further consideration of individual differences, see *supra*, pp. 57–60, 145–147.
[20] Cf. *supra*, pp. 229–230.
[21] G. B. Kelly, "Some Socialist and Anarchist Views of Education," *Educational Review*, 15:13–16, January, 1898; Benjamin R. Tucker, "Some Socialist and Anarchist Views of Education," *Educational Review*, 15:8–9, January, 1898; Leo N. Tolstoy, quoted in Albert Pinkevitch, *op. cit.*, p. 56.

which guides their research and practice. Since science reveals child nature as diverse rather than uniform, the child's individuality should be respected, even revered.

From such an exaltation of individuality, not a few vigorously dissent. The realization that nature is often ugly as well as beautiful puts them on their guard against a blanket endorsement of all its variations. Going further, some of these dissenters incline to think that social demands are about as rigid as their opponents hold individuality to be. Some, taking a supernatural point of view, decry the pedagogical naturalism of individualism as an undesirable weakening of the social prerogatives of the teacher, to say nothing of divine law itself.[22] Without appealing to authority so high, others say that reason, not man, is the measure of all things, that universality and not individuality, therefore, should be the norm of the educative process. If so, it follows that civilization cannot be transmitted by an overfaithful following of the individual in nature.

Yet another position finds the two foregoing views on individuality standing in false antithesis to each other. The falsity of this antithesis, so it is claimed, arises out of a misconception of the nature of individuality itself. The opposed camps seem to subscribe to a notion of individuality as something relatively fixed and rigid. On the contrary, the idea is advanced here that individuality is much more elastic and flexible. It is, in fact, merely a direction of movement, rather than something unvaryingly performed. Similarly, there is probably an exaggerated notion of the fixity of social demands too. The universal in the social heritage should be subject to amendment in the light of individual experience. If flexibility rather than fixity be the case, the educational problem is to discover within the individual's present experience the interests which are akin to what the community prizes. By cultivating these, a long step will have been taken in the direction of harmonizing individual and social interest in the classroom.

The question further arises, at this point, which individuals should be collected together in a given classroom. Should students be grouped according to their likenesses or their differences, homogeneously or heterogeneously? Both qualities have their advantages. The more heterogeneous the group, the greater variety of experience its members will have to share with one another, thus enriching the common experience of the whole group.[23] A certain homogeneity of the group, however, is also necessary and desirable, in order to ensure communication, to economize the instructor's effort, and to expedite the progress of the pupils. Yet, since indi-

---

[22] Pius XI, "The Christian Education of Youth," *Catholic Educational Review*, 28:149, March, 1930.

[23] *Supra*, pp. 67–69.

viduality is unique, it is at once obvious that there can be no such thing as a strictly homogeneous group. Furthermore, there is a considerable unevenness in the distribution of any single individual's abilities and aptitudes. Consequently, a group that might be relatively homogeneous as to one trait will more than likely be very heterogeneous as to some other. The ethical import of this situation is very great. Fairness to the individual requires that groups formed on one basis should not necessarily hold for all other purposes as well. Especially is this the case in so-called ability grouping.[24] A student placed in a low group for one purpose may belong in a much higher one for some other. The membership of a group, therefore, should be reconsidered and probably reformed almost every time there is a change in the area of instruction.

Whether the educator underwrites homogeneous or heterogeneous grouping of pupils, he must not overlook the importance of individuality as a source of originality or creativity.[25] Social progress as well as progressive education has a large stake here. But just what the teacher is justified in expecting in this connection needs careful delineation. If he judges originality or creativity in terms of a contribution to the world's stock of ideas, needless to say, there is perhaps little use to which pupil individuality can be put in the teacher's method, at least at the lower levels of the educational ladder. But if the teacher determines the novelty of a response from the standpoint of the student, the teacher's method can very profitably be organized about this point. Indeed, viewed in this way, all learning is necessarily creative. Whatever a unique individual learns in the time continuum of a contingent world must be the first occasion of that learning for him. Not only that, but there is a well-authenticated joy attendant upon such discovery and invention. If the teacher can organize the social environment of the class to capture this feeling for each individual as he learns, he can count his work well done.

It has been customary in some circles to associate creativity with a limited range of studies, particularly music, literature, and the fine arts. Obviously, in the light of the foregoing, this is too narrow a classification. There is no reason why creative learning should not occur in the shop, on the farm, and in the laboratory as well. Nevertheless, it is a good caution to remember that in none of these fields is any learning entirely original or creative. In each new act of learning a large proportion of elements of the process are bound to be drawn from habits and past experience. This well-established conclusion should betray no one into thinking that

24 Alice V. Keliher, *A Critical Study of Homogeneous Grouping* (Teachers College, Columbia University, New York, 1931), pp. 147–154.
25 Levi T. Hopkins, "Creative Education," *Educational Method*, 11:1–8, October, 1931.

learning the group culture and being creative are contradictory to each other. Learning the past is not just an appropriation of what already exists. Each individual, because he is an individual, creates his own response to the past. He reconstructs it as he uses it in the present. In this manner the future is the creative product of the present and the past.[26]

MEASUREMENT AND EVALUATION

We must return to aims again to orient ourselves with regard to measuring the results of teaching and learning. Only by referring to the values by which we steer education can the course be properly checked. In using aims to judge results, we must be very careful to distinguish whether we are judging achievement or aim. Thus in rating a teacher or accrediting a school or college, for instance, we might give a high rating for accomplishing the aims chosen but a low one for choosing those aims in the first place. Even with the utmost attention to the validity of our evaluation, student examinations and marks based on them seem to have an inescapable artificiality. Yet, while only life is a real test of educational results, the tests set in school are a pragmatic device for prognosticating results in daily life later on.

Our aims, as implied, provide our standards.[27] Since standards are standards of value, the question whether values are cognitive or emotive arises again.[28] As a matter of fact it is commonplace to recognize grades of almost any article, say, handwriting, composition, computation, and the like. The categories of excellent, good, fair, and poor are familiar to students and parents alike. Indeed it is possible to give descriptions of each category, remembering, of course, that the criterion of "good" will vary for different activities, such as debating, athletics, "merit scholarships," and the like. Once there is agreement on the description of each category, evaluation can go forward even without asking why the criteria are accepted. Obviously, therefore, to seek reform of grading probably means a disagreement on criteria. If it is irreconcilable, there may be need to resort to a majority vote.[29]

Before we consider categories, it will be well to note that there have been various theories as to when learning may be said to have taken place.

[26] See two articles by Ralph J. Hallman, "The Commonness of Creativity," Educational Theory, 13:132–136, April, 1963, and "Can Creativity Be Taught?" ibid., 14:15–23, January, 1964.
[27] John M. Rich, "A Philosophical Analysis of Educational Standards," Educational Theory, 17:160–166, April, 1967.
[28] Supra, pp. 211–212.
[29] J. O. Ormson, "On Grading," Mind, 59:145–169, April, 1950.

One of the most widely held views is that learning is the successful acquisition of material which has been set out to be learned. The teacher transmits the curriculum, and the pupil stores it away. His mind becomes a sort of warehouse. The logical test of such an objective is the ability to reproduce the material on demand, to re-cite it either orally or in a written examination. Sometimes, successful learning is measured by the pupil's ability to define the ideas involved. In practice, however, this does not change the essential nature of testing, for definitions are as easily stored away and brought forth for test purposes as other materials.

In either case, it is the storage or warehouse theory of learning which, on the whole, has been accepted as the basis of scientific measurement by its proponents. Their chief contribution has been to render the application of the theory more exact, for in spite of the rather external character of the curriculum implied by the storage concept, judgment of its mastery has usually been very subjective and hence unreliable. Consequently, the scientific-measurement movement has recommended itself to teachers chiefly because of the objectivity and reliability which it has introduced into assaying the educative process.

The initial introduction of scientific measuring devices into education more or less aped the same measurement techniques which produced such brilliant results in the physical sciences. Particularly did it borrow from mathematics as an instrument for interpreting educational data. Pure mathematics is a form of logic. Its basic proposition can be stated as "if p, then q" or "p implies q." The proposition merely states a relation between p and q. What p and q themselves stand for is immaterial. Their truth or falsity does not affect the proposition, nor does the proposition improve their truth or cure their falsity. This purely formal character of mathematics has led to the quip that in mathematics one never knows what he is talking about or whether what he says is true. The point, however, is worth making, for it immediately appears that any data, even such human data as education, can be poured into the molds of its rigorous logic.

In measurement, the propositional relation between p and q must express an arithmetical proportion. The distinguishing feature of arithmetic is the fact that these ratios are expressed in cardinal numbers. The critical feature of cardinal numbers as compared with ordinal ones, it will be recollected, is the fact that they can be added, subtracted, multiplied, and divided. These operations are possible because the units are equal to and interchangeable with one another.[30] The same operations would be im-

---

[30] Mark A. May, "Ten Tests of Measurement," *Educational Record*, 20:200–220, April, 1939.

possible, of course, with ordinal numbers. A person finishing second in a race might be just a pace behind the winner, while the person finishing third might be ten paces behind. In a system of cardinal numbers the distance, so to speak, between one and two or between two and three is the same. Not only do equal units separate them, but the units are therefore interchangeable. The unit one, for instance, has the same magnitude whether added to two or twenty-two. Cardinal numbers, thus, have the formal character of p and q; they apply to any data.

If education can be interpreted by such a logic as mathematics offers, it appears that an unequivocal judgment can at last be passed on learning achievement. The only question seems to arise whether the data of education can be reduced to such equal, interchangeable, homogeneous units. The first step in this reduction rests on one of the most fundamental assumptions in educational measurement. This assumption is that everything that exists, exists in some amount, and what exists in amount can be measured.[31] This assumption even extends to subtle and refined kinds of learning, such as growth in religion, although admittedly satisfactory results will be more difficult in this area.[32] And, needless to add, the measurement of amount implies equal units and the use of cardinal numbers. It means furthermore an objective and reliable estimate, one in which results agree for other observers and when repeated on other occasions.

Such a theory of measurement taken as a whole may imply a metaphysic. Some think measurement by cardinal numbers implies that the world is ultimately made up of preexistent entities, independent reals, and their relations.[33] It is atomistic, and it is these atoms which are so interchangeable that they can be subjected to such mathematical processes as addition and subtraction. The implication from educational measurement is similar. It assumes that the learning process can be broken down into equal units of subject matter, which are capable of measurement in cardinal numbers. Furthermore, it limits itself to test questions in which there can be little or no subjective variation of opinion. Of these, there are two sorts, those which deal with facts and those which deal with relations. In both instances, the correctness of answers depends on their correspondence to objective reality. Accuracy obviously involves the correspondence theory of truth.

Considerable exception has been taken to this philosophy of measure-

31 Edward L. Thorndike, quoted in William H. Kilpatrick (ed.), *Sourcebook in the Philosophy of Education* (The Macmillan Company, New York, 1934), No. 58, pp. 38–39.
32 Hugh Hartshorne, "Can Growth in Religion Be Measured?" *Religious Education*, 17:224–229, June, 1922.
33 *Supra*, pp. 136–137.

ment. To begin with, it has been pointed out that the application to education of the measurement techniques of the older, more established sciences
does not necessarily constitute a science of education.[34] The techniques are
merely borrowed and are not necessarily indigenous to the materials of
education. Such quantification would be possible only if mental or psychological phenomena could be reduced to units of space, time, motion, or
mass, a condition obviously unfulfilled at present. Furthermore, it needs
pointing out to those with an undue confidence in mathematics, that even
in mathematics quantity is not the basic concept.[35]

As repeatedly hinted, the critical question in quantifying educational
measurement is whether cardinal numbers applied to the products of learning actually do measure equal units of learning.[36] Does the vaunted equality
of educational units rest on experimental demonstration or on mere assumption? For the most part, educational measurement has only assumed
that the increment of difficulty from one problem of a test to another in
history, geography, or even arithmetic is equal. As a matter of fact, it is
doubtful whether, with the utmost exercise of care in this direction, these
increments could be rendered more than approximately equal. And if they
actually are not equal by however small a difference, then they cannot logically be the subject of arithmetical processes.

Every child knows that he cannot add apples and potatoes together.
But not many children, let alone many adults, stop to think that by the same
reasoning they cannot even add apples and apples together if some are
Baldwins and the rest are Greenings or if some apples are large and some
are small. All they can add are apples in the abstract which are hypotheti-
cally equal or equal by definition. Arithmetic, hence, in the concrete is only
true when we do not inquire too closely about the content with which we
are dealing. Yet in all fairness it must be said that, if educators bear this
limitation in mind, the arithmetic of measurement can still be of considerable use to them. They cannot rely on it with entire logical precision,
but they can make very good pragmatic use of it.

But, even granting measurement's fundamental tenet that what exists
in amount can be measured, by the same token it follows that what does
not exist cannot be measured. And education is fundamentally interested in
what does not yet exist, that is, in the student's future development and
growth. The judging of achievement where growth is incomplete and still
going on is bound to be different from measurement where growth is fin-

[34] John Dewey, The Sources of a Science of Education (Liveright Publishing Corporation,
New York, 1929), p. 26.
[35] Ibid., p. 27.
[36] James H. Blackhurst, "Do We Measure in Education?" Journal of Educational Research,
27:273–276, December, 1933.

ished, where its evidences already exist.[37] Besides, exact quantitative determination of educational results requires repetition and uniformity. The
school and college population, however, have individual differences. Not
only are no two exactly alike, but no one is exactly the same from day to
day. Even where overt performances or responses appear alike, the complexity of human nature and experience renders extremely unlikely that the
underlying subjective processes will be the same. No two educational situations, hence, are equally interchangeable, as measurement by cardinal
numbers requires.

Doubtless it is because of the dynamic, variable quality of the educative process that criticisms also directed at the way measurement tends to
fix its attention on clear, short- rather than long-range objectives of education. Only so, it appears, can reliable results be anticipated. Yet, as a
matter of fact, even the shortest-range objectives cannot be made entirely
dependable. By the time one gets to the end of measuring a child's achievement, one will find that the child has already changed in some aspects of
what has already been measured. The one administering the test cannot
measure fast enough, for the test itself seems to do something to alter the
very subject being measured.[38] Furthermore, even if one could bid time
stand still until the process of measurement is complete, one would yet
have the insuperable task of putting all the various results together to make
an adequately integrated picture of the whole child.

It is necessary, furthermore, to call attention to the fact that quantitative measurement thrives best where factors of the educative process can
be isolated, as in the case of learning specific skills or special bodies of
facts. Isolation of variables is the very basis of scientific control. But the
more numerous and interdependent these factors or variables become, the
less possible it is to isolate and measure them validly.[39] Many measurement people recognize this limitation. They recognize that their tests must
be valid as well as objective and reliable.[40] The tests must measure what
they purport to measure. If they do not, no amount of statistical treatment
of the test's data can improve the data's validity. The imminent danger,
where variables are complexly interdependent, is that in the interest of
validity one will try to measure only what can be measured and that
teachers will therefore teach only that which can be measured, namely, the

[37] John Dewey, "Progressive Education and the Science of Education," *Progressive Education,* 5:200, August, 1928.
[38] National Education Association, Department of Superintendence, Tenth Yearbook, p. 404.
[39] John Dewey, *The Sources of a Science of Education* (Liveright Publishing Corporation,
New York, 1929), pp. 64–65.
[40] Ernest E. Bayles, "The Philosophical Approach to Educational Measurement," *Educational
Administration and Supervision,* 26:455–461, September, 1940.

facts and skills which can be isolated. This situation, whenever it occurs, is lamentable indeed, for there is so much else that needs teaching.

Finally, the educational philosopher should not overlook the social significance of the movement to measure educational results scientifically. The rise of democracy has emphasized the unique worth of the individual and of the many rather than the few. But the many are so numerous that it taxes the ingenuity of educators to handle them with due regard to their individualities. Consequently the rise and development of statistics as a means of learning about large numbers of people through careful sampling is a virtual necessity and an educational value of the first magnitude.[41]

Realizing the limitations of arithmetic and cardinal numbers for measurement purposes and yet not abandoning them where appropriate, many educators have shifted from a quantitative to a more qualitative evaluation of learning results. To indicate this shift in emphasis, indeed, they have replaced the word "measurement" with the word "evaluation" in many cases. To a certain extent this shift in emphasis indicates a different theory of learning. Instead of regarding learning as putting one's achievements in storage, subject to delivery on demand at examination or recitation time, they regard learning more in the nature of a process of reconstruction of experience. At examination time they do not look to see whether the student can bring forth the exact goods that were deposited with him. Rather do they look to see whether he has been able to do anything with them, to see whether he realizes their consistency or inconsistency with other things he knows, or whether perchance he has even been capable of improving on them with some originality of his own. Hence the teacher watches for learning to arise not just out of an ongoing experience but also out of its tendency to reenter and reconstruct subsequent pupil experience.[42] But it will not be enough for learning to reenter experience for recitation purposes only; it must enter life outside of school and college as well, for one really learns only what he actually lives.

From such a viewpoint, obviously the total situation rather than isolated aspects of it is of first importance. But totality here is not just a matter of addition or multiplication. It is more than an arithmetical or algebraic sum of rights and wrongs. It is, rather, a matter of the reconstruction of old values in the light of new ones which have developed as the learner has pursued some accepted goal. Evaluation is an emergent and is therefore always more or less unique. Consequently, the goals in

[41] Helen M. Walker, "Democracy and Statistical Method," *Teachers College Record*, 32:599–607, April, 1931.

[42] William H. Kilpatrick, *A Reconstructed Theory of the Educative Process* (Teachers College, Columbia University, New York, 1935) pp. 29–30.

terms of which evaluation is made are themselves constantly undergoing redefinition. They do not stand still, as is required for measurement. Nor will adherents of this theory be dismayed if appraisal of such a process must needs be subjective. They refuse to abdicate personal judgment merely because it is difficult to make.

Such conclusions are almost sure to raise anxieties in those who staunchly believe in "holding up standards" and closing the gap between them and the mediocrity so often associated with democracy. The people who adhere rigidly to standards are likely as not the ones who limit educational change to means in achieving educational ends but exempt ends themselves from change. Once granted, however, that aims are also subject to constant reconstruction, there is no reason why there cannot be as many standards as aims. Instead of a single gold standard of achievement in studies, then, there may be a plurality of standards of excellence.

SELECTED BIBLIOGRAPHY

Dewey, John: *Art and Education* (The Barnes Foundation Press, Merion, Pa., 1934), pp. 32–40.

————: *Interest and Effort* (Houghton Mifflin Company, Boston, 1913).

Friedman, Bertha: *Foundations of the Measurement of Values* (Teachers College, Columbia University, New York, 1946).

Gardner, John: *Excellence* (Harper & Row, Publishers, Incorporated, New York, 1961).

Kandel, Isaac L.: *Conflicting Theories of Education* (The Macmillan Company, New York, 1938), Chap. 8.

Nash, Paul: *Authority and Freedom in Education* (John Wiley & Sons, Inc., New York, 1966), Chap. 7.

Peters, Richard S.: *Ethics and Education* (Scott Foresman and Company, Chicago, 1967), Chaps. 4–5, 8.

Scheffler, Israel (ed.): *Philosophy and Education* (Allyn and Bacon, Inc., Boston, 1966), Chap. 2.

Smith, B. Othanel: *Logical Aspects of Educational Measurement* (Teachers College Press, Columbia University, New York, 1938).

Thomas, Lawrence G.: *Mental Tests as Instruments of Science*, Psychological Monographs, Vol. 54, No. 3 (American Psychological Association, Evanston, Ill., 1942).

PART FIVE
Professional Rights and Duties

CHAPTER THIRTEEN

Academic Freedom and Civil Liberty

Change is undoubtedly the most obvious characteristic of history. For long, history was thought to be cyclic, and therefore, in spite of change, there was really nothing new under the sun. But Darwin's theory of evolution caused an abandonment of this theory. For more than a century now, man has interpreted history in terms of a theory of social progress. Indeed, since he is looking forward as well as backward now, the idea of progress dominates his thought. But the true direction of progress in the future is anything but clear in the moving present. As a matter of fact it might take any one of a variety of directions. It would seem, therefore, the more informed we are about the various possibilities, the more likely the chance of our making continued progress. Patent as this fact seems, there are many whom the uncertainties of history render insecure. Information about the road ahead is so dubious that they do not want to be confused by more information.

Whether to dispense information freely or to constrict it presents education with one of its most profound issues. Outcroppings of this issue have already occurred at a number of places in the preceding pages. It obviously came to the surface in our discussion of the role of the school as an agent of social change.[1] It surfaced again in the discussion of the role of truth in the curriculum[2] and once more in the method of instruction.[3] Reinforce these instances with the dedication of the scholar to truth as a matter of professional ethic,[4] and it is abundantly clear there is hardly a more significant issue in the whole philosophy of education.

Coincident to this issue, however, are knotty problems. How should we conceive of the verb "to teach"? Does it mean to settle thought or provoke it? And if the latter, how free should the teacher be? Are there any ground rules he should observe in the exercise of his freedom? What distinction, if any, should be drawn between academic freedom and civil liberty? And finally, are academic freedom and civil liberty proper concerns for the student as well as the teacher?

[1] *Supra*, pp. 9–11, 13–19, 21–24.
[2] *Supra*, pp. 167–168.
[3] *Supra*, pp. 143, 234, 267.
[4] *Infra*, p. 301.

INDOCTRINATION

The view one takes of the role of the school in the social order is heavily freighted with significance for the way in which the teacher teaches controversial issues in the classroom. As already indicated, much turns on how we define the infinitive "to teach." There are several possibilities.[5] Issues might be presented as if they had but one side to them. This is variously called education by imposition, authority, indoctrination, or propaganda. This method is an admirable instrument in the hands of those who know in advance the kind of social order they want, whether it be the old or a new one.[6] Another possibility is to present various contrary viewpoints but to assure a favorable outcome for a predetermined point of view. This sort of teaching registers some uneasiness about minority opinion but makes only a feeble gesture in its direction. Its long-term effect is but a slightly more circuitous route to regimenting a preconceived social order. A last option would define the infinitive "to teach" as to cause the pupil to investigate, to deliberate, to ponder. It would have all sides of a problem presented, so that students could independently think themselves through to their own personal conclusions. This would be the method of academic freedom. It fits very nicely, of course, with the theory that the school should be a fearless critic of the *status quo*. Certainly the public would support this role of the school more confidently and enthusiastically if it knew that to teach a very controversial issue like communism does not necessarily mean to advocate it but to weigh its pros and cons for what they are worth.

One-sided and even biased as the method of teaching by indoctrination may be, there are nonetheless substantial arguments in its favor. A frequent claim is that it is inevitable. Merely to be born into a culture settles some patterns of a child's conduct. It settles, for instance, his mother tongue and leaves him no option about the grammatical way in which to express his ideas.[7] The same is largely true of his manners and morals. Another claim is that indoctrination is not only inevitable, it is even necessary for the child. Thus when he goes to school the teacher chooses his text for him or arranges a syllabus of studies for him. It would be showing

---

[5] It has also been noted that there are several types of controversial issues: those which (1) once were controversial, (2) were controversial elsewhere, (3) are controversial only locally, (4) deal with highly dangerous problems, like religion, (5) are "dangerous but necessary," like economics. William H. Kilpatrick, "The Teacher's Place in the Social Life of Today," *School and Society*, 46:133, July, 1937.

[6] Earl Browder, "Education: An Ally of the Workers' Struggle," *Social Frontier*, 1:22–24, January, 1935.

[7] Edward B. Jordan, "The Bogey of Indoctrination," *Catholic Educational Review*, 37:20–29, January, 1939; and Helmer G. Johnson, "A Philosophy of Education for a Complex Civilization," *School and Society*, 71:34, January, 1950.

the child no favor to give him an option in these matters, for he is too inexperienced to have a basis for a valid choice. Similarly there are certain facts in science, history, geography, or mathematics which are so well settled that it would be a waste of valuable school time not to indoctrinate the child with them at once so that he can make a short cut to more puzzling problems in the field. In fact, we might lay down a general rule that it is proper to indoctrinate a child, teach him to accept the facts of the curriculum on authority, whenever experts are agreed on them or are convinced that the method they have used in validating the facts is the one the child would have used if he had been mature enough to investigate them.

So far probably most educators would go. The more debatable issue concerns using indoctrination and the method of authority where experts fail to reach common conclusions. Totalitarian states like those of fascism and communism do not stop indoctrinating at these points. Supremely confident in their political or economic doctrines for dialectical reasons sufficient to their leaders, totalitarian states teach a monolithic culture in their schools.[8] Opposing views may be considered but only to be mowed down by the official rebuttal.

Authoritarian churches with absolutistic religions are also prone to methods of indoctrination in their schools.[9] Believing themselves possessed of an infallible truth and often supported in their belief by a divine revelation, they go straight to the point in their instruction. True, certain vistas of speculation are closed by this kind of teaching, but this loss is more than compensated, they are certain, by the single-mindedness with which essential truths can be pursued and by the intensified energies released through overpowering loyalty to a changeless and eternal idea.[10] These churches may on appropriate occasion take up heretical doctrines in their schools, but they always do it with a sufficient antidote of orthodox doctrine so that the ultimate result is a strengthening of the student's faith.[11]

Not a few democratic educators believe that it is possible and desirable to indoctrinate the democratic method of free inquiry and discussion. Paradoxical as this may seem, it reveals that these educators are virtually as sure of their doctrine of freedom as totalitarian states and absolutistic churches are of their authoritarian doctrines. If one believes in democracy and freedom, why not propagandize for them? Must the pupil constantly restrain his enthusiasm for these ideals by constantly entertaining the

---

[8] See also *supra*, pp. 54–55.
[9] R. W. Condee, "Preaching or Teaching," *Christian Scholar*, 42:104–112, June, 1959.
[10] Edward B. Jordan, *op. cit.*
[11] Pius IX, "The Christian Education of Youth," *Catholic Educational Review*, 28:157, March, 1930.

hypothesis that perhaps he would be happier without them.[12] Of course, by hypothesis, freedom must always be ready for self-examination, but some of its supporters feel that in a world surrounded by its enemies freedom deserves an all-out defense. Subject to such examination, it should be taught with the same assurance that imbues the teaching of scientific findings.[13]

In teaching the democratic method of free inquiry some draw a distinction between the brighter and the duller halves of the school population.[14] They would teach both halves the slogans of democratic freedom, but they would teach the slogans critically to the brighter half and indoctrinate the duller half. They would teach the one group to think and the other group what to think. In making this distinction, however, they would not make the fatal error of segregating the two groups from each other. Both leaders and led can be effectively educated for their respective functions only when educated in relation to each other.

The critics of indoctrination have attacked it from several sides. Those impressed with the basically changing and unsettled nature of the world look very skeptically at any teaching bottomed on absolutism, whether that absolutism be political, religious, or scientific.[15] Inflexible viewpoints in a flexible world are unrealistic. In a contingent universe, there must be room for the critical weighing of alternative possibilities.[16] This also implies a theory of intelligence as an instrument for reconstructing the social order, in preference to the one which views mind as a mirror of immutable and unquestioned truth.[17]

Some critics think the teaching methods of indoctrination and propaganda are positively unethical. These methods, they say, treat the child as a means rather than as an end.[18] Instead of using his own intellect inde-

---

[12] Edward H. Reisner, "The Quality of School Experience Appropriate to a Democracy," *Teachers College Record*, 40:700–702, May, 1939.

[13] John L. Childs, "Should the School Seek Actively to Reconstruct Society?" *Annals of the American Academy of Political and Social Science*, 182:8–9, November, 1935. Theodore Brameld, "The Philosophy of Education as Philosophy of Politics," *School and Society*, 68:333–334, November, 1948. For a discussion of whether the school should make a similar commitment to a labor orientation, see John Dewey, "Class Struggle and the Democratic Way," *Social Frontier*, 2:241–242, May, 1936. See also John L. Childs, "Democracy, Education, and the Class Struggle," *Social Frontier*, 2:274–278, June, 1936; Boyd H. Bode, "Dr. Childs and Education for Democracy," *Social Frontier*, 5:38–40, November, 1938; John L. Childs, "Dr. Bode on Authentic Democracy," *Social Frontier*, 5:40–43, November, 1938.

[14] Ross Finney, *Sociological Philosophy of Education* (The Macmillan Company, New York, 1928), Chap. 20.

[15] Sidney Hook, "The Danger of Authoritarian Attitudes in Teaching Today," *School and Society*, 73:33–39, January, 1951.

[16] For analytical treatment here, see Robert H. Ennis, "A Concept of Critical Thinking," *Harvard Educational Review*, 32:81–111, Winter, 1962.

[17] *Supra*, p. 233.

[18] John Dewey, *Human Nature and Conduct* (Holt, Rinehart and Winston, Inc., New York, 1922), p. 64. See also *infra*, p. 298.

pendently, the pupil becomes dependent on the thinking of others. Of course, as already noted, these others are often justified in indoctrinating the child by making decisions for him because they are more competent or more experienced. But there is an inescapably grave risk here that the teacher may confuse the importance of his own convictions with the way his pupil should learn to think. This possible ambiguity is all the more insidious because the teacher may be utterly sincere in believing that the case at hand is one which imperatively demands that the pupil's judgment be supplanted by his own.

ACADEMIC FREEDOM

For those who flee from an instructional method predicated on indoctrination and propaganda, the logical recourse is to the method of free criticism and inquiry. The method of freedom is predicated on the theory that social progress occurs through individuals who depart from the conventional ways of thinking and acting. Of course not every such departure results in progress; many are abortive or even retrogressive. Nevertheless, the philosophy of this method holds that it is good for the teacher to provide a large measure of freedom in the educational program in order to liberate whatever genius is latent in any child's individuality. The method of freedom, thus, has a social as well as an individual significance. It is not only to let the student develop whatever unique capacities he is endowed with at birth, but perhaps even more significantly it is to make his unique contribution available for his fellows.[19]

Thus far there will probably be little or no disagreement in educational philosophy. But the difficult question next arises, just how far shall we go with this freedom? Should freedom have no limits to its exercise, or should it be exercised within a definite frame of reference? For instance, is freedom a condition of seeking the truth or is truth a condition of exercising freedom? Jesus seemed to imply the latter when he said, "Ye shall know the truth, and the truth shall make you free."[20] But whichever is the case, what is the truth? With the answering of this question serious disagreement begins. Educational philosophy, as already seen, is split wide apart by different theories of truth.[21] Those who maintain that there is a truth

---

[19] William C. Bagley, "Teachers' Rights, Academic Freedom, and the Teaching of Controversial Issues," *Teachers College Record*, 40:99–108, November, 1938; Glenn B. Negley, "Liberty and Lawlessness," *Journal of Higher Education*, 23:117–124, March, 1952.

[20] John 8:32. Note that this quotation is incomplete as it stands. Jesus' full statement is restrictive and runs, "If ye continue in my word, then are ye my disciples indeed; and ye shall know the truth, and the truth shall make you free."

[21] *Supra*, pp. 163–168.

eternal in the heavens tend to limit freedom to this frame of reference, while those who maintain that truth is contingent on what "works" tend to recognize no limiting frame of reference, not even that of freedom itself.

To ground freedom within the limits of eternal truth, Scholastic educational philosophy starts with a recognition of man's free will.[22] Liberty of the will, however, stands in need of direction, for otherwise it would almost certainly be man's ruin. Man directs his will through his reason, which judges what law should govern his conduct. To exercise freedom, therefore, does not mean to be exempt from law but rather to act in conformity with it. If to be free were to be exempt from law, then man would be deprived of the benefit of reason. It is of the utmost importance to note next that the law which man's reason declares to his will is not just of his own making. On the contrary, the prescription of human reason can have the force of binding law only if it approximates or is identical with the law of reason of God, the creator and ruler of the world upon whom man's existence is contingent.[23]

Some prefer to root academic freedom not so much in divine truth as in natural law. The scholar's obligation, they hold, is to truth itself. By trimming his sails to popular demand, Socrates might have escaped the hemlock cup, but he refused to make the accommodation. He refused to compromise his pursuit of truth. On his deathbed he declared his basic loyalty, not to the politics of the populace, but to the academy of scholarship. As truth is grounded in the nature of things, so is the right to search for it. Freedom, therefore, being of the natural law, is an inalienable right of man. If so, academic freedom can lay claim to a permanence and durability which it may well need in a day when authoritarian regimes like communism and fascism sweep it aside as a mere bourgeois fiction.

Probably academic freedom finds its *raison d'être* most frequently in moral prescription based on the necessities of modern scholarship. In learning the results of scholarly investigation scholars want assurance of the dependability of the results; that is, they want to know that the results are truly the outcome of professionally skilled handling of the sources of knowledge and that the results are unwarped by political, ecclesiastical, economic, racial, or other irrelevant factors. Yet, however well authenticated these results are by virtue of the academic freedom under which they

---

[22] *Supra,* pp. 125–126.

[23] John A. Ryan and Francis J. Boland, *Catholic Principles of Politics* (The Macmillan Company, New York, 1947), pp. 169–170; and John A. Ryan, "Truth and Freedom," *Journal of Higher Education,* 20:349–352, October, 1949. In criticism of this position, see Frederick E. Ellis, "The Conception of Liberty in the Papal Encyclical: *Libertas Praestantissimum,*" *Educational Theory,* 3:247–257, October, 1952; and Sidney Hook, "Academic Confusion," *Journal of Higher Education,* 20:423–424, November, 1949.

were reached, the public is not under the same compunction to accept them, as it is where academic freedom is grounded in natural or supernatural law. It can sweep them aside in a moment as have Nazis and Communists. We can only hope, therefore, that public opinion will be intelligent enough to be convinced of the reasonableness of this academic tradition.

This precarious state of academic freedom raises the question whether its exercise requires special political forms to support it. Some have advocated a school-state quite independent of the political one so that education would be free to initiate and carry out programs without reference to threatened interference from other social agencies.[24] Unlikely as is the adoption of such a proposal for the school system as a whole, it does not seem beyond possibility for that part which is the university. Some universities actually enjoy constitutional autonomy and all lay claim to being republics of scholars. The philosophy underlying this claim is that scholarly research involves expertise and that only scholars are expert judges of its proper exercise. If this is the case, then proper exercise can only occur under conditions of autonomy and freedom.

Whatever the ground for academic freedom, the question next arises whether this liberty extends only to the teaching of truth. Must the teacher or professor be intolerant of error? Some sincerely believe that he is not at liberty to teach anything he pleases. On the contrary, he is only at liberty to teach the truth. He must be intolerant of error. The fact that in good faith a teacher may be teaching error in the guise of truth will not justify his act. Error does not have the same right to be propagated as truth. If the skeptic or critic inquires how truth and error can be so sharply distinguished, suffice it to say that for Scholastic educational philosophers the law of God is in the safekeeping of the Catholic church, which is vested with a divine infallibility.[25] While this infallibility applies peculiarly to the divine order, it has repercussions in the natural order too. Yet this fact need occasion no surprise because there could be no possible contradiction between truth in the two spheres. Hence the academic world should take no alarm but rather comfort and assurance in any restraints which a supernatural frame of reference may place on freedom of inquiry and on teaching subjects in the curriculum which deal with the natural order.[26]

Others take a directly opposite view—that the instructor or professor must be free to err even about that which is known to be true.[27] For them

---

[24] National Education Association, Department of Superintendence, Twelfth Yearbook, *Critical Problems of School Administration* (National Education Association, Washington, D.C., 1934), pp. 65–66.

[25] Pius IX, *op. cit.*, pp. 133–134.

[26] John A. Ryan and Francis J. Boland, *op. cit.*, 175–177.

[27] George Boas and Sidney Hook, "The Ethics of Academic Freedom," in *Logic, Religion, and Academic Freedom* (University of Pennsylvania Press, Philadelphia, n.d.).

the *raison d'être* of academic freedom is not just the fact that all truth is not yet discovered. Academic freedom has a moral dimension as well. They would hold that finding out truths for oneself is morally more important than being right. Moreover, a society in which teachers and taught are free to err about truth is morally superior to one in which they are under compulsion to accept truths which they do not understand to be truths. This means that a competent scholar must be free to challenge *any* proposition in his field, even the most obvious and rudimentary. Thus it is more prudent to hope that a competent scholar will not urge absurdities than to provide against such a contingency by putting particular truths beyond jeopardy of challenge. Of course, to venture assertions which his peers may think nonsense, a scholar must really command their respect, and he can command it only by winning it.

In regarding academic freedom the tendency is to measure freedom by the latitude the teacher enjoys to set the limits of his teaching and investigation. But the question arises whether founders and donors of institutions of learning should not have as much latitude in determining the limits for which their benevolences are spent.[28] There can be no doubt that founders and donors, whether public or private, political or ecclesiastical, can found whatever kind of institution they wish. But if they want to claim it enjoys academic freedom, they must let the institution drift free and be autonomously ruled by the canons of truth, which are self-validating. Stated differently, the canons of truth are no respecters of institutions; they do not distinguish between secular and church-related colleges and universities. Recognition of this principle has caused Catholics to look askance at the clerical oath of obedience as possibly casting a shadow on the objective pursuit of truth in their academic institutions.[29]

The confusion or conflict between these two philosophies of freedom is serious enough when it divides men within academic institutions, but it could be much more serious where it divides society generally into opposing camps. The possibility of this danger is evident in the consequences of the intolerance with which those who think the teacher is only free to teach the truth must treat those who sincerely teach a contrary doctrine as truth. Here we might have the possibility of one champion of freedom aim-

---

[28] Alton B. Parker, "Rights of Donors," *Educational Review*, 23:5–21, January, 1902; Edmund D. Soper, "Academic Freedom in a Christian College," *School and Society*, 30:521–533, October, 1929. See also "Report of the Special Committee on Academic Freedom in Church Related Colleges," *American Association of University Professors Bulletin*, 53:369–370, Winter, 1967.

[29] Edward Manier and John Houck (eds.), *Academic Freedom and the Catholic University* (Fides Publishers, Notre Dame, Ind., 1967), pp. 169–173.

ing to put shackles on the other. Presumably, if they were to hold political power, they should suppress the teaching of false doctrine no matter how sincerely its proponents believed it to be the truth. Of course suppression is a game two can play. If those put under ban came into power, they might suppress their erstwhile suppressors. Unfortunately for them, however, their own principles would not permit them to do it. Regarding no truth as fixed, they must admit the possibility that their opponents are right and therefore should not be suppressed.[30]

Consequently we have a situation in which the advocates of one theory of truth may suppress the advocates of the other without fear of reprisal by the latter. While this conclusion seems sound enough in theory, it is difficult to believe that in fact the suppressed advocates of truth would not fly in the face of their theory and make reprisal just the same. All told, this prospect of internecine strife in the camp of freedom presents a depressing outlook on a world where the enemies of any freedom at all constantly threaten to overwhelm even modest evidence of it. Confronted with a common enemy, probably the two champions of freedom will get along well enough, but if they should definitely gain the upper hand, how they would settle the differences betwen themselves is a moot point.

Yet, even if academic freedom escapes these contradictions and confusions, there are still other precautionary measures it must face. One of these would limit the professor's or teacher's liberty to the field of his specialization. Within this confine, there seems general agreement that he should be quite free to investigate, publish, and teach the truth as he sees it. Indeed, this is the very core of academic freedom. Unless it be granted and protected, the avenue to social progress is seriously obstructed.

But suppose, now, that the instructor elects to speak outside the scope of his specialty. Policy here is not so clear. Some would guard against this by sharply restricting freedom at this point. Such excursions, it is said, are unfair to the student who elected the course for its announced content. They may also be misleading to the public, which will, like as not, indiscriminatingly associate the prestige of the teacher's official status with anything he may say. Others, however, would regret such a digression, but nevertheless would permit it. The harm that might result from misinforming students and public, they think, is outweighed by the heavier responsibilities which might arise from censorship. Once the latter

---

[30] Cf. John A. Ryan and Francis J. Boland, op. cit., pp. 318–319. Criticizing this view is James N. Vaughan, "On Modern Intolerance," Commonweal, 34:53–56, May, 1941; James M. O'Neill, Religion and Education under the Constitution (Harper & Row, Publishers, Incorporated, New York, 1949), p. 39; and Sidney Hook, "Academic Integrity and Academic Freedom," Commentary, 8:337–339, October, 1949.

is set up, there is an implicit institutional approval of anything the teacher does succeed in saying.

Even in the precincts of specialization, some think academic freedom is such a sharp tool that further safety devices should be installed against accidents in its use. Most notable here is the instructor's classroom method. The Socratic privilege of freely following an argument whithersoever it may lead is not unaccompanied by certain proprieties. The chief propriety to observe is to remember that the freedom accorded the teacher is not a purely personal privilege, but that it is primarily for the benefit of his students.[31] His method, therefore, should not be to hand out ready-made conclusions but to encourage freedom on the part of his students. Opportunity should be afforded them for the independent exercise of their own intellectual equipment. On the one hand, this will involve training in logical patterns of thought which will enable them to approach new problems. On the other hand, it will entail making accessible the more important sources of information. In this latter the teacher should be scrupulously careful to present without suppression or innuendo the divergent conclusions of competent investigators in the field. He must steer a careful course between the Scylla of the "right answer" complex and the Charybdis of leaving the student's mind in a state of confusion.[32]

As to whether the instructor should include a statement of his own convictions among others, there seems to be some difference of opinion. Since the teaching function, especially in a public school, is representative rather than personal, some would carefully warn instructors against the injection of their own individual opinions into the discussion of controversial issues. They think it just as undesirable for the teacher to call his students' attention to his Republican, Democratic, or communist sympathies as to his Catholic, Protestant, or Jewish faith. Some would not even have the students take sides, since there is no effective action which they can take until they grow older. For the interim, they recommend suspended judgment. Others think that the instructor's opinion should be thrown into the balance along with the rest. The only thing he must vigilantly guard against is that his position as teacher does not unduly influence his students in coming to their personal conclusions. This he can encompass by various artifices, such as delaying the presentation of his own views, encouraging students to be present where members of the faculty disagree,

[31] John Dewey, "The Social Significance of Academic Freedom," *Social Frontier*, 2:165–166, March, 1936; and Melvin E. Haggerty, "The Paramount Service of Education to Society," *Annals of the American Political and Social Sciences*, 182:10–20, November, 1935.
[32] Cf. John L. Childs, *op. cit.*, pp. 6–9.

and when opponents are likely to be evenly matched in knowledge and persuasiveness, but above all by tempering both his written and oral statements with a certain dispassionateness and self-restraint—a professional and scholarly decorum.

But suppose, now, that teachers were to be successful in cultivating this even-tempered method of teaching, and suppose, further, that they were to succeed in getting their students to weigh controversial issues in the cool temperature of reason, is there danger that both will lose their ultimate effectiveness by sublimating their energizing emotions? Emotions may becloud reason, but they are also the dynamos of energy which can move mountains. Again, if students are taught to face a world of flux and contingency in which there are no ideals to cling to unwaveringly, where shall one look for the strength of conviction which makes martyrs? To these questions there are no immediate or easy answers. History records no society that has been managed on such rational democratic principles, from school to legislature. The chief hope in the future seems to lie in seeing whether the principle of the open mind can find nourishment in the soil of emotional zeal, as have other great faiths like nationalism and religion.[33]

The further question arises in connection with academic freedom, as with all other delicate and finely wrought instruments: What levels of the educational ladder shall be permitted to exercise it? Originally, academic freedom was associated with instruction of university grade. There are those who would still confine it to that level and who hold it inapplicable to the work of the secondary and elementary levels. There is some doubt, however, about the adequacy of this view. So small a percentage of students attend higher institutions of learning, and the exactions of democracy from the average man are so great, that schools can hardly start early enough to train the citizenry in habits of free criticism. At the opposite pole are those who would extend complete freedom to all the teachers throughout the whole school system. Even though children of tender years cannot understand the complex issues of the modern politico-economic system, nevertheless it is felt by this pole of thought that it will be a grave misfortune for children to learn—as it is feared they too soon will—that their teachers believe one thing and teach another.

The majority of those who have given this problem thought would be inclined to graduate the amount of academic freedom.[34] Some would make

[33] Beryl Pring, *Education, Capitalist and Socialist* (Methuen & Co., Ltd., London, 1937), pp. 265–266, 269.
[34] For a detailed consideration of freedom at the various levels of the educational ladder, see John Dewey Society, Second Yearbook, *Educational Freedom and Democracy* (Appleton-Century-Crofts, Inc., New York, 1938), Chaps. 4–7.

the degree of academic freedom dependent upon the maturity of the learner. In the graduate school of the university, freedom would be greatest because it trains men to do research on the very boundaries between present knowledge and ignorance. The undergraduate college, not quite so close to the intellectual frontier, should have only slightly if any reduction in its academic freedom. Below that, there would be a further gradual reduction down to the earliest grades. Others, commencing in the same way, would make concessions further down the educational ladder in proportion to the pressure from local custom and prejudice, especially from the parents concerned. Still others would take into account what is all too frequently overlooked in defending the claims of academic freedom, the qualifications of the teacher. They would hold that if a teacher is to enjoy a special privilege, such as academic freedom, he must earn or deserve it by virtue of his training and experience. If the social order is to be criticized with the school as a sounding board, the community must have assurance of the competence of the educational leadership.[35]

Reference has just been made to the traditions and idiosyncrasies of the community. Perhaps a further word is in order with regard to the way in which they condition academic freedom. If one takes the democratic point of view that the community is the ultimate judge of its own mores, then the predispositions of the community are an inescapable dimension of the problem of academic freedom. The most painstaking formulation of the principle of freedom will be of no avail, if parents and citizens will have none of it. Teachers must, therefore, practice the golden rule and treat the community even as they would be treated in return. If the teacher craves freedom to express his own individuality, so too, he must remember, does the community. But if the teacher takes a tactless delight in shocking and irritating local sympathies, he must not be surprised or provoked at any consequent alienation of public support. Such inconsiderate teachers do more harm to the cause of freedom than do many of its avowed enemies. Courteous persuasion, not insolent defiance, should be the teacher's manner.[36]

Yet, even where freedom is hedged about by carefully thought-out precautions, there are still obstacles aplenty to surmount. Not infrequently the teacher himself stands in his own light. The inertia of the folkways is often strong upon him, and he complacently submits to restrictions which

---

[35] Abram R. Brubacher, "Public Schools and Political Purposes," *Harvard Educational Review*, 8:179–190, March, 1938.

[36] Edgar W. Knight, "Academic Freedom and Noblesse Oblige," *Teachers College Record*, 37:186, December, 1935; Thomas H. Briggs, "Propaganda and the Curriculum," *Teachers College Record*, 34:471–472, March, 1934; and M. M. Chambers, "The Signposts Sometimes Shift," *Educational Forum*, 23:447–452, May, 1959.

a little pluck on his part might have escaped. In spite of this probability, just where to stand one's ground and where to make a graceful retreat is a most difficult problem. Tact may be such an easy screen for lack of courage, and courage can so easily become foolhardiness. A few American folkways or habits of mind have particularly tended to put fear, rather than enterprise, in teachers' hearts and minds. Among these might be listed the survival of a certain authoritarianism from evangelical religion, the feeling that the school has a paternalistic responsibility for the beliefs of children, a corresponding blind spot to the fact that loyalty to institutions cannot be legislated but must be won by persuasion and conviction, and a confidence in majority rule in matters of intellectual investigation as well as in those of politics. This latter is still manifest in some places where Jacksonian democracy makes the teacher's position a spoils of office.

In the foregoing treatment, academic freedom has been considered apart from any specification of a social time dimension. Nothing has been assumed as to the contemporary state of law and order. Suppose, now, that there is either the external threat of foreign war or the internal menace of insurrection. Should these conditions lead to any compromise on the principles of academic freedom? Some think that these circumstances more than ever imperatively demand every variety of intellectual resource for meeting the common danger. Others fear that too great variety will lead to disunity, and disunion to weakness. Doubtless, in the end, this is an issue of fact. However that may be, communities pretty generally take the more conservative view and, at least temporarily, curtail the guarantees of academic freedom.[37]

CIVIL LIBERTY

Up to this point, we have discussed freedom as a perquisite of the teacher or professor. Freedom, however, also belongs to the citizen. And let no one forget that the teacher is a citizen as well as a teacher. He would like to be as free as other citizens in deciding to join a church or a political party, to wear a style of clothes, to dance, and to drink or smoke. So long as he exercises freedom in these matters in conformity with the mores of his community, no trouble will arise. But let him depart from the norm or stereotype of his community and alas, if anything, he is likely to find his fellow citizens more critical of his exercise of civil liberties than of his exercise of academic freedom.

[37] Harold W. Stoke, "Freedom Is Not Academic," *Journal of Higher Education,* 20:346–347, October, 1949.

On the side of the right of the community to prescribe the way in which the teacher is to exercise his civil liberties, it may be said that the teacher teaches by example as well as by precept. Not only that, but he teaches by example out of school hours and off the school grounds just as well as during the time he is officially at school. Since a democratic community has the right to prescribe the curriculum it wants taught, it is only proper that the teacher should conform to its dictates in exercising his liberties as a citizen. If it seems hard for the teacher to make this sacrifice, he should remember that high office in any community carries with it responsibilities as well as rights. On elevation to the bench, a lawyer must forgo strong partisanship in controversial matters open to the average citizenry so that no possible reflection can be cast on the judicial temper of his mind. So, too, any man or woman on becoming a teacher may well feel honored to ascend any pedestal of civic virtue on which the community wishes to place him. If he is unwilling to do this, then perhaps he should resign and seek a position in some other community or perhaps in some other profession.

There are many laymen as well as teachers who do not side with the community in dominating the private life of the teacher as a citizen. They do not think that being a teacher should in any way handicap a person as a citizen. How, they inquire, can a teacher produce good citizenship through teaching, unless he himself can participate to the full in the duties of being a citizen and make these experiences available for his students? For them, the question answers itself. For them, the citizen-schoolmaster must be an incarnation of the better self of the populace. They would have no restrictions placed on teachers, as teachers, to which other citizens are not subjected as citizens.

Particularly would they press this point in the matter of teacher loyalty oaths. They see no reason why they should be singled out, as teachers, to be compelled to avow their loyalty to state and national constitutions, when other citizens are not required to do so. If it be said that they should swear an oath like other officers of the state, the technical objection must be raised that teachers are not public officers. Certainly, to say that teachers as a class are peculiarly susceptible to disloyalty is contrary to fact. If it is the permanence of the *status quo* which is in danger, it needs pointing out that these very constitutions generally not only guarantee free inquiry and discussion, but, what is decisively significant, they contemplate their own amendment. Furthermore, when a pluralistic state engages the services of a teacher, it acts as the representative of society. The obligation of the teacher is to serve society, not to protect the existing state from change.

A number of administrative devices have found their way into practice to ensure teachers' independence of action in both their official and unofficial lives. Chief among these have been tenure laws, regulations for a larger share for teachers in the administration of the schools, stronger professional organizations, and recognition of the right to collective bargaining.[38] These devices have sought to protect teachers from dismissal for reasons irrelevant to their professional efficiency. While such enactments may reveal a certain outward form of independence, unfortunately they do not always result in encouraging the critical attitude inside the school. Perhaps this is because there is some doubt about their real defensive strength, were an aroused public opinion to beat upon them. Perhaps, too, this security has sometimes been purchased at the price of freedom. In the long run probably there is nothing so important as educating public opinion to the paramount significance of academic freedom and civil liberty.

Teachers, however, let alone the public, are not always able to distinguish clearly between their academic freedom and their civil liberty. Frequently, when they have exercised their civil liberties in such a way as to offend the community and the community demands their dismissal, they claim that dismissal would be an infringement of their academic freedom. A professor speaking outside his chair or field of specialization is a good case in point. When the professor of chemistry puts himself on public record as to his views on communism he is really speaking as a citizen and not as a professor. On the topic of communism he is no more competent than any other layman. Therefore the only protection he can expect is the protection of his civil liberties, not of his academic freedom.

What is the difference between the protection afforded the professor through academic freedom and the protection afforded him through his civil liberties? As a citizen the professor has the right to deliver himself of any opinion he wishes without fear of arrest, fine, or incarceration, provided that his opinion is short of incitement to violence or of palpable moral turpitude. But if he loses fame or fortune as a result of his utterance, it is just one of the risks attendant on the exercise of his civil liberties. On the other hand if the professor speaks *ex cathedra,* within his field of specialization, then he can be neither arrested, fined, nor imprisoned, nor can he be made to suffer loss of his position. We do not protect the citizen against economic loss of position if he exercises his civil liberties in an unpopular fashion, but we do protect the professor. Why? Because the professor has made a life study of his field; he is an expert in it. What he says is much more likely to be true than what the lay citizen says. If we want

---

[38] For a brief review of the pros and cons of some of these devices, see Howard K. Beale, *Are American Teachers Free?* (Charles Scribner's Sons, New York, 1936), pp. 686–688.

to guarantee ourselves this probably superior insight into the most likely direction of future social progress, we must throw a cloak of economic security around him so that he will be able to continue his researches. Perhaps the citizen should have a similar immunity to economic loss so as to fulfill his office as a citizen more effectively, but to date the community has not yet reached this ethical level. Indeed, the professor has a hard enough time maintaining his own unique privilege.

So far our discussion of academic freedom and civil liberty has been confined to the teacher or professor. Yet, what of the students, do they have a stake in these freedoms too? Clearly most students, especially college and university ones, think they do. If professors must be free to teach then correlatively students must be free to learn. If unpopular views on social affairs are not ventilated by the faculty in their courses, then students must be free to invite proponents of these views to expound them on the campus. Unlike the faculty some student "activists" go so far as to claim that the university should take sides on social issues. Instead of its traditional role of objectively investigating and disseminating truth, the university should adopt an adversary position polarized on moral principles.

But it is in the area of civil liberties, perhaps, that students have been most active. The basic question is whether students enjoy all the freedom citizens do, except in such instances where it is incompatible with the purposes of the university, or whether they enjoy freedom only as a privilege extended in certain circumstances. Whichever assumption governs, students tend to be impatient and often try to achieve their purposes, not as a matter of right, but through naked "student power." Such power, however, challenges the power resident in the faculty and administration, who can hardly brook defeat. That such a confrontation has occurred probably heralds the end of the university's long-time exercise of arbitrary authority over students on campus and the need for a kind of campus law consisting of ordered and articulated legal controls ultimately calculated to enlarge rather than restrict the ambit of freedom.

In exercising their civil liberties off campus, students must expect to run the risks of ordinary citizens which is, indeed, all they are. If they challenge the authority of civil officers, they will have to abide the consequences. Nor should campus authorities put students in double jeopardy by taking jurisdiction of the same offense when students return to the campus. Although under extreme provocation civil police may have to invade the campus or school, it is much better if these academic precincts remain inviolate as a guarantee of the freedom which properly obtains there.

Whether the teacher be relying on his academic freedom or his liberty as a citizen, the question is bound to arise, sooner or later, who is to determine whether or not he has violated his trust. Some think that the lay representatives of the community, notably the board of education, should be the judges. This is frequently the case. On the other hand, if the teacher's privilege of freedom is predicated on recondite expertise, it may be doubted that laymen are capable of judging whether a teacher has exceeded his authority or been unfaithful to his trust. Indeed, the profession is quite unanimous in insisting that such questions should be settled by a jury composed in whole, or at least in part, of the teacher's professional peers.

This leaves two final points.[39] Is it ever ethical to deny academic freedom or civil liberty to a teacher who is a professed critic or even an enemy of freedom? Take someone who does not accept democracy as the political frame of reference in which education should operate. Suppose we know that if he were in a position of authority he would be the first to suppress independent thinking and judgment. When such a one outrages us with his criticism of our frame of reference, shall we envelop him with the protecting cloak of academic freedom or civil liberty? So long as he confines himself to the rational and orderly procedures of discussion and voting, it seems we should protect any sincere critic of our system. So long as he uses the relatively slow procedures of trying to educate the majority to his point of view, we need take no especial alarm. We have only to guard ourselves by stipulating that no point of view be taught in an atmosphere where others are excluded. Even if one point of view seems to threaten violence, still we should insist on freedom to assert it so long as there is no clear and present danger of violence occurring.[40]

But what of the professor who conforms his teaching to the point of view of a political party or religious sect to which he belongs? If he sincerely and independently surrenders his own individual convictions to party or sectarian discipline, there seems no reason to criticize him for his position.[41] But if, on the other hand, the professor insincerely conforms his teaching to what he does not believe, then there is danger of betraying the academic community. Not being a genuinely free agent himself, he is hardly entitled to the privileges of academic freedom.[42] And what now of the pro-

---

[39] Harry L. Weinberg, "Prejudice$_1$, Prejudice$_2$," *Bulletin of the American Association of versity Professors*, 41:470–475, Autumn, 1955.

[40] George E. Axtelle, "Should Communists Teach in American Universities?" *Educational Forum*, 13:425–432, May, 1949.

[41] Alexander Meiklejohn, "Should Communists Be Allowed to Teach?" *New York Times* (Magazine), Mar. 27, 1949.

[42] Sidney Hook, "Should Communists Be Permitted to Teach?" *New York Times* (Magazine), Feb. 27, 1949; John L. Childs, "Communists and the Right to Teach," *Nation*, 168:230–233, February, 1949; Vivian T. Thayer, "Should Communists and Fascists Teach in the Schools?" *Harvard Educational Review*, 12:7–19, January, 1942; Arthur O. Lovejoy, "Communism versus Academic Freedom," *American Scholar*, 18:332–337, Summer, 1949; and Harold W. Stoke, *op. cit.*, pp. 347–349.

fessor who belongs or has belonged to such a party or sect but conceals his membership behind the shield of the Fifth Amendment of the Federal Constitution? Such concealment may be quite justified before a legislative investigating committee but not at all before the professor's students or colleagues. While the committee is not entitled to evidence which might be self-incriminating, the campus is entitled to know without reservation exactly what influences make up the professor's mind or condition his teaching. Concealment may be necessary to the enjoyment of civil liberties, but it is quite inconsistent with academic freedom.

The danger grows distinctly worse, of course, where the teacher is ready at any moment to execute a *coup d'état*, that is, take a sudden short cut to the overthrow of democracy through the use of force. If he is insincerely hiding in the folds of the mantle of academic freedom or civil liberty till such an opportune time, then there seems no ethical objection to denying him the protection of these privileges.[43]

SELECTED BIBLIOGRAPHY

American Civil Liberties Union: *Academic Freedom and Civil Liberties of Students in Colleges and Universities* (1964).

Bantock, Geoffrey H.: *Freedom and Authority in Education* (Henry Regnery Company, Chicago, 1953).

Beale, H. K.: *Are American Teachers Free?* (Charles Scribner's Sons, New York, 1936), Chaps. 20–22.

Berkson, Isaac B.: *The Ideal and the Community* (Harper & Row, Publishers, Incorporated, New York, 1958), Chaps. 12, 15.

Bunting, David E.: *Liberty and Learning* (Public Affairs Press, Washington, D.C., 1942).

Coe, George A.: *Educating for Citizenship* (Charles Scribner's Sons, New York, 1932), Chap. 4.

Gorovitz, Samuel (ed.): *Freedom and Order in the University* (Press of Western Reserve University, Cleveland, 1967) Chaps. 3–4.

Hollins, T. H. B. (ed.): *Aims in Education: The Philosophic Approach* (University of Manchester Press, Manchester, 1964), Chaps. 2–3.

Hutchins, Robert M.: *The Conflict in Education* (Harper & Row, Publishers, Incorporated, New York, 1953), Chap. 3.

John Dewey Society: Second Yearbook, *Educational Freedom and Democracy* (Appleton-Century-Crofts, Inc., New York, 1938).

Jones, Howard Mumford: *Primer of Intellectual Freedom* (Harvard University Press, Cambridge, Mass., 1949).

---

[43] Thomas V. Smith, "Academic Expediency as Democratic Justice *in re* Communists," *American Scholar*, 18:342–346, Summer, 1949. Holding much the same point of view but thinking it more important to encourage the friends of freedom than to discourage its communist enemies, is Max Lerner, "The Mandarins and the Pariahs," *American Scholar*, 18:337–342, Summer, 1949.

Kilpatrick, William H.: *Education and the Social Crisis* (Liveright Publishing Corporation, New York, 1932).

Kirk, Russell: *Academic Freedom* (Henry Regnery Company, Chicago, 1955).

Law and Contemporary Problems, Vol. 28, Summer, 1962.

Lovejoy, Arthur O.: *Encyclopedia of the Social Sciences* (The Macmillan Company, New York, 1954), s.v., "Academic Freedom."

Lowell, A. Lawrence: *At War with Academic Traditions in America* (Harvard University Press, Cambridge, Mass., 1934), pp. 267–272.

Machlup, Fritz: "On Some Misconceptions concerning Academic Freedom," *Bulletin of the American Association of University Professors*, 41:753–784, Winter, 1955.

Manier, Edward, and John Houck (eds.): *Academic Freedom and the Catholic University* (Fides Publishers, Notre Dame, Ind., 1967), Chaps. 3, 4, 7.

Nash, Paul: *Authority and Freedom in Education* (John Wiley & Sons, Inc., New York, 1965), Chap. 2.

Peters, Richard S.: *Ethics and Education* (Scott Foresman and Company, Chicago, 1967), pp. 121–127.

Pittenger, Benjamin F.: *Indoctrination for American Democracy* (The Macmillan Company, New York, 1941).

Progressive Education, March, 1948.

Ryan, John A., and Francis J. Boland: *Catholic Principles of Politics* (The Macmillan Company, New York, 1940), Chap. 13.

Social Frontier, January 1935 and March 1936.

Tos, Aldo: *A Critical Study of American Views on Academic Freedom* (The Catholic University of America Press, Washington, D.C., 1958).

CHAPTER FOURTEEN

Professional Ethics

The normative function of educational philosophy would be incomplete without mention of the ethical tactics of the teacher in giving effect to the overall strategy of education. The teacher must negotiate many personal relationships with his students, colleagues, and lay public—notably parents and school-board members—in which conflicts of interest arise. What ethical standards shall the professional and the layman employ in resolving these conflicts?

To be more concrete about the kinds of personal relations which involve ethical considerations, we might sample a number of situations. However, to point to but one very striking illustration, let us take the teachers' strike. Is it ethical for the teacher to withhold his services from the pupil? Ostensibly the teacher withholds instruction in order to bring pressure to bear on the community to ensure the sort of working conditions which make it possible for the teacher to lead his pupils to the achievement of the values incorporated into the ultimate and proximate aims of education. But in spite of that high purpose an inevitable ambiguity arises. When he strikes, is the teacher really acting in the interest of his pupil or rather in his own personal interest? Obviously the interests of pupil and teacher overlap and interpenetrate so that it is not easy to discriminate the exact motivation. How is the teacher to disentangle and sort out these interests to ensure a judgment about them that is just and fair? This is clearly an ethical problem.

Undoubtedly there are general ethical principles which could be invoked to guide the teacher's conduct. But the question arises whether such general principles are enough or whether the practice of education presents special circumstances which require some added qualification of general ethical principles. Does the relation of pupil and teacher present unique problems not ordinarily found or recognized in the relations of people generally to one another? Such a unique relationship is recognized in the relation of the doctor and his patient, of the lawyer and his client, and of the clergyman and his parishioner. Do the same or similar circumstances obtain in the case of education, which warrant our going beyond a general to a professional ethic?

PRINCIPAL DIMENSIONS OF A PROFESSIONAL ETHIC

If the professional person were to consult only the maxims of general ethics he would have at hand a very good rule by which to guide his relations with laymen seeking his services. That rule is embodied in the famous imperative of Immanuel Kant. "So act as to treat humanity," he enjoined, "whether in thine own person or that of another, in every case as an end withal, never as a means only."[1] By treating the individual as an end, we may assume that Kant considered the individual to have intrinsic value.[2] His injunction, therefore, charges us to respect this value and *always* to act with the other fellow's best interests in mind. So long as we remember this directive it will be unobjectionable if incidentally we use others to our own advantage, that is, make them means to the realization of our ends.

The Kantian imperative is addressed to everyone without qualification. Nothing is said about one imperative for laymen and another for professional people. Since the Kantian standard is of the highest, we may well wonder in just what way the adjective "professional" is intended to modify the noun "ethic." To meet this query it will first be necessary to explicate the nature of a profession. What distinguishes a profession from other occupations is the fact that it is learnèd. Its members possess a special competence based upon a long period of rigorous theoretical training. Note that special competence alone without exacting intellectual preparation is not enough, for a craftsman might have that. The *ad hoc* routine of the craftsman is foreign to the professional, whose actions constantly require recondite and frequently creative judgment.[3]

In what way, then, does this definition of a profession modify the ethic requiring that persons be treated as ends? We may note several different directions which modification might take. Ordinarily the layman can be trusted to be the judge of whether he is being treated as an end, whether his best interests are being served by another. Self-reliance in judging one's own interest works reasonably well as long as both parties have approximately equal knowledge of the probable motivations and consequences involved in social interaction. But obviously this is not the situation where a professional exercises his peculiar competence for a layman. The professional knows so much more than the layman that the latter is almost completely at a disadvantage in determining whether the professional service he is receiving is to his best interest or not. As a matter of fact, only the professional has a sound basis for judging the best interests of the lay-

[1] Immanuel Kant, *Metaphysics of Morals*, Part I, Book II, Chap. 1, Sec. 25.
[2] Cf. *supra*, pp. 57–59.
[3] Harry Broudy, "Teaching: Craft or Profession?" *Educational Forum*, 20:175–184, January, 1956.

man. Hence, since the layman's judgment is an inadequate check against the professional's, the professional person must take almost sole responsibility himself to see that the Kantian ethic is fulfilled. This is a heavy responsibility. The adjective "professional," therefore, modifies the noun "ethic," not by restricting its content, but by adding to the professional's obligation to abide by it.

An important corollary of this obligation is the necessity for recognizing the autonomy of the professional. As his expert knowledge makes him alone competent to determine what service is good for a particular layman, so too it must be left to him to set appropriate standards for professional practice in general. Naturally this autonomy must extend also to determining criteria for admission to the profession and programs of training suitable for that purpose. For the layman to prescribe through the legislature or otherwise for the professional in these areas would be assuming ethical prerogatives for which he is unfitted.

As the professional seems uniquely charged with being the exclusive custodian of a large segment of public welfare, the question may arise, quis custodiet ipsos custodes—who takes custody of the custodians themselves? In other words, what assurance has society that professional people are faithfully executing the weighty ethical obligation which their advanced training has thrust upon them? Ordinarily the guarantee of professional integrity is found in the professional's disinterested dedication to the welfare of his public. Presumably he proves this disinterested dedication by dispensing his expert services primarily for the benefit of others. His own personal advancement and material comfort must be unequivocally subordinated to the public he serves. He must positively leave no confusion in his own or the public's mind as to whose interests he is primarily serving.

This brings forward the question of financial remuneration for the professional. It has often been stated that the essential difference between a craft and a profession is that the former is carried on primarily for financial gain, while the latter always counts financial remuneration of secondary importance. This denigration of crafts was extended at one time to professions also and to some extent still attaches to them. As evidence, note that another meaning of the word "professional" has quite a different emphasis from the one employed so far. This meaning denotes a person who not only takes pay for his services but probably would not perform at all except for pay. In this vein Socrates denounced the Sophists of his day for accepting pay for their teaching; and we can easily understand that pay was demeaning in a society where freemen lived off the labor of slaves. Even though today it is considered dignified to live by the sweat of one's brow, good form still demands that the professional be motivated primarily by the idea of service rather than of gain.

To account for good form on ethical rather than socioeconomic grounds, we may commence with a distinction made by Aristotle between activities that are "honorable" and those that are merely "useful." The value of honorable activities is that they are self-contained; they result in perfecting the self of the doer. The value of useful activities, on the other hand, is that they lie outside the self; they are contingent on someone or something else. Which kind of activity is teaching? When a student earns his way through college, for instance, he usually performs a service for someone for which he is recompensed. The transaction is obviously a "useful" one. Does the same situation obtain when the teacher teaches? Does he teach for his pay check? No doubt there are teachers who do just this, and to the extent that they do, we can at least say their actions are "useful." But if the teacher teaches out of a sense of self-fulfillment, if he feels that he must teach to realize himself, we can add that his action is "honorable." He is like Professor George Herbert Palmer, who once said that if Harvard did not pay him to teach, he would gladly pay Harvard for the privilege of teaching. Teaching is more fully professional, some think, if the teacher is propelled by "honorable" rather than utilitarian motives.[4]

The kind of pay the teacher gets may even have subtle ethical implications. If he is paid a salary—a polite word for wages—there is a strong inference that he is being compensated for energies expended and therefore that the transaction falls in the category of usefulness. Ordinarily the professional person is paid a fee or an honorarium. An honorarium, particularly, implies that it is difficult or impossible to compute the value of the service performed and therefore to recompense it. Services that are honorable—that redound to the development of the performer quite apart from their usefulness to someone else—can hardly be assigned a price. For this additional reason, perhaps, the professional person may be expected not only to place pecuniary motives second but on occasion to dispense with them altogether.

APPLICATIONS OF PROFESSIONAL ETHICS

How does teaching stack up to these general ethical requirements? In the first place, does the teacher possess a body of highly expert knowledge which is so beyond the layman's ken that a special ethical obligation devolves on the teacher to be quite single-minded in looking after the educational welfare of his public? There is no doubt that this situation obtains

---

[4] Mortimer J. Adler, "Labor, Leisure, and Liberal Education," *Journal of General Education,* 6:41–43, October, 1951.

vis-à-vis the pupil. Vis-à-vis the parent, however, some qualifications may be necessary. The parent may frequently know as much subject matter as the teacher, if not more. Whether in addition the teacher commands a body of technical information and skill in the science, philosophy, and art of teaching which quite exceeds that of the parent will no doubt vary with the mother's vocation before she was married and with the teacher's length of training and years of experience. As long as the training of teachers was accomplished in a two-year period in normal school, teaching could make little claim to being a learnèd profession. As that period, however, has lengthened into four years at a teachers' college, a fifth year for a master's degree, and particularly two further years for a doctor's degree, teaching has made great strides toward the dignity of a learnèd profession with all the ethical obligations that designation has been seen to entail.

There are three directions in which to note the application of our professional ethic. One is in the dedication of the teacher to his subject matter, that is, to knowledge, and in the last analysis to truth itself. A second is expressed in the relations of the teacher and pupil, and the third in the relations of the teacher and his colleagues. No attempt will be made to cover all the cases but merely to indicate a few principal ones.

The chief ethical obligation of the teacher to his subject matter is to be as objective as possible about it. Expertise manifests itself in thorough knowledge, and thorough knowledge is the product of conscientiously weighing the evidence for and against such conclusions as he may teach. If his teaching includes and results in any modest research, he should publish the results, because only as scholars are able to stand on the shoulders of each other's expertise can they see farther ahead.[5]

In the course of his contact with the child, the teacher is bound to pick up considerable information about the student and perhaps even about his home. Following the ethical principle of always acting in the best interests of his client, the teacher will regard it an ethical obligation to treat this information as strictly confidential. If he does not do so, he is likely to find the main avenue of approach to indispensable pedagogical information cut off, for no one likes to learn that his private affairs have been discussed before a curious and gossipy public of youngsters or adults. On the other hand, if the teacher's ingenuity leads him to the discovery of some new pedagogical technique, the teacher will find it unethical to keep such information a closed secret and even more unethical if he discloses the secret only for a price. There must be no ambiguity in the mind of the teacher or

---

[5] For a more extended discussion of these ideas, see A. C. Benjamin, "The Ethics of Scholarship," *Journal of Higher Education*, 31:471–480, December, 1960.

the public on the precedence of the student's growth and development over the teacher's fame and fortune.

If the teacher's fortune is secondary here, it is no less so in the case where he is asked to give a pupil special tutoring. It is distinctly unethical to accept pay for this extra service because otherwise ambiguity arises as to whether the teacher has not neglected this pupil in order that his parents might ask him to undertake this service and thus enable him to add to his usually meager compensation. Even where the circumstances are unusual, as when a pupil has fallen behind because of illness, the teacher should accept pay for tutoring only under the surveillance of school authorities. The ethical rule which holds for tutoring one's own pupils holds, furthermore, for accepting any kind of gratuity which is offered the teacher for fulfilling his usual line of duty. If he does not, for instance, reject a gratuity offered by a publisher to influence the teacher's selection of a textbook, it will never be clear, even if he picks a good text, whether he might not have picked a better one if he had refused the favor.

To turn now in the direction of the ethical relations of the teacher with his fellows, it is important to note at the outset that, though these relations only indirectly affect the child, ultimately they are governed by the same ethical imperative of keeping one's eye single to the best interests of the child. As already seen, to keep his best interests to the fore requires considerable sacrifice of personal fame and fortune on the part of the teacher. It will be difficult for any one teacher to continue to make this sacrifice if he observes colleagues who do not seem to restrict themselves similarly. Therefore, in order to reinforce every teacher in his high ethical resolve toward the pupil, each must owe a duty to the other not to act in any way which will make it difficult or embarrassing to maintain a high level of professional ethics.

A number of stratagems illustrate the point. For example, a teacher must not apply for a particular position till a vacancy occurs in that position. Furthermore, an applicant must not underbid for a vacancy and offer to teach for less than the salary schedule stipulates. Practices of this sort undermine the props which make it possible for the professional teacher to refuse emoluments like gratuities from publishers or fees from private tutoring. Of course it almost goes without saying that it is not only unethical but positively illegal for a teacher unilaterally to break an existing contract even though it is to accept another position offering better opportunities for professional advancement. And again, to emphasize the advancement of the pupil's rather than the teacher's interests, the teacher should neither apply for nor accept a position from a superintendent or board of education where he, the teacher, is a blood relation of one of these public officials.

Teachers must also be very careful about adversely reflecting on their profession by disparaging their colleagues. If the profession is to stand high in the regard of the public, it must have a professional solidarity born of mutual respect and loyalty. It will be a long step toward this mutual respect if the profession will discipline itself by keeping high at all times the standards of admission into its fellowship. On the other hand, in writing testimonials for fellow teachers the teacher or administrator should be at least as honest as he is ordinarily kind. After all, as he writes his testimonial, it is the benefit of the children to come under the influence of this teacher, even more than the prospects of the candidate himself, that the writer should have in mind.

Again, if a teacher has been helped by one of his colleagues to achieve some success and public notice, it is only proper to acknowledge the help. Especially is such acknowledgement owing from the author of a professional publication when he has received help in arriving at his conclusions. One can almost say that this is true no matter what the circumstances of the help. Thus it will not matter that the teacher's wife helped him or that he paid for the assistance he received. Neither will it matter that the technical assistance he received was or was not work of a sort he could have done himself, had he wished to take the time. Neither will it matter, again, if he picked up help incidental to shoptalk with his colleagues or at a professional conference specially called to consider his problem. In every case it is the better part of ethics, to say nothing of good manners, to give credit where credit is due.

THE ENFORCEMENT OF PROFESSIONAL ETHICS

Obviously a breach of professional ethics not only rings up a moral lapse for an individual teacher, but casts a shadow on and weakens the whole corporate body of the profession. In most breaches of professional ethics, however, there is no infraction of any statute law. Hence no remedies are enforceable at law. This is just as well, for there are nuances of ethical relations which perhaps the grosser and more cumbersome machinery of the law could never judge anyhow. Professional organizations have long taken the view that the organization itself is the only effective agency for disciplining its members. It is the ethical duty of every member, therefore, to report instances of unprofessional or unethical conduct to the committee in charge, to be dealt with as the rules of the organization provide.

The most difficult cases of enforcement arise where the profession disciplines, not its own membership for infractions of its code of ethics, but the community for tolerating conditions inimical to the maintenance of high professional standards. The reference here is chiefly to the case of the teachers' strike. Strikes have principally occurred over salaries. At first glance it would appear conclusive, from the principles already laid down, that a teachers' strike is definitely unethical. To strike for higher pay appears not only to put the teachers' personal interests ahead of those of their pupils but at the same time to do the pupils positive harm by withholding instruction from them. This harm is the more threatening since by reason of their advanced training and state certification teachers have a virtual monopoly over their art.

To this indictment defenders of the strike reply that, although the immediate incidence of the strike is to advance the teachers' private interests, the long-run effect is to benefit the child. By insisting on salaries which enable teachers to afford the personal sacrifices incidental to high ethical standards, teachers are really putting the interests of their pupils first. This is well said, if true, but even at best an inherent ambiguity remains in the situation which lies open to misinterpretation even by the well-intentioned.

Teachers would not be caught in this embarrassing dilemma if they really enjoyed all the prerogatives of a professional person. If they were members of an autonomous profession, they would have the prerogatives of setting their own hours of employment, owning their own professional equipment, and above all, regulating their own rate of compensation. Because of these circumstances the conventional professional person has within his own control the financial conditions necessary to maintaining professional standards. Public school teachers, on the contrary, do not. They are employees whose hours and wages are regulated by the board of education. If negotiations to raise subprofessional conditions of employment fail, teachers can protest only by striking or quitting the profession. If the strike of public employees is outlawed by statute, then the only protest left teachers is to seek employment in some other line. This, of course, is an intolerable conclusion for both teachers and the community to reach. Teachers are thwarted in their calling, and the community loses talented teachers. To avoid such an admittedly intolerable situation, many think the strike, while still unethical and an evil, is at least the lesser evil.

Less apologetic are those who forthrightly claim that teachers should recognize themselves, not as professional persons, but as members of the laboring classes.[6] Hence they should organize themselves along economic rather than professional lines; they should organize as a union rather than as a profession. If they were to do so, then they would be less hampered

---

6 Cf. Henry R. Linville, "The American Federation of Teachers," School and Society, 40:616–621, November, 1934; and cf. Samuel P. Capen, "The Teaching Profession and Labor Unions," Journal of General Education, 1:275–278, July, 1947.

by the sort of ethical misgivings considered so far. Indeed, there are substantial reasons for making this reappraisal of themselves. As already indicated, teachers do not regulate their fees; they are paid a salary or wage as in the case of other laboring groups. Today, furthermore, when nearly every calling is becoming increasingly complicated by science and technology, the line between trades and professions is growing very thin. It grows even thinner, excessively thin in fact, when any occupational group finds itself exploited by another social group, whether private employers or government authorities. Hence teachers' ethics may be due for amendment. Indeed a first step in that direction is the increasing recognition of the right of teachers to bargain collectively. After all, professional codes of ethics are no more than the expression of the best ethical practice of the times. When times change, codes must change with them. But if historical precedent were needed for the strike, it can easily be found in the right of *cessatio* at the medieval university. There the profession of scholars did not hesitate to cease holding classes if the townfolk did not provide satisfactory conditions for carrying them on.

SELECTED BIBLIOGRAPHY

Brubacher, Abram R.: *Teaching: Profession and Practice* (Appleton-Century-Crofts, Inc., New York, 1927).

Brubacher, John S.: *Bases for Policy in Higher Education* (McGraw-Hill Book Company, New York, 1965), Chap. 4.

Heermance, Edgar L.: *Codes of Ethics* (Free Press Burlington, Vt., 1924), pp. 489–504.

Kelley, Truman L.: *Scientific Method* (The Ohio State University Press, Columbus, Ohio, 1929), pp. 42–80.

Landis, Benson Y.: *Professional Codes* (Teachers College, Columbia University, New York, 1927).

Lieberman, Myron: *Education as a Profession* (Prentice-Hall, Inc., Englewood Cliffs, N.J., 1956), Chaps. 2–4, 9–10, 13.

National Education Association: *Ethics in the Teaching Profession*, Research Bulletin, January, 1931.

————: *Report of the Professional Ethics Committee, 1948.*

Taeusch, Carl F.: *Professional and Business Ethics* (Holt, Rinehart and Winston, Inc., New York, 1926), Chaps. 1, 5, 10.

Walsh, Matthew J.: *Teaching as a Profession* (Holt, Rinehart and Winston, Inc., New York, 1926).

Wilson, Logan: *Academic Man* (Oxford University Press, Fair Lawn, N.J., 1942), Chap. 7.

PART SIX

Systematic Educational Philosophy

CHAPTER FIFTEEN

Educational Philosophy as a Discipline

So far, as indicated in the preface, our strategy has been to commence each section of our exposition with an examination of problems of educational practice. In almost every instance we found we could penetrate only a short distance before encountering philosophical issues. In the social context of education, for example, we considered political theory; in the aims of education, value theory; in curriculum and method, knowledge theory. At every point, however, we have been philosophizing as if there were little doubt what philosophizing is. Since philosophical differences have appeared on nearly every issue taken up, it should surprise no one that differences exist also on the role of educational philosophy. These differences have protruded from time to time from below the surface of our discussion, but we passed them by. Now, instead of neglecting them, we must give them our direct and full attention.

One may wonder why such a discussion has been postponed so long. Would it not have clarified the preceding problems if we had defined at the outset the nature of the philosophical enterprise? Perhaps so, but it is equally possible that such definition might have been so abstract as to be actually baffling to the uninitiated. The situation is not unlike learning a foreign tongue. When should one take up grammar? At the outset or after some facility has been gained in actual communication? Ultimately, of course, the two must go hand in hand, but it is generally agreed that good pedagogy makes formal structure of a language of secondary importance at the beginning. So too of philosophy. It is well to gain some familiarity with handling philosophical issues before studying the intricacies of philosophical method itself.

COMMON SENSE

On a number of occasions our discussion of educational problems must have seemed little more than good common sense. Indeed, it is because there is such a close similarity between common sense and philosophy that we have been able to postpone the discussion of the more formal aspects of philosophy till now. Ask the average layman or teacher untrained in philosophy what action to take in meeting many educational problems, and he will, in all probability, have a ready answer for you. Where did he get the resources for such an answer? From common sense, we say, from the common allowance of wits which everyone has to understand practical affairs. But it is more than that; it is also a capacity of wit armed with a mass of accumulated convictions which he shares with his fellows and which social convention endorses. Thus common-sense decisions on educational matters are the individual expression of a kind of underlying public opinion. Or, stated differently, common sense is the theoretical group premise or bias by which everyone undergirds his decisions and conducts his practical affairs.

It is often remarked that every teacher has a philosophy of education whether he is aware of it or not. This is probably true if what is meant is that every teacher has a common-sense outlook on education. Doubtless, common sense as a homespun philosophy of education is often adequate to make immediate resolutions of conflicting demands on the teacher's attention, but it easily breaks down if the severe strain is placed on it of formulating long-range educational policies. Properly speaking, the philosophical outlook results from much more rigorous thinking—from giving thinking much greater scope and also from making it much more logical. Although this is true, it would be a mistake to conclude that the difference between philosophy and common sense is so abrupt or sharp as to amount to a difference in kind. The difference is rather one of degree. Yet even here we must exercise caution in the use of our terminology. While on occasion we may be justified in using the term philosophy to cover a common-sense viewpoint, we should beware of using it to describe every sort of educational viewpoint from mere fancy to severe logical reasoning.[1]

Yet, however ready or in vogue common-sense decisions on education may be, they have their shortcomings. When we stop to do the uncommonsense thing of asking common sense for its credentials, we perceive at once how unsatisfactory is their authenticity. A critical examination of the past of common sense alone quickly reveals its fickleness. It has vacillated from time to time and place to place. While yesterday it may have been common sense to make a dull child wear a dunce cap, today this practice would not make sense to the community at all. And while it may have been common sense in ancient Greece to practice educational eugenics by exposing deformed infants to death, in modern America this custom would seem monstrous to current standards of common sense. Consequently as

---

[1] The *reductio ad absurdum* here is the teacher who said she overcame her professional anxieties philosophically, that is, she did not think about them.

good a point of departure as common sense may be for the solution of educational controversies, it can hardly be a satisfactory court of final appeal.

Obviously the earnest professional student of education must go beyond the common sense of the lay community if he is to form educational policies which are to have any scope and stability. The way for him to do this is to subject common sense to careful refinement, that is, to bring in further data so that his judgment can reach conclusions which will be valid for more people in more times and more places. There are two principal methods of achieving this further refinement of common sense, the one scientific and the other philosophic. The way in which the scientist improves on common sense is well known. He selects for experimentation an educational problem which can be narrowly and precisely defined. That is, he selects a problem in which the number of factors or variables involved is very limited and in which these factors or variables can be easily isolated from the context in which they occur. The reason for this careful selection of factors is to enable the scientist to gain rigid control over their variation. If he is experimenting with homogeneous grouping of pupils according to ability, for instance, he must be sure that such factors as the teacher, the sex of the student, the community, the size of the class, and the like do not vary sufficiently to upset the homogeneity of the groups he is studying. Just let one such factor elude control and the educational scientist cannot tell whether such results as better scores on tests are due to the homogeneity of his groups or to the extraneous factor which has escaped his control. The point at which he is most likely to depart from common sense is in the hypotheses he formulates. In advanced science, hypotheses may be cast in anything but common-sense language. To make the dependability of his conclusions a further refinement on common sense, the scientist usually repeats his experiment and encourages others to conduct the same experiment. Then, if the results are uniform, he can claim that his conclusions are not only reliable but objective, both prime characteristics of dependability. It is by the employment of these refinements that science enjoys the wide popular confidence it does today.

The philosophic method of extending and refining common sense moves in a quite different direction from the scientific one. It aims not at a solution of just a limited number of the factors and variables which inhere in an educational problem and which can be rigidly controlled experimentally, but at one which includes every factor or variable which is either directly or remotely relevant to the problem. Thus, in studying the feasibility of homogeneous grouping, the philosophic interest concerns more than just the limited data to which the scientist must confine himself.

Beyond improved test scores, for example, the philosopher is also interested in the personal attitudes of superiority or inferiority that children learn when homogeneously grouped, in the out-of-school as well as the in-school effect of these groupings, and in the impact of these groups on the democratic outlook.[2] Or take another instance from the field of moral education. Admittedly we all want to teach traits of character such as courage, loyalty, perseverance, obedience, and the like. Taken singly, however, these are each traits which a band of gangsters might also cultivate among its members. Consequently we cannot confidently assert that any of these traits is a worthy aim of moral education until we refer it to some over-all purpose of education, for instance, what kind of society we live in or want to live in.

For such an overview philosophy must feel free to draw on a varied mix of materials. As often as not it may start with the humble data of common sense and that stolid first cousin of common sense, tradition. The facts of common sense and tradition, however, will not be exact enough for the thoroughgoing conclusions at which philosophy aims. Consequently philosophy will gather into its bag those more critical editions of common sense and tradition, science and history. Among the sciences, educational philosophy will pay high regard to the life sciences of biology and psychology but no less high regard to the social sciences of sociology, politics, and economics as they bear on the problem at hand. Last but not least, the data of religion and morals should become an ingredient of the comprehensive outlook of educational philosophy. Indeed, religion itself is closely akin to the philosophical enterprise in that it too is interested in exploring the most inclusive ramifications of educational problems, even in exploring those boundaries of the problem which border on the most sublime speculation. In taking advantage of all these data, however, one should note that philosophy itself uncovers no new facts. It processes the facts of other disciplines but owns none of its own.

The totality of circumstances considered relevant for philosophical study should not be considered a mere quantitative affair such as an encyclopedia might total up. Merely to multiply circumstances which the educator should take into account is as likely to confuse as to enlighten the educational practitioner. In treating such a wide range of factors or circumstances as bear on an educational problem, philosophical method traditionally tries to perform three functions. One is speculative; another is normative; and the last is critical.

---

[2] For example, see the philosophical critique of scientific results in homogeneous grouping in Alice V. Keliher, *A Critical Study of Homogeneous Grouping* (Teachers College, Columbia University, New York, 1931).

EDUCATIONAL PHILOSOPHY AS SPECULATIVE

In its speculative phase educational philosophy makes an endeavor to be synoptic. Given the array of facts from science, history, and other areas mentioned above, philosophy tries to get an overview of the whole field. From this vantage point it tries to put the various parts together into some synthesis or mosaic. For this reason, indeed, some call this function of philosophy synthetic rather than speculative. Where there are gaps in the data, philosophy may venture more or less tentative inferences to fill out a meaning where none is obvious. In a sense, speculative philosophy tries to sketch a map of the universe and man's place in it. Figuratively, with such a guide at hand, it should be easier to make a design for an educational program.

While it is generally agreed that a speculative wholeness of outlook is a legitimate objective of educational philosophy, the manifold details with which it deals may or may not reduce to a single consistent pattern. Some philosophies actually succeed in achieving a unitary or monistic point of view or synthesis, as, for instance, the totalitarianism of fascist education. But other philosophies, paradoxically, find unity in diversity. Those reducing to two principles are called dualistic. This type is illustrated in religious philosophies of education such as Catholicism or Scholasticism, where educational practice is determined by two distinct orders of thought, the natural and the supernatural. All other philosophies which are neither monistic nor dualistic go under the title of pluralism. Such is the educational philosophy of democracy, which protects and promotes the cultivation of diverse personalities and cultures as a matter of central principle.

Whether in principle unity be one or many, the question next arises whether this unity serves current educational experience and is, consequently, always forming and reforming to meet the shifting demands of education or whether this unity outruns the experience of the moment to take lodgment in ultimate and final reality.[3] Some think the demand for unity takes its point of origin in ordinary educational experience, in some circumstance which has arisen to interrupt the continuity of the educational process. Perhaps different pressure groups, such as the parent-teacher association, the chamber of commerce, or the American Legion are making conflicting demands on the program of the school. Perhaps the faculty is in doubt whether to introduce some new theory or technique or cling to traditional procedures. In such situations philosophy considers its function to clarify the various factors of experience involved, to reduce con-

---

[3] Cf. John Dewey, in National Society for the Study of Education, Thirty-seventh Yearbook, Part II, *The Scientific Movement in Education* (Public School Publishing Company, Bloomington, Ill., 1938), Chap. 38.

flicts, where found, by finding some larger common denominator of their differences. Thus, in the end, it restores the continuity of the educative process by continuing the former process of education together with a readaptation of it which will keep it vital and growing. The decision on whether philosophy thus succeeds in lifting educational practice to some broader, more unified level of meaning will be grounded, finally, in the test of further experience.[4]

Other philosophies, while they accept experience, regard it as inadequate by itself to afford a completely synoptic view of education. Where experience fails to afford the necessary data about the ultimate nature of reality they will fill in the gaps with speculation. In some cases, particularly where speculation invokes theology, they claim to have a kind of knowledge superior to experience by which to guide educational policy. To them the philosophical quest for wholeness is not just a reduction of conflicting educational tendencies to some temporal harmony but a quest for wholeness or unity that is eternal. Since the whole is naturally interrelated and since education is but a fragment of this interrelated whole, a major justification for the philosophical study of education is the clue it offers in regard to the nature of the perfected whole of reality. The way to gain insight into such complete and perfected knowledge is through a priori intuition or through a rational faculty which has the unique ability to grasp directly absolute non-empirical truth.

This rift between basically empirical and non-empirical educational philosophies poses problems all too evident as the exposition of this book has proceeded. Suffice it here to point out that, if the claims of educational philosophy to being grounded in ultimate reality are justified, then there can be only one true philosophy of education. There cannot be a number of equally true competing philosophies, each with its own peculiar set of assumptions and definitions. Perhaps no great difficulty will arise from this situation so long as proponents of true philosophies of education are modest enough to confess that they are not sure that theirs is the true philosophy of education. More difficulty will arise where such modesty gives way to absolute assurance. In that case two teachers, motivated by different but absolutely right educational philosophies, will find it extraordinarily difficult to cooperate in a joint school program. Neither will be able to persuade or convince the other because any concession toward community of opinion by either must be a betrayal of his absolute conviction that he alone is right. The two might as well be talking two different languages.

[4] For a treatment of this sort of unity, see Ephraim V. Sayers, *Education and the Unity of Experience* (Teachers College, Columbia University, New York, 1929).

What to do in such an impasse? Some are tempted to charge their opponents with being merely contentious or even morally perverse.[5] Others appeal for a decision to external authority, such as church or state. But if backed by such powerful institutions, they are under the further temptation of being "justly" intolerant of rival educational philosophies.[6]

EDUCATIONAL PHILOSOPHY AS NORMATIVE

In addition to providing a world view to guide the pilgrim through this uncharted land, educational philosophy has also traditionally assumed the burden of formulating goals, norms, or standards by which to conduct the educative process. Some place their norms within the speculative frame already mentioned. For them philosophy is a cloud by day and a pillar of flame by night to lead the pilgrim out of the educational wilderness. Others, however, think that philosophy follows rather than leads educational practice.[7] They view educational philosophy as a rationalization of usages already familiar in practice. From their point of view, educational practices arise in random, informal fashion. On the face of it these practices do not appear to be parts of a large-scale coordinated plan. By the artful use of logic and a little imagination the philosopher manages to supply the intellectual coordinating structure. He states with as much consistency as he can what seems to be the common theory underlying these diverse practices. But in so doing philosophy is retrospective rather than prospective in character. It is more conservative than progressive.

The place of John Dewey's *Democracy and Education* in the literature of American education may be a case in point.[8] Most readers of this justly famous book view it as the single best statement of the democratic ideal in education. And there can be little doubt that subsequent to its publication it had a profound effect on education not only in America but in the world at large. Yet, valid as it is to regard the book as setting a goal to be achieved, this could easily be a superficial view. It bears noting at this point that *Democracy and Education* appeared at the end and not at the beginning of America's first century and a quarter of experience with democratic institutions. Coming at this time, it makes explicit for education what was implicit in the social, economic, and political developments of

---

[5] Mortimer J. Adler, "Tradition and Communication," *Proceedings of the American Catholic Philosophical Association*, 1937, pp. 110–111.

[6] Cf. John A. Ryan and Francis S. Boland, *Catholic Principles of Politics* (The Macmillan Company, New York, 1947), p. 318.

[7] Isaac L. Kandel, *Comparative Education* (Houghton Mifflin Company, Boston, 1933), p. 24.

[8] John Dewey, *Democracy and Education* (The Macmillan Company, New York, 1916).

the country up to this time. On this account it is doubtful indeed whether the book could have been written one hundred and twenty-five years earlier. In a deep sense, therefore, the book is a rationalization of past national experience as well as an inspiring ideal for the future.

In performing its normative function, educational philosophy may draw on other areas of the culture just as it does in fulfilling its speculative function. Yet in drawing from literature, morals, and the like but particularly from history and the behavioral sciences, a problem arises. It is the relation of facts and values. Some think that philosophy should have exclusive jurisdiction over values and science over facts. Yet, time-honored as this statement is, it is not quite accurate. It needs qualification. Values are sometimes facts in a situation. Communities, for instance, do as a matter of fact have certain values or aims which they seek to realize in their school systems. There are scientific techniques which can determine quite accurately what these aims or values are at any given time or place. But while the scientist is qualified to determine what values are in fact held, he must be scrupulously careful not to allow his own scheme of values to bias his judgment in ascertaining any fact. If he did that, another scientist confronting the same situation with a different scheme of values might find a different set of facts, thereby greatly interfering with scientific objectivity.

Although science may properly aid in determining what the aims or values of a community *are,* it is obviously quite another question to determine whether existing aims or values are good or the aims the schools *ought* to have. To answer this question we must go beyond science to philosophy. Starting with the description of what values actually obtain in an educational situation, philosophy goes on to a critique of them in terms of a norm of value. The critique or evaluation of values is a very complicated affair. The variables are many and so intricately interwoven with the social and cultural context that they cannot be easily, if at all, isolated for study but must be treated comprehensively in the light of the total situation. Indeed, apart from some comprehensive or philosophical theory, it will be next to impossible to decide whether the schools should perpetuate the *status quo* in educational aims or whether they should amend it. If the philosopher's personal set of values enters into his final judgment there will be no complaint, as there would be if the scientist permitted his bias to affect his conclusions, for the philosopher himself is bound to be part of any total situation.

Finally there are those who would deny a normative role in education not only to scientists but to philosophers as well. Using strict canons of verification, logical positivists find it impossible to authenticate value assertions. No wonder they are disparaging of philosophers when they ask, "Whoever heard of anyone changing his basic values as a result of argument?"

EDUCATIONAL PHILOSOPHY AS CRITICAL

In its critical phase educational philosophy subjects the terms and propositions undergirding educational thought and practice to rigorous scrutiny as to the form in which they are stated.[9] The educator wants to be assured not only of the substance of the program of the schools but of its formal validity. This assurance may be sought in several directions. In one direction, critical philosophy examines the logical premises on which educational conclusions rest.[10] In another, it closely examines the language used to be sure its meaning is clear and unambiguous. In still a third direction, critical philosophy takes a penetrating look at the kind of evidence which will be acceptable for confirming or refuting statements of fact about education.

A good illustration of subjecting educational positions to logical analysis is the critical examination of assumptions. In delving into any educational problem, we find that there are some aspects of it which by their very nature force the investigator to make the comprehensive approach of the philosopher rather than the limited approach of the scientist. One of these aspects is the critical examination of basic assumptions on which the solution of a problem may depend. Assumptions which can be tested by an appeal to experience are more in the nature of hypotheses and probably should be called hypotheses. The kind of assumption we have in mind here, however, is that on which the solution of a problem rests but which itself cannot be demonstrated by an appeal to experience.[11]

Educational measurement is a case in point. The scientific measurement of, say, intelligence or achievement depends ultimately on whether the data of intelligence or achievement can be treated arithmetically, that is, whether they can be added or subtracted. In order that such psychological data may be added or subtracted, they must be capable of being

[9] For a general background of this aspect of educational philosophy, see Brand Blanshard, "The Changing Climate of Philosophy," *Liberal Education*, 47:229–254, May, 1961.

[10] Joe R. Burnett, "An Analysis of Some Philosophical and Theological Approaches to Formation of Educational Policy and Practice," *Proceedings of the Philosophy of Education Society*, 1961, pp. 7–22.

[11] Cf. Boyd H. Bode, "Where Does One Go for Fundamental Assumptions in Education?" *Educational Administration and Supervision*, 14:361–370, September, 1928; and A. Stafford Clayton, "On Probing the Assumptions of Educational Theories," *Proceedings of the Philosophy of Education Society*, 1959, pp. 41–48.

stated in cardinal numbers, that is, in equal units. Now it is customary to state the scores of intelligence and achievement tests in cardinal numbers, but how do we know that the items on the test are actually of equal difficulty? As a matter of fact we do not know, nor with the greatest of care can we make them exactly equal. Failing such precision, we assume that our units are equal. This assumption, though unproved, is nevertheless very useful in supporting practical results in educational measurement.[12]

Since there is an unproved core at the heart of every genuine assumption, obviously someone must stand guard against too great dilution of sound educational argument by a lavish or unwarranted use of assumptions. This is the more important since assumptions are often so innocently unobtrusive that their significance is quite overlooked. At any rate this task of challenging assumptions and letting only those pass which can stand rigid scrutiny is one which the philosopher has long claimed for himself. He has, however, no monopoly on the post. Scientists, too, are often as scrupulously critical about assumptions in common use as are philosophers. Naturally the more philosophically trained the scientist is, the more fruitful is his criticism likely to be.[13]

If philosophy is critical of assumptions, it is no less critical of the precise use of basic terms and concepts. So interested has it become in the meaning of meaning that it has developed a whole discipline of semantics. This discipline is governed by the principle that the meaning of a word or phrase is created and controlled by the way in which it is used. That is, social conventions of communication endow words, phrases, and sentences with whatever meaning they have.

We may illustrate this syntax of language by examining a statement of Horace Mann's. "I believe," he said, "in the existence of a great, immortal, immutable principle of natural law . . . which proves the *absolute right* to an education of every human being. . . ."[14] When Horace Mann wrote that statement in an annual report to his state board of education, what did he mean? Was he just recognizing and describing a fact? Or was he giving voice to his feeling of enthusiasm or commitment for the principle he asserted? Or, again, was he really trying to incite or persuade the board and his fellow citizens to accept and act on his conviction?

---

[12] For a fuller treatment of the philosophy of measurement, see *supra*, p. 271.
[13] Cf. Clark L. Hull, "The Conflicting Psychologies of Learning: A Way Out," *Psychological Review*, 42:491–516, November, 1935; and L. O. Kattsoff, "Philosophy, Psychology, and Postulational Technique," *Psychological Review*, 46:62–74, January, 1939.
[14] Tenth Annual Report of the Secretary to the Massachusetts State Board of Education, in Mary Mann, *Life and Works of Horace Mann* (Horace B. Fuller, Boston, 1868), Vol. 3, p. 533.

EDUCATIONAL PHILOSOPHY IN A "NEW KEY"

The answer to these questions is not free from ambiguity. Much depends on what Mann meant by such pregnant words as "believe," "existence," "law," "order of nature," and the like. There must be clarity not only of thought but of language too.[15] If there is confusion or disagreement about language, we must ascertain whether it is due to difference of opinion about matters of fact, misunderstanding of logical implications or conflict of values. One early group, calling themselves linguistic analysts and having a predilection for logical positivism, thinks the first two difficulties can be settled to anyone's satisfaction, the first by empirical verification and the second by rigorous application of logical syntax. The third, being non-cognitive, they set aside as unsolvable.

Indeed, this group go so far as to insist that philosophy forswear its traditional roles of explaining the universe and making prescriptions for the good life. The former, to the extent it is factual, should be surrendered to science. The latter, not being subject to empirical verification and therefore unsolvable, incurs an unwarranted expenditure of time. Instead of its traditional tasks, philosophy should confine itself to a clarification of terms and propositions. To attack on a narrow front such as this might enable philosophy to achieve some consensus after centuries of proverbial disagreement. So promising does such a redefinition of philosophy seem to many linguistic analysts that they have termed it a "revolution" in philosophy or at least philosophy in a "new key."[16]

Confident as many linguist analysts are about their revolution, they are not without opposition.[17] No one denies that linguistic analysis has greatly sharpened the philosophical tools of criticism. But the idea that philosophy should surrender its speculative and normative functions and cleave only unto its critical ones has met considerable resistance. Those engaged in education are inescapably submerged in problems involving moral values of one sort and another. If moral values such as academic freedom and professional ethics cannot be justified, the position of the teacher is dismaying indeed. Not only is the teacher's work necessarily normative, but he needs a map, even a speculative map, of the educational

---

[15] For illustrations see B. Othanel Smith and Robert H. Ennis (eds.), *Language and Concepts in Education* (Rand McNally & Company, Chicago, 1961); and Israel Scheffler, *The Language of Education* (Charles C Thomas, Publisher, Springfield, Ill., 1960).

[16] Charles D. Hardie, "The Philosophy of Education in a New Key," *Educational Theory*, 10:255–261, October, 1960.

[17] John P. Strain, "A Critique of Philosophical Analysis in Education," *Educational Theory*, 14:186–193, July, 1964. See also Harry Broudy, "The Role of Analysis in Educational Philosophy," *ibid.*, 14:261–269, October, 1964.

terrain by which to plan his strategies. Linguistic analysis is too nominalistic, too piecemeal, to give him this kind of assistance. In fact, linguistic analysis, if it is to remain an ally of education, must concern itself with "ordinary" rather than "meta-language" and with a less rigorous and more informal logic.[18]

Many think that linguistic analysis is so obsessed with the empirical verification of meaning that it has virtually sold out to science. Such a possibility raises shades of a sharp controversy whether scientific interests are palpably encroaching on educational philosophy.[19] The roles of science and philosophy must be separated, it seems, as they apply to the field of pedagogy. Thus the art of education, or pedagogy, differs from the science of education because the latter is concerned with universal principles which are applicable to all learners. The art of education may be and usually is based on such principles, but often there is some slack between principle and practice. It is through the art of the teacher that this slack is taken up, that an adjustment is made between general principle and the peculiarities of the individual learner.

There is a similar relation between pedagogy and the philosophy of education. Thus it is on philosophy that the art of education must wait for a design of action. Conversely, educational philosophy, whose solutions can be achieved only in action, will have urgent need for the art of education. Philosophy cannot bring its theories into existence merely by thinking them. This the art of education can do and in so doing can make education a laboratory where philosophical distinctions can be empirically tested. A philosophy of education that constantly appeals its validity to practice is in that degree necessarily dependent on the art of education. In fact only a philosophy truncated from practice can be clearly distinguished from education as an art.

PHILOSOPHY AND SCIENCE

But how does philosophy differ from science if philosophical theory bears a strong experimental relation to educational practice?[20] The main difference lies not so much in the experimental test of theory but, as already

[18] D. Bob Gowin, "Can Educational Theory Guide Practice?" Educational Theory, 13:6–12, January, 1963; and George L. Newsome, "Ordinary Language, Philosophy, and Education," Proceedings of the Philosophy of Education Society, 1962, pp. 90–99. See also James E. McClellan and Paul B. Komisar's introduction to the American edition of Charles D. Hardie's Truth and Fallacy in Educational Theory (Teachers College Press, Columbia University, New York, 1962).
[19] Mortimer J. Adler and Milton Mayer, The Revolution in Education (University of Chicago Press, Chicago, 1958), Chap. 17.
[20] This question has provoked much discussion in educational literature. See Theodore

indicated, in the scope of the theory. Science prefers an educational problem in which it need propose a theory to cover no more variables than can be rigidly controlled. Philosophy, on the other hand, makes no such limitation. It is willing to handle educational problems in which it must propose a theory for uncontrolled as well as controlled variables. While scientific and philosophic theory cover different ranges of fact, there is no reason why both should not test their theories by an appeal to practice. Yet, though both science and philosophy may test their theories by the same method, they will differ widely in the extent to which their results can command assent from other workers in the field. By limiting its variables, science is able to win wide and almost universal support for its conclusions. By refusing to limit variables, especially normative ones, philosophy has become almost notorious for its disagreements.

Can one conclude, therefore, that scientific theory and practice is more dependable than philosophic theory and practice? No, the fact rather seems to be that science and philosophy each has its unique advantages and limitations. In reaching the prized advantage of reliability and objectivity, science sacrifices the breadth of scope of its conclusions. In achieving the no less prized advantage of a comprehensive solution, philosophy gives up any hope of general agreement on its conclusions. Apparently the practical educator cannot expect solutions that are at once reliable, objective, *and* comprehensive. Educational philosophy and educational science, therefore, are to be considered complementary disciplines. Perhaps better, they are but different aspects of a single discipline, the discipline of inquiry. The educational practitioner will need them both.

There are some, however, who do not draw this balanced conclusion from the various incidental comparisons of educational science and philosophy made so far. Instead of assigning each a unique function of its own to perform, they insist on arranging science and philosophy in a hierarchical order. In this group some regard science as the premier discipline

Brameld, "The Relation of Philosophy and Science from the Perspective of Education," *Educational Trends*, 9:5–10, July–August, 1941; John Dewey, in National Society for the Study of Education, *loc. cit.*; Ross Finney, "Philosophy versus Science Again," *Educational Administration and Supervision*, 16:161–173, March, 1930; Frank N. Freeman, "Scientific and Philosophic Method in Education," *Science*, 73:54–59, January, 1931; H. Gordon Hullfish, "The Relation of Philosophy and Science in Education," *Journal of Educational Research*, 20:159–165, October, 1929; E. B. Jordan, "Respective Roles of Science and Philosophy in Education," *Proceedings of the American Catholic Philosophical Association*, 1947, pp. 38–49; Truman L. Kelley, "A Defense of Science in Education," *Harvard Teachers Record*, 1:123–130, November, 1931; Truman L. Kelley, "The Philosophic vs. the Scientific Approach to the Novel Problem," *Science*, 71:295–302, March, 1930; William H. Kilpatrick, "A Defense of Philosophy in Education," *Harvard Teachers Record*, 1:117–122, November, 1931; William H. Kilpatrick, "The Relation of Philosophy to Scientific Research," *Journal of Educational Research*, 24:97–114, September, 1931.

while others put philosophy at the top. Those who claim that philosophy is paramount assert that philosophical truth is not only demonstrable but even much more so than are scientific findings.[21]

Those who subordinate philosophy to science do so because of the exalted importance they attach to experimentalism. The test of experiment or practice, they hold, is the final arbiter of all doubts and perplexities in education. It is science, furthermore, that has made the most brilliant and permanent conquests by this method. To be sure, philosophy, particularly pragmatic philosophy, has employed this same method but confessedly without the same commanding results. Philosophy is all right but only as a temporary expedient till science has had time to mature a more thorough and enduring solution. In fact, as these scientific solutions accumulate there will be progressively less and less need for philosophy.

The atrophy and ultimate obsequies of educational philosophy seem to its friends rather premature. When science purports to exclude the need for philosophy in the solution of educational problems, it is, they declare, paradoxically asserting a philosophy. Unwittingly it is making a speculative statement as to the totality of circumstances which affect the educational process. On the one hand, it is assuming that the variables or factors which compose the educational situation are of such a character as to lend themselves to the technique of isolation and description. On the other hand, it is assuming that the number of variable factors in the educational universe is limited. If these assumptions were warranted, perhaps science could ultimately look forward to overcoming all educational difficulties one by one. But there seems to be a growing conviction, even among scientists, that the world is more than a sum of finite parts; that, on the contrary, the world seems to possess an infinitely variegated structure. Hence each scientific solution of an educational difficulty seems to beget as many problems as it solves—and often more. Indeed, new solutions frequently unsettle old ones and thus add to, rather than diminish, the problems awaiting solution. If this is the case, the need for educational philosophy will last as long as the need for science.

Those who subordinate science to philosophy do so because they think that both theoretically and practically philosophy is superior to science in explaining the educational process. As science gives a more refined explanation than practice, so philosophy, they declare, gives a more adequate explanation than does science. The study of the sciences of biology and psychology, for example, is superior to the practical study of education,

---

but in turn the study of such philosophic branches as ontology or metaphysics is superior to biology and psychology. The basic reason why these studies can be arranged in this hierarchy is that science is interested in the proximate or efficient causes of practice, while philosophy is concerned with its ultimate or final causes. But in addition it should be noted that in every case the superior study is of greater general interest and more worth studying as an end in itself. The inferior study, on the other hand, is in each case of more practical value and only worth study on that account. Not only that, but the inferior study in each case presupposes the principles of the next higher range of studies. Thus a study of education presupposes a knowledge of the psychological principles of learning or the biological principles of the interaction of heredity and environment. But the study of psychology and biology in turn take for granted an understanding of such basic concepts as life, adaptation, regeneration, and the like. For an adequate understanding of these terms one must turn to ontology or general metaphysics, the absolute top in the hierarchy of studies, for it is the one discipline which does not presuppose any other, inasmuch as it studies pure being as such.[22] The way in which philosophy thus tops the sciences has earned it among its devotees the title of queen of the sciences.

THEORY AND PRACTICE

As can readily be seen, the further our quest for fundamental or comprehensive principle extends beyond common sense, the more theoretical our conclusions become. In fact, not a few educators think that philosophical conclusions are too theoretical. The growing dependence on theory strikes them as a distinct liability. Interesting as the excursion into theory may be, it too easily causes these men to slip their moorings to the practical realities of the educational situation. Losing sight of the connection between theory and practice, they rail against theory as remote, vague, and idealistic.

In lodging this complaint against philosophy, educators are all too likely to forget that it may still be practice that is at fault. Generally we have plenty of practice, but practice is often confused and contradictory, a circumstance already seen to have been almost the continual state of affairs since the time of Aristotle. What we need is not more practical remedies but, as Aristotle pointed out, some theory to guide practice. It is on

---

[22] See two statements of Mortimer J. Adler, "God and the Professors," in *Conference on Science, Philosophy, and Religion* (Published by the Conference, 1941), p. 129; and "The Crisis in Contemporary Education," *Social Frontier*, 5:142–143, February, 1939.

this account that the defenders of philosophy have stated that theory is in the end the most practical of expedients.

The conflict between theory and practice should really be capable of some solution. Perhaps we can start by recognizing that the critics of both theory and practice are each really criticizing straw men. One is criticizing ineffective theory and the other thoughtless practice. It is not likely that any one will object to burning up both these straw men. But what sort of men should be installed in their places? What is the proper relation of theory and practice, of educational philosophy and the conduct of the schools?

At first glance there seem two ways in which philosophy might enter educational practice.[23] One is that followed in the foregoing chapters— probe into educational problems, and when you come on philosophical issues, go to philosophy for resources to dispose of them. The other is to go to philosophy first and then with its principles firmly in mind decide on an educational pattern to follow. Notable exception has been taken to this view on the ground that one cannot formally deduce educational practice from a given system of philosophy.[24] On the contrary, it would appear that a variety of philosophies can be logically erected on the base of given metaphysical or epistemological premises. Take the Christian metaphysics as a good example; it has supported a number of different educational philosophies, from the Thomistic Aristotelianism of Catholicism to the Froebelian idealism and Herbartian realism of Protestantism. Perhaps it is fortunate that this is so, for it is a favorite trick of some educational critics to try to discredit an educational philosophy by claiming it is inescapably based on a general philosophy which is presumably in disfavor. Happily the converse also seems true: The diverse philosophies of education often agree on certain practices such as recognizing the importance of interest and individual differences.

Although it may be conceded that no educational practice follows by logical necessity from philosophy, this does not mean that philosophical presuppositions are useless. Thus they may at least have psychological connections which the teacher may find meaningful.[25] Or, still retaining them, they may be reduced to only one component of a theory of edu-

---

23 Harry Broudy, "How Philosophical Can Philosophy of Education Be?" *Journal of Philosophy*, 152:612–622, October, 1955.

24 Hobert W. Burns, "The Logic of the Educational Implication," *Educational Theory*, 12:53–63, January, 1962.

25 *Ibid*. See also Joe R. Burnet, "Observations on the Logical Implications of Philosophic Theory or Educational Theory and Practice," *Educational Theory*, 11:65–70, April, 1961. Unless there is some justification for this procedure, we would be unable to include Whitehead's "organic" philosophy of education. See *infra*, p. 341n.

cation in which other components might be psychology, sociology, history, and the like.[26] This, however, runs counter to the theory that philosophy itself is the comprehensive matrix which binds all the other components together. Dewey, for instance, defines philosophy as the theory of education in its most general phases.[27]

The clearly controversial relation between philosophy and educational practice, raises a question in the minds of some whether education can stand as an autonomous discipline. Some hold it can,[28] while others take a contrary view.[29] If educational theory consists of many components, as was suggested, then certainly education is not autonomous but a composite of various disciplines.

CATEGORIES OF EDUCATIONAL PHILOSOPHY

The difficulty we find in delineating the proper spheres of philosophy and science in education is not one of ancient origin. Originally all advanced study was philosophical. Philosophy was, as its etymology from the Greek words $\phi\iota\lambda\circ\varsigma$ and $\sigma\circ\phi\iota\alpha$ suggests, love of wisdom or learning. Moreover it was love of learning in general; it subsumed under one heading what today we call science as well as what we now call philosophy. It is for this reason that philosophy is often referred to as the mother as well as the queen of the sciences. This philosophical lineage of science was still quite clear as late as the nineteenth century when the various divisions of science were still spoken of as branches of philosophy. At that time the growing sciences of physics and chemistry went under the title of "natural philosophy"; psychology had the title of "mental philosophy"; and the budding social sciences of politics, economics, and sociology were subheadings under "moral philosophy."

Of course, it is common knowledge that one by one the various sciences have come of age and have left the maternal household to engage independently in building the temple of learning. This exodus includes

---

[26] Paul H. Hirst, "Philosophy and Educational Theory," *British Journal of Educational Studies*, 12:51–64, November, 1963. Cf. Elizabeth S. Maccia, "The Separation of Philosophy from Theory of Education," *Studies in Philosophy and Education*, 2:158–169, Spring, 1962.

[27] John Dewey, *Democracy and Education* (The Macmillan Company, New York, 1916), p. 386.

[28] Foster McMurray, "Preface to an Autonomous Discipline of Education," *Educational Theory*, 5:129–140, July, 1955, and 6:10–20, January, 1956. See also Marc Belth, *Education as a Discipline* (Allyn and Bacon, Inc., Boston, 1966).

[29] John Walton and James L. Kuethe (eds.), *The Discipline of Education* (University of Wisconsin Press, Madison, Wis., 1963).

practically all the fact-finding disciplines. As a result no one today expects philosophy to contribute to the finding or determination of facts. Instead, philosophy now generally takes its exact facts from history and the sciences. It is the critical analysis of these facts, their normative connotations, and the speculative theories that they support with which philosophy does its characteristic work.

Whichever of these views is most appealing, it still remains to consider just what disciplines are left under the philosophic roof with which to attack educational problems after the exodus of the sciences. There are three which principally concern education. They are ethics, or the theory of values; epistemology, or the theory of knowledge; and metaphysics, or the general theory of being or reality. Ethical considerations come up unavoidably in examining the social or political setting of the educative process, to say nothing of its religious and moral dimensions. In examining the aims of education, the motivation of learning, or the measurement of its results we are inescapably dealing with ethical problems, problems of value. Values also are an important consideration in selecting which studies shall be included in the curriculum. But the curriculum also raises very important questions of epistemology. The curriculum being the student's avenue of approach to knowledge, it behooves us to understand the nature of knowledge. The nature of knowledge will not only have an influence on the way in which the curriculum is organized and taught, but it will also undergird the conception of truth and the freedom with which it is taught. Ultimately, difficulties in the problems of knowledge and value, epistemology and ethics, will rest back on our notions of what kind of world we live in anyhow, that is, the study of metaphysics. Here we will have to consider the nature of human nature as well as the world in which it abides and whether the whole story may be had from an examination of nature or whether there is a supernatural realm affecting education as well.

SELECTED BIBLIOGRAPHY

Adler, Mortimer J.: "In Defense of the Philosophy of Education," in National Society for the Study of Education, Forty-first Yearbook, Part I, *Philosophies of Education* (Public School Publishing Company, Bloomington, Ill., 1942), Chap. 5.

American Council on Education Studies: Series I, Vol. 3, *Educational Research*, Chaps. 1, 7.

Brown, L. M.: *General Philosophy in Education* (McGraw-Hill Book Company, New York, 1966), Chaps. 1–4, 9.

Dewey, John: *Sources of a Science of Education* (Liveright Publishing Corporation, New York, 1931).

Hardie, Charles D.: *Truth and Fallacy in Educational Theory* (Cambridge University Press, New York, 1942), Chap. 4.

Harvard Educational Review, 26:94–203, Spring, 1956.

Kneller, George F.: *Logic and Language of Education* (John Wiley & Sons, Inc., New York, 1966), Chap. 9.

Lepley, Ray: *Dependability in Philosophy of Education* (Teachers College, Columbia University, New York, 1938).

O'Connor, Daniel J.: *An Introduction to the Philosophy of Education* (Philosophical Library, Inc., New York, 1957), Chaps. 1–2, 4–5.

CHAPTER SIXTEEN

Schools of Educational Philosophy

Up to this point the exposition of philosophy has been organized to shed light on specific problems which arise in the study and practice of education. Each problem has served as a nucleus for organizing the different theories or philosophies on which its solution has been based. So far, however, no attempt has been made to maintain continuity in the discourse in terms of particular philosophies of education themselves. It is time now to assemble the like segments of these various educational philosophies into their respective systems of thought. It is chiefly in the light of some total consistency that the strength of any individual stand can be assured. If any stand contradicts others in the system, then one must be on his guard against weakness somewhere. But the search for this larger comprehensive statement is just what the purpose of philosophy is. Indeed, one would fail to be true to the spirit of philosophy if he did not endeavor to reduce his manifold convictions to some single, inclusive, consistent scheme of thought.

A number of systematic statements are on record, of which some are much more fully developed than others. Because of the many shades of opinion, there is, as might be expected, no little overlapping. This overlapping poses a significant problem in classification. In the preceding chapters the exposition has on the whole epitomized philosophical positions in education for the most part under two headings, progressive and conservative. While our emphasis was on educational categories, this simple, general classification was adequate enough. But now that our emphasis is shifting to philosophical categories, which are many and diverse, this dichotomous division will no longer suffice. Furthermore, complete systems of educational philosophy are rarely if ever wholly progressive or wholly conservative.

PRAGMATIC NATURALISM[1]

Until the appearance of "progressive education" in the early part of the twentieth century, educational philosophy was more or less moribund. The

---

[1] This title might as well have been "instrumental" or "experimental naturalism." Indeed, the three words pragmatism, instrumentalism, and experimentalism will be used interchangeably in this section. The single best statement of this point of view is to be found in John Dewey's *Democracy and Education* (The Macmillan Company, New York, 1916). Good

innovations of progressive education, however, made so strong a protest against the conventional wisdom inherited from the nineteenth century that educators were forced to resort to philosophy to decide whether to join the progressives or to remain with the traditionalists and essentialists. Since "progressive education" spurred the present extensive interest in educational philosophy, we may well commence our systematic summaries with an epitome of its rationale.

The best clue to the philosophy of progressive education lies in the adjective "progressive." Progress is naturalistic; it implies change. Change implies novelty. And novelty lays claim to being genuine rather than the revelation of an antecedently complete reality. Since things change neither at the same time nor at the same rate, novelty is relative to the familiar. In fact, the world which confronts the pupil is a peculiar mixture of these two characteristics. Given such a metaphysic, it is small wonder that progressive education should emphasize the problem-solving attitude of mind, or that it should try to develop initiative and self-reliance in its devotees. The challenge to the intellect calls for employment of the familiar as a means of exploring the novel and bringing it under control in order to meet future novel situations.

One of the chief channels through which an emergent evolution works is that of individual differences. Both biological and social reproduction always occur with variations. Each variation, each species, however, is not necessarily a new genus. Yet, on the other hand, neither does subsuming the species under a genus exhaust the unique individuality of the species. Its individuality is still incomparably precious; without it, there could be no progress at all. Consequently, the stress laid by progressive education on a cultivation of individual differences of pupils is easily understood. Their development is not only indispensable to self-realization but of inestimable value as a resource for social progress.

But the question arises, how is one to know when change and individual variation will lead to progress? Progress is, after all, a value word. From the pragmatic point of view values are instrumental. They are mea-

but less important are John L. Child's two books, *Pragmatism and American Education* (Holt, Rinehart and Winston, Inc., New York, 1956), and *Education and Morals* (Appleton-Century-Crofts, Inc., New York, 1950); William H. Kilpatrick, *Philosophy of Education* (The Macmillan Company, New York, 1951); and Ernest E. Bayles, *Pragmatism in Education* (Harper & Row, Publishers, Incorporated, New York, 1966). For systematic criticisms, see Herman H. Horne, *The Democratic Philosophy of Education* (The Macmillan Company, New York, 1936); Alexander Meiklejohn, *Education between Two Worlds* (Harper & Row, Publishers, Incorporated, New York, 1942), Chaps. 10–14; Isaac B. Berkson, *The Ideal and the Community* (Harper & Row, Publishers, Incorporated, New York, 1958), Chaps. 1–2; Joseph McGlade, *Progressive Educators and the Catholic Church* (The Newman Press, Westminster, Md., 1953).

sured by their efficacy in gaining ends. Progress occurs if these ends are achieved. But, of course, the inquiring mind will still want to know whether the ends were worthy or good. The pragmatist can answer this question only by asking again, good for what? In other words, the value of any particular ends must themselves be instrumentally judged against yet other ends. Such a process is endless unless one is willing to start with some simple desire as the given or accepted invaluable of that situation. Which of several lines of conduct is most likely to lead to progress will then be *judged* in terms of that specific situation. The criterion of the progressive, then, is always specific. He has no general formula for net progress because he has no final or fixed values. Indeed, how could he in a world in which he sees a constantly emerging novelty?

From this it is easy to see why the progressive educator gives so much attention to pupil interest. It is, after all, the core of educational value theory. It is one guide to the selection of curriculum materials and the single best dynamo by which to motivate them. Of course, the danger with this theory is that interest, like progress, will have a very limited application or duration. Children's interests are, for instance, notorious for their vacillation and lack of sustained drive. The defect, however, is not fatal, but something against which to guard. Some interests as they novelly emerge are, to be sure, only ephemeral. Others are much more intense, grip attention longer, and even change little, if any, over long periods of time. The pragmatist senses no contradiction in his position in entertaining such long-range interests. The point at which he wants to save his integrity is in being able to adhere to these values tentatively or experimentally. Consequently, the pragmatist or progressive would count it very shortsighted if young people were not taught persistence and stick-to-it-iveness. The distinctive merit which he ascribes to his position is the fact that the child is driven to persevere by values which he himself sees and voluntarily accepts as his own.

The progressive's or pragmatist's theory of value not only lends importance to the role of interest in learning but also adds significance to several aspects of educational aims. Most readily deducible is the fact that the progressive has no fixed aims or values in advance. Educational aims, no matter how well authenticated by the past, are not to be projected indefinitely into the future. In a world rendered precarious and contingent by a compounding of the novel and the customary, educational aims must be held subject to revision as one advances into the future. If education has any general aim in the light of which these successive revisions can take place, it is only that of pupil growth. But growth itself has no end beyond further growth. In other words, education is its own end. Progressive education is not progressive because it is making steady advance toward some definite goal but because it is growing in whatever direction a novelly emerging future promises most development.

From the foregoing, it must further be evident by now that educational ends are not termini to the road of education, but that they are, paradoxically enough, employed as means or instruments for finding the way. As such, they are used experimentally. No way to education is the true way. Rather it becomes true. To the pragmatist, truth is to be conceived dynamically. Veri-fication is not just figuratively, but literally, truth-making. Education is creative. This does not mean, however, that pupil or teacher makes or creates external reality. Yet, while the pragmatist accepts the existence of an external objective world, nevertheless he does aim to manipulate it to see what the consequences will be. These consequences, in so far as they corroborate anticipated fact, become the truth.

This pragmatic theory of truth implies a very distinctive role for intelligence in the world order. It is to be thought of as an instrument of verification. In a precariously shifting environment, intelligence implements satisfactory adaptations, enables one to use the old and familiar as a tool for subjugating the novel and contingent. It is the chief means of survival. This is its biological evolution and its epistemological significance. Again, this background of pragmatism sheds light on the emphasis which progressive education places on the experimental way of both learning and teaching. When student and instructor enter on a project, there are no preconceived ends at which they must come out. The mutual challenge is to think their way out.

Crucial in the pragmatic or experimental way of gaining truth is its methodology. As already noted several times, a precarious universe sets the problem. After defining the difficulty as precisely as possible and surveying the resources available for its solution, a hypothesis is proposed. After this has been dramatically acted out in imagination, it is put to the test. Activities are overtly initiated in the precarious environment to see whether their consequences will square with those anticipated. The importance of the "activity" curriculum centers right here. Activities are necessary both to make education lifelike and to make life yield the truth.

The pragmatic theory of knowledge is further strategic in the progressive's conception of the curriculum. For the pragmatist, knowledge is something which is wrought out in action. Before it is used, it is merely information. Information becomes knowledge when it is judged to be relevant to the solution of a particular problem, and that judgment is tested in the crucible of experience. It is for reasons such as these that the progressive educator tends to distinguish between the curriculum drawn up in advance and the curriculum which the child actually learns in action. For him, knowledge does not antedate learning but is forged as the pupil and teacher adapt means to ends as their project develops.

Because the pragmatist approaches both value and truth through the concrete experience of some individual, it must not be thought that he is overlooking the experience of others. As a matter of fact, he rates the social very highly. Simply stated, society is a mode of shared experience. Participation in society is one of the most important ways in which education takes place. The way in which society is organized for sharing is, of course, the critical point. The more free and unimpeded this sharing is, the more democratic the society is said to be, and certainly the greater is the educational opportunity. Herein one can see at a glance the great dependency of a democracy on education. All this is very pragmatic, because the free flow of social intercourse makes more experience available for judging what is true and good in the individual's experience.

It is not surprising, therefore, that the progressive educator is warmly attached to the democratic process. The two have much in common because both encourage the individual to specialize in cultivating his unique talents. Happily, the more differently individuals develop, the more things they have to share and the more socially interdependent they necessarily become. Consequently, progressive education is opposed to any barriers which inhibit the easy interchange of diverse cultural viewpoints, such as segregation on racial and religious lines or separate high schools for vocational and college preparation. Besides, in the classroom the progressive teacher democratically shares with the children as many decisions as to obectives, curriculum, and discipline as possible. The sharing he expects between pupil and teacher he also recommends between teacher and administrative or supervisory staff.

Of course, all this means a larger measure of freedom in the progressive school. Freedom will be predicated upon the importance of individuality. Its effectiveness, however, will be enhanced in proportion to the richness of the culture that is appropriated through democratic sharing. Furthermore, freedom is not just for the student, but for the instructor as well. The progressive will especially value his academic freedom, for without it the school is powerless to be an effective instrument of social progress. But on the question whether the school should lead the way to building a new social order, progressives themselves disagree. Suffice it to say that the efficiency of the democratic school in meeting social change lies in its insistence on a free flow of social intercourse. In this way it is able to mobilize the maximum resources at any given point of the front of social progress.

Further to ensure a maximum of freedom for each individual, the pragmatic progressive favors a pluralistic view of society, that is, a society in which the state is but one among many different forms of social organization providing educational opportunities. By preventing any one agency, such as the state or the church, from obtaining a monopoly over education, society ensures freedom for the individual to choose among a variety of different educational aims, methods, and curriculums. Yet, although betraying a deep commitment to the idea of freedom, the pragmatic progressive does not think he contradicts himself in yielding to greater and greater participation by the state in the educational enterprise. Indeed, only if the state expands such services as free transportation to and from school, free medical examinations, and free texts and supplies, will the whole of the younger generation be free to make the most of their capacities.

This social orientation is, finally, the characteristic feature of the progressive's religious and moral education. Moral education is education in the mores. But, like a good pragmatist, he wants the child to be intelligent about the mores. The mores, in other words, are to be applied tentatively and experimentally. Their sanction is to depend on their consequences, not on religion. Indeed, religious education is as naturalistic as youth's secular education. It, too, consists in a zealous participation in the enterprises of the community. If it has a distinguishing feature, it is an endeavor to get youth to undertake their activities in the light of the most inclusive meaning possible.

RECONSTRUCTIONISM[2]

Reared in the progressive philosophy of education and still adhering to the pragmatism which undergirds it is a group of "reconstructionists," who are impatient with the pace and scope of the educational reform characteristic of progressivism. Progressive education, the reconstructionist thinks, is all right in a fairly stable society where, to be sure, changes do occur, but the adjustments they require to maintain stability are rather limited. If the pursuit of academic freedom or civil liberty leaves one undecided as to alternative adjustments or at least without strong commitment to one of

---

[2] The principal reconstructionist is Theodore Brameld, who first gave a synopsis of his views in Ends and Means in Education: A Mid-century Appraisal (Harper & Row, Publishers, Incorporated, New York, 1950), and later expounded them at full length in Patterns of Educational Philosophy: A Democratic Interpretation (World Book Company, Tarrytown-on-Hudson, N.Y., 1950). See also his Toward a Reconstructed Philosophy of Education (The Dryden Press, Inc., New York, 1956) and Cultural Foundations of Education (Harper & Row, Publishers, Incorporated, New York, 1957). For a critique of his view, see James E. McClellan, Toward an Effective Critique of American Education (J. B. Lippincott Company, Philadelphia, 1968), Chap. 4.

them, no great harm results. Such uncertainty is the normal expectancy in a society which is in transition. But those who call themselves reconstructionists do not think they are living during a mild period of smooth social transition. Quite the contrary, they think the conditions resulting from world war, from the continuing strife between communism and capitalism, and from the peacetime as well as military significance of atomic fission are volcanic, even revolutionary, with possibilities. Minor and retail adjustments will no longer suffice. The times demand major and wholesale "reconstruction." Progressive education may have been adequate for an era of *laissez faire* liberalism, but it is high time now to take a bold step beyond it as we move toward the collective-welfare state.

Nothing reveals the radical boldness of the reconstructionists better than the importance they attach to taking a utopian view of education. They favor criticizing and guiding contemporary educational efforts from the point of view of the finest idealization of education they can possibly form. Because they are utopian, however, they are not unrealistic. They expect to put their utopia to work and not to retreat to it as to some ivory tower in the dim past or remote future. In main outline their utopian conception of education calls for the maximum possible self-realization of the great mass of the people. Since the great mass of the people are workers—farm workers, wage earners, salaried employes—education will have an undoubted labor orientation. Such an education will only be possible in an economy of abundance and under the aegis of a positive or welfare state, from both of which human exploitation is excluded and under both of which there is thoroughgoing democratic control.

On the whole, the reconstructionist leans heavily on pragmatic philosophy for strategy and tactics to achieve his utopia. Yet his utopianism is sufficiently different to require some amendments and some different emphases. Perhaps first is the orientation toward the future which his utopianism gives him. If the pragmatist is accused of presentism, the reconstructionist may be accused of futurism. However, there is nothing merely fanciful about the reconstructionist's preoccupation with the future. To him the future, as he sees it, is a proper part of his ontology, a generic trait of existence. If we speculate on what the future might be like and then take these future possibilities into account in planning the present, the future becomes a force in the present and takes on genuine reality.

It is perhaps next in order to note the emphasis which the reconstructionist places on goal seeking. Not only does he regard goal seeking as basic to human nature, but he also regards it as central in a theory of learning. Obviously, goal-seeking behavior is future-oriented. Hence it is ideally suited to supporting a utopian philosophy of education. But in addition, goal seeking makes another emphasis which the reconstructionist regards as highly important. Goals or values are immediately known un-mediated by reason. They have a nonrational quality which the reconstruc-tionist thinks has been much neglected in knowledge and value theory. Because of this immediacy these goals are prehended rather than appre-hended. On this account they tap human powers of tremendous force. Hence if a social consensus on utopia and the means thereto can be achieved, powerful energies are at hand to bring utopia into being.

Such a consensus is already to be found in a people's ideology—the system of beliefs, habits, prejudices on which it joins in acting. To the reconstructionist this ideology is a kind of group mind and as a social structure forms one of the generic traits of existence which a philosophy of education must take into account. In pointing to a group mind, the reconstructionist is not invoking any mystical entity different from or other than the individual mind. He is merely describing the fact that groups of people do remember their common experiences, criticize them, and use them as norms for future experience. But groups are at odds on their ideological norms. In fact, intergroup struggle, with its contraction and expansion of freedom, seems to be as much a part of the reconstruc-tionist's ontology as social structure itself. The possibility of achieving utopia through education can be effective only as there is social consensus on utopia. Yet the reconstructionist insists that this consensus must be voluntary; it must wait on the voluntary testimony of individuals and groups approving the goals it sets forth. Consequently the reconstructionist does not believe that the school should indoctrinate students with the principles of his utopia, although he does believe it defensible partiality for the pupil or teacher to propagandize for it once he has considered all the evidence pro and con and made a commitment to it.

ROMANTIC NATURALISM[3]

Not a few progressives find philosophical support for their educational con-victions, not so much in pragmatism as in a romantic naturalism. For them the main tenets of progressive education spring from the thinking, not of Dewey and his followers, but of Rousseau and his adherents. Pragmatists like Dewey ground the main progressive tenets of interest and freedom in

[3] The classical exposition of this educational philosophy is to be found in Jean Jacques Rousseau, *Emile*, and in Friedrich Froebel, *Menschenerziehung*. In the twentieth century there has been both some talk and some practice of this educational philosophy but practically no systematic writing about it. Yet see James J. Bernard, "Romanticism and the Ivory Tower," *School and Society*, 87:137–138, March, 1959.

a theory of democracy. The activity program which embodies these tenets is basically a method of testing the truth. The romantic followers of Rousseau, on the other hand, ground the tenets of progressive education principally in a theory of human nature. Since the child is spontaneously self-active, interest and freedom follow as the chief vehicle of self-expression.

The romantic naturalist has a profound reverence for nature, as witness that famous assumption of Rousseau's that child nature is good, rather than fallen, as his contemporaries generally maintained. The implication here is that human nature develops according to laws as inexorable as those which heavenly bodies obey in their orbits. The duty of educators is to learn what these laws are. It is their further duty, once they know the laws, to invoke, rather than interfere with, their operation. From this origin, then, stems the whole child-study movement. Child nature becomes the norm.

From these premises the romantic naturalist draws the conclusion that what is, is right. Whatever the child is striving to do must be because of some basic urge that is trying to assert itself. The attention, therefore, paid to children's interests is entirely proper and natural. Indeed, one must be very careful not to thwart these native drives any more than can possibly be avoided. To reinforce this caution, an educator today frequently invokes Freud rather than Rousseau in support of romantic naturalism. At home and in school he approves a greater permissiveness both to avoid and to cure neuroses resulting from the frustrating inhibitions of social convention. Furthermore, if he would fashion a list of the objectives of the school, he should have immediate recourse to child psychology. From its inventory of the instincts which are seeking expression, the educator can make up a catalogue of child needs. These, then, become the objectives which education should try to liberate and satisfy.

The romantic naturalist not only has a high regard for nature as represented in child needs, but he has an especially high regard for nature as represented in individual child needs. He reverences the unique as well as the universal in human nature. Consequently he is ready to organize the school program around the individual interests of the child. He gives high priority to what the individual child thinks and feels, to what he desires and values. If this seems like undue attention to the subjective moods of the child, it is because we fail to attach sufficient worth to the rich diversities of nature.

Sentimental regard for the unique and subjective has even infected the pragmatism of some progressives. After defining the true as what works, they proceed to define "works" as achieving what they set out to do. What turns out to be true thus depends in part, at least, on the aims or values with which they started. That is, there is a certain wishful quality about the truth. If what they will to believe turns out well, then they are inclined to regard it as the truth in so far forth. With such premises it is easy to comprehend why learning in the progressive school must be purposeful, why in the project method the child should have a dominating purpose or inner urge which fixes the aim, guides the process, and furnishes the motivation.

The modern romantic naturalist probably accords the social process a more natural status in the education of the child than did its famous earlier advocate, Rousseau. But even so, the center of gravity of the educational process is still quite heavily weighted toward the independence and autonomy of the individual. The natural rights of man are matched with a bill of rights of childhood. Indeed, these rights often seem to crowd his duties off to the back or side of the educational stage. The inhibitions of social taboos are sometimes rejected as unnatural. The natural state of man is supposed to be freedom. While discipline and self-restraint are worthy objectives, they are incidental to the more positive virtues of a school program emphasizing self-expression.

This thinly veiled injunction laid on parents and teachers not to interfere with the natural development of their offspring blossoms into the doctrine of *laissez faire* on the larger social scale. A governmental hands-off policy toward education has more than once been advocated on naturalistic grounds. In place of the artificial promptings of government, the natural self-interest of people is relied on to provide schools when needed. Where the natural instincts of parenthood fail, those of philanthropy will come forward. If the government steps in at all, it should be only as a last resort in order to see that no injustice is done to any child. Such a philosophy of education, of course, accentuates opportunities for the self-assertiveness of the strong and capable. But even this aggressiveness evinces a sort of natural justice. It seems to be a social application of natural selection and survival of the fittest.

Underlying both pragmatism and romantic naturalism is a certain presentism or temporalism, which finds an easy lodgment in a naturalistic philosophy of education. In a novelly developing universe, one can hardly afford to take his eye off the point at which the new emergents are constantly coming into view. That point, of course, is the ever-moving present. If he averts his gaze too long to the past or future, the rush of oncoming events may run him down. This being the case, it is small wonder that progressives advocate that education be life now rather than a preparation for adulthood or life at some contingent future date. If the child lives well in the present, then as the future imperceptibly grows out of the present, he will be as well prepared as he can be for whatever the future has in store.

EXISTENTIALISM[4]

The emphasis on the individual, which is common to pragmatic naturalism and romantic naturalism, is also present in existentialism. But while an optimism is native to pragmatism and romanticism, existentialism sounds, if not a pessimistic, at least a very sober note. As might be surmised, the ultimate concern of existentialists is with the meaning of existence. They are, of course, hardly alone in this concern. Classical idealists shared it too. Indeed, so wholehearted was their concern for the Ultimate, that they had no doubt the Ultimate was equally concerned with them. Existentialists, on the contrary, have not been so sure that the concern is mutual. Fearing that it is not, they see man's situation in the world as one of loneliness and anxiety. Unsure of his meaning and destiny, man faces the future and ultimately death with understandable feelings of disquietude. What he dreads most, perhaps, is the annihilation of his own existence. Classical philosophers took refuge from this fear in finding the essence of existence in rational principles of metaphysics. By contrast, existentialists find the essence of existence in the very tensions and contradictions which condition their loneliness and anxiety.

Central to an understanding of existentialism is the notion that existence precedes essence, that is, that man first exists and only later defines or conceptualizes himself. The reason for this order lies in existentialism's theory of knowledge. The conventional approach to knowledge permits some separation of knower and known. The existentialist approach, however, overcomes this separation. In this view knowledge is not *about* existence; it *is* existence. Indeed, one knows subjectively only what one uniquely is. But one not only is, he is constantly becoming, he is making choices. Just as he intuits knowledge, so too he intuits values. He has an almost instant access to value with little or no recourse to criteria—the latter, of course, would smack of essence. Yet it is noteworthy that while the existentialist is completely free to choose his values, he holds himself responsible for the consequences of his choice. In the end the learner's identity is found in his commitments. What he chooses, that he becomes.

Since traditional schools have put essence ahead of existence—con-

---

[4] Several accounts of the impact of existentialism on education are available in George F. Kneller, *Existentialism and Education* (Philosophical Library, Inc., New York, 1958); Van Cleve Morris, *Existentialism in Education* (Harper & Row, Publishers, Incorporated, New York, 1966); and Harold O. Soderquist, *The Person and Education* (Charles E. Merrill Books, Inc., Columbus, Ohio, 1964). For a shorter account relating existentialism (1) to teaching, see Austin Patty, "Existential Teaching," *Educational Theory*, 17:329–334, October, 1967, and (2) to phenomenology, see L. F. Troutner, "Existentialism, Phenomenology, and the Philosophy of Education," *Proceedings of the Philosophy of Education Society*, 1964, pp. 118–124.

cept and theory ahead of experience—they seem to children abstract and unrealistic. The existentialist school must be quite the contrary. Instead of retailing vicarious or generalized experience, it insists on experience first hand. It puts emphasis on the child's raw, unmediated reactions. On this account the child's unique individuality receives prime consideration. In the argot of the day each child must "do his own thing." Hence a school which tries to capture the child's own inner "moment of truth" will obviously give a vitality to motivation and an "authenticity" to the curriculum which, to say the least, will be refreshing. Yet, while inviting, this is extremely difficult—some say impossible—for the school to do. Because the reactions of both pupil and teacher are unique, they tend to be inscrutable, ineffable. This amounts to saying that neither teacher nor pupil has windows on to the experience of the other. If that is so, interaction and communication, the kernel of the educative process, are in serious jeopardy.

Oddly enough the existentialist philosophy of education has found its greatest popularity among students rather than teachers. Thus some restless elements of the younger generation, especially in college, have sometimes justified their abrasive behavior on existentialist principles. Exposition of this position takes two directions, one that of the "activists" and the other that of the "hippies."

Activists stress existence as choosing, taking action—especially rebellious action because it so strikingly sharpens personal awareness as existence. The college, too, they think should turn activist; it should promote a heuristic spirit and take an adversary position on the moral and political issues of the day. The traditional idea that the proper role of the college is intellectual (concerned with essences) they repudiate. Moreover, because of existentialism's private and immediate access to knowledge and value, activists make a passionate, relentless, uncompromising, and often humorless insistence on the choices they make on current issues. Holed up in such an almost solipsistic epistemology, it is no surprise that they feel lonely, complain of a "generation gap," or protest the "straight world" and the "establishment." For the same reason existentialism forms a base from which to demand freedom to manage their own affairs and to discard the traditional doctrine that school and college stand in loco parentis to them. Virtually "condemned" to freedom by existentialism, many students are despairingly uncertain how to exercise it and hence suffer an "identity" crisis which in some cases festers into "alienation."

In its second form existentialism seems to undergird an anti-intellectual and hedonistic cult of presentism. The demand of "hippies" in this cult is to experience things now, to have immediate satisfactions. Away with restraint and postponement. Here the self is defined, not by action and protest, but by receptivity and awareness. The way to make existence more

set instruction is exploratory, adventurous, interesting. The second phase is that of "precision." Organization and systematization of data occur here. If the first phase is exciting, the second is exacting. The final stage of the rhythm is "generalization." One can now return to the first stage with classified ideas and relevant techniques, for that experience will be meaningless unless guided by conceptualization. This last aspect of the rhythm of instruction is like the synthesis of an Hegelian triad. It is not only the end of a cycle but the point of beginning a new one.

Progressives found themselves attracted by the first phase, conservatives by the second. When progressive education overflowed the banks of conservatism, many, both progressives and conservatives, turned to the organic philosophy of education as an escape from the excesses of progressive education and the intransigeance of the reactionaries.

IDEALISM[6]

Over against the philosophy of progressive education, with its main props in pragmatism, reconstructionism, and romantic naturalism, stands that of essentialism or traditionalism. The spirit of this educational view can, perhaps, best be caught from the word "essentialism."[7] In the midst of the welter of change and diversity the essentialist believes there are some points of the educational compass which are more or less fixed. Convinced of what are the essentials in education, he firmly and resolutely insists that youth learn them. Essentialism has several philosophical props, one of the principal being idealism.

Parent to much of the educational innovation of the nineteenth century, idealism has been unwilling to acknowledge its twentieth-century offspring, pragmatism. Idealism is to be credited with a high regard for individuality and freedom in education. Moreover, its activity program has been voluntaristic and developmental. Yet in spite of even a tinge of ro-

---

6 Idealistic educational philosophy has several representatives, most notable of whom is probably J. Donald Butler. See his *Idealism in Education* (Harper & Row, Publishers, Incorporated, New York, 1966). For other accounts see Herman H. Horne, *Philosophy of Education*, rev. ed. (The Macmillan Company, New York, 1927), and *The Democratic Philosophy of Education* (The Macmillan Company, New York, 1935). Theodore Greene's "A Liberal Christian Idealist Philosophy of Education" is the best short statement; see National Society for the Study of Education, Fifty-fourth Yearbook, Part I, *Modern Philosophies and Education* (Published by the Society, Chicago, 1955), Chap. 4. Good but more limited are William E. Hocking, *Human Nature and Its Remaking* (Yale University Press, New Haven, Conn., 1923), and Alexander Meiklejohn, *Education between Two Worlds* (Harper & Row, Publishers, Incorporated, New York, 1942). For a limited assessment of the idealistic philosophy of education, see Hubert E. Langan, *The Philosophy of Personalism and Its Educational Applications* (The Catholic University of America Press, Washington, D.C., 1935).
7 William C. Bagley, "An Essentialist's Platform for the Advancement of American Education," *Educational Administration and Supervision*, 24:241–256, April, 1938.

manticism, there is a measure of absolutism in the idealistic philosophy of education, which seems more properly to align it with the essentialists.

This classification seems clearly justified where the idealistic pattern of modern educational philosophy is Platonic. Here ideas are of ultimate, cosmic significance. But by ideas much more is meant than mere mental states. Ideas are rather the essences of archetypes which give form to the cosmos. They are the immaterial molds into which all matter is cast. Moreover, they are the ideals or standards by which the things of sense are to be judged. While matter is known through the senses, its idea or principle is grasped by the mind. But most important for the educational philosophy of essentialism is the fact that these ideas or forms are eternal, unchanging. The objects of sense, on the other hand, seem to be in a continual state of process or flux. Archetypal ideas do not become; they simply are.

If the ideas conditioning the very pattern of the world in which the child lives are in fixed and final form, they must necessarily constitute the essentials of his education. There can be no avoiding them as the backbone of the curriculum. They become a "must" program for the school. This does not mean that education of the senses, and particularly physical and vocational education, is to be neglected. But in any hierarchy of educational values it will not be surprising if such fields of study occupy a lower status. Formal intellectual studies and methods will rank highest.

Moreover, there seems to be a definite organismic bearing to the idealistic essentialist's educational philosophy.[8] It appears to side with Aristotle in declaring that what a developing organism is to become the organism already latently is. The idea or ideal toward which his mind matures must potentially exist within the child before he starts to learn. Learning merely makes definite what formerly was inchoate. This position, clearly, is cousin to the account of learning given by Gestalt psychology.

Modern idealism has given a somewhat different turn to educational philosophy. In its modern meaning, idealism has more to do with ideas as mental states. In this sense idealism might more properly be called a philosophy of idea-ism, the "I" of idealism being inserted for euphony. On careful analysis, it has occurred to some that the only knowledge one has of his environment is his idea of it. The environment in itself can never be known directly. It can be known only through the intermediary ideas of a human knower. The form which the learner's knowledge takes, therefore, is bound to be in part the product of his human way of apprehending it.

---

[8] Although much indebted to the idealism of Plato, Frank C. Wegener claims that *The Organic Philosophy of Education, op. cit.* is not idealistic. According to him, it transcends dualisms such as idealism and realism by embracing them in an organic unity.

The space or time occupied by a learning activity affords a good illustration. Whether space or time has an external objective existence is beyond human proof. Nonetheless, men do have definite ideas of space and time. The conclusion, therefore, is that such concepts are supplied by the mind of the human learner. They are a priori categories of thought.

If such a theory of knowledge be sound, some idealists have gone a step further to argue that reality itself must be idea-istic. What the more exact nature of reality as idea happens to be, is answered by a variety of idealisms. The one which has most found its way into educational philosophy is that of absolute idealism. According to this view, the heart of reality is to be found in thought or reason. Reason is absolute; in fact it is *the* Absolute. Being absolute, it is also One, monistic. In it, everything is interrelated, all contradictions reconciled. Furthermore, the complete cause of any single occurrence involves the whole of reality. The cosmos, then, is a great thought process, and the Absolute is God thinking. Whatever has happened or whatever will happen, is the result of the self-willed idea of the Absolute. Yet, at the same time, the Absolute is already complete, self-realized. Nature, not to forget it, is the medium through which the Absolute progressively reveals itself in external form. Mind in man partakes of the nature of this Absolute Mind. The mind of man, however, is but a part of this absolute whole. It is, therefore, finite and incomplete. Consequently, its objective is to strive to realize itself, to become what it was meant to be.

On the whole, the essentialist's philosophy of education is quite appropriately enclosed in this frame of reference. Obviously, what is absolute is essential. This unmistakably sets the end of the educational process. It is the ever-increasing realization of the Absolute Idea. This statement of objectives also determines the function and purpose of educational philosophy. Its quest is an understanding of ultimate reality. The Absolute being the whole and education being a part thereof, it may be that study of the fragment may reveal important facets of the totality.

The Absolute Idea, of course, is never fully learned because the Absolute is infinite. Hence, each learning achievement of the educator but reveals that his goal is farther off. At this point the idealistic philosophy of education not only seems to satisfy essentialism but to be progressive as well. It seems at once to be both stable and flexible. But the weight of this philosophy rests more heavily on the one foot than on the other. Its Absolute is infinite, limitless, only in the sense of being all-inclusive. This means that absolute Mind requires no further development. It is already complete and fully self-realized. Development or learning is only for the mind of the child, of finite man. And even he becomes, in time, what he eternally is.

Nothing evolves which was not already involved. Thus, in the end, essentialism prevails over progressivism.

Since the Absolute is all-inclusive of everything that ever has been or ever will be, truth and goodness must be an open book to the mind of the Absolute. This extension of the idealist position further increases the gap between essentialism and progressivism. It at once determines a different and distinct pattern for the educative process. Truth and goodness set the models to which the child's learning should conform. They set the bounds of what is essential. Learning is not a creation, but a realization, of the absolute idea of truth and goodness. In the idealistic school, ideas do not become true because of the value they have for accomplishing some pupil project. Rather, ideas work well there because they are true. Their worth is intrinsic, not instrumental. They are representative of ultimate reality and are, therefore, worth learning as ends in and of themselves. Truth has always been true; it does not become true. Hence, the essentialist's curriculum, in so far as it is constituted of knowledge that is consistently true, can be made up and learned in advance of its use.

Exact and direct correspondence of the child's efforts with objective truth, of course, is impossible for the idealistic essentialist. For him, the test of truth is better derived from the logical consistency among his various ideas about truth. From this and the foregoing, one can deduce the role of mind in both the educative and world process. Mind is not merely a recent biological acquisition. Rather is it a primordial stuff which is the very essence of reality itself. Since the world is the learner's idea, education is a sort of world building in which the learner tries to construct an inner world-view which as nearly as possible approximates outer reality, the Absolute. He endeavors to form a *Weltanschauung*, world-view, to use the German word which has so precisely and popularly expressed the philosophy of idealism.

The mentalistic approach to idealism on the whole has committed this educational philosophy to the preeminent importance of consciousness. Mind is ultimately spiritual, not materialistic. Partaking of the nature of the Absolute, it could not be otherwise. A body and an environment there are, to be sure, but ultimately these are reducible to mind. Consequently, any educational psychology which overlooks the data revealed by introspection must necessarily be untrustworthy. Human nature is to be viewed as more than a behaving organism responding to the stimuli of its environment. This is too atomistic. Idealism stresses a certain wholeness. Nothing happens in any part of the system that does not affect all the rest. Herein lies theoretical support both for education of the whole child and, to a degree, organismic educational psychology.

Some idealists are inclined to exalt will rather than intellect or reason to the position of Absolute. On analysis, they find that primacy must be awarded to a certain activity or striving as the heart of reality. This theory is notably different from the pragmatic in accounting for the activity principle in education. It puts an education squarely up to the individual. Neither teacher nor parent, school nor church can educate him. Only through a voluntary effort of his will can he educate himself. He will be particularly called upon to make this effort when interest fails to motivate his learning activities. This assures the essentialist that essentials will be learned despite the failure of easier approaches.

Whether idea or will be made the Absolute, each is peculiarly private to the individual. The idealist must therefore be at especial pains to avoid the egocentric predicament of solipsism. His educational theory must avoid the uncompromising insistence of the pupil or teacher that reality exists exclusively as he views it. Otherwise, the operation of mind on mind would be impossible and both the social and educational processes would be without meaning. The idealist escapes this predicament by objectifying mind, that is, he reduces everything to mind but admits that there are other minds than his. Most important here, of course, is Absolute Mind. All individual minds are encompassed in the Absolute Mind. Out of this grows a conception of the social mind. In addition to individual minds is the over-mind of society in which all share. It is the whole, of which the rest are parts.

The educational significance of this rather abstruse and compact statement is tremendous. On the one hand, it projects individuality to front-rank importance. Much is made of the spiritual autonomy of the individual. In this respect idealism can lay definite claim to favoring a democracy as the social soil in which its educational theory is to grow. On the other hand, the individual seems subordinated to the social whole. About this whole there is a definite oneness; it is monistic. This has led to invoking idealism as the underpinning for totalitarian theories of education, especially that of fascism. Of course not all essentialists are fascists, but there is an undeniable essentialism about fascism.

Little need be said, in conclusion, about the idealistic point of view on religious and moral education. Its definition of the Absolute has unmistakable theistic characteristics. Since the aim of education is the increasing realization of the Absolute, all education appears tinged with religious significance. This includes moral education as well. Reason being absolute, the universe is one of law and order. So, too, there is a moral law in the universe backed by the authority of the Absolute. This lays an inescapable moral imperative on education.

REALISM[9]

So far the stability and firmness on which the essentialist philosophy of education prides itself has been rooted in a reality that has been idealistic. Ideas rather than external objects have constituted ultimate reality. Some essentialists, however, think that a more solid foundation can be built for their philosophy of education in a theory that these objects have a reality independent of mental phenomena. This philosophy is known as realism. In its more materialistic phases, it even reduces mind itself to an aspect of matter. Possibly excepting this last statement, realism seems a very common-sense point of view. It seems essentialist in that it bluntly recognizes the uncompromising limits within which human educational endeavors must be undertaken.

Education, for the naturalistic realist, is primarily concerned with the world as it is here and now. The universe, for him, is not only external to him, but it is governed by inexorable law. If this seems less true in the social as compared with the natural sciences, it is only because man has not yet perfected techniques for ascertaining and stating the laws of social phenomena. In any event, man has only his intelligence to depend on to survive in his struggle with external nature. Fortunately for him, his intelligence is thoroughly at home in the natural order because its pedigree shows its evolution as an instrument of adaptation to a changing environment.

This reference to mind indicates a further affirmation of a naturalistic realism. Instead of standing outside nature, mind is a naturalized product within it. Mind is biological in origin and developed as a way of adjusting to a precarious and contingent nature. Furthermore, the mind of *Homo sapiens* is a comparatively recent addition to nature. It appeared late in evolutionary history and is not some primordial stuff which has antedated nature herself. In place of merely contemplating the glory of God's handiwork, mind is in and of nature, reconstructing it as well as comprehending it. The natural classroom method, therefore, is that of exposition and persuasion.

[9] The best full-length statement of the realistic position is that of Harry Broudy, *Building a Philosophy of Education* (Prentice-Hall, Inc., Englewood Cliffs, N.J., 1961). For an excellent shorter statement, see John Wild, "Education and Human Society: A Realistic View," in National Society for the Study of Education, Fifty-fourth Yearbook, Part I, *Modern Philosophies and Education* (Published by the Society, Chicago, 1955), Chap. 2. Less well knit is Frederick Breed's *Education and the New Realism* (The Macmillan Company, New York, 1939). For realism with emphasis on biology, see William C. Bagley, *Education and Emergent Man* (Thomas Nelson & Sons, New York, 1935), and with emphasis on sociology, Ross Finney, *Sociological Philosophy of Education* (The Macmillan Company, New York, 1929). Theodore Brameld offers an interesting critique of realism in his *Philosophies of Education in Cultural Perspective* (The Dryden Press, Inc., New York, 1955), Chap. 9.

One very important group of educational realists are the scientific realists. The fundamental assumption lying back of most educational science is that the object of research has a definite external physical reality. The educational scientist may fail to describe it accurately, but he never doubts the objective existence of what he is trying to study. This is true whether he is studying the material or the social environment. In either case their external existence sets an undeniably common point of reference for the educational enterprise. It is here that subjective differences of opinion must ultimately come for arbitration. Not even the fact that the objective reality so revered may be subject to evolutionary processes alters this conclusion. Under such conditions education, especially its scientific study, should endeavor to approximate the laws according to which these changes take place. Clearly, the realism depicted in these rugged and un-yielding terms has a strong essential flavor.

Reality so defined is to be distinguished from truth. Reality simply is; truth is its image. The test of truth, hence, is its correspondence to reality. If ideas work, it is because they are true to reality and not vice versa. Truth may be the product of the human mind, but not so reality. A creative intelligence, which creates reality, is discounted in advance. Consequently, the theory of education as a reconstruction of the universe around us must give way to a theory of education as conformity to it. The curriculum, therefore, is composed of the best data on reality to date. Because this must be determined by the most competent investigators, the realist's curriculum tends to be sponsored in an authoritarian manner. For the same reason, it can readily be required as essential. Indeed there is an inherent and welcome discipline in letting the learner know that his education is conditioned by the inexorable quality of an external reality.

This point of view is, furthermore, the attitude of much scientific study of educational psychology. Particularly is it true of behaviorism. Here, the investigator contents himself only with what he sees in the way of overt behavior. The idea that the psyche of the learner has a supernature, a soul, finds no place in his account. Pretty much the same comment is in order for the neurological and physiological approaches to educational psychology. There is often a materialism and mechanism inherent here which is congenial with a naturalistic realism.

Given such premises, the educational realist is quite naturally committed to a stimulus-response type of learning and human nature. In the strictest sense stimuli are objective. On this account each stimulus and its response is capable of objective study. This in turn paves the way to the theory underlying scientific measurement in education. Tests are found to measure the qualities objectively observable in pupil reactions. The quality most frequently measured is that of accuracy, and it hardly needs mention what the standard of accuracy is where the correspondence theory of truth is assumed.

The same philosophy is implied in the movement to make a scientific determination of educational objectives. What a community values is held to be an objective fact. As such, it should be as susceptible to investigation and definition as any other object of scientific research. And once given the authenticity of science—to most minds incontestable—it becomes invested with the spirit of essentialism. The social or cultural tradition stands for external reality as it is best known to date.

The principal concern of the school is to examine things as they really are in themselves. The examination is most effectively made in terms of pure theory. To ensure the purity of theory the school must be detached from the special needs or particular interests of the concrete life of practice. Vocational and professional education will, to be sure, have their place, yet both should be taught, not pragmatically, but in relation to the pure theories which undergird them. Vocational and professional education cannot be trusted to occupy the forestage, because the practical man of action too often has no time for long-range, theoretical perspective.

By confining educational aims within the bounds of the here and now, one but fits his educational philosophy to the dimensions of nature. He omits the eternal, the timeless, from his space-time frame of reference. Man does this because he feels at home in nature. He may not have a complete list of answers to all his problems, but he takes comfort and gains confidence in thinking that none of them is hidden in mysterious riddles of a superhuman or supernatural character. If religion enters his philosophy of education, it is only as a deified nature. God is immanent in nature, and nature is His temple of worship.

Moral education likewise is put on a naturalistic basis. Morals originate in the folkways or mores. These are either enforced by social pressures or are self-enforcing through their natural consequences. Character education, therefore, has no need of an appeal to an authority external to nature. Conscience becomes an echo of social custom rather than divine command.

RATIONAL HUMANISM[10]

Essentialism probably finds its sturdiest support from those who refer to their philosophy as the *philosophia perennis*. Aristotle was the principal author of this philosophy and St. Thomas Aquinas its chief subsequent

---

[10] The reader should distinguish between rational humanism and the humanism of the "religious educators," *supra*, pp. 190–193. Humanism emphasizes human nature and the

modifier. So soundly did these men lay the basis of this philosophy that it has remained substantially unchanged since the Middle Ages. In spite of the rise and fall of rival systems, it has continued to appeal to generation after generation down through the centuries. It is indeed, literally, the perennial philosophy.

Aristotle developed the *philosophia perennis* about as far as one can go on human reason alone. St. Thomas made such modifications in Aristotle's position as the advent of Christianity seemed to demand. Some modern perennialists think they can maintain the perennial philosophy by leaning on Aristotle alone. Others, probably the majority, think this philosophy a more hardy perennial when it draws strength from St. Thomas as well. We shall here refer to the educational philosophy of the former as rational humanism and to that of the latter as scholastic realism.[11]

The major premise of rational humanism is an assertion that the essence of human nature is its rational character. His vegetative and animal nature man shares with other animate forms of life. Like plants and animals, he takes nourishment, and like the brute, he is sentient and capable of feelings. But unlike the plant or the brute, he can reason, judge, discriminate. In respect of reason man has not his like anywhere. In this he is unique, *sui generis*. If reason is the essence of man's nature—the quintessence, we might even add—then wherever and whenever we find

---

human point of view. Some humanists think man's humanity lies in a rationality with which he was invested from the beginning of time. Other more recent humanists think man's rationality the natural product of evolution according to Darwin. The former humanists tend to think of the character and quality of rationality as fixed from the beginning, while the latter regard it as subject to further modification. The older humanists are concerned with an educational role for mind as knowing the world as it is constituted, while the newer ones formulate the role of mind as not only adapting to the world as it is but adapting the world so far as possible to suit themselves.

No one has yet set forth a full-length comprehensive exposition of the educational philosophy of rational humanism. The reader must depend, therefore, on a number of short brochures stating various aspects of it. Chief exponent of this position is Mortimer J. Adler, who has principally expounded his position in "The Crisis in Contemporary Education," *Social Frontier*, 5:140–145, February, 1939; "Are There Absolute and Universal Principles on Which Education Should Be Founded?" *Educational Trends*, 9:11–18, July–August, 1941; "The Order of Learning," *Proceedings of the Western Division of the American Catholic Philosophical Association*, 1941, pp. 103–125; and "In Defense of Philosophy of Education," National Society for the Study of Education, Forty-first Yearbook, *Philosophies of Education*, Chap. 5. Robert M. Hutchins, another capable exponent of rational humanism, has stated his position most explicitly in "The Philosophy of Education," in Robert N. Montgomery (ed.), *William Rainey Harper Memorial Conference* (The University of Chicago Press, Chicago, 1938), pp. 35–50. Major criticisms of the position of these men occur in Sidney Hook, *Education for Modern Man* (The Dial Press, Inc., New York, 1963), and in the published papers of the Second Conference on the Scientific Spirit and Democratic Faith, *The Authoritarian Attempt to Capture Education* (King's Crown Press, New York, 1945), as well as in Theodore Brameld, *Patterns of Educational Philosophy: A Democratic Interpretation*, Chaps. 10–12.

11 Cf. Robert H. Beck, "Neo-Thomism and Rational Humanism in Educational Philosophy," *Harvard Educational Review*, 19:16–29, Winter, 1949.

man we shall expect him to be possessed of the faculty of reason. Changing the emphasis somewhat, we shall expect human nature to be the same everywhere and always. We shall invariably expect rational humanism, therefore, to weigh educational policy and practice by the standard of rational man.

Equipped with the unique faculty of reason, man's main business is to use this faculty, to know the world in which he lives. Happily, the world is intelligible so that it can be known by the proper exercise of reason. Starting with self-evident principles like the principle of self-contradiction (a thing cannot both be and not be at one and the same time), man can reach absolute and universal truth. Truth, of course, is everywhere the same. Reason distills truth from its study of nature by distinguishing between what is essential and what is accidental in nature. The essential is concerned with the uniform; the accidental is concerned with the variable. The variable is an indication of change, but change as things will, they never change as to their essential nature. This does not mean that the accidental and variable are unimportant but merely that they are less important for the educational philosophy of the rational humanist than are the essential and uniform.

Obviously a philosophy which is so preoccupied with the essence, whether of human nature or nature in general, is bound to offer staunch support to essentialism in education. Since rationality is the essence of man's nature, the principal aim of his education must necessarily be intellectual. Moreover, since human nature is the same everywhere and always, it follows that this aim of education must be the same for all men in all times and in all places. This does not mean that the humanistic rationalist overlooks or disregards the individual differences psychological research has so convincingly revealed; sex and vocational differences, to mention but two, are important also. But they are accidental; they are not of the essence. Furthermore, cultivation of the intellect is important not just as a means to an end, as in problem solving, but more significantly as an end in itself. It is the educational *summum bonum.*

In selecting his materials for the curriculum, the rational humanist is again interested in choosing the essentials. The essentials, of course, consist in what is uniform and recurrent in human experience. But the school day is not long enough to include everything which meets this criterion. There must be a further hierarchy of value. This is found in the rational nature of man. The larger the rational content of subject matter, the greater its claim to preference in the curriculum. This is as it should be if the universal aim of education is the cultivation of intelligence. The subjects with the greatest rational content, of course, are the liberal arts, and among the liberal arts, the humanities. These are best exemplified in the "great books" of our culture.

A curriculum so composed is likely to admit of little election by the student. The fact, however, that, conversely, such a curriculum is likely to be largely prescribed does not deprive the student of freedom but rather gains it for him. "Education for freedom," a popular phrase and principal objective of rational humanists, is achieved by conformity to the truth and not by a *laissez faire* attitude toward the student's election of it or by the license to deviate from it.

As a matter of pedagogy, it will be well for the teacher to recognize two orders of knowledge or learning. One is the inherent, essential order of subject matter itself as logically descriptive of the part of nature with which it deals. The objective of teaching and learning is to discover this order. Some essentialists conform the order of the lesson directly to this essential order of subject matter. Much like the progressives, however, the leading rational humanists recognize a second order of learning which takes its cue from the nature of the learner himself. They recognize that learning is a historical process which is relative to the point that the child has presently reached in his education. Consequently, still aiming to reach the essence of the subject matter under consideration, the teacher makes concessions to the temporary and accidental by starting with child experience. Instead of ordering the lesson according to the abstract and universal he commences with the concrete and particular.

SCHOLASTIC REALISM[12]

Scholastic realists, for the most part Roman Catholics, agree with the rational humanists as far as they go, but declare that they do not go far enough. The latter go as far as natural reason and metaphysics permit, but

---

[12] It may surprise some that scholastic realism is the only religious philosophy of education to be presented systematically in this chapter. The fact is that neither Protestants nor Jews have systematically developed a philosophy of education. Perhaps the divisive nature of Protestantism is one obstacle here. Nevertheless, see George W. Forell, "Some Implications of the Axioms of Classical Protestantism for the Philosophy of Education," *Proceedings of the Philosophy of Education Society*, 1959, pp. 92–100. It would be interesting to present Buddhist and Moslem philosophies of education, too, but again, neither religion has spun a systematic philosophy of education; or to the extent that representatives have attempted a formulation, they have been so preoccupied with stating religious objectives that they have failed to develop the full range of their educational implications. See A. L. Tibawi, "Philosophy of Moslem Education," and A. Basu, "Hinduism and Buddhism," The Yearbook of Education, 1957, *Education and Philosophy* (World Book Company, Tarrytown-on-Hudson, N.Y., 1957), Chaps. 5 and 6.

The single most comprehensive treatment of the educational philosophy of scholastic realism is that of John D. Redden and Francis A. Ryan, *A Catholic Philosophy of Education*

they stop short of the further vista which revelation and theology open up. Down this further vista the scholastic realist seeks deeper meanings for his educational philosophy.

The educational philosophy of scholastic realism is fundamentally dualistic. It recognizes both an order of nature and a supernatural order. Central in the latter is the divine being of God, the Author of all. While change and time characterize the former, God Himself is changeless and eternal. Novelty, so evident in the natural order, turns out to be apparent only when viewed from the standpoint of an immutable eternity. Individuality, likewise, is accidental and merely an instance of an already complete reality. Indeed, God could not be omniscient and omnipotent if He were to grow or learn, if He did not both antedate and postdate time, and if there were anything that could be novel to Him.

With such premises granted, it is easy to understand why many educators insist on essentialism. What is fixed and unalterable through all time is undeniably essential. It is so essential that failure to insist on it would be folly indeed. It justifies any educator in holding to certain unwavering educational objectives. Furthermore, it is sufficient warrant for a prescribed curriculum. Educational values which partake of an immutable character remove any difficulty from selecting a program of minimum essentials.

Of course, change is not completely eliminated from this scholastic system. If there were no change, there could be no learning. But learning is a necessity of finite man in the natural order. Education is the process by which he lifts himself up to the eternal. Progress is measured by advance toward this goal. This progress, however, is primarily a matter of improving the means of gaining the final objective. It takes place within nature. There is no progress in the ultimate end or supernatural destiny of

(The Bruce Publishing Company, Milwaukee, 1955). Other good accounts are Herbert Johnson, *A Philosophy of Education* (McGraw-Hill Book Company, New York, 1963); Leo Ward, *Philosophy of Education* (Henry Regnery Company, Chicago, 1966); William F. Cunningham, *Pivotal Problems of Education* (The Macmillan Company, New York, 1940); and Edward A. Fitzpatrick, *Philosophy of Education* (The Bruce Publishing Company, Milwaukee, 1953). To these books should be added two very good sets of essays, *The Philosophy of Christian Education*, being the *Proceedings of the Western Division of the American Catholic Philosophical Association*, 1941; and Hunter Guthrie and Gerald G. Walsh, *A Philosophical Symposium on American Catholic Education* (Fordham University Press, New York, 1941). One may also add an anthology of the educational philosophy of Jacques Maritain gathered together in Donald Gallagher and Idella Gallagher (eds.), *The Education of Man* (Doubleday & Company, Inc., Garden City, N.Y., 1962). The nearest approach to a systematic criticism of scholastic or Catholic educational philosophy is to be found in the published papers of the Second Conference on the Scientific Spirit and Democratic Faith, *The Authoritarian Attempt to Capture Education* (Kings Crown Press, New York, 1945), and in Theodore Brameld, *Patterns of Educational Philosophy: A Democratic Interpretation* (World Book Company, Tarrytown-on-Hudson, N.Y., 1950), Chaps. 10–12.

man. This is final, unchangeable, eternal. The supernatural essentialist, thus, is progressive only within very definite and fixed boundaries. He rejects the radical philosophy of progressive education, in which there are no limits or ends that are not subject to further evolution. Indeed, without the eternal verities as a fixed point of reference, the theological essentialist finds it impossible to calculate progress at all.

Among these verities, the nature of truth and goodness has peculiar significance for the philosophy of education. To commence with the former, it is obvious that knowledge, the chief commerce of the school, should be true. But when is knowledge true? If truth is an eternal verity to be regarded as forever the same, an objective external reality is imputed to truth. Truth is not the victim of subjective personal opinion or mental states. Rather is it universal. This characteristic of truth is especially congenial to the essentialist. Learning it does not alter its character. Learning experimentally involves verification, but verification is not literally truthmaking. Truth is not made—much less is it manufactured by a child learning. Verification is merely testing the correspondence of what is learned with objective truth. But learning is more than just copying or mirroring the truth as it is in idealism and realism. It is a direct apprehension of reality; it is an entering into or laying hold on the very essence or being of the subject matter under study.

Of course, the entire truth has never been vouchsafed to man's keeping, not even to that of the essentialist. Much of man's knowledge is only an approximation of truth itself. Nevertheless, the assumption that there is a prototype of truth leaves its mark on the way the curriculum is conceived. The fact that truth is ever the same enables the teacher to make the curriculum up in advance of any learning activity. Essentials can be determined before school opens. Moreover, the knowledge of truth to be imbibed can be set out to be learned. The formal knowledge of the school is rarely something to be learned incidentally or indirectly as the outcome of fulfilling a pupil's purpose. It antedates any project he may wish to carry out. It is waiting to be learned. Consequently, it is something which can be appropriated directly. Being objectively conceived, it can, when learned, be stored away till called up on demand.

Accordingly, the primary role of mind in the world order is that of cognition. Its primordial business is to know. Since the truth is not always clear, it may first have to find out, to judge, what corresponds to the truth. But ultimately, its function is to record what is true. So school becomes the place where mind masters the essentials of culture. With training acquired from the sciences and humanities in the curriculum, mind can accurately penetrate much that is profoundly true. But, suffering finite limitations, it will fail to grasp some of the profoundest truths of all, those of religion. Fortunately, however, aided by supernatural revelation, the human mind can penetrate the truth of even some of these divine mysteries.

The nature of mind further bears out the perennial dualism in the Catholic philosophy of education. Mind is to be carefully distinguished from the body or matter. One must be especially on his guard in identifying mind with the brain or any other part of the neural system of physiology. The dualism of mind and body consists chiefly in that the latter is a material, while the former is an immaterial, substance. This difference should not lead one to think that there is a schism in the learner's personality. The oneness of the learner is fundamental in spite of the fact that that oneness is compounded of an immaterial mind with a material body. Just how an immaterial substance can interact with a material one or vice versa is a mystery of the dualism. But, in any event, the difference between mind and body is sufficiently great to warn the teacher not to place too great confidence in the conclusions of behavioristic and materialistic psychology.

It is, of course, not enough for the educator to know what is true. He must also know what is good. Truth and goodness are separate categories. Much that is true is not good. Happily for the essentialist, values are to be regarded just as externally and objectively as truth. They inhere in the form of objects or studies even though unrecognized by pupils or teachers. Values, indeed, are convertible with being. If they originated solely in bodily states, they would be too vacillating, for the instability of feelings is notorious. Besides, man's original nature is fallen, not wholly in order, thus undermining any assumption that what he desires is *ipso facto* good. What is good must also be judged good. Through reason, one will be able to apprehend what it is in any object or study that endows it with inherent and abiding value. Of course, it is this objectivity of value, it is the fact that the good is eternally good, that recommends it to the perennial essentialist of Catholic persuasion.

This philosophy of educational values has an important bearing on the employment of interest in learning. Interest is an assertion by the learner of a recognition of value in the object of his studies. As such, it is entirely normal and should be capitalized on if possible. But if the learner manifests no interest in the eternal verities presented to him in the curriculum, which should take precedence, interest or curriculum? The scholastic realist definitely aligns himself with the latter. In this he is consistent with the rest of the scholastic position. The permanent obviously is to be preferred to the transient. Because it is permanent and enduring, it generates an obligation. It must, or ought to, be learned even in the absence of interest. Effort must be summoned up so that duty may be discharged.

The immutability of truth and goodness lays yet a further imperative upon the teacher. If he is imparting what is unmistakable and eternal truth or what are well-known essentials, it will be legitimate for him to indoctrinate. He will even be inclined to this procedure where there is uncertainty as to the final form of truth or goodness, for then his duty will be to pass on the most approved view to date. To let a youth arrive at his own conclusions independently may result in an extravagant waste of time, to say nothing of his running the risk of failing to put in at the proper port in the end. If this method of instruction seems to disregard minority or contrary opinions, suffice it to say that the truth, if it really is the truth, must be intolerant of error.

At first glance it may appear as if there were no room for freedom in the Catholic philosophy of education. However, there are two important points at which it is quite marked. In the first place, there is individual freedom of the will. The will of the pupil is free to accept or reject the authority of the teacher. To have to choose between the true and the false, or between the good and the bad, may not seem to be a difficult option, but its exercise is nonetheless a fateful decision. In the second place, freedom is a social privilege. It is awarded to pupils in proportion to their command of the accumulated wisdom of social ages past. In this sense freedom is an outcome or end of education. It is predicated on a knowledge of, and respect for, the essentials of tradition. Academic freedom thus is not absolute, but proportioned to expertise.

The importance of individuality in the Catholic philosophy of education may be inferred from its position on freedom. Individuality is obviously recognized. Indeed, individuals are of supreme worth. Individual differences in school children, however, are accidental, to use the word in its technical meaning. These differences are cultivated, to be sure, but they are not of the essence of childhood or humanity. It is the pupil's immortal soul that is most important to save through education. There is no difference in the quality of immortality. Salvation through education is accomplished by enabling the child to perceive and act on what is universal in truth and goodness, not what is accidental or transient. It is the universal that is essential, not the particular.

The sort of social structure in which the Catholic philosophy of education most readily roots may be either aristocratic or democratic. Its dependence on authority and the people who know best ordinarily enables it to work well in states where political power is rather narrowly and autocratically held. At the same time, the fact that it opens the highest careers to talent, in whatever social strata it is born, has a sound democratic ring. But in the relation of state and church the Catholic philosophy of education maintains its fundamental dualism between the natural and the supernatural, the temporal and the spiritual. The state's interest in education being of the natural order, therefore, is of a lower estate than that of the church. The educational philosophy of essentialism reaches its most extreme point in the supreme sureness of the Catholic church in the infallibility of its mandate to teach.

The Catholic philosophy of education comes to a final focus in religious and moral education. Although religion and morals are to be included right along with the secular or lay subjects, nonetheless the fundamental dualism of scholasticism is recognized in the distinction between profane and sacred studies. The approach to the latter, as might be expected, is from the supernatural side. The lay teaching of morals, independent of religious instruction, is thought woefully inadequate. Goodness is commended to children as a divine command. Religious education is orienting the child toward his Creator and final destiny.

FASCISM[13]

Reference is often made to fascism as an offshoot of idealism. Offshoot or not, it has had an importance for educational philosophy which entitles it to independent consideration. In spite of the destruction of the two principal fascist powers in the Second World War, the fascist mentality still persists and not always in formerly fascist countries. It seems to suit itself to regimes which can maintain themselves only by bold and even brutal authoritarian means.

Primarily, fascism is a political philosophy of education. To aid in clarifying a positive statement of its position, it may be well first to outline a negative statement of what it opposes. In large part fascism is a protest against what it believes to be weakness in the democratic philosophy of education. The principal weakness of democracy, it holds, is its individualism, born of the Protestant Reformation and the French Revolution. Thus the democratic state is merely the atomistic sum of the wills of the individuals which compose it; it has no ends of its own. Government, consequently, is merely a convenient device for maintaining individual interests in some balance of justice. Rule by majority gives effect to the selfish interests of those individuals able to maintain themselves in power. As majorities are notoriously unstable, society is ruled by no fixed or stable ideals.

---

[13] The outstanding fascist philosopher of education was the Italian, Giovanni Gentile. See his *The Reform of Education* (Harcourt, Brace & World, Inc., New York, 1922), and Merrit M. Thompson, *The Educational Philosophy of Giovanni Gentile* (University of Southern California Press, Los Angeles, 1934). For the German influence, see George F. Kneller, *The Educational Philosophy of National Socialism* (Yale University Press, New Haven, Conn., 1941). For the United States, see Lawrence Dennis, *The Coming American Fascism* (Harper & Row, Publishers, Incorporated, New York, 1936), Chap. 17.

The liberal state exists merely as a means for promoting the welfare of the individual, who finds his happiness in liberty, not in sacrifice or discipline.

Against this individualistic, atomistic, pluralistic conception, fascism sets up a positive, organic theory of the state with not only purposes of its own but purposes superior to those of the individual. In this conception the state becomes the end and the individual, the means. The function of liberty under such circumstances is not to provide the means for individual self-realization and self-expression, but rather for sacrifice of the self in the interests of the state. Liberty is not a natural right but a concession of the state; furthermore, it ranks ethically lower than duty. And why not? The state is more than the sum of the individuals who compose it. It has ends which are always superior because the state is the link between succeeding generations and therefore is more farseeing and more unselfish. Hence control of the state rests, not with majorities of individuals, but with an elite capable of subordinating their own immediate private interests to those of the national ideal. This elite is chosen, not from below but from above. Its values are validated by its power to enforce them and are not stalled by interminable parliamentary debate.

Naturally education in the fascist state gives first priority to the elite of exceptional endowment. Yet the school does not make or unmake the elite; it merely increases their social distance from the masses. To face these facts realistically should not be depressing. Neither should it afford an argument against more and better education for everyone. The aim of fascist education is not to equalize educational opportunities but rather to differentiate them. If liberal democratic education claims that it, too, has always sought to realize each student's maximum potentialities, the protest is vitiated because liberal democratic education teaches individuals to be maximally effective in realizing their own material advantage rather than in giving unselfish devotion to state interests.

The identification of the individual's with the state's interests is a prime principle of fascist education. The individual learns to exercise true volition when the will of his state acts in his personal will, that is, when his will is the realization of the will of his state. Hence, in learning to realize the ends of the state, which, as has been said, are less selfish and more far-reaching than his own, the individual realizes a more significant selfhood than would ever be possible in the liberal democratic state. This same spirit pervades the classroom. The teacher must establish himself as that unique superior personality in whom the spiritual life of the students and teacher is fused and organically united. If he fails to do this, then the discipline and respect for authority so characteristic of the fascist hierarchy is lacking.

COMMUNISM[14]

If fascist educational philosophy seems to have an affinity for idealism, perhaps communist educational philosophy has more of an affinity for realism. This may seem strange since Karl Marx, communism's earliest theoretician, was so indebted to the German idealist, Hegel, for the seminal notions in his system. But certain communist tenets are definitely realistic. In the first place, the communist grounds his faith in communism on its scientific inevitability. This expectation may be as metaphysical a theory of history as Hegel's, but since communistic science presupposes a physical reality independent of man's mind, the realistic implications are obvious, to say nothing of the firmness, even rigidity, of conviction it supports. In the second place, communist educational philosophy seems to be materialistic like the rest of its economic outlook. The postulates for its theory of learning rest in a materialistic view of human nature. If the child does not do well in school, he is sent, not to the psychologist to be examined and interviewed, but to the physician to see whether he is well. Furthermore, the communist has extraordinary confidence in the extent to which the physical environment can alter physical nature. As nothing is immovable or intractable, communists have every hope of erasing all traces of capitalist mentality and of producing a "new" communist man.

The most important aspect of the physical environment as it impinges on the student is the economic. Thus it is a cardinal tenet of communist philosophy that the mode of production of material things determines the character of social and political institutions. Man deceives himself if he thinks his institutions are the product of purely rational principles. Consequently, as the communist believes that the value of goods is measured by the labor expended on them, so he believes labor must have an important role to play in education. But he means by labor much more than is included in bourgeois capitalist schools. He means much more than manual training, arts and crafts, or even shopwork. The school which treats labor as valuable merely for motor training does not deserve the name communistic. Moreover, communism vigorously rejects any artificial dualism between the work of head and hand, and naturally, therefore, it rejects the wider dualism between cultural and vocational curriculums.

In communist society, socially useful labor must form the central pivot

[14] Literature in English on communist educational philosophy is meagre. Somewhat out of date now is the formerly leading statement of Albert P. Pinkevitch, *The New Education in the Soviet Republic* (The John Day Company, Inc., New York, 1929). For a good, chapter-long statement by a non-communist, see Robert S. Cohen, "On the Marxist Philosophy of Education," in National Society for the Study of Education, Fifty-fourth Yearbook, Part I, *Modern Philosophies and Education* (Published by the Society, Chicago, 1955), Chap. 6. For an excellent account of the theory of work in communist education, see John W. Donohue, *Work and Education* (Loyola University Press, Chicago, 1959), Chap. 3.

of the entire school. The student must feel himself a worker in a laboring society. From this demand it becomes understandable why communism insists on a close relation between the school, the local factory or office, and the nearest state or cooperative farm. It should not escape attention here that polytechnical education is to be developed in the full context of general education. That is, labor as the central preoccupation of the school is to be studied in all its economic, political, scientific, social, and aesthetic aspects. Indeed one might say that polytechnical education so conceived is a communist form of liberal education.

Of course the institution of such an advanced program for the schools is impossible until such time as the injustices and contradictions of capitalism are swept away. These evils are only too evident in the bourgeois hypocrisy which exalts education but persists in the material impoverishment of both its schools and its teachers, to say nothing of denying the latter an important role in the determination of educational policy. Indeed, the ineptness of educational leaders in self-criticism reveals that they are not doctors diagnosing the ailing social system but are symptoms of the disease itself. The basic cure is to replace that form of society where an owning class can exploit another that is propertyless by one that is altogether classless. Hence it is only when the workingman comes to power, as inevitably he must, that labor can assume its proper role in the educative process.

Communism does not deceive itself into thinking, as some liberal democrats do, that the school can take the initiative in building this new social order. Neither is communism taken in by that other liberal democratic contention—that the school can stand above politics and disinterestedly serve society as a whole. On the contrary, communism quite frankly treats the school as a deliberate instrument of state policy. Indeed, the school is a weapon in the hands of the ruling class, and teachers are soldiers in the battle for communism. If communist educational policy has seemed pragmatic and progressive at times, it is only because such a policy has served the expediency of the moment. Basically, communist education is guided by bedrock realism, where the external course of events is already clear to any one who understands the dialectic of history.

Confident of the way in which history will eventuate, communists do not hestitate to indoctrinate their students, especially in matters of party policy. In controversial issues there is no possibility of following an argument whithersoever it may lead, unless perhaps this occurs in the Central Committee of the party, whose proceedings are for the most part secret. The idea of an objective truth, unaffected by the interests of the state or the party, is foreign to the communist philosophy of education. The absence of academic freedom as commonly understood, however, does not mean that the communists lay no claim at all to freedom in their system. If they do have freedom, it is a freedom born of regulation rather than a freedom to criticize.

Although communism actively teaches an atheistic outlook, it by no means neglects the moral instruction of the young. The morals taught, however, originate in social-class thinking. Communism rejects a moral education grounded in divine ordinance. Such a moral is too likely to be-cloud the minds of workers and peasants to a subtle sanctioning of the economic interests of the exploiting class. Since morals are social-class in origin, let the working classes create their own class morals. To ensure the victory of their cause, however, they will undoubtedly have need of such old-fashioned virtues as bravery, loyalty, steadfastness, and discipline.

DEMOCRACY[15]

The social philosophy which undergirds most of the preceding philosophies of education is neither fascism nor communism but democracy. Although each philosophy of education which claims democracy as its own probably does so for different reasons, nevertheless, in spite of these differences there seems to be a denominator common to them all which deserves separate systematic exposition. Perhaps the core of the democratic phi-losophy of education can best be explicated from the etymology of "de-mocracy," which is a combination of two Greek roots that, added together, mean rule by the people. If people are to rule themselves and no longer be ruled by kings, tyrants, aristocrats, oligarchs, or plutocrats, they must educate themselves for the task. Noble as the aspiration to self-rule may be, the people are an unsafe respository of political power without knowl-edge and training. The shouldering of power by the people themselves, let it be noted, is not just a political formula but a way of life. Democracy, thus, is a rule to be applied not only to the state but to the family, the school, and other social institutions.

Vesting power in the people raises at the outset a question as to just how the people conceive of themselves and their government. Quite gen-erally they regard themselves as having intrinsic worth. Having intrinsic

15 Without doubt the classic exposition of the democratic philosophy of education is to be found in John Dewey's *Democracy and Education* (The Macmillan Company, New York, 1916). Good but lesser accounts are Ernest E. Bayles, *Democratic Philosophy of Education* (Harper & Row, Publishers, Incorporated, New York, 1960); Isaac B. Berkson, *The Ideal and the Community* (Harper & Row, Publishers, Incorporated, New York, 1958); Horace M. Kallen, *The Education of Free Men* (Farrar, Straus and Cudahy, Inc., New York, 1949); Ephraim V. Sayres and Ward Madden, *Education and the Democratic Faith* (Appleton-Century-Crofts, Inc., New York, 1959); John L. Childs, *Education and Morals* (Appleton-Century-Crofts, Inc., New York, 1950); and Boyd H. Bode, *Democracy as a Way of Life* (The Macmillan Company, New York, 1921). For an idealistic critique of Dewey's view, see Herman Harrell Horne, *The Democratic Philosophy of Education* (The Macmillan Company, New York, 1935).

worth, everyone must be considered when educational opportunities are passed around. Everyone not only has intrinsic worth, but he has unique worth as an individual. Individuality is precious in a democratic philosophy of education both on its own account and because it is the very source of social progress. If schools regimented individuals to a common mold, there would be no escaping the *status quo.*

Democracy, consequently, makes a great point of freedom in education. The basic purpose of freedom is to ensure for the individual an opportunity to express his unique personality, to be different from his neighbors. The right to be free, the right to be different, finds its principal expression in academic freedom and civil liberty. Democratic education, however, is not licentious. There are occasions, as in compulsory education, when collective action must be taken to ensure that the individual realizes his intrinsic worth.

If there were unlimited resources of money and trained personnel, everyone in a democracy might expect to have his unique talents developed to their maximum extent. The optimistic assumption that there are such unlimited resources has given rise to the further democratic theory that everyone should have an equal educational opportunity. Easy as it was for this theory to establish itself in America in previous centuries, it is having a more difficult time clinging to the twentieth. With even the vast resources of this century subject to so many humanitarian demands, from hospitals to world peace, the present spirit of democracy is to provide a just rather than an equal opportunity for education. Under modern circumstances it seems unfair to give equal opportunities to youth of unequal abilities.

The conception the people have of themselves is a clue to the conception they have of the role of government in education. Regarding themselves as possessed of intrinsic worth, they expect the state to be the means by which they realize their worth. To make the state the end and the individual the means would be a denial of that intrinsic worth. To treat the individual always as an end and never as a means merely demands that education be so managed that the individual is consulted as to what ends he shall pursue and what values he shall choose.

The theory that the state is a means rather than an end of the educational process leads to another important aspect of democratic education. The democratic philosophy of education posits a pluralistic state; that is, the state is only one among several societies which provide educational opportunities and in which the individual may have membership. If the state were the only agency, it might become totalitarian, and the individual might stand in the shadow of its tyranny. In the pluralistic state, however, he is free to turn to schools maintained by the church or other private agencies as an alternative to state or public education.

Product and guarantee of freedom that the private school is, democracy must be on its guard against barriers growing up between public and private schools. Anything like socioeconomic class, race, or religious creed which interrupts the free flow of communication between people is inimical to the best interests of democracy. In a democracy society not only exists in and by communication, but is rated by increase in communication. The norm of the good society—whether the home, the classroom, the school or college—is the number and variety of interests shared both in the group and between that group and other groups.

While we might expect to find general agreement on the foregoing features of the democratic philosophy of education, we should be likely to encounter considerable disagreement on the way in which these values are grounded. Some think that democracy is a challenge to any and all forms of absolutism. Others think that unless democracy is founded on fixed principles and inalienable rights it will be so internally incoherent that it will succumb to whatever group is able to gain power. Whether democracy is capable of generating its own lay ethic or whether it must depend on religious norms presents something of an internal contradiction. Perhaps in the end it is the genius of the democratic system that communication can go on in spite of metaphysical incompatibilities.

SELECTED BIBLIOGRAPHY

Brameld, Theodore: *Patterns of Educational Philosophy: A Democratic Interpretation* (World Book Company, Tarrytown-on-Hudson, N.Y., 1950).
————: *Philosophies of Education in Cultural Perspective* (The Dryden Press, Inc., New York, 1955).
Butler, J. Donald: *Four Philosophies of Education and Their Practice in Education and Religion* (Harper & Row, Publishers, Incorporated, New York, 1967).
Gallagher, Donald A. (ed.): *Some Philosophies of Education* (Marquette University Press, Milwaukee, 1956).
International Institute: *Educational Yearbook, 1929* (Teachers College, Columbia University, New York, 1930).
Lodge, Rupert C.: *Philosophy of Education* (Harper & Row, Publishers, Incorporated, New York, 1947).
Morris, Van Cleve: *Philosophy and the American School* (Houghton Mifflin Company, Boston, 1961).
National Society for the Study of Education: Forty-first Yearbook, Part I, *Philosophies of Education* (Public School Publishing Company, Bloomington, Ill., 1942).
————: Fifty-fourth Yearbook, Part I, *Modern Philosophies and Education* (Published by the Society, Chicago, 1955).
Wingo, Max: *The Philosophy of American Education* (D. C. Heath and Company, Boston, 1965).
Wynne, John: *Philosophies of Education* (Prentice-Hall, Inc., Englewood Cliffs, N.J., 1947).
Yearbook of Education, 1957, *Education and Philosophy* (World Book Company, Tarrytown-on-Hudson, N.Y., 1957).

CHAPTER SEVENTEEN

Consensus among
Philosophies of Education

By far the greater part of the foregoing exposition sets forth the differences in philosophic approach to educational problems. This great emphasis on differences could easily obscure the fact that there are also many genuine agreements. Moreover, it could easily obscure the tremendous importance of continually searching for more and more agreement. Indeed it might be said that the attention paid to differences or disagreements so far has been occasioned by trying to understand why there is not more agreement or consensus among educators and by trying to find some common denominator of their differences as a means of enlarging the areas of professional cooperation.

IMPORTANCE OF CONSENSUS

The endeavor to resolve differences in political, economic, scientific, and religious points of view in order to arrive at a common line of action in the schools has an importance which runs beyond local or even national boundaries. It is truly worldwide in significance. If world order is ever to arise from the ashes of nationalistic rivalries, any permanence it may have must root in the ability of men to think alike to a greater degree than has been their wont to date. Or, as the preamble to UNESCO (the United Nations Educational, Scientific, and Cultural Organization) puts it, since wars arise in the minds of men, it is in the minds of men that we shall have to lay the foundations of peace. To undergird world order with enduring peace will require more than an international police force, important as that may be. It will require emotional attitudes of peace incorporated into the habit patterns of boys and girls, men and women, the world over. Of course many agencies like the church, labor unions, movies, radio, and the press can help build these habits, but the major portion of this undertaking must fall to the schools. Educators will not be able to fulfill this great function if they are preoccupied with stressing the divisions among their philosophies of education. They must rise above these divisions and achieve some consensus if they are to become molders of the new world order.[1]

---

[1] George E. Axtelle, "Philosophic Consensus, World Order, and Education," *Educational Theory*, 1:251–261, 268, December, 1951. Sidney Hook claims that agreement on fundamental questions is not prerequisite to a viable philosophy of education. See Horace T. Morse (ed.), *General Education in Transition* (University of Minnesota Press, Minneapolis, Minn., 1951). pp. 69–70.

Attempts to put forward a philosophy of education which gathers up the frayed ends of educational controversy in a unitary pattern congenial to the warring factions have not met with much success to date. Obviously such a philosophy of education cannot center in any of the great world religions, such as Buddhism, Islam, or Christianity. Neither can it take its origin in such politico-economic systems as democracy or communism. None of these is catholic enough.[2] Perhaps the most comprehensive proposal has been an "organic" philosophy of education.[3] The genius of this educational philosophy is that it is bipolar. It recognizes that many ingredients of the educational process stand in opposition to each other. They are described as free and authoritative, logical and psychological, empirical and intellectual, progressive and conservative, ideal and real, to mention but a few. The bipolar view of these opposites, however, does not consider them in either-or fashion. Being bipolar, they are reciprocal, complementary; both are necessary to an organic whole. Yet the whole is not the result of a Hegelian synthesis nor is it a Deweyan continuity based on Darwinian evolution. Rather is it bipolar, organic. This conclusion might settle conflicts if it were not for the fact that the rhythm of educational practice tends to oscillate between these two poles, depending on time, place, and circumstance. But in just which direction to oscillate and how much? It is controversy over these questions which leads to the whole philosophical argument. This brings us back to about where we started.

Even if it does, we must press toward greater agreement or consensus among warring educational philosophies; consensus is indispensable to any sort of social cohesion. Indeed we may lay down the fundamental proposition that educators cannot successfully disagree with each other unless they start with some agreements. Paradoxical though it may seem, we must agree in order to disagree, that is, we must agree in order to disagree significantly.[4] The administration of justice in our courts furnishes a good example. However sharply plaintiff and defendant disagree, they at least agree to accept the jurisdiction of the court to which they carry their quarrel. In accepting the jurisdiction of the court, they accept its rules of procedure and its precedents as a basis for handing down a verdict or decision in their own controversy. If they did not accept so much in common, there would be no way to terminate their quarrel except by an appeal

[2] Julian Huxley, UNESCO: Its Purpose and Its Philosophy (Public Affairs Press, Washington, D.C., 1948).

[3] Frank C. Wegener, "The End of an Educational Epoch: What Next?" Educational Theory, 9:129–139, July, 1959. See also Frank C. Wegener, The Organic Philosophy of Education (William C. Brown, Dubuque, Iowa, 1957).

[4] Mortimer J. Adler, in Forty-first Yearbook of the National Society for the Study of Education, Part I, Philosophies of Education (Public School Publishing Company, Bloomington, Ill., 1942), p. 201.

to physical force, and that would disturb the peace of the community and in the long run conceivably lead to an enduring quarrel or feud. A civilized community is one where people learn to disagree without being disagreeable.

The same proposition holds in school and college. An interscholastic debate would be quite meaningless if the affirmative and negative did not define the issue between them the same way. However they differ on resolving the issue, they must at least agree what the issue is. Similarly in interscholastic athletic rivalry, however keen the strife, the rival teams must agree on the interpretation of the rules. The case is no different in the management of the academic program. If teachers did not predicate their policies on some common philosophic principles, promotion through the various grades would lose all sense of continuity. The unity of the pupil's experience of the curriculum would be seriously interrupted.

Important as enlarging the area of common agreement is, whether establishing the community of debate, sport, justice, school, or what have you, it hardly needs saying that our objective is not a community of complete agreement. That is probably as undesirable as it is impossible. If all differences were to be eliminated, there could be no growing edge to our agreements. What we seek is simply an orderly basis of agreement in order that we may reap the creative product of our differences and disagreements. And of course we would prefer that the orderly basis of any underlying unity should well up from the voluntary consent of those involved rather than be thrust on us from above or from without by liquidating dissenters.

PRACTICAL AGREEMENTS

In searching for some consensus among competing philosophies of education, it seems best to start where right now, as a matter of fact, we find the greatest number of agreements. This place is the concrete field of educational practice rather than the abstract field of educational theory, the area of educational tactics rather than that of educational strategy. Since we differ on the theoretical implications of educational practice, the agreements on practice may be more apparent than real. Nevertheless, even if that is the case, it seems best to start with practice where the greatest area of apparent agreement lies. At best it will be possible only to describe areas of agreement. Almost as certainly as we try to expand single areas of agreement we are likely to find that they border on other areas of disagreement. Moreover, we are unlikely to find clear-cut boundary lines precisely dividing black and white areas of agreement and disagreement. These lines, instead, are more likely to be wide bands of mixed agreement and disagreement.

Without attempting to be exhaustive, we might mention the following areas of significant agreement in the everyday practice of the schools. At the very outset there is wide agreement on such obvious matters as making school buildings safe against fire hazards, protecting children against traffic hazards on the way to school, and providing children with glasses if they need them. There is general agreement on compulsory attendance up to a minimum level. There is also quite general agreement that children should be vaccinated before they come to school. Moreover there is wide assent to the fact that only teachers who can meet certification requirements by virtue of professional preparation should be allowed to teach.

Beyond such practical matters of common agreement, there is an area where congruity of opinion might least be expected, the area of educational aims. Restricting ourselves to the proximate aims of education,[5] we find that nearly every educational philosophy accepts such objectives as the Seven Cardinal Principles of Education—command of the fundamental processes of communication and computation; health; competency in family, civic, and vocational relations; worthy use of leisure; and ethical sensitivity. If not this exact list, then some modification of it or some similar list usually offers unexceptionable educational objectives to nearly everyone. Educators will differ on how these aims serve realization of the ultimate aims of education, and they will also differ on what any one of these aims demands when broken down into more specific detail.

Although educators differ on how the specific or proximate aims of education are to be broken down into the detail which constitutes the curriculum, there is, nevertheless, a considerable area of agreement on the curriculum itself. There is pretty general agreement, for instance, that a sizable portion of the race experience should be the common heritage of all. This is most clear in the program of the elementary school. But if less clear at the secondary and higher levels of education, there is nonetheless a common patrimony there too, which educators insist upon. The three R's at the lower level and the trivium—grammar, logic, and rhetoric—at the upper levels are generally agreed to be indispensable for all. There is wide consensus, too, that to these essentials must be added a basic knowledge of history and of social and physical science. And, very promising for future consensus, there is a growing unanimity of sentiment favorable to the inclusion in the curriculum of some of the sharper controversial social issues which divide the body politic. We should not be surprised, however, if after agreeing that all should learn to write, for instance, we should disagree on

[5] *Supra,* pp. 100–102.

what they should write, or after agreeing to include controversial issues, we find that it is inappropriate to include religion as such an issue.

To be added to these important agreements in the areas of aims and curriculum happily are further agreements on the matter of methods of instruction. Perhaps the principal agreement here is that there are several methods and that their selection and use depend upon circumstance. Nearly everyone is agreed there is a proper time and place for drill. Beyond that there seems to be a notable common endorsement of the problem method. Life is undeniably problematical in many of its aspects; what could be more appropriate, therefore, than to pose this part of life to children in problematical form? Indeed so important is training in problem solving that many advocate the problem method where answers are already well known in advance. Where certain answers are almost universally accepted throughout the population, as in the fields of arithmetic, grammar, or health, there is considerable consensus that it is proper to make the efficient short cut of indoctrinating such answers. But whether any answers are to be regarded as final or indisputable, there consensus begins to wear thin.

Where problems are genuinely precarious in outcome, the problem method, of course, presupposes or perhaps even demands a certain amount of freedom for the individual in arriving at his solution of the problem. Fortunately again, we can say that most philosophies of education concede the preeminent importance of freedom both as an end of the educative process and as a method of achieving that end. Probably there is more agreement on freedom as an end than there is on freedom as a means. But even on freedom as a method, notably in the form of academic freedom, there is wide consensus—at least in democratic nations. Few educators have confidence in any assent won from students under coercion. Yet whether or not freedom has reasonable limits and just where these limits lie states an issue which indicates that we are getting beyond the area of common agreement.

A further cardinal point of agreement in the realm of method or technique of instruction is the general acceptance of need for motivating instruction. Indeed there is much more agreement than ordinarily thought that the most effective learning occurs where children are interested in their studies. Furthermore, it is generally conceded that students are more likely stirred to interest where the curriculum grows out of their present experiences. This amount of agreement is tremendously hopeful. But of course there are all degrees of enthusiasm and conviction with which the theory of interest is endorsed. Faced with lack of interest or difficulty in obtaining it, some educators abandon it much more quickly than others. At just what point to abandon interest and what to substitute in its place is a question which again indicates that we have reached the fringe between an area of agreement and one of disagreement.

Just as nearly everyone recognizes the practical importance of interest, so nearly everyone, too, recognizes that interest varies with individuals. Indeed, individual differences are so well authenticated now that educational philosophy would have to fly in the face of science to disregard them in the practical administration of the classroom. Yet, widespread as is the willingness to be guided by this obvious fact, the point of disagreement is not far off. Ask the question whether it is more important to educate a man in respect to his individuality or in respect to his common humanity, and a sizable disturbance develops. No little of the disturbance arises over failing to distinguish between an education which cultivates individuality and one which makes a cult of individualism.

It is perhaps well at this point to observe that most educational philosophies have come to terms with the science of education. There is a general willingness to admit that, where variables can be isolated and controlled, science can do a commendable job of describing reliably and objectively what the consequences are of engaging in certain practices. Thus educational philosophers are quite in concert in accepting the pragmatic results of intelligence testing although they differ quite severely on the nature of intelligence and what its function is in the world order. Disagreements multiply when we must decide whether or not scientific techniques of measurement can be extended to cover religious and moral education as well as secular.

To carry the matter of individual differences a point further, we must note the general acceptance of the practice of trying to equalize educational opportunities, of trying to prevent accidental inequalities in the geographical distribution of economic resources from becoming insuperable obstacles to a child's realizing and developing the unique talents of his individual heredity. This acceptance, however, points to neither an identity of educational opportunity nor to a race in which the hindmost drop out. Nor is this attempt to share economic resources more equitably the only way in which educators try to practice the democratic philosophy of education. There is also a growing tendency to share practical decisions of classroom management with children in so far as they are mature enough to make decisions. Thus the teacher may consult children as to problems to include in the curriculum, and the superintendent may invite his staff to help form important educational policies for the whole system of schools. The basic item in this sort of democratic practice, which commands such wide endorsement, is the fact that neither children nor adults like to be pushed around against their consent. They like to be consulted, to have their interests respected. But even so, it is surprising how often teachers and administrators think their own unaided judgment better than conforming to a shared decision at variance with it.

A final sample area of agreement might be the approval given to the role of the school in conserving the social order. There is virtually no disagreement that the school should conserve the social heritage of race experience. Unless each generation knows the successes and failures of preceding generations, it will be at an unnecessary disadvantage in the struggle for existence. But of course it is impractical for everyone to learn the whole long record of these successes and failures. Consequently there is also wide agreement that the school must exercise a normative as well as a conservative function in selecting the curriculum of the schools. But at this point agreement begins to fade out, for, what shall that norm be? And how rapidly shall we expect to achieve the norm educationally?

PHILOSOPHICAL AGREEMENTS

Happily, in addition to the foregoing agreements at the level of educational practice, there are also a number of points of agreement at the level of theory or philosophy. Where there is indication of so much agreement of a practical nature, it would be surprising indeed if there were not a corresponding degree of consensus in theory or philosophy as well. Some indication of the concurrence of philosophies can first be seen in the way in which they conceive the nature of education itself. Following are statements of a pragmatist, an idealist, a rational humanist, and a scholastic realist. Which is which?

Education should be thought of as the process of man's reciprocal adjustment to nature, to his fellows, and to the ultimate nature of the cosmos.

Education is the organized development and equipment of all the powers of a human being, moral, intellectual, and physical, by and for their individual and social uses, directed toward the union of these activities with their creator as their final end.

Education is the process in which these powers (abilities, capacities) of men which are susceptible to habituation are perfected by *good* habits, by *means artistically contrived*, and employed by a man to help another or himself achieve the *end* in view (i.e., good habits).

Any adequate educational program will thus be concerned to help each individual child grow up from his state of initial dependence into full participation in the richest available group life, including in a democratic country a full share in the active management of group affairs. Such an adequate program will besides go on further to an active effort to improve the group culture.[6]

---

[6] National Society for the Study of Education, Forty-first Yearbook, Part I, *Philosophies of Education* (Public School Publishing Company, Bloomington, Ill., 1942), p. 320.

Of course a close analysis of these statements will betray different schools of thought. Yet in spite of these differences there is a striking similarity of expression. Doubtless much of the consensus that appears is due to the generality of each statement. If the statements were less broad, the differences would doubtless be accentuated. Yet, stated broadly, these generalizations seem to approach a common denominator into which each is divisible.

It is particularly easy for philosophies to tend toward agreement on the nature of education when they confine themselves to the natural order. The proximate aims of education, for instance, rest on an analysis of life and culture here and now. The employment of interest for motivation rests on an understanding of the basic drives of human nature. There is a public quality about examining educational aims and motivation in the natural order. The presence or absence of uniformity in the facts are there for anyone to see. Anyone can test his conclusions against those of others. In fact the ultimate test of any conclusion is its success in getting itself accepted by competent students in the field. Although the natural order is very matter-of-fact, it nevertheless is not wanting in a certain sublimity. Plato and his *Republic*, St. Thomas and his *De Magistro*, Dewey and his *Democracy and Education* were all products of nature, perennially stimulating gifts to unnumbered generations of teachers yet to come.

When confining ourselves to knowledge in the natural order, we find a rather significant agreement possible on the theory of knowledge underlying the curriculum. Two principal theories of the way of knowing, the morphological and the operational or experimental, have already been described at some length.[7] The former tries to get at the essential form of the material undergoing learning so that it can be described or defined in the most precise and unambiguous way. The latter is concerned with successfully adapting means to ends in the solution of some problem which is obstructing action. Happily, these two ways of learning or knowing are not mutually exclusive or antagonistic to each other. Consequently, as long as we are dealing with learning the secular curriculum, there should be a growing area of philisophical consensus. Particularly is this the case where the resulting knowledge is held to be tentatively true rather than a genuinely true copy of antecedent reality.

Again restricting ourselves to the natural order, we can find a significant area of agreement in the field of educational values. This area of agreement lies principally in the field of instrumental or utilitarian values.

[7] *Supra*, pp. 227–231.

Nearly every educational philosophy holds that the value of studies in the curriculum or of equipment in the schoolroom very often depends on the use to which these items are put. Whether they have an intrinsic value in addition to, and independent of use is another matter. Disagreement on this point, however, need be no bar to extend agreement about values at the level of use. Similarly, irrespective of whether or not some educational values are intrinsic, all educational philosophies seem agreed that some educational values are aesthetic and consummatory and are enjoyable on their own account.

Even more gratifying is the degree of consensus that has been reached in the difficult to define area of spiritual values which are and can be taught in the public schools.[8] Not least among these spiritual values is knowledge itself. This is true whether knowledge is pursued in the form of science, philosophy, or art. Indeed, naturalists and supernaturalists may find to their surprise that their ultimate aims of education may tend to coincide in this area of knowledge as its own end. Thus Catholic supernaturalists often think of the highest end of man as union with God and this union as a glimpse of the beatific vision. This vision is an essentially intellectual vision, since to look upon God is to behold perfect reason or understanding. The pragmatic naturalist, in stating that education is subordinate to nothing save more education, seems to be formulating an ultimate aim of education which is not unlike that of the supernaturalist. Since education can be pursued indefinitely as its own end, the search for education becomes an infinite quest. But since God is infinite, the beatific vision, too, is without limit. Hence naturalism and supernaturalism do not seem far apart in their ultimate aims of education when these are projected indefinitely into the future.

Of course the principal object of value in the whole educational program is the pupil himself. On this point—the dignity of the individual, respect for human personality—there is as wide agreement among philosophies of education as it is possible to get. Certainly democratic philosophies of education are unanimous in identifying themselves with this concept. It is easy to see why they should agree here since democracy is the form of social organization in which individuals freely manage their own affairs. It is the form of social organization which is most consonant with the autonomy of human nature. An important corollary of this agreement

---

[8] John Dewey Society, Seventh Yearbook, *The Public School and Spiritual Values* (Harper & Row, Publishers, Incorporated, New York, 1944). See also American Council on Education, "The Relation of Religion to Public Education," *Religious Education*, 42:129–190, May–June, 1947.

is an endorsement of a theory of freedom, a theory in which freedom comes with understanding but in which the pupil is still free to experiment with deviations from common understanding.

Because of its commitment to the worth of the individual as an end democratic philosophies of education are generally united in favoring a pluralistic theory of the state. Accordingly, the state is but one among other social agencies interested in providing educational opportunities for the child. This leads to the further commonly accepted theory of approving private as well as public schools and colleges because, in having a choice of schools to attend, the individual is able to guard himself to an important degree against any tyranny of the mind. The communist philosophy of education also professes an interest in the dignity of the individual, but, professing a totalitarian rather than a pluralistic state, the freedom it guarantees is only the freedom to do what the state thinks best for him.

PHILOSOPHICAL DISAGREEMENTS

With such an extensive basis laid for consensus among philosophies of education, it is time to remind ourselves that there are still profound points of disagreement between them which prevent their adherents from achieving even more unified cooperation in the conduct of the schools. The purpose of recalling our differences, however, is not to strike a note of discord. On the contrary, perhaps it will be in the ultimate interests of consensus to narrow down the major points which stand in the way of even greater consensus. Indeed, to be able to agree on no more than a definition of our disagreements proves at least that the parties thereto are still in communication, a point of tremendous importance for, without communication, there can be no hope at all for consensus.

The foregoing philosophical concert of opinion has been largely in the nature of working or practical agreements. No doubt such agreements are better than none at all. And perhaps they are better than theoretic agreements which, oddly enough, find conflicting practical expression.[9] At any rate the extended area of agreement seems to come to an end when we try to reach agreements of more than a working nature. When we ask whether the warrant for our agreements is to be found in this working consensus itself or whether it rests on more certain ground, we ask the question which generally starts the great schism between educational philosophies.[10]

9 National Society for the Study of Education, op. cit., pp. 32–37.
10 Cf. Laurence J. O'Connell, Are Catholic Schools Progressive? (B. Herder Book Co., St. Louis, 1946).

So long as they confine themselves to the order of nature a number of educational philosophies feel insecure in their conclusions about educational policy, even though others are in consensus with them this far. To be sure, the temporal order of nature is characterized by change and contingency. Conclusions about the aims of education or about a suitable curriculum to fulfill these aims, therefore, must be constantly subject to amendment in the light of changes wrought by the passage of time. Yet this precarious quality of life and education at the level of nature makes them uneasy. For good and sufficient reasons they are confident that the world of apparent change and contingency is undergirded by another which is changeless and eternal. To those content with the natural order the proof of such a world is speculative at best, logical rather than empirical. The quest for certainty beyond what is known in the natural order can therefore lead but to uncertain pretensions to certainty and to divisiveness among educational philosophers. So the budding consensus begins to wither.

The schism in metaphysics between educational philosophies emphasizing change and those emphasizing the changeless widens and becomes more unbridgeable when reinforced by theological considerations. Those who seek to overcome the uncertainties of education in the natural order by an appeal to certainty in the supernatural order almost put themselves out of communication with those who insist on restricting the universe of educational discourse to the natural order. Yet, in all sincerity, the supernaturalist does not see, for instance, how consensus on the dignity of man can hold any secure place at the center of educational philosophy unless it has a divine authorship. Similarly moral education is precarious at best unless the child learns that in conforming to moral values he is obeying divine ordinance. Yet the naturalist, in all sincerity, does not see any more warrant for the theologically supernatural than he does for the metaphysically changeless. It may be supreme egotism on his part to trust his natural capacities in their struggle with the uncertainties of the natural order, but he sees no other resource if he is to be honest with himself. He must himself bear his cosmic anxieties; he cannot shift them to supernatural shoulders.

The critical question in these metaphysical and theological disagreements is how do we know? Obviously the naturalist trusts his own experience; he cannot transcend it. Since his experience is the product of interacting with a more or less changing environment, he accepts no truths as fixed or final. All truths are subject to amendment in the light of further consequences. The supernaturalist, on the other hand, accepts some truths as fixed, even self-evident. But more than that he supports his human experience with divine revelation, which he believes to be factually verifiable. Indeed it is principally through revelation that he has knowledge of the supernatural. Because of his confidence in the supernatural he believes that human learning results from more than human initiative, that there is also a divine initiative through grace.

Intransigeant differences in educational philosophy take root in other soil than just that of metaphysics, theology, and epistemology. They also take root in racial and economic differences as well. To some educators the fact that there are children black of skin constitutes as inalterable a reason for a different sort of educational program as metaphysics constitutes for others. Similarly other educators gear their policies so closely with an economic system like capitalism or communism or with a theory of government like *laissez faire* or the welfare state that they find it utterly impossible to achieve any basic consensus with their adversaries.

Whatever the reason for taking a rigid or intransigeant stand in one's educational philosophy, the ultimate and deplorable result is to break down communication between the adherents of conflicting philosophies of education. Each group seems to have its own universe of discourse. Consequently they do not speak the same educational language. Community breaks down into several communities each with its own separate system of schools. The danger here is that separate school systems will breed suspicion and mis-understanding. Yet, deplorable and dangerous as this situation is, what can be done about it? How can we endeavor to reconcile the irreconcilable?

METHODS FOR CONSENSUS

What agreements have been achieved so far have been largely substantive agreements. We must now try to enlarge the area of agreement to include the method of determining agreement and disagreement. First let us note that consensus presents us with a problem in learning. The philosophical differences like experimentalism, rational humanism, and the rest, which divide and separate us, are not biologically inherent. For the most part they are learned. Consensus, therefore, may also be a matter of learning or perhaps better, relearning. Second, let us remark that we have learned our divisions in a social setting and that much of the rigidity of these differ-ences may come in part from the satisfaction we derive in sharing them with others. If these divisions were strictly a matter of individual personal differences, they might be more readily reduced. But it is the social rein-forcement of sharing them with others which provides the most effective resistance to their modification. Learning consensus, therefore, may pri-marily be a matter of forming a new and different set of group relations, and of emphasizing their importance.

Again, in trying to set up new social relations conducive to consensus, we shall do well to be as sensitive as possible to any and all barriers to communication. For instance, we should be careful about setting up straw men for purposes of knocking them down. In directing the shafts of our criticism at straw men we are aiming at the wrong target; we are, in fact, preventing ourselves from seeing the real men opposite us. Perhaps nothing corrects such distortions or so reveals the real opposition as does face-to-face discussion of issues. Yet even in direct communication educational philosophers will do well to moderate their philosophies with a due sense of humility. That virtue may be a necessary prelude to being able to understand what some other philosopher is saying.

Two noneducational illustrations may make the desirability of moderation more plausible. A notable poster during the Second World War showed a fallen soldier with a member of the Red Cross unit rushing up to his side. The question the poster asked was: Did it make any difference to the member of the Red Cross whether the fallen soldier was a Catholic, Protestant, or Jew? Of course it did not. A person's philosophy is important but not that important. So, too, in another illustration, again taken from court procedure. When a person takes the witness stand, do his philosophical reasons for telling the truth matter so long as he is committed to telling the truth, the whole truth, and nothing but the truth? Again, of course not. Naturally we feel more confidence in someone who thinks as we do, but we are far from making that a condition precedent to hearing his testimony.

The significance of these illustrations will serve to point out that conduct is as important if not more important that the theory which undergirds it. Theory, the verbalization of conduct, is undoubtedly very important, especially to its formulator, but it should not overshadow conduct. If we can manage to act in concert on the battlefield and in the courts, or in the classroom, should that not teach us to revaluate the significance of verbal or theoretical disagreements? May not theoretical differences, which do not noticeably alter action or conduct, be trivial or purely verbal at best? Doubtless some theoretical differences stem from temperamental differences and do have important aesthetic consequences for the individual. But if so, should we not take these differences for what they are and not stake the issue of "one world" and its social cohesion and stability on their acceptance?

On the other hand, suppose we insist that our theoretical disagreements are as important as we think they are, that we cannot sacrifice or compromise them for practical agreement, just how far are we prepared to carry this insistence? Are we ready, for instance, to insist that our peculiar theoretical formulation of life or education prevail over others, though to do so will bring on civil or international war in which civilization comes tumbling into ruins about us? Is it better that libraries, laboratories, schools, and museums—to say nothing of factories, governmental buildings, and homes—should come crashing down rather than that we should give up one iota of principle in our educational philosophies in order to compromise on some common line of conduct? Is it humanly possible for one of us to be so unquestionably sure of his position that he would be warranted in paying such a price? And the price could be terrible to pay because in an atomic age another holocaust of war might very well reduce the material basis of civilization to such a low level that it might be centuries or even milleniums before we would have the surplus wealth and consequent leisure to cultivate education in high principle as we do at present. Certainly these are questions which any of us must answer before he is ready to be rigidly uncompromising to the bitter end of philosophical controversy.

Proceeding now on the assumption that educational philosophers will be willing to be at least a little tractable in negotiating their diverse viewpoints, we may inquire as to the probable directions of improving consensus. The place to look for consensus, some venture, is not in the stars, lofty as that aim may be, but in the practical affairs of men. Trying to negotiate agreement in some practical area may yield only limited unity, but that unity will engender more confidence than the construction of logical formulas which fail to win inclusive allegiance.

The area today where men *actually* have the greatest common denominator of human agreement is science. When there is confusion as to a matter of fact there is well-nigh universal agreement on what to do. It matters not at all whether the disputants are Japanese or Australian, communist or democrat, Hindu or Buddhist, the procedure is the same. Scientists may not always agree on specific facts, but they do not disagree on the ultimate way to arbitrate these differences. Furthermore, scientists continue to make brilliant scientific advances in spite of the fact that philosophers are not agreed on the theory of scientific knowledge because they cannot agree on the nature of man as a knower. The fact that scientists are in consensus on conquest after conquest of their discipline despite the philosopher should be a challenge to the latter to achieve a similar consensus in knowledge theory or epistemology.[11]

But if it is clear that consensus can be built only in the atmosphere of cautious scientific objectivity, why is there little inclination and less effort to establish science as the basis for consensus in educational philosophy? In large part it is because some will immediately shout the old cliché that science may be effective in determining disputed questions of fact but not of values, and that the obstacles to philosophical consensus are more often

---

[11] Cf. the attempt of Filmer S. C. Northrop, *The Meeting of East and West* (The Macmillan Company, New York, 1946).

disagreements about value than about facts. No doubt this is a time-honored objection, but just how much of it can be whittled away?[12]

In the first place, facts and values cannot be kept in logic-tight compartments. History attests to many instances where scientific facts have altered existing values or created new ones. Data from psychiatry have provided the educator with a whole new set of norms and imperatives to direct him in dealing with the young from the kindergarten to the university. Behavior formerly viewed as insubordination to be controlled by "breaking the child's will" now often calls, not for negative thwarting, but for positive guidance.

Yet, in the second place, can science help us choose values prospectively? It is a platitude that science can determine what "is" but not what "ought to be." Yet again, can anything be whittled off this objection? Suppose an educator is confronted with a choice between two possible educational programs, each based on a different value. Could he not at least employ the services of the scientist to find out what, as a matter of fact, would be the actual consequences of acting first on one value and then on the other? In other words, values are facts, and to the extent they are, they should be capable of being reduced to a common denominator of scientific handling.

But now in the third place, suppose the facts about the proposed values are all in, can science determine which set the educator "ought" to choose? Much turns on what is meant by the word "ought." A semantic analysis of this imperative can reduce it to the indicative mood: "I like this value and I wish you would too." Still there is no obligation in this statement. There will be obligation only *if* there is a community of persuasion, only *if* the person addressed accepts the point of view, the set of values, the authority of the person endorsing them. But again, can science give the sanction which pushes one over the brink of indifference into the depth of conviction? Certainly not in the sense that some value is so incontestably established that the individual is overwhelmed into obeying it. But then, is there any theory of values which provides such an overwhelming sanction?

Perhaps religious values—values ordained by God—may be suggested as having such obligation. Yet even under God's rule man's will has not always been vanquished. Adam disobeyed God's explicit commandment not to eat of the tree of knowledge. His act may have been unreasonable and the consequences dire, but Adam did it and some of his descendants are still doing it. Actually the role of science is not very different from religion

12 Lawrence G. Thomas, "Prospects of Scientific Research into Values," *Educational Theory*, 6:193–205, October, 1956.

at this point. As already stated, science can amass facts about values. Not always but sometimes these facts point inescapably in one direction. If they do, the individual is just as palpably unreasonable to fly in the face of science as Adam was in rebelling against God. However incomprehensible their conduct, there always seem to be rebels who refuse to obey values, no matter by whom they are sanctioned, God or science.

Till recently there has been no long-standing and well-recognized method for settling differences in the optative or imperative mood of values as there has been in the indicative mood of fact. However, an elaborate attempt has now been made to work out a discipline of practical judgment which would compare favorably with the discipline of scientific judgment.[13] Given a "community of persuasion," a community of people voluntarily disposed to overcoming personal rigidities of viewpoint, much can be done. But given optative rigidity, the outlook is not so hopeful for a discipline of practical judgment.[14]

In an educational impasse brought on by optative rigidity, about the best that can be done is to compromise or submit the issue to majority vote. Of course compromise does not offer a real consensus. However, where a dispute resolves itself into optative rigidity on each side, perhaps the best that can be expected is negotiation of an educational *modus vivendi*. In sincere search for some sort of practical working conditions, there is bound to be a modicum of reconstructed theory. Negotiation, if carried on by equals who are mutually interdependent, comes as near as anything can to bringing about some lessening of rigidity. In compromise a rigid educational philosophy may be just bending to spring back into position when the tension is released, but to bend at all is something; and if the tension is kept up long enough, the structure of an otherwise rigid position may be enduringly warped.

If no compromise is possible, then perhaps the only way to break the impasse is through majority vote. In removing the controversy from the arena of education to that of politics, it is necessary here to appreciate the role of majority rule. To make a majority determination in coming to a practical decision does not resolve the merits of a dispute over values. It rather recognizes the rigidities involved, but instead of letting them stall or stalemate the course of instruction indefinitely, it provides a way of releasing some action. It does not say that the majority is right; it merely

[13] R. Bruce Raup, George Axtelle, Kenneth D. Benne, and B. Othanel Smith, The Improvement of Practical Intelligence (Harper & Row, Publishers, Incorporated, New York, 1949).
[14] Observe the note of caution against overoptimism on achieving consensus in Charles F. Donovan, "Anti-intellectualism in American Schools," Catholic Educational Review, 48: 150–151, March, 1950. See also William O. Stanley, Education and Social Integration (Teachers College, Columbia University, New York, 1953).

says let the majority organize us for action. Even so, majority action should be taken in the interests of the whole group and not just for the majority, because only so will the minority be able to acquiesce in it. And even then the majority must realize that there are some things, like religious instruction, on which it is better not to take action for fear of stirring up implacable rigidity in the minority.

Finally we must remember that no worthwhile consensus is possible which violates the integrity of any party thereto. In seeking for consensus we must have entire respect for the personality of those who differ from us, even where our differences stiffen into rigidity. If a consensus of educational philosophies is to be forthcoming in the twentieth century, as was a medieval synthesis in the thirteenth century, it will in all probability have to be the cooperative product of many minds. Some one man, like St. Thomas, may succeed in summing it all up, but the groundwork will have to be laid by many lesser minds. With appropriate humility by all and appropriate charity to all the success of such a consensus or synthesis does not appear impossible.

SELECTED BIBLIOGRAPHY

Adler, Mortimer J.: The Revolution in Education (The University of Chicago Press, Chicago, 1958).

Smith, Huston: The Purposes of Higher Education (Harper & Row, Publishers, Incorporated, New York, 1955).

BIBLIOGRAPHY

GENERAL WORKS IN EDUCATIONAL PHILOSOPHY

Arnstine, Donald: *Philosophy of Education* (Harper & Row, Publishers, Incorporated, New York, 1967).

Berkson, Isaac B.: *Preface to an Educational Philosophy* (Teachers College Press, Columbia University, New York, 1940).

————: *The Ideal and the Community* (Harper & Row, Publishers, Inc., New York, 1958).

Bode, Boyd H.: *Fundamentals of Education* (The Macmillan Company, New York, 1931).

Brameld, Theodore: *Patterns of Educational Philosophy: A Democratic Interpretation* (World Book Company, Tarrytown-on-Hudson, N.Y., 1950).

————: *Philosophies of Education in Cultural Perspective* (The Dryden Press, Inc., New York, 1955).

————: *Toward a Reconstructed Philosophy of Education* (The Dryden Press, Inc., New York, 1956).

Broudy, Harry: *Building a Philosophy of Education* (Prentice-Hall, Inc., Englewood Cliffs, N.J., 1961).

———— et al: *Philosophy of Education* (University of Illinois Press, Urbana, Ill., 1967).

Brown, L. M.: *General Philosophy in Education* (McGraw-Hill Book Company, New York, 1966).

Butler, J. Donald: *Four Philosophies and Their Practice in Education and Religion* (Harper & Row, Publishers, Incorporated, New York, 1967).

Childs, John L.: *Education and Morals* (Appleton-Century-Crofts, Inc., New York, 1950).

————: *Pragmatism and American Education* (Holt, Rinehart and Winston, Inc., New York, 1956).

Cunningham, William F.: *Pivotal Problems of Education* (The Macmillan Company, New York, 1940).

Demiashkevich, Michael: *An Introduction to the Philosophy of Education* (The Macmillan Company, New York, 1935).

Dewey, John: *Democracy and Education* (The Macmillan Company, New York, 1916).

Dupuis, Adrian, and Robert Norberg: *Philosophy and Education* (The Bruce Publishing Company, Milwaukee, 1964).

Finney, Ross: *A Sociological Philosophy of Education* (The Macmillan Company, New York, 1928).

Horne, Herman H.: *Philosophy of Education*, rev. ed. (The Macmillan Company, New York, 1927).

————: *The Democratic Philosophy of Education* (The Macmillan Company, New York, 1935).

Johnson, Herbert: *A Philosophy of Education* (McGraw-Hill Book Company, New York, 1963).

Kneller, George F.: *Introduction to the Philosophy of Education* (John Wiley & Sons, Inc., New York, 1964).

Lodge, Rupert C.: *Philosophy of Education* (Harper & Row, Publishers, Incorporated, New York, 1947).

MacDonald, John: *A Philosophy of Education* (Scott Foresman and Company, Chicago, 1967).

Mason, Robert E.: *Educational Ideals in American Society* (Allyn and Bacon, Inc., Boston, 1960).

Morris, Van Cleve: *Philosophy and the American School* (Houghton Mifflin Company, Boston, 1961).

Munk, Arthur W.: *A Synoptic Philosophy of Education* (Abingdon Press, Nashville, Tenn., 1965).

Nash, Paul: *Authority and Freedom in Education* (John Wiley & Sons, Inc., New York, 1965).

Newsome, George: *Philosophical Perspectives* (University of Georgia Press, Athens, Ga., 1961).

Phenix, Philip H.: *Philosophy of Education* (Holt, Rinehart and Winston, Inc., New York, 1958).

Redden, John D., and Francis A. Ryan: *A Catholic Philosophy of Education* (The Bruce Publishing Company, Milwaukee, 1955).

Reid, Louis A.: *Philosophy and Education* (William Heinemann, Ltd., London, 1962).

Rusk, Robert R.: *Philosophical Bases of Education* (Houghton Mifflin Company, Boston, 1956).

Smith, Philip G.: *Philosophy of Education* (Harper & Row, Publishers, Incorporated, New York, 1965).

Thomson, Godfrey H.: *A Modern Philosophy of Education* (George Allen & Unwin, Ltd., London, 1929).

Ulich, Robert: *Fundamentals of Democratic Education* (American Book Company, New York, 1940).

————: *Philosophy of Education* (American Book Company, New York, 1961).

Ward, Leo: *Philosophy of Education* (Henry Regnery Company, Chicago, 1966).

Weber, Christian O.: *Basic Philosophies of Education* (Holt, Rinehart and Winston, Inc., New York, 1960).

Wegener, Frank C.: *The Organic Philosophy of Education* (William C. Brown Company, Dubuque, Iowa, 1957).

Wingo, Max: *The Philosophy of American Education* (D. C. Heath and Company, Boston, 1965).

Wynne, John: *Philosophies of Education* (Prentice-Hall, Inc., Englewood Cliffs, N.J., 1947).

SOURCE BOOKS

Brubacher, John S. (ed.): *Eclectic Philosophy of Education* (Prentice-Hall, Inc., Englewood Cliffs, N.J., 1962).

Burns, Hobert, and Charles J. Brauner (eds.): *Philosophy of Education* (The Ronald Press Company, New York, 1962).

Fitzpatrick, Edward A. (ed.): *Readings in Philosophy of Education* (Appleton-Century-Crofts, Inc., New York, 1936).

Kilpatrick, William H. (ed.): *Source Book in the Philosophy of Education* (The Macmillan Company, New York, 1934).

Pai, Young, and Joseph T. Myers (eds.): *Philosophic Problems of Education* (J. B. Lippincott Company, Philadelphia, 1967).

Park, Joe (ed.): *The Philosophy of Education: Selected Readings* (The Macmillan Company, New York, 1958).

Rich, John (ed.): *Readings in the Philosophy of Education* (Wadsworth Publishing Company, Belmont, Calif., 1966).

Scheffler, Israel (ed.): *Philosophy and Education: Modern Readings* (Allyn and Bacon, Inc., Boston, 1958).

YEARBOOKS

International Institute: *Educational Yearbook, 1929* (Teachers College, Columbia University, New York, 1930).

National Society for the Study of Education: Forty-first Yearbook, Part I, *Philosophies of Education* (Public School Publishing Company, Bloomington, Ill., 1942).

————: Fifty-fourth Yearbook, Part I, *Modern Philosophies and Education* (Published by the Society, Chicago, 1955).

Yearbook of Education, 1957, *Education and Philosophy* (World Book Company, Tarrytown-on-Hudson, N.Y., 1957).

HISTORIES

Brumbaugh, Robert S., and Nathaniel Lawrence: *Philosophers on Education* (Houghton Mifflin Company, Boston, 1963).

Dupuis, Adrian: *Philosophy of Education in Historical Perspective* (Rand McNally & Company, Chicago, 1966).

Frankena, William K.: *Three Historical Philosophies of Education* (Scott Foresman and Company, Chicago, 1965).

Gruber, Frederick C.: *Foundations for a Philosophy of Education* (Thomas Y. Crowell Company, New York, 1961).

Price, Kingsley: *Education and Philosophical Thought* (Allyn and Bacon, Inc., Boston, 1962).

Thut, I. N.: *The Story of Education: Philosophical and Historical Foundations* (McGraw-Hill Book Company, New York, 1957).

Wynne, John: *Theories of Education* (Harper & Row, Publishers, Incorporated, New York, 1963).

INDEX